THE GREEKS AND TH

The Greeks have long been regarded as innovators across a wide range of fields in literature, culture, philosophy, politics and science. However, little attention has been paid to how they thought and felt about novelty and innovation itself, and to relating this to the forces of traditionalism and conservatism which were also present across all the various societies within ancient Greece. What inspired the Greeks to embark on their unique and enduring innovations? How did they think and feel about the new? This book represents the first serious attempt to address these issues, and deals with the phenomenon across all periods and areas of classical Greek history and thought. Each chapter concentrates on a different area of culture or thought, while the book as a whole argues that much of the impulse towards innovation came from the life of the polis which provided its setting.

ARMAND D'ANGOUR is Fellow and Tutor in Classics at Jesus College Oxford.

THE GREEKS AND THE NEW

Novelty in ancient Greek imagination and experience

ARMAND D'ANGOUR

CAMBRIDGE UNIVERSITY PRESS
Cambridge, New York, Melbourne, Madrid, Cape Town,
Singapore, São Paulo, Delhi, Tokyo, Mexico City

Cambridge University Press
The Edinburgh Building, Cambridge CB2 8RU, UK

Published in the United States of America by Cambridge University Press, New York

www.cambridge.org
Information on this title: www.cambridge.org/9780521616485

© Armand D'Angour 2011

This publication is in copyright. Subject to statutory exception
and to the provisions of relevant collective licensing agreements,
no reproduction of any part may take place without the written
permission of Cambridge University Press.

First published 2011

Printed in the United Kingdom at the University Press, Cambridge

A catalogue record for this publication is available from the British Library

ISBN 978-0-521-85097-1 Hardback
ISBN 978-0-521-61648-5 Paperback

Cambridge University Press has no responsibility for the persistence or
accuracy of URLs for external or third-party internet websites referred to
in this publication, and does not guarantee that any content on such
websites is, or will remain, accurate or appropriate.

τοῖς τε νέοις τόδ' ἔθηκα τὸ βιβλίον τοῖς τε παλαιοῖς·
καὶ γὰρ γηράσκω καινὰ διδασκόμενος.

I've made this book with young and old in view:
for I grow old discovering what's new.

Contents

Acknowledgements — *page* ix

Introduction — 1

1. New, new, new — 11
   - Novelty in Greek Culture — 12
   - 'New': word and concept — 19
   - The psychology of novelty — 27
   - Dimensions of novelty — 32

2. Loosening the grip of the past — 36
   - The grip of the past — 41
   - Novelty and time — 43
   - Novelty and multiplicity — 49
   - Nothing new — 52
   - Song's new chariot? — 57
   - Conclusions — 61

3. The transformations of Kaineus — 64
   - Two words for new — 66
   - The emergence of *kainos* — 71
   - The myth of Kaineus — 74
   - The mark of *qāyin* — 79

4. Old and new — 85
   - The Pythagorean table — 90
   - Old and young — 98
   - Old versus new — 102
   - *Kaina kai palaia* — 104

5. Nothing new under the sun — 108
   - What's new under the sun — 109
   - Cycles of novelty — 112
   - Cycles of nature — 116
   - *Ex arkhēs* — 119

	Thinking new thoughts (1)	122
	Thinking new thoughts (2)	126
	Ex oriente novitas	129
6	The birth of Athena	134
	The brainchild of Zeus	138
	The radiance of the new	141
	Novelty and wonder	148
	The shock of the new	150
	Birth into the new	157
7	Inventions of Eris	162
	Serious play	166
	The gleam of glory	170
	Innovation in battle	173
	Inventions of war	177
	Inventions of peace	179
	Conclusions	181
8	The newest song	184
	The discourse of novelty	190
	Prin and *nūn* – then and now	195
	A tradition of innovation	198
	New music, new sounds	202
9	Constructions of novelty	207
	Novelty in the air	211
	The innovationist turn	216
10	So what's new?	225

References 233
General index 247
Index of Greek terms 253
Index locorum 255

Acknowledgements

The germ of this book was my doctoral research at University College London, undertaken in 1994–8 with the help of a Fellowship from the British Academy and a one-year interdisciplinary Fellowship in UCL's Department of Psychology. Those from whom I benefited in the course of that research were my thesis supervisors Richard Janko and Alan Griffiths, examiners Chris Carey and Paul Cartledge, and others including Anthony Cantle, Paddy Considine, Simon Hornblower, Chris Kraus, Steven Instone, Herwig Maehler, Vivian Nutton and Bob Sharples. Others who have since been generous in conversation or correspondence include Lauren Apfel, John Birchall, Louise Braddock, Coline Covington, Eric Csapo, David Fearn, Robert Fowler, Laurel Fulkerson, Monica Gale, Gregory Hutchinson, Chris Kraus, Francesca Martelli, Kieran McGroarty, Robin Osborne, Robert Parker, Tom Phillips, Jim Porter, Andrew Pratt, Philomen Probert, David Scourfield, Richard Seaford, Julia Shear, Michael Vickers, Neil Vickers, Martin West and Stephen Wolfram. I am grateful to my friends and colleagues at Jesus College Oxford for granting me two terms of research leave, and to James Téboul, Stephan Chambers and Michael Anderson for arranging invitations to me to speak on innovation at INSEAD, the Said Business School and London Business School.

I am deeply indebted to Ben Henry and to Paul Cartledge for reading through the first draft and saving me from many errors and infelicities, and to John Birchall and Malcolm Todd for their careful help at the editing stage. The patience of Michael Sharp, Commissioning Editor at Cambridge University Press, and the increasing impatience of my wife, Karen Ciclitira, have both helped me bring this project to completion. Since I began teaching at Oxford in 1998, my students at Oxford, both undergraduate and graduate, have contributed in many ways to my thinking, and more recently have humoured the delayed publication of my thoughts on novelty. I include them among the young and old to whom I dedicate this book, along with my late parents, my daughter Samantha and the many teachers (including John Evans, Martin Hammond, John Roberts, John Lewis, Michael Atkinson, David Bostock, Tom Braun and Nicholas Richardson) who laid the foundations of my knowledge and love of the classics.

NOTE ON SPELLINGS

All Greek is transliterated, with macrons placed over long vowels (*ā*, *ē*), *k* for κ and *kh* for χ. I have used Greek-style spellings of names wherever I feel it to be possible without infringing norms of English usage and pronunciation: thus I write Alkaios and Herodotos, but Aeschylus, Homer, Thucydides, Plato etc.; and I retain Latin spellings for the titles of ancient texts.

Introduction

> Everything clever has already been thought, one must only try to think it again.
>
> Goethe

The original idea for this book came to me when I was working in a family-run manufacturing company in the 1980s. The constant pressure to innovate in products, designs and organisational structures aroused in me a mixture of feelings, positive and negative, about the generation and reception of novelty. This experience led me to wonder whether the Greeks in classical times had encountered a similar ambivalence about innovation. It seemed likely that, although the acknowledged artistic and intellectual innovations attributed to the ancient Greeks fell into a different category from novelty in a modern commercial context, the principles of innovation and the range of human responses to it would at some level have been similar. Above all, I was bound to learn something interesting and useful about processes of innovation, the nature of novelty and the sensibility of newness from studying these things in the ancient context.

My initial investigations showed that although the exceptionally innovative nature of the Greek achievement was taken for granted by students of Greek history and culture, little scholarly consideration was given to how the Greeks felt about and reacted to the new in its wide range of manifestations. One reason for this neglect appeared to be the general consensus among classical scholars and historians that the Greeks were averse to innovation and shunned the new. I regularly found views to this effect expressed, if only *en passant*, in books, articles and commentaries. The supposition that the Greeks did not care for the new seemed strikingly at odds with the widely acknowledged innovativeness of classical Greek thought, art and literature. 'If novelty had been as much detested by the Greeks as it is by us, what classics would there be?' Horace asks in his *Epistle to Augustus* (written *c*.12 BCE).¹ The Roman poet's focus is on literary novelty, but the same question could be asked in respect of the other classics that comprise the Greeks' enduring legacy of art, science and philosophy.²

This apparent dissonance recalled to my mind the episode that had inspired E.R. Dodds' classic study *The Greeks and the Irrational*, the book of his 1950 Sather Classical Lectures. Dodds tells how a viewer of Greek sculptures in the British Museum commented to him that classical statuary was 'so terribly *rational*', rousing him to wonder 'whether the Greeks were in fact quite so blind to the importance of nonrational factors in man's experience and behaviour as is commonly assumed'.³ In similar vein, I doubted that the Greeks could have been as unconcerned with the new or as disinclined to innovate as had generally been supposed.⁴ Two decades after Dodds' book, when Hugh Lloyd-Jones published *The Justice of Zeus* (also derived from a series of Sather Lectures), Dodds wrote to him: 'I stressed the element of change in Greek beliefs, you stress the element of continuity; we are both of us right, though both of us at times exaggerate the partial truth we are stressing.'⁵ It seemed to me that the natural scholarly tendency to seek continuity rather than change, to identify historical links rather than ruptures, might be partly responsible for the dismissal of the Greeks' innovationism – their deliberate pursuit of novelty and acclaim of the new.⁶ Coming from a decade of varied experiences outside academia, I wondered if a new approach to the ancient evidence might help to dislodge inherited assumptions and prejudices about Hellenic traditionalism. What was needed, I felt, to redress the emphasis was a thorough reappraisal of the Greeks' responses to the new, beginning with an attempt to distinguish those spheres in which novelty was rejected from those in which it was welcomed. While the body of evidence itself was not new, a new perspective could be brought to the interpretation of familiar texts if one read them with an eye to what novelty meant for their authors.

---

[1] Hor. *Epist.* 2.1.90–1: *quod si tam Graecis novitas invisa fuisset / quam nobis, quid nunc esset vetus?*
[2] The wider scope of the question is implicit in Horace, who goes on (93–100) to pinpoint the period after the Persian Wars (*positis bellis*) as one in which the Greeks began to 'trifle and play' (*nugari, ludere*) in areas ranging from athletics and horsemanship to art and music.
[3] Dodds (1951) 1.
[4] Of Athens, Dover writes (1974: 111) 'it may seem surprising that a culture which had itself made so many innovations in the arts and in political organisation should have reacted with such undiscriminating hostility against innovations in morality and religion.' Few scholars have sought to go beyond such expressions of surprise.
[5] Lloyd-Jones (1971) xi.
[6] Cf. Foucault (1989: 23): the notion of tradition 'allows a reduction of the difference proper to every beginning, in order to pursue without discontinuity the endless search for the origin; tradition enables us to isolate the new against a background of permanence, and to transfer its merit to originality, to genius, to the decisions proper to individuals'.

Introduction 3

When I embarked on doctoral research in the 1990s, I initially proposed to explore how the Greeks had spoken and felt about novelty. This broad objective immediately raised confusing preliminary questions. Which Greeks, in which period? Intellectuals or peasants, soldiers or traders, men or women, inhabitants of the Greek East or residents of southern Italy and Sicily? What kind of novelty – small-scale or large-scale, literary or artistic, scientific or cultural? Should I take into consideration new sights, sounds and experiences, as well as new ideas, techniques and institutions? It would be hard for a researcher using carefully designed questionnaires to find a uniform and meaningful answer to what novelty means to people in contemporary society. Answers would vary depending on personal circumstances and inclinations, on how the inquiries were framed, on the prevailing social, intellectual and political conditions in which people found themselves at the time of asking, and on a multitude of other factors. These considerations point to the ineluctably subjective aspect of the idea of newness, of which my own personal experience made me constantly aware. I wanted to find a way of interrogating the textual witnesses so as not to lose sight of the underlying complexity and subjectivity of individuals' experience of newness.

Our access to the Greeks is selective and uncertain, our worlds separated by a gulf of time, language and cultural difference; and it is increasingly recognised that a monolithic notion of 'Greek culture' is untenable.[7] Nonetheless, sufficient evidence exists to make such an investigation feasible. The Greeks' legacy of innovation in art and drama, logic and mathematics, medicine and historiography is embodied in surviving artefacts, living traditions and an unparalleled assortment of written texts. The latter indicate, implicitly and explicitly, numerous ways in which people thought about and reacted to the notion of the new in matters great and small, and in relation both to lasting innovations and fleetingly ephemeral novelties. In view of the wealth of evidence that survives for Athenian history and culture from the mid fifth century on, it was practical to make classical Athens the initial focus of a doctoral investigation of the 'dynamics' of innovation – that is, the way attitudes to the new both affected, and were affected by, the incidence of novelty and innovation in the chosen period.[8] The city's unprecedented sociopolitical trajectory, exposure to new ideas and experiences, and acknowledged receptivity to innovative pursuits, were

---

[7] Dougherty and Kurke (2003) 1–6.
[8] The title of my thesis, *The Dynamics of Innovation: newness and novelty in the Athens of Aristophanes* (Ph.D. Lond. 1998) echoes that of Storr's psychoanalytically informed study of creativity (1972), *The Dynamics of Creation*.

noted in antiquity, and make Athens potentially unrepresentative of Greek views generally.[9] But attitudes to the new were by no means uniform in Athens, and from the fifth century on non-Athenian intellectuals and artists had a significant presence and influence in the city. My aim was to consider divergent viewpoints, those of ordinary citizens as well as intellectuals, of laymen no less than specialists. What did it feel like to be surrounded by new objects and ideas? What did it mean to be conscious of new experiences and eventualities? Did all these forms of novelty encourage the seeking out of new paths of thought and action, or were they a disincentive to innovation?

I eventually restricted the scope of my doctoral thesis to roughly the half century 430–380 BCE, for which surviving written evidence is particularly plentiful. The chronological bounds of the inquiry were chosen to coincide with the half century during which Aristophanes' brilliant comedies were written and performed. While other sources reflect and report non-elite viewpoints, Old Comedy does so with a particularly unselfconscious freshness and immediacy. For all their humour, absurdity and potential unreliability as raw data, the surviving plays constitute an indispensable body of source material for popular thought and everyday experience in the city.[10] As well as indicating different viewpoints on specific innovations in fields such as music, philosophy and science, the comedies mostly revolve around larger themes of old and new in Athenian society – moral, political and generational. Supplemented with other texts from the fifth and fourth centuries, they provide a core of vital evidence for ways in which Greeks of the time thought, felt and acted with regard to the new.

An initial survey of words for 'new' and expressions for 'newness' in the chosen texts guided the choice of areas in which I might pursue evidence for Greek innovationism and the experience of novelty.[11] I then sought to find other ways in which novelty and innovation might be expressed or implied. The way a society experiences the new may be indicated, for instance, not only by what people say about it, but by the sounds and sights

---

[9] In this respect it is ironic that the oft-noted (and often inevitable) Athenocentricity of classical Greek scholarship has done so little to counteract the assumption that the Greeks rejected novelty. Ober (2008) singles out Athenian democratic institutions as uniquely effective for distributing information and generating new kinds of knowledge.

[10] Ehrenberg's (1951) useful compilation suffers from treating Aristophanic data as plain fact: Dover (1987).

[11] Dover (1974: 46–50) indicates the virtues and limitations of the lexical approach in studies of this kind. Schmidt (1967 [1876]: 77–123) provides a comprehensive schematic analysis of Greek words for 'old' and 'new'.

to which they are exposed, and by the evidence of material changes and associated behaviours.[12] In the course of the first millennium BCE, social innovations included the introduction of 'silver and bronze coins, money taxes, chattel slavery, writing, schools, written contracts, commercial loans, technical handbooks, large sailing ships, shared risk investment, absentee landlordism'.[13] Such matters are rarely identified as 'innovations' by Greek authors, but they will have contributed to the general consciousness of novelty in their environment no less than demographic changes, linguistic shifts and intercultural borrowings. Rather than attempting to construct a uniform Greek 'attitude to novelty', I compiled recurring themes that had a bearing on the Greeks' receptivity to new ideas and experiences: notions as disparate as artificiality, brightness, chance, commercialism, diversity, excitement, fashion, memory, play and youth. The list of associations to newness indicates the richness and complexity surrounding the meaning of 'new', as well as the potential for confusion owing to the scope of the word's connotations.

The wealth of perspectives revealed by my doctoral research called for a wider investigation of the Greeks' responses to 'the new'. Novelty in manifold guises – change and metamorphosis, emergence and genesis, strangeness and wonder, difference and plurality – inhabits a key place in the landscape of Greek imagination. In classical Greek writings an engagement with novelty can be discerned that is usually subtle and sometimes intense: epic and lyric poetry, tragic drama, medical and philosophical treatises, historiographical and oratorical prose all evince an imaginative commitment to the new in both their form and content. The Athenians were and are singled out as lovers of novelty (see Chapter 9 below); but the Panhellenic outlook of Greek poetry and literature from Homer onwards makes it reasonable to suppose that, local differences notwithstanding, ancient Greeks in general experienced a similar range of thoughts and feelings in respect of, among other things, the new. Unlike with the much-debated question of 'progress', a word for which no satisfactory equivalent exists in classical Greek, the two main Greek words for 'new' (*neos* and *kainos*) are explicit and commonly found. However, the awareness of the new in thought, word and deed also revolves around and embraces a range of other lexical signifiers – 'first', 'different', 'unprecedented', 'original' and

---

[12] In D'Angour (2007) I suggest ways in which new auditory stimuli may have contributed to the sense of novelty experienced by Athenians in the late fifth century.
[13] Hopkins (1983) xv.

so on.[14] Naturally, the Greek equivalents of these terms had domains of signification that often differ from the way they are used in modern contexts. 'Innovation' in particular, signifying the intentional pursuit of novelty and the products of that pursuit, has lexical counterparts in Greek terms such as *kainopoiiā*, *kainotomiā*, *kainotēs*, *kīnein*, *metabolē* and *neōterismos*; but the technical and political spheres in which these terms are generally found differ from the scientific and material technologies with which the term 'innovation' is so heavily associated nowadays.[15]

Aristotle cautions that 'it is the mark of a trained mind never to look for more precision in the treatment of any subject than the nature of that subject permits'.[16] One can only pursue the question of what 'new' means in the directions in which our sources point, and attempt to avoid overprecise categorisation of the admittedly select and selective evidence. It requires consideration not only of what Greeks did in relation to novelty, but how they felt about it and imagined it. Newness inhabits a complex, timeless and ultimately indefinable fusion of ideas, symbols and fantasies (a domain comprised by the French term *l'imaginaire*).[17] How are the lineaments of human imagination to be adequately captured and represented? The exploration of the vagaries of collective fantasy deals with indeterminate phenomena which are not obviously conducive to the establishment of historical or even psychological 'facts'. Historians may seek to present and evaluate evidence and sources; literary investigators may aim to illuminate the meaning of a text through analysis of such elements as verbal structures and intertextual relations; but the investigator of the Greek 'imaginary' who attempts to combine empirical and hermeneutic methodologies risks straddling the opposite poles of positivistic rigour and imaginative flexibility. This topic is not susceptible to the confident (or naive) historicism expressed by the nineteenth-century German historian Ranke's *wie es eigentlich gewesen*, 'how it actually happened'. The focus cannot only or even principally be on the realities, such as they are, of novelty and innovation, since these are largely matters of perception, whether

---

[14] Edelstein (1967: xxx) observes that 'in tracing the history of a concept one cannot be bound by lexicographical considerations but must look for identity of content'. But on the whole neither verbal nor conceptual identity is to be found, and one must be content with Wittgensteinian 'family resemblance'.

[15] See further Chapter 7. The terminology in English for demarcating the general area of this study, whose scope and complexity I further indicate in Chapter 1, is markedly unsatisfactory. 'Novelty' has specific and often pejorative associations, 'innovation' is linked to technology, and 'newness' is an awkward-sounding abstraction. I have settled on 'the new' (equivalent to the Greek *to neon* or *to kainon*) as the most neutral and convenient term for the range of notions under investigation.

[16] Arist. *EN* 1094b23–5. [17] On the use of this term see Buxton (1994) 4–5.

contemporary or retrospective. Insights provided by modern psychology and psychoanalysis regarding the perceived salience of stimuli, the role of play and competition in human life, the creative impulse, the innate desire for understanding or unconscious sense of loss can offer some help in understanding how to think about the genesis, production and reception of novelty. While such notions have informed my investigation at every stage, and seem no less pertinent to ancient Greek behaviours and attitudes to the new than to modern ones, I have not sought to apply them in any systematic way. Where the psychoanalytic mode of inquiry has had its strongest impact is on my supposition that texts and verbal expressions reveal unconscious as well as conscious assumptions and preoccupations.[18]

My aim, then, is not so much to try to determine the historical vicissitudes of newness or of its conceptualisation as to present and elucidate its manifestations and intimations in ancient texts. Any account is destined to be partial and diffuse; but by observing the interplay of texts and ideas one may recognise the richness and variety of the landscape of novelty in the classical Greek context.[19] Philological and historical inquiry need to be combined in such a project, which is akin to the anthropologist's 'searching out and analysing the symbolic forms – words, images, institutions, behaviors – in terms of which, in each place, people actually represented themselves as themselves and to one another'.[20] The heterogeneous scope and subject matter of the investigation raise questions that may be assigned to different approaches and methodologies as follows:

1. *Logico-lexical*
   How did the Greek words for 'new' arise and what is their etymology? What is the range of meanings of 'new' and related words in Greek (*neos, kainos* etc.)? In what contexts are these words found, and with what different significations (original, recent, young, modern etc.)?

2. *Psychological-philosophical*
   What impact does the new have, positive or negative, on different percipients? How do specific reactions inform us about the Greeks' feelings about novelty? How is a sense of 'newness' unconsciously indicated, and

---

[18] Unlike some uses of intertextuality, this approach supposes that we may posit relations between signifiers and what may be *unconsciously* signified; cf. my discussion (2003) of Horace's 'Archytas ode' (*Odes* 1.28), where I delve beneath the surface of the poem to explore implicit sources of meaning. Oliensis (2009: 5–11) gives an elegant exposition of what she calls the 'textual unconscious'.

[19] 'Classical' here roughly covers the period 750–350 BCE. Much remains to be said about the Hellenistic period, with its sophisticated and multifaceted approach to innovation in art and literature, for which see e.g. Fowler (1989), Fantuzzi and Hunter (2004).

[20] Geertz (1983) 58.

how is it exploited for rhetorical purposes? To what extent is the perception of novelty engendered by a shift in the position of the perceiver?
3. *Literary-symbolic*
How is newness imagined and represented in Greek? What symbols of novelty may be found in myth, art and literature? How does the new relate to metaphors of birth and enlightenment, or to notions of youth and change, emergence and recurrence, diversity and multiplicity?
4. *Social-historical*
What narratives of innovation exist in technical and intellectual domains? What do accounts of new inventions, discoveries and institutions tell us about the impact of the new? What part is played by the historical introduction (acknowledged or otherwise) of ideas and techniques from 'outside'?

The different and often unrelated methodologies that may be brought to bear on the notion of the new can lead to discussions which appear to have scant bearing on one another. Linguistic analysis of 'new', for instance, may seem to have little in common with consideration of the impulse towards political or medical novelty; and mechanisms of artistic and technical originality may be felt to have few points of intersection with the way 'new' is invoked in narratives of social and historical change.

Can the elusive and many-sided aspects of the Greeks' imaginative understanding of novelty be productively explored, rather than reductively anatomised? A unifying perspective on this Protean subject is hard to achieve. While a focus on 'the new' avoids the linguistic and conceptual obstacles of the question of 'progress', it raises definitional problems that are no less problematic. It is not easy even to determine the relations between the disparate categories, ideas and experiences signified by the word 'new', if these are taken to include recency, modernity, youthfulness, otherness, diversity, the unfamiliar, the unexpected and the future. In view of such terminological and semantic indeterminacy, no tidy anatomisation of the concept can be made without arbitrariness or artificiality, and despite some provisional schemas (such as that on p. 22) this book makes no attempt to do so. One can only hope for a more or less coherent and illuminating picture to emerge cumulatively from a composite methodology that takes into account an appropriately disparate range of questions, texts and analyses.[21]

---

[21] An increased (and welcome) critical self-consciousness among classicists has tended to shift the focus away from studying innovations *in* antiquity to generating innovations *of* antiquity (Hexter and Selden 1992); the scope of this study embraces both objectives.

Given the potential scope of their interpretation, newness and novelty may be found in most areas of ancient life. I have selected areas where either explicit indications or suggestive indications permit some productive consideration of the notion. In Chapter 1, I outline previous approaches to Greek creativity and innovation, and indicate the breadth of the investigation by discussing issues of logic, psychology and imagery that surround the notion of the new. In Chapter 2, I propose that newness may be imaginatively reconceptualised in ways that challenge the traditional view that the Greeks were held 'in the grip of the past'. Chapter 3 links the broad notion of metamorphosis to the linguistic and cultural transformations out of which emerged a principal (and arguably, at one stage, new) Greek word for 'new', *kainos*. In Chapter 4, I consider 'new' in relation to its antonym 'old', and explore different aspects of the opposition, arguing that it is less straightforward in Greek than in English because of the close linguistic association of 'new' with 'young'. In Chapter 5, discussion of the familiar proverb 'there's nothing new under the sun' connects the sentiment to the views of Presocratic thinkers, which leads to a consideration of the sources of new ideas and knowledge. In Chapter 6, the imagery associated with the birth of Athena and other Greek divinities is the basis of an exploration of literary and psychological associations to novelty (in particular those of genesis, light and wonder) and of attitudes to innovation in the visual arts. In Chapter 7, I consider the link between innovation and competition, and explore its elusive manifestations in various contexts in ancient Greece. In Chapter 8 I focus on Greek *mousikē*, which presents a notable 'tradition of innovation' in the explicit claims of musico-literary artists from the time of Homer onwards, but requires us to draw distinctions between claims to be doing something new in music and poetry. In Chapter 9 I consider the way novelty relates to literary constructions and discuss how the Greek literary imagination was both an expression of and a spur to innovative developments, particularly with regard to the 'innovationist turn' that characterises late fifth-century Athens.

The composition of this book itself illustrates approaches to innovation that can be derived from an examination of the ancient Greek experience: the criticism and contestation of earlier ideas, the recombination and reinterpretation of familiar material, the presentation of existing evidence in a new light, the novelty produced by profusion and variety, and so on. In writing about novelty, I naturally hope to say something new; but there are always new things to say and new ways of saying them – and since the passage of time itself brings about the new, the newest thing is what remains to be said. The topic potentially covers innumerable areas of thought and investigation, and I am conscious of having only touched the surface of many areas, texts and periods in which innovation of various kinds featured in antiquity – religion and politics, architecture and theatre, the Hellenistic era, the Second Sophistic, etc.[22] My omissions and inadequacies will be a spur to me and, I hope, to others to explore new avenues. But it may be that, to misquote T.S. Eliot, humankind cannot bear very much novelty, and what is true for humankind will go for me and my readers.

---

[22] Whitmarsh (2005) comments briefly on rhetorical *kainotēs* in the Second Sophistic (54–6) and in the Greek novel (86–9). The latter draws attention to itself owing to its homonymy, though 'novel' in this sense derives from the sixteenth-century Italian *novella storia*. Tilg (2010: 164–97) examines how Khariton and other novelists draw attention to their own originality in developing their 'novel' genre.

CHAPTER I

New, new, new

Au fond de l'inconnu pour trouver du nouveau...
                                               Baudelaire

In today's world, with its unprecedented technological capabilities and global interconnections, novelty is a constant and inescapable feature of everyday life. The pursuit of the new drives commerce, science, education and the arts. Creativity is commodified, originality is considered the key to success. Novelty is sought out by inventors, extolled by advertisers, devoured by consumers. 'Innovation' is the buzzword of modernity. 'News' is a term so implicated with rapid and sophisticated communications media that its semantic connection to 'new' is often all but forgotten. Words such as *newness, news, novelty* and *innovation*, despite their very different connotations, exhibit a family resemblance in that they all in some way converge upon the everyday, if deceptively simple-seeming, notion of 'the new'. This notion retains the power to arouse a range of responses, negative as well as positive. It evokes pleasure and excitement, anxiety and resignation. Newness entails change, an inescapable aspect of the world and of the human condition. But to experience the *new* is to register a change that is in some way heightened, striking, or salient.

Can we validly relate our own disparate experiences of the new to the experience of societies and individuals in Greek antiquity? In marked contrast to the way the modern world is seen to rely on and celebrate newness across so many areas of life, the ancient Greeks are commonly characterised as having been unconcerned with and even averse to novelty. Propositions to the effect that the Greeks 'did not like novelty' or 'shunned the new' are widely found in studies of classical literature, history and thought. B.A. van Groningen's 1953 monograph *In the Grip of the Past*, which argues that conservatism and disinclination to the new are evident in all aspects of Hellenic thought and culture, is still respectfully cited.[1] His conclusions, however, pose something of a paradox. How can the overriding traditionalism he and others attribute to 'the Greek mind' be reconciled with the undoubted profusion of novelty, the often unprecedented and unsurpassed innovations, produced by Greek thinkers, writers and artists?

NOVELTY IN GREEK CULTURE

'Time as it grows old teaches all things' was a Greek commonplace.[2] If the passage of time itself gives rise to the new, the experience of novelty will be keener for societies and individuals who perceive a visible growth in capacity and opportunity as each year passes. The Hellenic world from the eighth to the fourth century BCE (the period broadly referred to as 'classical Greece') underwent and generated decisive changes in politics, society, art and thought. Few inhabitants of the thousand or so Greek *poleis* (city-states) can have avoided some experience of the novelties that emerged. The Greek alphabet, a brilliant adaptation of Phoenician script, rapidly became established as an incomparably convenient medium for recording literature for wide dissemination. The use of coined money, introduced in the seventh century from Lydia, spread across the Greek world and led to its eventual monetisation to an unprecedented level. The city-state emerged as a unique political unit, operating with new legal systems and forms of citizenship, and promoting innovative notions such as political equality (*isonomiā*) and, in due course, democracy (*dēmokratiā*). Numerous new 'colonies' (*apoikiai*) were founded as independent offshoots of their mother-cities, expanding and diversifying the Greeks' geographical knowledge and exposure to the products of different cultures. Athletic and artistic competitions were established, acquiring such Panhellenic prestige that it made sense for the earliest standard dating system for Greek history (devised by Hippias around 400 BCE) to begin with the supposed date of the first Olympic Games in 776 BCE.[3]

In parallel with these developments, philosophers, physicians and political thinkers ventured on revolutionary new kinds of reasoning and reflection about the natural world and the nature of man. Human knowledge was organised into specialist disciplines such as music, mathematics and

---

[1] E.g. in Csapo and Miller (1998: 94–5), Dunn (2007: 197 n. 5), Grethlein (2010: 2). I offer a critique of van Groningen's approach and conclusions in Chapter 2.
[2] The words are spoken by Prometheus in [Aesch.] *PV* 982 as a warning that Zeus will come to grief. Cf. Eur. fr. 945: *aei ti kainon hēmerā paideuetai*, 'each day always teaches something new'.
[3] Christensen (2007) 46–9.

medicine, and a host of sub-disciplines such as grammar, metre and acoustics. Pictorial perspective was invented, and forms of sculpture and architecture were created that were to become canonical. The growing diversity of human experience was represented in an explosion of new forms and genres of literature – notably lyric poetry, tragic and comic drama, and historiographical and philosophical prose. The scale and nature of these innovations have been felt to mark a wholesale transformation in human capacities and psychology:

Modes of symbolic expression and the manipulation of signs, ideas of time and space, causality, memory, imagination, the organization of acts, will, and personality – all these categories of mind undergo a fundamental change in terms of both their internal structure and their interrelationships.[4]

The magnitude and character of these achievements have been felt to distinguish Greek culture from previous cultures, giving rise to the term 'Greek miracle'.[5] In recent times scholars have questioned this notion, enumerating the contributions of other ancient peoples to Greek culture, and stressing how the traditional narratives of Greek history have been selectively constructed since the European Renaissance.[6] What is unassailable is the evidence of contemporary and subsequent sources that during the archaic and classical periods changes of diverse kinds and consequences, some transient and some lasting, were made across a wide range of disciplines and activities. Multiple forms of novelty, both generated within Greek society and adopted from without, made an impact on societies and individuals throughout the Hellenic world. These different kinds of novelty are remarked on by Greek poets, artists and thinkers in a more direct, ample and self-conscious manner than can be found in the surviving documents of any other ancient culture; and the notion of innovation (*kainotomiā, to kainon*) is more regularly and explicitly raised by Greek authors than in any earlier corpus of ancient texts.

The effusion of novel and original expressions in art, literature, politics and science fundamentally calls into question the view that the Greeks rejected novelty wholesale. Nor was it always supposed that they did so. Among scholars reared in the Victorian era, when the spirit of innovation and discovery flourished against a background of austere traditionalism, views of the following kind were not uncommon:

---

[4] Vernant (2006) 15.
[5] The term derives from Renan's (1948: 393) 'Prayer on the Acropolis' of 1876: Lloyd (1990) 14.
[6] Papenfuss and Strocka (2001); Osborne (2006) 4–5.

Freedom of development and joy in the quest attended the creation of new ideas in literature and science. Greek literature is the only absolutely original literature of Europe. In a rapid succession of inventive crises nearly every known species of poetry and prose was developed. Greece gave birth to the critical instinct applied to all knowledge and to the desire to compass all knowledge; to the science of theory; to the organization of society into all its various forms; to the philosophy of government and to the dream of an ideal state; to the science of ethics; to the search for the causes of Being; to the analysis of the functions of mind; to the distinction between mind and matter... On every hand the Greeks seem always to be adventuring the unknown, forever to be 'voyaging through strange seas of thought alone'. The fruition of their prerogative of possession of the field was the orderly but rapid conquest of the territory still unsubdued by their intellect. In Hellenic thought there is always a passion for change, for some reaction from national ideals.[7]

Herbert Weir Smyth, the author of this paean to Hellenic innovationism – and also the compiler of a standard Greek grammar – goes on to stress that these selfsame Greeks were conservative in outlook and character. The 'seeming paradox' has been summed up (in the context of Greek politics) by Paul Cartledge:

On the one hand, there is easily detectable in much Greek thinking, not only political, an all-pervasive conservatism. Greeks often found themselves or perceived themselves as being in the grip of the past, with the linguistic consequence that political ideas and practices which we might want to label positively as 'revolution', such as the invention of democracy, they would habitually and automatically anathematise as 'new' or 'newer things', opposing them unfavourably to that which was traditional (*patrion*), in accordance with ancestral custom and practice, even – or especially – when the supposed tradition was perceptibly or demonstrably an invented one. On the other hand, the Greeks did actually achieve revolutions or at any rate profound and lasting transformations in both their political practice and their political consciousness, something structurally far deeper and more permanent than is conveyed by the terms *metabolē* or *metastasis* (transformation) employed by the author of the 'Constitution of the Athenians' attributed to Aristotle.[8]

Cartledge proposes three possible ways of resolving the paradox. One is to suppose that the changes were evolutionary rather than revolutionary: the gradual emergence of new things would have allowed the manifestations of novelty to be more easily absorbed by traditionally minded recipients. Another is to argue that the agents of change were atypical individuals, whose thoughts and activities went against the grain of a more common

---

[7] Smyth (1906) 49–50. [8] Cartledge (1998b) 381.

attitude of traditionalism. The third is to suggest that innovations due to such exceptional individuals were 'crucially facilitated by conditions peculiar to Greek political life'.[9] This seeks to account for how changes in Greek social and political institutions, generally devised by undoubtedly exceptional men such as Solon and Kleisthenes, were adopted by and took root among Greeks who were themselves not thinkers of equally radical inclinations. But the question then arises as to how the 'peculiar conditions' that facilitated such changes may themselves be thought to have pertained.

Questions about the deeper roots of Greek innovation have long formed a part of attempts to account for their celebrated cultural achievements. Some investigators have been content to note historical contingencies; others have sought to analyse cultural tendencies or to elucidate the Hellenic 'mentality'.[10] In evaluating the conditions that led to an intellectual flowering in archaic Greece, scholars such as Pierre Lévêque, Jean-Pierre Vernant and Pierre Vidal-Naquet have emphasised the development of political relations, temporal structures and personal interactions.[11] Jack Goody and Ian Watt have argued that the advent of alphabetic writing brought about a change in cognitive capacity, spurring the development of logic and reasoning, the growth of individualism and democracy, and the shift from a mythical to a historical perspective on the past.[12] In *Magic, Reason and Experience*, Geoffrey Lloyd has illustrated how the introduction of money, curiosity about other societies and the advent of literacy were interrelated with Greek practices of open debate, critical scrutiny and rational justification.[13] Subsequently, in the second of a series of Sather Lectures published as *The Revolutions of Wisdom* (1987), Lloyd offered a concise outline of Greek innovationism, focussing on Greek medicine and science and highlighting such indicators as first-person claims by medical practitioners, criticism of predecessors, and practices of contestation in public arenas.[14]

Other scholars have emphasised the way material conditions underpinned the unique cultural trajectory attributed to the Greeks. Robert

---

[9] Ibid. 382.
[10] On the difficulties associated with the notion of 'mentality' see Lloyd (1990), who cautions that 'just how recurrent and pervasive a set of characteristics has to be in order to be considered evidence of a distinct underlying mentality will be a matter of judgement, but that judgement should, in principle, depend on whether or how far other accounts might appear to offer adequate ways of describing and explaining the data concerned' (5).
[11] Lévêque and Vidal-Naquet (1996), Vernant and Vidal-Naquet (1988) etc.
[12] Goody and Watt (1963). Havelock, E. (1963) and Ong (1982) also note ways in which the use of writing transformed the nature of Greek thought and literature, stressing that orality continued to shape patterns of thought down to the fourth century BCE.
[13] Lloyd (1979). [14] 'Tradition and Innovation, Text and Context': Lloyd (1987) 50–108.

Hahn has argued that techniques of archaic monumental architecture, imitated from Egyptian models, inspired the rational world-view that emerges in the thought of Presocratic philosophers and in the creation of Greek political structures.[15] More recently, Richard Seaford has made a bold case for the crucial impact of monetisation in sixth-century Greece on the development of Greek culture and ideology. Analysing the formal characteristics of money, such as its function in social exchange and its status as the provider of a guaranteed and generally accepted measure of value, Seaford argues that the advent of money was the prime influence on the evolution of abstract thought, philosophy and tragedy.[16] Explanations of this kind can seem over-schematic, but they demonstrate ways in which practical and material innovations undoubtedly interacted with and influenced the Greeks' artistic and intellectual development.

What have been less systematically investigated are the Greeks' consciously expressed views on the new, and the way these relate to their novel achievements in various spheres. Expressions of innovationism have, however, been regularly adduced and discussed in scholarly studies of the 'idea of progress'.[17] In a valuable monograph (published posthumously), Ludwig Edelstein analysed the material and psychological conditions that encouraged some forms of the notion of progress to emerge in the Greek world, compiling numerous intimations and indications of the idea from the Presocratics to late antiquity.[18] He was careful to note that the absence of a direct equivalent to 'progress' in Greek meant that 'one is sometimes constrained to use language that sounds strange to modern ears and often to speak in categories unknown to the ancients'.[19] But Edelstein presented – in opposition to earlier studies such as that of Bury (1932) – a convincing array of instances to show that 'there is abundant and unimpeachable evidence for ancient progressivism'.[20] Subsequently E.R. Dodds summarised the lexical and literary evidence for the idea of progress, and concluded that 'only during a limited period in the fifth century was it widely accepted by the educated public at large', and drew attention to the 'broad correlation between the expectation of progress and the actual experience of

---

[15] Hahn (2001).
[16] Seaford (2004); cf. Seaford (1994), which traces how notions of reciprocity in epic and tragedy are connected to Greek ritual and civic practices.
[17] E.g. Bury (1932), Edelstein (1967), Dodds (1973), Burkert (1997). [18] Edelstein (1967).
[19] Ibid. xxx–xxxi; the evidence adduced is often equally relevant to the 'new', for which Greek terms abound.
[20] Ibid. xv. Cf. Zhmud (2006) 16: 'the idea of the progressive growth of knowledge (as well as many others) can well be expressed without being labeled with a specific term'.

progress'.[21] Subsequent discussions of the question have added little to his conclusions.[22]

In an important attempt to address the question of progress from a fresh perspective, Christian Meier has argued that Greeks of the fifth century were conscious not so much of continuing advances over time but of the augmentation (*auxēsis*) of human knowledge and technical capacities in their period.[23] The recognition that the experience of growth and diversity may be equated with a sense of novelty and progress provides a corrective to narrower approaches such as that of van Groningen, whose conclusion that the Greeks were antipathetic to novelty rests partly on the assumption that a temporal (mainly future-oriented) connotation is intrinsic to 'new'. However, even the assumption that newness might include non-temporal qualities such as those of 'difference' or 'otherness' has not prevented scholars taking similar positions to that of van Groningen. Arlene Saxonhouse, for instance, has sought to interpret expressions in Greek philosophy and Attic drama as showing that the Greeks in general feared and strove against manifestations of diversity, and were inclined to seek the reassurance of unity beneath the multiplicity of appearances and the plurality of moral, social and existential possibilities.[24]

Unpacking a distinction briefly raised by van Groningen between 'mythical' and 'historical' perspectives on time, Eric Csapo and Margaret Miller have contributed a subtle and complex exploration of Greek attitudes to temporality. They note Meier's reference to the emergence of 'political time' in fifth-century Athens ('a consciousness of time predicated upon a faith in the ability of humans to master their destiny through the political process')[25] and demonstrate how the evidence of classical art and literature points to the simultaneous coexistence of different understandings of time. The emergence of a new 'democratic' sense of temporality, accompanying and only eventually replacing 'aristocratic' temporality, is related to political and sociological developments in the fifth century:

In opposition to the dominant temporality of the Archaic period which privileged the distant past, the new dominant privileged the present. To the Archaic dominant the present continued or repeated the past and was determined by it, but to the

---

[21] Dodds (1973) 24–5.   [22] E.g. Burkert (1997), Zhmud (2006).
[23] Meier (1990) 186–221; he proposes extending the use of *auxēsis* to stand for 'an ancient equivalent of progress', while admitting that the Greeks did not use the term for this purpose.
[24] Saxonhouse (1992). Much the same evidence may be used to argue a diametrically opposite conclusion: thus Apfel (2011) views the writings of historians, sophists and tragedians as demonstrating the 'advent of pluralism' (moral, intellectual and cultural) in fifth-century Greece.
[25] Csapo and Miller (1998) 95.

new temporality the present was its own moment which could be freed from past determinations by knowledge of historical causality, and this knowledge could be put toward shaping the future. Time became historical.[26]

Francis Dunn has also recently explored aspects of the shift to a present-centred temporality in the fifth century. He argues that the experience of diversity evoked ambivalent responses in the Greeks: a new sense of 'present shock' – 'radical disorientation at living in a present no longer shaped and given meaning by the authority of the past' – is detectable in the way texts of the fifth century increasingly concentrate on the here-and-now.[27]

The texts in question are predominantly literary works composed by Athenian authors or with Athenian readership in mind. This is significant, because while scholars have long seemed united in attributing to the Greeks an overridingly traditionalistic outlook, there are two areas of widely (if tacitly) admitted exception: the trajectory of Greek literature, and the history of Athens. Both narratives exhibit numerous and unmistakable manifestations of deliberate and often wilful innovation. In Greek literature, scholars have identified such innovation as stemming from mechanisms of creative imitation, selective borrowing, the reconfiguring of familiar stories and themes, the modification and adaptation of particular styles and tropes. These strategies involve imaginative and often adventurous choices in relation to familiar conventions, often with the express intention of departing from the constraints of tradition and creating something new and original.[28] The political, educational and artistic directions pursued by Athens over the course of the classical period have also been recognised not just as novel but as strikingly innovatory. If these features are so readily discernible in the Panhellenic area of musico-literary composition and so apparent in the city dubbed 'an education to Greece', 'the Central Office of Hellenic wisdom', and 'the Greece of Greece', why might they not be seen as integral to the capacities and imaginative orientations of the ancient Greeks?[29] A closer look at Greek responses to the new, expressed and

---

[26] Ibid. 100.
[27] Dunn (2007); his starting-point (4) is the figure of Strepsiades in Aristophanes' *Clouds*, who at different junctures rejects and embraces the new freedom from traditional moral and religious constraints.
[28] See e.g. Bowra (1966) 17–18: 'the Greeks saw that tradition must not be followed too slavishly and should rather be a guide to new work at an agreed level in accord with accepted standards. They knew that it was not enough simply to copy the achievements of the past, that they must always adapt and assimilate them and add something to them and give a new turn to an old tale or a new interpretation of a much-told event'. Hose (2000) discusses explicit manifestations of the musico-literary promotion of novelty.
[29] *Paideusis tēs Hellados*, Thuc. 2.41.1; *tēs Hellados auto to prutaneion tēs sophiās*, Pl. *Prot.* 337d; *Vit. Eur.* p.3 Schwartz.

implied, combined with a reconsideration of the psychological tendencies these represent, is needed to throw light on the question.

'NEW': WORD AND CONCEPT

Innovation is not the only way in which novelty presents itself. Since we are concerned to inquire into the Greeks' experience of the new no less than its explicit expression, an initial indication of the range of the concept is required. Newness in everyday speech is predicated of a bewilderingly disparate variety of subjects, abstract and concrete: ideas, events, experiences, roles and institutions, as well as people, places, physical objects, artefacts and material structures. While 'new' presents itself as an objective and descriptive term, its meanings are essentially relative to and dependent on its locus of utterance (one may compare the use of the word 'now', to which 'new' is etymologically related, cf. Greek *neos* and *nūn*). The connotations of the word 'new' range from recent, young, different, other, next in sequence and additional, to novel, unusual, unfamiliar, extraneous, unprecedented, hitherto non-existent and hitherto unknown. It is regularly used in English, as were its equivalents in Greek, in two distinct but related senses, which may be termed 'temporal' and 'qualitative'. The temporal sense (new 'in time') makes it equivalent to 'young', 'recent' and so on; the qualitative sense (new 'in kind') aligns its meaning with 'different' or 'unfamiliar'.[30] The distinction is seldom explicit, and the senses are often conflated.

The concept of newness appears inherently relative and multifaceted, and gives rise to what look like puzzling contradictions. Something new can invariably be said to be new in one sense and not another. Thus a 'new chapter' may be the next one in sequence, but have nothing original about it. A 'new book' need not be lately authored, only one not yet read by a particular reader. Spurious novelties are hailed as exemplary, genuine innovations are dismissed as 'nothing new'. The exercise of skill (*tekhnē*) gives rise to the new, but so do eventualities of chance (*tukhē*).[31] What is new may be recent, but what is recent is not always new; a 'new poem by Sappho' may refer to a poem recently discovered rather than one newly composed. Some things are called 'innovative' but are not; others are novel but are not innovations. Aristophanes' new ideas (*kainai ideai*) may be

---

[30] Cf. the French distinction (though again there is some semantic overlap) between 'nouveau' ('another') and 'neuf' ('brand-new').

[31] The opposition may be collapsed: 'Chance loves skill, and skill chance' runs a line from the dramatist Agathon (Arist. *EN* 1140a17); cf. Ion of Khios, fr. 3.

original ideas, or simply ideas that, on his own claim, have not previously been presented to his audience.[32]

The quality of novelty may be predicated of a perceived object, but the feeling of newness may rather be located in the perceiver. When Theognis rejects any 'newer concern' (*neōteron meledēma*) in favour of the pursuit of poetry, he is rejecting the thought of a different pursuit, not one that is more up to date.[33] In contexts of this kind, 'new' simply carries a weak sense of otherness, an indication that some unspecified degree of change or difference should be registered. A 'new' idea may strike people from time to time, but the newness in question need not be of the kind for which Einstein is celebrated. In Euripides' satyr-play *Cyclops*, when Polyphemos complains about his monotonous diet of lions and deer, the thought that new human flesh might make a nice change for him seems to Silenos somewhat overdue:

> After everyday fare, master, something new (*ta kaina*)
> is all the sweeter; it's not a recent matter (*neōsti*)
> that strangers have come to your house.[34]

In English we often find 'new' used in a way where in Greek one might find *heteros* or *allos* ('other') or simply a future tense. We may talk, for instance, about acquiring a 'new' (i.e. another) job, home or partner, or about encountering a new idea, making a new plan, or starting a new chapter. The appropriate term of opposition to 'new' in such cases may be 'the same': 'atomism is not a *new* idea, ancient thinkers had the *same* concept', 'the actor is performing the *same* part, not a *new* one'. In that the later occurrence is identified as potentially 'newer', a degree of temporality is involved; an object so perceived may possess no intrinsic quality of novelty or recency. Greek often uses expressions lacking a specific word for 'new'. When Telemakhos in the *Odyssey* proclaims that he will permit Penelope to remarry if Odysseus is found to have died, he promises (in effect) 'I shall give her to a new husband', but the Greek phrase *āneri dōsō* does not have any lexical equivalent of 'new'.[35] Similarly, in the short poem in which Arkhilokhos dismisses the loss of his shield on the battlefield, we might translate 'I'll get a new one just as good' where the Greek text (*exautis ktēsomai ou kakiō*) contains no word literally to be translated 'new'.[36] The difference in usage is sufficiently common to suggest that the Greeks may have used *neos* or *kainos* less casually, and with a more precise connotation,

---

[32] Ar. *Nub.* 547. [33] Thgn. 789. [34] Eur. *Cycl.* 250–2. [35] *Od.* 2.223. [36] Arkhil. fr. 5.4.

than is often the case with English 'new'. This species of newness might be considered a form of *differentiation*.

Diversity of form, appearance or experience (*poikiliā*, *polupeiriā*) is also associated with the sense of the new, even if these notions are not strictly considered to form part of the word's semantic properties. What gives rise to the sense of novelty may be the fact that one thing appears in different guise from another thing that has been viewed or perceived earlier, though the sequence of temporal occurrence may be arbitrary or accidental. A form of novelty may accordingly arise when different aspects of a plurality are perceived in sequence. Observers presented with great diversity may be unable to take in a multiplicity of differences simultaneously, so will range across the domain encountering one 'new' thing after another.

Loosened from temporal connotations, *kainotēs* can come to be associated with artificiality, excess and supervenience, something that goes outside or beyond what is natural or normal. This form of *to kainon* emerges *ex nihilo* in a way that defies expectation or anticipation. Qualitative newness may be manifested as radical difference or otherness, a startling intrusion, an unheralded epiphany; it may indicate a revolutionary change in structures of knowledge or experience, a 'paradigm shift'.[37] The term 'radical innovation' is occasionally used to draw a contrast with 'incremental innovation'.[38] Where the latter term is used to describe the way one may build on known and existing elements to create something new, 'radical' implies by contrast that innovation begins with a clean slate, owing nothing to a previous or existing state of affairs. From a logical viewpoint, however, the notion of a newness that is genuinely radical ('new from the root up'), altogether transcending existent structures, verges on paradox.[39] Modern complexity theory may offer the best account of radical innovation, analysing it in terms of the way complex systems produce outcomes which, though entirely dependent on foregoing conditions, are wholly unpredictable in form.[40] But the expression is more often found when novelty is simply felt by the utterer to be unprecedented, or as a rhetorical means of emphasising the extent to which something departs from past experience.

---

[37] Kuhn (1970).   [38] E.g. in Bronk (2009) 208–9.
[39] Supposedly 'radical' innovators may themselves explicitly reject the notion; e.g. Isaac Newton wrote in a letter to Robert Hooke (15 February 1676) 'If I have seen a little further, it is by standing on the shoulders of Giants.'
[40] Wolfram (2002); for suggestions for modelling social innovation see Spratt (1989), McGlade and McGlade (1989).

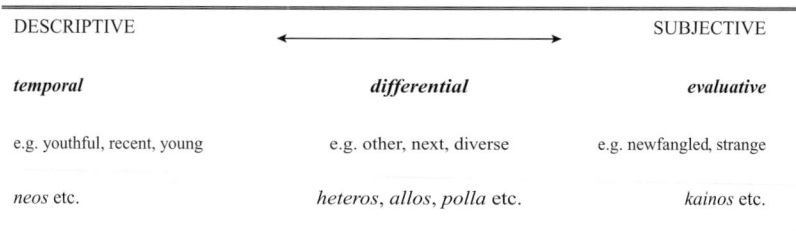

Figure 1 The semantic domain of 'new'

The semantic domain of 'new' thus extends along a spectrum of signification from trivial difference to wholesale alterity. The various aspects discussed may be schematically presented as ranging from temporal notions at one end to evaluative or emotive connotations at the other (see Figure 1). Words at the 'descriptive' end of the spectrum relate the meaning of 'young', 'new' etc. to their position on a notionally objective timescale. Those on the 'subjective' end are related more closely, if not entirely, to the effect on a percipient. The centre is occupied by more neutral meanings, including the use of 'new' to mean 'another'. At both ends of the spectrum, what is new may be defined in relation to what is old. At the temporal end the relationship is more naturally understood as one of continuity: young becomes old, the recent past is continuous with the remoter past. At the other end, it is more readily seen as one of opposition: new is not old, novel is not familiar.

Such a scheme inevitably requires oversimplification. In fact, rather than comprising a single spectrum, it can be shown that 'new' intersects numerous matrices of sense and reference, with subtle gradations of meaning for which everyday speech lacks adequately precise means of expression. It may, for instance, be a useful rule of thumb to distinguish weak from strong varieties of newness, the former comprising less salient kinds of change or difference, the latter requiring the recognition of a marked quality of novelty. But it is no easier to assess degrees of salience with any precision than to insist on clear-cut distinctions between 'new' and synonyms such as 'young', 'recent' and 'next'.

In Greek too, lexical data do not support rigidly determinate distinctions in the meaning or status of expressions of newness. In cases where the Greek expression uses *neos* and *kainos*, however, we find that a general (if not consistent) distinction can be drawn between the principal connotations of the Greek words. Where what is new is essentially a young or recent variant of something, *neos* is generally found to be the appropriate signifier. In that the word primarily represents 'young', whether in terms of natural growth or development in time, it is less apt to suggest a sense of unfamiliarity or unpredictability. Even the adverb *neon*, 'recently', refers to the past, albeit what is *just* past.[41] By contrast, the notion of a quality of novelty or difference that arises from human intention or creation, for instance in objects that are 'brand-new' and ideas that appear 'newfangled', is more appropriately (though in practice not exclusively) expressed by *kainos*. Novelty of this kind partakes of an aspect of temporality insofar as it implies a deliberate break from the past; but the focus is not on newness in time but on newness in kind.

The rhetorical dimension of the term is ever-present. 'New' attached to objects, institutions and other predicates whose newness may lie in the future or in the past depending on the time of utterance: 'new year', 'new pence', 'New Deal' etc. It notoriously survives as a fossilised element in proper names, where its original temporal signification has passed. Just as New College, the New Forest and New York are no longer 'new', in Greek we find such appellations as *to Kainon*, the nickname of the new Athenian lawcourt built in the late fifth century;[42] and Neapolis ('new city'), the name given to numerous cities on their first foundation, including the seventh-century Greek foundation of Naples.[43]

In his dialogue *Theaetetus*, Plato presents Sokrates discussing a theory according to which 'passive' qualities do not exist independently of the activity of a perceiver:

All the [perceptible qualities] – hard, hot, and so on – must be regarded in the same way. We must assume, as we said, that nothing exists in itself, but all things of all sorts arise out of motion, by engagement with each other. It is impossible, as they say, to form a firm conception of the active or the passive element as separate, for there is no active element until it is unified with the passive element, nor passive except in conjunction with the active.[44]

It may be argued, on these lines, that the concept of the new indicates a quality that is neither wholly objective nor wholly subjective. It is to be

---

[41] *Palai* is also found with this connotation, e.g. in Sophoklean tragedy (Dawe 1978: 208).
[42] Ar. *Vesp.* 120.
[43] Cf. Carthage (Greek *Kalkhēdōn*), from Phoenician *qart-hadasht*, 'new city' (Hoyos 2010: 6), also used for Kition in Cyprus, Panormos in Sicily, Kalkhedon in Bithynia etc.; the description of Carthage by Virgil as *urbs antiqua* in *Aen.* 1.12 may be knowingly ironic, since in 4.260 he has Aeneas assisting in 'laying the foundations of the city and building new houses' (*fundantem arces ac tecta novantem*).
[44] Pl. *Tht.* 156e–157a.

sought at the point at which the phenomenon of the new and the experience of novelty intersect. An individual percipient may choose to privilege one particular kind of novelty over another, or to try to judge whether something is really new or merely perceived as such. A sharp dichotomy between the old and the new, or between the traditional and the innovative, can rarely be sustained. The semantic range of the Greek words *neos* and *kainos*, which can both signify 'new' and 'young', adds to the potential inexactitude of sense and reference. A new leader need not be a young leader; a young wine need not be a new wine (i.e. a new *kind* of wine). It is possible for one person to argue that the novelty of a particular phenomenon is salient, another to dismiss the same phenomenon as 'nothing new', or to claim that there is 'nothing new under the sun'. While there are ways of reaching a consensus or ascertaining for practical purposes whether something is to be called 'new', the manipulation of conventional parameters within which something is identified as a new idea, object or experience allows for widely different constructions of novelty.

While the contexts and associations of newness were different for the Greeks from those of today, the vexed logic of the concept seems to have raised similar problems and paradoxes. Confusion may also arise from uncertainty or disagreement about the structure of relationship between old and new, past and present. In speaking of 'new wine in old bottles', one may seek to privilege the newness of the wine or the age of the container. The equivalent phrase is used in the Gospels ('new wine in old wineskins') to stress the importance of keeping old and new apart.[45] The issue is often not whether the new is or should be wholly distinct from the old, but the extent to which it depends on it, or the particular manner in which it departs from it. The idea that there can be absolute novelty is dubious on a purely experiential as well as logical level. If something has no roots in the past, in pre-existent experiences or faculties, it can hardly exist for us in a meaningful way: 'innovation with no tradition at all would produce unintelligibility'.[46] The philosopher John Locke noted that the taste of a pineapple was something one could not know before actually experiencing it.[47] The taste would have to be something new when experienced for the first time; but we could not entertain its novelty were it something to which we had no prior point of reference. When Captain Cook's *Endeavour* sailed in October 1769 into Poverty Bay, New Zealand, the sight was so novel to the indigenous islanders that some took it to be a

---

[45] Matthew 9.17, Mark 2.22, Luke 5.37–8.   [46] Lloyd (1987) 50, with reference to science.
[47] Locke (1972 [1689]) 424–5.

floating island, others a giant bird; however alien the encounter, the viewers could use as points of comparison objects that featured in their world-view and mythological traditions.[48] Pheidias' colossal statues aroused wonder in fifth-century observers, though they were innovative neither in form nor in the materials used for their construction; what was new to Greek viewers was the unprecedented scale of their construction. Even in this respect Pheidias was not doing something wholly novel, but was seeking to imitate Persian and Near Eastern statuary of similar magnitude.[49]

'Innovation' as an abstract term refers to the process by which something new is produced. The concept may be taken as secondary to 'novelty', in that it refers to conscious activity undertaken with the new as its goal – though the result is not always or necessarily 'innovative'. *An* innovation, however, tends to be evaluated less as the outcome of a process than as something perceived as new by a viewing subject. In the context of today's novelty-driven business and technology, an innovation is defined as

any idea, practice or object perceived as new by an individual. It matters little, so far as human behaviour is concerned, whether an idea is objectively new as measured by the lapse of time since its first use or discovery. It is the perceived or subjective newness of the idea for the individual that determines his reaction to it. If the idea seems new to the individual it is an innovation.[50]

This definition recognises that the ascription of novelty need not appeal to objectivity. Distinctions between what is 'new' and what is 'newfangled', between what is 'novel' and what is 'innovative', depend heavily on *who* is judging, acting or observing. 'O brave new world that has such people in't', exclaims Miranda in Shakespeare's *Tempest*, on seeing young men for the first time on her magical island. ''Tis new to thee', her father Prospero replies.[51] For the young woman the novelty is an objective attribute of the world; for the father it is a function of his daughter's youth, ignorance and inexperience.

While styles of imagination may not be timeless, they are arguably less temporally definable than many aspects of culture. Up to the mid fifth century BCE, the textual evidence for Greek history is largely in the form of verse, and poetic imagery no less than prose descriptions indicates how novelty was perceived. Aristotle supposed poetry to be a more 'philosophical

---

[48] King (2003) 10; cf. Humphreys (1982: 200), who quotes Joseph Banks' journal report on indigenous fishermen's lack of reaction ('they scarce lifted their eyes from their employment') to the *Endeavour*'s arrival in Botany Bay, Australia (April 1770), and comments: 'In the experience of these people nothing so monstrous had ever been seen upon the survace of the waters – and now it seems they could not see it when it came.'
[49] Lapatin (2001). [50] Rogers and Shoemaker (1971) 19. [51] Shakespeare, *Tempest* Act 5 Scene 1.

and serious' pursuit than history on the grounds that the latter tells us what has happened, the former tells us what *can* happen. Poetry deals with universals, while history records the particulars of 'what Alkibiades did or underwent'.[52] Those particulars may, of course, indicate more universal attitudes; as it happens, Thucydides records Alkibiades' positive advocacy of gaining 'new experience' in war, an indication of the impact of new approaches to military *tekhnē* found elsewhere in the historian's work.[53] Three centuries earlier, the reaction of a character in a poem by Arkhilokhos to the novelty of a solar eclipse suggests a more negative view of the effect of the new; but with regard to such natural phenomena, many contemporaries of Alkibiades were equally prone to superstitious views.[54]

In a letter written by Julian the Apostate, the Roman emperor (361–3 CE) and zealous restorer of ancient pagan religion affirmed his general dislike of innovation (*kainotomiā*).[55] His attitude to the notion contrasts with the earliest attestation of the word *kainotomeō*, 'innovate', in Aristophanes' *Wasps* of 422 BCE. There it is used by the chorus approvingly of the 'new rite' (*kainē teletē*) devised by Bdelykleon to assuage his father's mania for jury service; the perceived Athenian zeal for innovation is, as elsewhere, a target for comic satire.[56] In contrast to religious ritual, however, novelty is often an explicit desideratum in literature. An Egyptian poem from the second millennium BCE provides a point of comparison with the lament of the early fourth-century poet Khoirilos of Samos that it is impossible to find 'new paths' for poetry (see p. 58). One might be tempted to conclude that, in the ways human beings respond to novelty, there's 'nothing new under the sun' (see further Chapter 5). These literary responses to novelty, with their repeated resonances in poetry and proverb, themselves manifest a kind of exemplarity that draws attention to the relationship of the new with the timeless and 'classic'.[57]

Since the experience of the new cannot be determinately described or evaluated, no straightforward narrative of innovation can be constructed. Observing characteristic ways in which Greeks reacted to novelty can be more helpful than trying to determine dates of innovations. We cannot,

---

[52] Arist. *Poet.* 1451a36–b11.
[53] *Proslēpsesthai tēn empeiriān*, Thuc. 6.18.6; cf. the Corinthian ambassador's advocacy of *epitekhnēsis* in Thuc. 1.71.3 (p. 221 below).
[54] Arkhil. fr. 122 (see p. 45 below). In 413 BCE, Nikias' superstitious response to a lunar eclipse was to have disastrous practical consequences (Thuc. 7.50.4).
[55] Julian *Epist.* 20.453b: 'I shun innovation in general, but especially where it concerns the gods'. Cf. Littlewood (1995) 5 (introducing a volume that considers from different angles how the notions of innovation and originality apply in the Byzantine period).
[56] Ar. *Vesp.* 876; cf. *Eccl.* 583–7. [57] Cf. D'Angour (2005).

for instance, be certain that chryselephantine statuary was a new practice in the 440s, or that rhetoric was a new *tekhnē* in the 420s. But we might recognise the novelty of both in their time by comparing, say, the astonishment (*ekplēxis*) that Gorgias' 'alien-sounding' rhetoric (*to xenizon tēs lexeōs*) was said to have aroused in Athens in 427 with the unprecedented effect of Pheidias' colossal sculpture of Zeus Olympios.[58] The innovationism that features most prominently in the fifth-century Athenian context, as in the latter examples, need not be dismissed as unrepresentative of Greek attitudes generally. Attempts at political innovation may be no less characteristic of 'the Greek mind' than attempts to resist it, despite – and perhaps in view of – the general antipathy to political change expressed by many Greek authors.

THE PSYCHOLOGY OF NOVELTY

Since the objective status of novelty is questionable, its psychological and rhetorical dimensions are often paramount. These dimensions were recognised and exploited by both the promoters and decriers of innovation in antiquity. When something is new and unfamiliar to one person but not to another, the ascription of newness may be more a matter of belief or persuasion than indicative of an intrinsic property. The frame of reference is all-important: if it comprises the present, the new is the past or the future, if it embraces what is local and known, the new is the foreign and unfamiliar. A corollary is that for something to be 'new', all that may be required is for observers to shift their own position, viewpoint or frame of reference. This process is exemplified in Greek experience by the transformations that are felt to take place within individuals, whether via the acquisition of knowledge from outside sources, changes of mind and exposure to new experience, or in mythical metamorphoses and mystic initiations (see Chapter 5).

Whether the new is organically connected to the old, or felt to spring into existence ungenerated, is a matter both of perception and presentation. The perception of newness in practice entails the recognition of what has gone before, either as continuity or difference. 'Whether in science or the arts,' observed the poet Paul Valéry, 'if we look for the source of an achievement we can observe that *what a man does* either repeats or refutes *what someone else has done* – repeats it in other tones, refines or amplifies it or simplifies it, loads or overloads it with meaning; or else rebuts, overturns,

[58] D.S. 12.53.2–3, Strabo 8.3.30.

destroys and denies it, but thereby assumes it and has invisibly used it.'[59] Since the new may appear to pose a threat to the old, or to represent a loss or reversal of the status quo, this may be rhetorically exploited by presenting something desirable as 'old' (or 'nothing new'; see p. 53 below) or branding something unwelcome as 'new'. In other contexts, 'new' may indicate some kind of renewal, while leaving obscure whether that renewal partakes in, improves on or updates the earlier identity – whether the new manifestation supersedes or merely augments the earlier one. Thus the New Testament (*Kainē Diathēkē*) is intended both to build on and to supersede the Old.[60] In a modern consumerist context, where the ascription of newness is frequently used to promote a product (new Persil, new Coke, new Labour), 'new' is used to indicate both continuity with the past and a break with a previous identity.

Linguistic usage provides a prima facie case for there being something inherently ominous about novelty. Words for 'new' in Greek (and other Indo-European languages) may be associated with positive emotions, but are more often associated with the expression of danger or anxiety: *ti kainon* or *ti neon* ('something new') in tragedy may denote 'a calamity', Greek *neōtera prāgmata* ('newer things' or 'too new things'), like Latin *res nova(e)*, connotes political revolution. The fact that people react to the new positively or negatively, rather than with indifference, indicates its psychological salience. What is new is something that makes a difference or creates an impact. Novelty testifies to the operation, for good or bad, of a vital force or current in personal life, art, society or intellectual endeavour. The ambivalent possibilities of the new are grounded in human psychology. An infant's reaction to new stimuli will sometimes be fearful, sometimes curious; both the desire for novelty and the fear of the new are enduring human characteristics. Plato and Aristotle traced the beginnings of philosophical thought to *thauma*, the wonder that leads to curiosity and the desire to know.[61] Human beings are, it seems, innately geared towards seeking out novelty (the German *neugierig* 'curious', literally means 'greedy for the new'); the psychoanalyst Melanie Klein posited an 'epistemophilic' instinct to explain observed tendencies in infant development.[62] From the moment of birth, our encounters with the world within or outside ourselves hold out the promise or threat of novelty. As infancy progresses,

---

[59] 'Letter about Mallarmé' (1927): Cowley and Lawler (1972) 241.
[60] Cf. Matthew 5.18, 'Till heaven and earth pass, one jot or one tittle shall in no wise pass from the law, till all be fulfilled.' In that innovation is incompatible with Judaic religious structures (Greek religion is more fluid, see p. 49), Christianity must present innovation as fulfilment.
[61] Pl. *Tht.* 155d, Arist. *Meta.* 982b12–13.   [62] Klein (1928).

what has once seemed novel is increasingly experienced as neutral and unremarkable. It is absorbed or suppressed, sapped of its salience by the memory of previous encounters, diminished by the familiarity of regular recurrence or by the assimilation of the new to the old. Yet newer pursuits and experiences follow, originating from within and from without one's mind and body.

The same 'novelty' may be viewed with pleasure by some and alarm by others; 'new' by itself cannot guarantee positive or negative associations, but its affective impact must be evaluated in relation to its environment and its perceiver. The locus of utterance will have a major and often decisive influence on the word's emotional charge. In the context of Greek tragedy, the nature of the genre creates an expectation that 'new' represents an untoward disturbance, presaging disaster in the minds of character, author and audience. Conversely, in Greek literature and music, novelty can be presented as a desideratum, and asserting one's newness may be used to *create* inclinations and expectations in reader or audience. When something may be experienced as new simply because it is said to be new, rhetoric creates its own version of reality.

Innovation means change, and change means loss.[63] The psychology of novelty therefore brings into consideration ideas of memory and forgetting, of loss and mourning of what is past, of instances of cultural amnesia and creative destruction.[64] From a psychoanalytic viewpoint, the inability to acknowledge and mourn loss is apt to lead to a shutdown of vital creative impulses: in Freudian theory, unresolved trauma leads to stasis and to a compulsion to repeat thoughts or actions associated with the trauma.[65] Only the resolution of loss allows for a fresh start and renewed access to sources of creativity. Mourning provides the psychological closure needed to make a new start. While the theory applies to individuals, it may have a broader application: constructions of discourse, ritual activities and physical monuments may all be used to mourn, and to a degree compensate for, physical and emotional loss.[66] These functions were fulfilled performatively in ancient Greece by public activities such as funeral games, ritual laments, funeral speeches and the celebration of rites of passage – birth, coming of age, marriage and so on. More obliquely, the idealisation of the

---

[63] Cf. Montaigne, 'I do not change easily, for fear of losing in the change': Frame (1958) 428.
[64] For the notion of cultural amnesia (in America) cf. Bertman (2000); that of creative destruction goes back to Nietzsche, and was popularised by the economist Joseph Schumpeter (1975 [1942]).
[65] Freud (1914).
[66] It is not evident, however, that societies which have the time, space or inclination to mourn the dead or honour the past are necessarily more creative or more open to innovation than societies which do not; a host of social and cultural variables complicates the picture.

good old days expressed by Nestor in the *Iliad*, in Aristophanes' comedies and in the speeches of fourth-century Athenian orators could serve to acknowledge and mourn the loss of a past that was felt to have value. A similar function may have been fulfilled by the most notable literary innovation of classical Greece, tragic drama, in its enabling of *katharsis*, the purgation of the emotions of pity and fear.

In his essay 'Of Custom', written in the wake of the European Reformation, Montaigne wrote approvingly of the Greeks' (sometimes avowed) disinclination to alter their laws, adding 'I am disgusted with innovation (*nouvelleté*), in whatever guise, and with reason, for I have seen very harmful effects of it.'[67] Since the political aspect of the new may raise the spectre of revolution (Greek *neōterismos*) with its associated turbulence and danger, political innovation is often presented as a return to the past, pursued in the guise of renovation. Similarly, in matters touching on religion, since new ideas and practices may seem to threaten eternal truths, innovators are apt to appeal to the past (in sixteenth-century Christian Europe, Copernicus presented his revolutionary science as a rediscovery of ancient knowledge).[68] At the other end of the spectrum, 'new' may indicate little more than the latest fashion, a function of changing attitudes to dress, music or forms of social interaction. In these cases, the new is identified with what is current, i.e. the most recent trend (Greek *neōteros*, *neōtatos*), while the fashions of previous years are considered outdated and *passé* (Greek *arkhaios*). What is seen to be short-lived has correspondingly limited value; the distinction between spurious and genuine, transient and enduring, often leads to 'novelty' being associated with superficiality.

A keen engagement with the past may be understood not simply as a way of reducing the scope of one's imagination to the old, but as allowing a secure and productive basis for the exploration of the new. From this viewpoint, the notion that the Greeks did not innovate, only renovated, may be turned on its head. Even if innovation is indeed widely presented as renovation, the appeal to the past often tends to reveal, rather than obscure, the fact of innovation. An example of this in the political sphere is visible in the accounts of the two short-lived revolutions at Athens in the latter stages of the Peloponnesian War. The first, in 411 BCE, arose out of dissatisfaction in upper-class circles with the radical democracy that had voted to launch the disastrous Sicilian campaign. Some planned to impose an outright oligarchy, but a 'moderate' party under Theramenes sought to limit the franchise and abolish indemnities (introduced by Perikles) for

---

[67] Frame (1958) 86.   [68] Eisenstein (1980) 613–14.

those holding public office. These proposals were commended as a return to the 'ancestral constitution' (*patrios polīteiā*), the same slogan used by the restorers of democracy after the regime of the Thirty was overthrown in 403. Both Aristotle and Thucydides praise the 'moderate' programme of 411 as creating an eminently sensible basis for Athenian democratic decision-making. Given that Solon and Kleisthenes themselves were recognised not as renovators but as innovators, Theramenes' appeal to the 'ancestral constitution' (whether it was supposed to be that of Drakon, Solon, or Kleisthenes) was arguably less a call to 'turn the clock' back than to remind Athenians of the bold innovations that had created their democratic system in the preceding century.[69]

The psychological responses to changing conditions in the ancient world raise suggestive parallels with responses to the changes in modern society. The sense of radical discontinuity in contemporary forms of knowledge and experience has given rise to the notion of the 'postmodern', whether this is taken to mean after, beyond, or outside the structures of the modern.[70] A comparable sense of constant novelty in late fifth-century Athens has led to the ascription of 'postmodernity' as well as 'modernity' to aspects of the age and its expressions.[71] 'Modern' is not itself an ancient term; *modernus* first appears in Latin in the sixth century meaning 'fashionable', and in sixteenth-century England the word meant 'contemporary'. In that it connects the 'new' with the 'now', Greek counterparts may be found in terms like *nūn* (now, nowadays) and *ta paronta* (the present). Modernity is the container of the new, but when change is experienced as excessively rapid and pervasive, the new bids to exceed the bounds of its container and to encroach on the future. Terms like 'New World Order' and 'New Age' express a positive sense of hope for a state of affairs that may be imminent rather than exactly present. In practice, however, an intense sense of novelty is more likely to lead to symptoms of anxiety than to euphoria. The inability to digest, absorb or come to terms with the loss of the old can result in disorientation, inertia and anomie (the term used by the French sociologist Durkheim to indicate a loss of social norms, with the corresponding sense in individuals of alienation and lack of purpose).[72] It can lead to the conviction that individuals are powerless to influence change, because it is hard enough just to keep up with it. In such circumstances, a defiant individualism can

---

[69] Cf. D'Angour (1999a), in which I argue that the 'reform' of Attic script in 403 was essentially a conservative measure that affirmed the literary status quo and offered political reassurance to Athens' allies.
[70] Bertens (1995).   [71] E.g. Connor (1977), Cartledge (1990) 29.
[72] Durkheim (2006 [1897]) 297–8.

assert itself, or a sense of resignation in the face of an apparently irreversible direction of events. Both kinds of response are portrayed in Aristophanic comedies such as *Acharnians*, *Knights* and *Birds*, with their individualistic anti-heroes, utopian scenarios and satirical commentary on contemporary politics.[73]

It is one thing to experience novelty as an aspect of the passing of time or as part of a natural cycle, another to experience change that has been deliberately brought about or artificially engineered (a distinction that, as I show in Chapter 3, may be broadly represented by the difference in the connotations of *neos* and *kainos*). Accordingly, attitudes to and perceptions of the new are likely to differ between agents and recipients, between those who make it their business to innovate and those who are on the receiving or perceiving end of such innovation. We see this, for example, when Aristophanes in *Clouds* boasts of the novelty of his ideas, a standard trope in comedy, while at the same time lamenting the fact that his audience has not appreciated them. Conversely, the author of the Hippocratic treatise *On Ancient Medicine* is at pains to promote empirical medical practice as being 'nothing new' (*ouden kainon*), while other treatises observe how laymen are naively enthusiastic in their embrace of bizarre medical novelties.[74]

DIMENSIONS OF NOVELTY

A range of ideas and images is structurally and symbolically associated with newness of various forms, even if they do not directly signify the new. Metaphors for the new in Greek literature and poetry regularly include notions of birth and origins (*genesis*, *arkhē*), as elaborated in cosmogonical and theogonical accounts of elemental origins (see Chapter 5). In the political and social arena the consideration of novelty is often expressed in terms of upheaval and revolution (*metabolē*, *kīnēsis*). Greek myths offer a wealth of material relevant to the study of their imagination in respect of new beginnings, experiences and discoveries. In myth and art, Athena, goddess of *tekhnē* (skill) and *sophiā* (wisdom) springs fully formed from the head of Zeus. The city of Athens, a preeminent locus of novelty for Greek onlookers and commentators, was devoted to a divine patron whose mythical origins offer a symbolic, if not explicit, validation for the creation of innovation via handicraft and intellect.

As the new dawn emerges from the dark of night, so the new is regularly correlated with images of light and brightness (*phōs*, *lamprotēs* etc.). Since

---

[73] On comic utopias see Ruffell (2000).   [74] Lloyd (1987) 64–9.

conditions of diversity manifest and are productive of novelty, expressions of variety, plurality and multiplicity (*poikiliā, to polu* etc.) are often highly suggestive of the new. Awe, wonder and amazement (*sebas, thauma, thambos*) indicate receptivity to newness by expressing the surprise of the novel and the unexpected. In that novelty is a perception of difference, it may be associated with exoticism and the experience of foreignness (*to xenon, to allotrion*); in that it is about the unexpected, it may be indicated by words signifying hope or the failure of anticipation (*elpis, aelpton*). The feminine is often symbolic of otherness in male-centred cultures; in fantasy, if not in reality, women can be associated with new and politically subversive modes of action, as depicted in Euripides' *Bacchae* and Aristophanes' *Lysistrata* and *Ecclesiazusae* (see p. 94).

Insofar as the emergence of the new involves processes of change, it relates to fantasies of metamorphosis and to the transformation of personal identity. Numerous Greek accounts tell of the assumption of new identities through some process of transformation, spiritual or physical, internal or external. Myths about discovery and invention (*heuresis, heurēmata*) serve to validate the kind of novelty that emerges from inquiry and inventiveness, and may have encouraged the pursuit of innovation. Newness in principle and in practice has connections with the notions of play and playthings (*paidiā, paignia, athurmata*), risk and daring (*kindūnos, tolma*), youth and youthfulness (*neotēs*); its relationship to the future (*to mellon*) raises the notions of prediction and foresight (*prophēteiā, pronoia*), the anticipation of things to come. The promotion of the new raises the theme of sources of inspiration (*enthousiasmos*), with its potentially uneasy alliance to madness (*maniā*).

The question of novelty overlaps with preoccupations central to ancient thinkers. How anything new may arise is one of the earliest philosophical concerns. The first philosophers concerned themselves with questions of cosmic origins and first principles (*arkhai*). The attempt to find answers to questions about change and *genesis* is represented by Presocratic thinkers such as Xenophanes, Parmenides and Herakleitos. The temporal significance of 'new' requires us to take into consideration ancient conceptions of, and confusions over, time. 'What, then, is time?' St. Augustine asks. 'If no one asks me, I know. If someone asks me to explain it, I know not.'[75] The Pythagorean doctrine that time is cyclical entails that everything is in some sense a repetition of the past; in the words of the biblical Ecclesiastes,

---

[75] Aug. *Conf.* 11.15.

'What has been will be and what has happened will happen; there is nothing new under the sun.'[76] For Herakleitos, by contrast, the ceaseless flow of the universe would make everything constantly new. 'You could not step twice into the same river' is how Plato reports his doctrine; 'not even once' allegedly rejoined his pupil Kratylos, since one's identity too is subject to ceaseless alteration. Both the subject matter of Presocratic thinking and the dialectical process presented in their critical evaluation and rejection of others' ideas demonstrate their engagement with the generation of the new (see Chapter 5).

The dissemination of news (*nea, angeliā*) in the ancient world was largely oral. In the fourth century BCE, the orator Demosthenes, frustrated by the Athenians' apparent inability to see the truth of Philip II of Macedon's hostile activities and intentions, berated the Athenians for wandering about in the agora asking 'is there any news?'[77] Centuries later, when the apostle Paul visited Athens in the first century CE, he was struck that 'all the Athenians and strangers that were there spent their time in nothing else other than telling or hearing some newer thing (*ti kainoteron*)'.[78] The Athenians' long-recorded desire for news chimes with Thucydides' account of the Periklean funeral speech, which emphasises, in more respectful terms than in Demosthenes' caricature, Athenians' inclinations to curiosity, openness and *polupragmosunē* ('busy-ness'). A modern definition of the term, 'new information of recent events', emphasises the temporality of the novelty of the information received.[79] But events long past may be 'news' to those who have never heard of them; what makes them news is dependent on the state of knowledge of the recipient. When we say 'that's stale news' we are denying that it is new to *us*. What the Watchman in Aeschylus' *Agamemnon* sees from his lookout is news to him, and will be news to those to whom he will report it; and the tragedian presents it in such a way that the long-familiar tale of Troy's destruction has all the thrill of fresh news for his audience.

News and newness may be largely a matter of individual perception. But within the conscious pursuit or process that is 'innovation' we may identify a number of common mechanisms. These include such strategies as the recombination, retheorisation, or re-presentation of previous ideas or practices. All these suggest a logical dependence on the past, and indicate ways in which pre-existing elements may be manipulated or shown in a new light. In practice, the analysis of such mechanisms as producers of innovation tends to be retrospective. Innovators themselves are often

---

[76] Ecclesiastes 1.9.   [77] Dem. 4.10.   [78] Acts 17.21.   [79] Cf. Lewis (1996) 3.

unaware of the roots of their creative ideas, or the particular conditions which have enabled them to emerge and flourish. Those conditions may be seen to include such features as an openness to novelty and innovation on the part of both individual innovators and the societies to which they belong; a capacity and willingness to take risks; the exposure to varied perspectives and experiences; a cultural embrace of competition and critique; the existence of education or formal instructional methods in technical specialisations; the presence of rewards and incentives for innovation; the availability of media that facilitate the communication of ideas; the economic resources to exploit such media and their objects; the creation of circumstances that foster individual creativity and inspiration; and a sense of the value and importance of the new as a positive element in human life. With such principles in mind, we may attempt to relax the grip of the commonly held view that the Greeks did not like novelty, and then proceed to consider more fully the variety of ways in which they engaged with all forms of the new.

CHAPTER 2

Loosening the grip of the past

> The more definite a mind is, the more it needs the new.
>
> Elias Canetti

Aristotle's second book of *Politics* offers a useful starting-point for the investigator who seeks to distinguish Greek attitudes to novelty in different spheres of activity. He begins by outlining and criticising various theories of 'ideal states' starting with Plato's *Republic* and *Laws*, and examines in particular the latter's arguments for owning property, wives and children in common. Seemingly new ideas of this kind, he suggests, may already have been tested and found wanting in the past:

> We are bound to pay some regard to the long past and the passage of the years, in which these things [advocated by Plato as new discoveries] would not have gone unnoticed if they had been really good. Almost everything has been discovered (*heurētai*) already: though some of the things discovered have not been co-ordinated, and some, though known, are not put into practice.[1]

Aristotle gives guarded praise to his teacher's clever if impracticable proposals: 'All the writings of Plato are original: they show ingenuity (*kompson*), novelty of view (*kainotomon*), and a spirit of inquiry (*zētētikon*). But perfection in everything is perhaps a difficult thing.'[2] No other thinker, he notes,

> has proposed such novelties (*kekainotomēken*) as community of wives and children or common meals for women: on the contrary, thinkers have rather started from the immediate necessities of life. Thus there are some who hold that the proper regulation of property is more important than any other object, because this is the

---

[1] Arist. *Pol.* 1264a1–5. Translations are by Barker (1946).
[2] Ibid. 1265a: 'writings of Plato' here is a translation *hoi tou Sōkratous logoi*, 'the words/ideas of Sokrates'. Aristotle elsewhere claims (fr. 72 Rose = *Ath.* 11.505a) that the Platonic dialogue form followed the example of Sophron's mimes, and names Alexamenos of Teos as the inventor of the genre of *Sōkratikoi logoi*: Clay (1994) 32–7.

issue on which civil discords always arise. Phaleas of Khalkedon was the first to suggest regulation of property for the purpose of preventing discord.[3]

After rejecting the ideas of Phaleas (an otherwise unknown political thinker of the late fifth century BCE), Aristotle goes on to discuss the ideas of the flamboyant fifth-century city-designer, Hippodamos of Miletos, 'the first man without practical experience of politics who attempted to handle the theme of the best form of constitution'.[4] Hippodamos also proposed that a reward should be offered for 'inventions of benefit to the state', and anticipated the Athenian law that the children of men who died in battle should be supported at public expense.[5]

From this background Aristotle proceeds to reflect briefly on the question of political innovation in general, concluding that a distinction should be drawn between *tekhnē*, the sphere of specialist disciplines, and *nomos*, that of law and politics. Regarding laws, he says,

a case may be made for the view that change (*kīnein*) is the better policy. Certainly in other branches of knowledge change has proved beneficial. We may cite in evidence the changes from traditional practice which have been made in medicine, in physical training, and generally in all the arts and forms of human skill; and since politics is to be counted as an art or form of skill, it can be argued logically that the same must also be true of politics.[6]

This analysis recalls the words attributed by Thucydides to the Corinthian envoy to Sparta in 431:

In politics as in technology (*tekhnē*), the new (*epigignomena*) must always prevail over the old. The established traditions may be best in a settled society, but when there is much change demanding a response there must be much innovative thinking also.[7]

However, Aristotle ends his discussion by rejecting the parallel between law and *tekhnē*, and poses a series of questions about pertinent differences in the implementation of political innovation:

We must also notice that the analogy drawn from the arts is false. To change the practice of an art is not the same as to change the operation of a law. It is from habit, and only from habit, that law derives the validity which secures obedience. But habit can be created only by the passage of time; and a readiness to change from existing to new and different laws will accordingly tend to weaken the general power of law. Further questions may also be raised. Even if we admit that it is allowable to make a change, does this hold true, or not, of all laws and in all

---

[3] Arist. *Pol.* 1266a34–40. [4] Phaleas: Arist. *Pol.* 1266a39–1267b21; Hippodamos: ibid. 1267b29.
[5] Ibid. 1268a6–11. [6] Ibid. 1268b33–8. [7] Thuc. 1.71.3. See further Chapter 9, p. 221.

constitutions? And again, should change be attempted by any person whatsoever, or only by certain persons? It makes a great difference which of these different alternatives is adopted... We may therefore dismiss this question for the present. It belongs to a different occasion.[8]

In the event no further discussion survives; neither Aristotle nor any other extant ancient author discusses novelty or innovation in any depth, or provides any extended analysis of the meaning to the Greeks of their encounters with the new. In other contexts, however, Aristotle was inclined to view the notion of novelty in organic, evolutionary terms: the roots of novelty lie in what has gone before, the seeds of the old give birth to the new. Underlying such metaphors is the notion of development in terms of potentiality (*dunamis*) and fulfilment (*energeia*).[9] From a historical vantage-point, events and experiences arise naturally and inexorably from the past; in retrospect, societies, institutions and ideas appear to have developed from seed to full flowering with the inevitability and directionality of natural growth.[10]

Following Aristotle's brief analysis, one might initially be tempted to draw a distinction between those areas in which innovation tended to be espoused by the Greeks and those in which it was rejected. To his specific examples of medicine and gymnastics one could add, for instance, philosophy, art, literature and science, disciplines for whose continued vitality some palpable degree of innovation is desirable if not necessary. Circumscribed technical subjects of this kind, which require teaching and can be mastered only through intensive application by their practitioners, appear at first sight to differ substantially from practices and activities that characterise the world of society and politics.[11] *Tekhnai* tend to comprise the privileged pursuits of a minority of individuals with special expertise, whereas activities such as religious observance, participation in farming, war or athletics, and political activity of varying degrees were incumbent on and practised by most citizens in a Greek polis.[12] Since the very existence of

---

[8] Arist. *Pol.* 1269a19–28.   [9] Lloyd (1968) 62–7.
[10] E.g. regarding the genre of tragedy and the development of the polis, Aristotle is less interested in these being innovations than in the fact that they have attained their *phusis*: *Poet.* 1449a10–15, *Pol.* 1252b33–6. It might be argued that the idea of the new, no less than that of tragedy, achieves its fullest expression in relation to Athens (see Chapter 9).
[11] Aristotle elsewhere draws a distinction between 'art' and 'life', e.g. in his *Poetics*, where he notes that 'correctness (*orthotēs*) is not the same thing in *politikē* and *poiētikē*' (1460b13–15); and in general he is concerned to distinguish the products of reason from those of nature (*Phys.* 198a9–10, *Met.* 1032a12–13 etc.).
[12] In *Laws* (889d1–6), Plato similarly draws a distinction between serious *tekhnai* which 'give service to nature' e.g. medicine, husbandry and gymnastics, and those which are mere playthings (*paidiai*) such as painting, music and so on; innovation in the former is curtailed by natural limits.

collective structures, institutions and activities appears to be threatened by change, novelty is often repudiated in areas of social practice, in contrast to the way it is considered *de rigueur* in technical domains.[13]

Proper account should be taken, therefore, of differences between domains and genres of activity in which novelty arises. Unfortunately we are very poorly informed about many areas of specialised activity in which we might expect innovation to have been a particular feature. Craftsmanship and the production of new goods, for example, are only infrequently and sporadically discussed in Greek sources (see further Chapter 7). This reticence reflects the lowly status of 'banausic' and commercial pursuits in the eyes of predominantly elite authors, who generally consider novelty to be an issue worth remarking upon only in artistic, intellectual and political domains. However, the manner in which the idea of innovation is treated in such areas as music and literature can throw light on modes and mechanisms of the Greeks' understanding and reception of the new in general. It is above all apparent that Greek society and politics are areas in which we invariably find consistency and stability approved, while innovation is rejected.[14] But these domains are precisely those in which we should expect nothing other than that the notion of novelty should be regarded with concern and anxiety. 'Too new' affairs (*neōtera pragmata*) and political 'novelty-making' (*neōterizein, neōterismos*) are terms used from at least the fifth century to denote revolution or the kind of violent political activity which offers a threat to the status quo. These terms are used by authors who were either themselves of high birth and status, or who had internalised an upper-class outlook that shuns social and political change. The views held by individuals, educated or otherwise, for whom 'newer actions' may have been necessary and beneficial, go unrecorded.[15]

Aristotle's cursory comments on innovation come at the end of a discussion of the value of deliberate efforts at political change. As his argument shows, one needs to be aware of precisely how and where the issue of innovation arises. What counts as a *tekhnē* is also important: many practices of law and sociopolitical activity, not least rhetorical practices that were central to the face-to-face societies of ancient Greece, fall in the course of time

---

[13] Cf. Vidal-Naquet (1986) 93: '*tekhnē* implies continual innovation'.
[14] On an individual level, Demokritos advises against envying those perceived as better off, since this 'constantly forces one to try to do something new (*epikainourgein*) and to be driven to do what is forbidden by law' (B191).
[15] The term *neōterismos* primarily refers to 'new' political notions, but may also be related to the action of 'younger men', *neōteroi*: Davidson (2006). I consider connections of novelty with youth below (p. 100).

into that category.[16] Politics, warfare and religion all exhibit some points of innovationism as undeniably as medicine, music and sculpture; while in overtly innovationist disciplines such as music and poetry, the uses of tradition are significant and far-reaching (see Chapters 8 and 9). In the analysis of texts and passages regarding novelty and innovation, individual authors' values, purposes and predilections should also be taken into account. When the disapproval voiced by an author regarding musical, medical or religious innovation is seen to be a reaction to actual manifestations of such innovation, the other side of the picture begs consideration. Who were the upstart innovators? What were their attitudes to novelty in these areas? How did they and the recipients of their innovations feel about it?

Rather than anatomising novelty with regard to different spheres of experience, therefore, it makes sense to explore the way tradition and change are negotiated and represented in particular cases and periods. In doing so, one should be wary about taking at face value expressions of traditionalism or conservatism no less than of innovationism. When a particular opinion is subjected to closer interpretation, new possibilities emerge: conservative expressions can be recognised as offering a direction for novelty rather than rejection of it, while claims to innovation on one's own or another's behalf come to seem less convincing when we recognise their rhetorical motivation. The disavowal of the new can at times be a means of camouflaging or disguising a genuinely original initiative. Equally, it may be used to sanction an incontrovertibly novel approach. An example of the latter kind of 'invention of tradition' comes towards the end of Xenophon's *Ways and Means*, a pamphlet proposing a radically new system of state-run economy for Athens in the early fourth century BCE:

> Now, since none of my proposals is impossible or even hard to put into practice, since by doing so we will improve our relations with the rest of Greece, live in greater security and gain a more glorious reputation, since the general populace of Athens will never go short of subsistence and the wealthy members of society will no longer have to spend money to support the war effort, since a generous surplus will enable us to celebrate our festivals on an even more magnificent scale than we do now, to repair our temples, rebuild the walls and dockyards, and return our priests, Council, functionaries and cavalry *to the traditional ways of doing things* (*ta patria*), what could be wrong with setting this programme in motion straight away, in order to see prosperity and security come to the state in our time?[17]

---

[16] 'Face-to-face' society: see Ober (1989) 31–3.
[17] Xen. *Vect.* 6.1, trans. in Waterfield (1997), italics added. In Hobsbawm and Ranger (1983), 'invented tradition' is defined as 'a set of practices . . . [which] normally attempt to establish continuity with a suitable historical past' (1).

The disavowal of innovation via a 'rhetoric of reaction' is most clearly to be found in broadly political contexts.[18] In technical and intellectual fields, by contrast, the use of terms related to innovation often points to the way novelty was not only openly sought by creative individuals, but readily accepted by observers and beneficiaries, audiences and readers. The simple fact that innovation was promoted and espoused in some of the most important areas of the Greeks' cultural self-expression – their music and poetry, visual arts and prose literature – is arguably as characteristic an aspect of the Greeks' mentality as the traditionalism manifest in their approach to society and politics.

THE GRIP OF THE PAST

In his study *In the Grip of the Past*, B. van Groningen presents a sustained argument for the Greeks' attachment to the past at the expense of the new in all areas of their life and thought. In Greek literature, for instance, he proposes that 'there is nothing essentially new, although there is renovation, and new wine is always put into old vessels... Imitation, return to the past, restoration of ancient things is the accepted rule.' In the visual and plastic arts 'the Greek limits himself in principle to a variation of the existing norms. Again and again we meet a certain fear of breaking with the acknowledged forms.'[19] A disinclination to novelty, he argues, is intimated by the structures of the Greek language itself: 'the great number of forms used for the past (imperfect, aorist, perfect, pluperfect, future perfect) proves in itself a certain orientation towards the past'.[20] The founder of historical inquiry is seen as exemplifying the Greek tendency to look back rather than forward: Herodotos is 'the type of historian who appeals to the past and exclusively to the past'.[21] Greek politics, philosophy and myth allegedly tell the same story. The fact that Perikles' funeral oration, as composed by Thucydides, 'begins with the ancestors' suggests a retrospective inclination. Political revolution is an anomaly; in Athens, 'the cry to introduce something new never was heard in difficult times; then the watchword was always a return to the government of the fathers'.[22] The Presocratic philosophers' fascination with *arkhai* (origins or first principles) indicates that 'the Greek tendency to regressive thinking was active and decisive'. The backward-looking direction of

---

[18] For an account of the 'rhetoric of reaction' in the modern context see Hirschmann (1991), who identifies 'futile', 'perverse' and 'dangerous' as key terms used in the rhetorical opposition to political change.
[19] van Groningen (1953) 4–5.   [20] Ibid. 22.   [21] Ibid. 27.   [22] Ibid. 7, 10.

Greek imagination and fantasy is demonstrated by the way that 'all the decisive events which myth relates happened "once upon a time", "in the past"'.[23]

Van Groningen arrives at uncompromising conclusions: 'the Greek did not like anything totally new: real revolutions were exceedingly rare in his public as well as his cultural life'. He considers the antipathy towards the new to be not just incidental to the Greeks' outlook, but fundamental to their psychology:

[in] the world of the Greek mind no sudden impetuous change of course occurs; nothing but developments and alterations take place, the later events may always be easily connected with the preceding ones. The present offers him, it is true, the opportunity to form his life again and again, but he borrows the material from the past.[24]

The suspicion arises that the author has projected wholesale his individual perspective and inclinations onto the subjects of his investigation.[25] The retrospective discovery of connections is, after all, a favoured pursuit of classical scholars, and the 'material of the past' is the very material with which ancient historians engage. In view of the Greeks' acknowledged originality and demonstrable receptivity to the new, evidence that appears solely to demonstrate such a resolutely backward-facing perspective cannot tell the whole story. The philosopher Kierkegaard observed: 'It is perfectly true, as philosophers say, that life must be understood backwards. But they forget the other proposition, that it must be lived forwards.'[26] For the conscious and experiencing human subject, the unfolding of life presents at any particular moment the possibility of an encounter with the new. It may be denied or negotiated in different ways, but it cannot be avoided or excised from consciousness.

The relentless case for Greek traditionalism and conservatism finds an immediate challenge from no less an authority than Aristotle, whose own observation in his *Politics* is that 'as a rule everyone seeks to follow not tradition (*to patrion*) but the good (*t'āgathon*)'.[27] The notion that the Greeks

---

[23] Ibid. 76, 96.   [24] Ibid. 5, 122.
[25] Dodds (1951: 170 n. 88) similarly remarks on 'the kind of historical mirage which arises when men unknowingly project their own preoccupations into the distant past'.
[26] So Kierkegaard in his journal for 1843: Dru (1938) 127. The 'Weber–Fechner law' (to which John Krebs has drawn my attention) quantifies the way stimuli become less differentiated the further they recede. This process is helpful for historians who seek to generalise about the ancient world, but indicates that caution must be exercised when viewing events through, as it were, an inverted telescope.
[27] Arist. *Pol.* 1269a3–4.

felt that the good lay solely in the past or the old is impossible to sustain. The specific arguments employed by van Groningen to prove his point vary in force and plausibility. His tendentious explication of Greek tense structure is evident from his suggestion that the aorist and perfect tenses, which so often have an immediate and present aspect, are 'past-oriented'. His suggestion that the Presocratic search for *arkhai* illustrates 'a tendency to regressive thinking' is dubious both philosophically and psychologically: it is just as likely (as I suggest in Chapter 5) to represent a reaction to burgeoning novelty, an urge to account for the notion of emergence in a period in which the phenomenon was increasingly evident. He omits, above all, to cite key passages from ancient texts which explicitly or implicitly indicate the existence of a different and opposing vision of novelty from the one he projects wholesale onto the Greeks. Such omissions include the 'novel (*kainai*) hypotheses' proposed by medical theorists and criticised by Hippocratic authors who see the only future for medicine as lying in empirical research (see p. 55); the keenness to innovate in military and political arenas ascribed to the Athenians in the Thucydidean speech assigned to the Corinthian envoy (p. 221); and Telemakhos' promotion of the 'newest song' in the *Odyssey*, most boldly recapitulated by the much-vaunted novelty of the fifth-century musician Timotheos of Miletos (Chapter 8 below). An impartial consideration of such expressions and attitudes would suggest that van Groningen's dogmatism regarding the Greeks' refusal to entertain the new is untenable.[28] In addition, his analysis seems inadequate in principle, in that he neglects the synchronic aspect of novelty as *difference* and makes the questionable assumption that what is 'new' is solely to be located in the future.

NOVELTY AND TIME

For van Groningen 'the new' is the opposite of 'the past'. Insofar as 'new' is used to signify what comes next or what has not yet happened, the idea of newness is frequently associated with the notions of futurity and the unknown. The Greeks were extremely concerned to know what the future held, though seldom confident about their capacity to predict or to influence events. The growth of technical knowledge and experience in the fifth century engendered some unusual expressions of confidence

---

[28] Kullmann (2001 [1968]: 408 n. 54) judges van Groningen generously, simply noting that 'his investigation still needs amplifying on the future side'.

in man's ability to control nature (notably the 'ode to man' in Sophokles' *Antigone*).²⁹ But through the scenarios depicted in Greek myth, ritual and literature, Greeks could project their imagination into situations and experiences which might affect them in the future as they had affected real or fictional characters in the past. Personal identification with figures of myth and history could allow individuals a foretaste of how they might react to events that lay in the future; and the description of actions and events in the past could provide a lively impression of new situations. By locating themselves, their circumstances or surroundings in times and places remote from their location in the here-and-now, the Greeks continually evoked and explored the experience of the new.

The popularity of prediction, prophecy and divination, and the frequent incidence of teleological thinking and utopian fantasy, belie any notion that the Greeks had no appetite for thinking about the future. In the *Iliad*, the fall of Troy is predicted by both Agamemnon and Hektor with the words 'the day will come (*essetai ēmar*) when holy Troy will perish, and Priam, and the people of Priam of the strong ash spear'.³⁰ Both leaders anticipate the future, from contrasting perspectives; they foresee new battles in store, and new sorrows and triumphs awaiting them. 'Look to the end' was a proverbial sentiment. In Herodotos' account, Solon warns Kroisos that change is inevitable with the words 'of all the days of a man's life, not one brings to him anything at all the same as another. So, Kroisos . . . in every matter one must look to the end and how it will turn out.'³¹ Thucydides praises Themistokles as 'supreme in conjecturing the future . . . he foresaw better than any the possible advantage and disadvantage in a yet uncertain future.'³² In 431 BCE, after the Athenians had rebuffed King Arkhidamos' last-minute peace proposals, the Spartan envoy Melesippos recalled the verses of Homer with the solemn prediction 'This day will be the beginning (*arxei*) of great misfortunes to the Hellenes.'³³ A similarly ominous tone is struck by the sophist Antiphon, though in the rather different context of offering guidance on marriage: 'This day, this night, begin a new destiny (*kainou daimonos arkhei*), a new fate. Marriage is a great challenge for a man.'³⁴ Poetry and historiography affirmed the general recognition that while the shape of the future might be uncertain, new experiences, whether

---

[29] See p. 127. But fragment 761 from Euripides' *Hypsipyle*, 'nothing is beyond expectation (*aelpton*), one should expect everything', may be an expression of despair or alarm akin to those of Arkhilokhos' speaker (p. 45) and Sophokles' Ajax (p. 118).
[30] *Il.* 4.164–5, 6.448–9. [31] Hdt. 1.32. [32] Thuc. 1.138.
[33] Thuc. 2.12.3; *arxei* raises specific verbal echoes of *Il.* 5.63, 11.604. [34] Antiphon fr. 49.

Novelty and time

similar or divergent in nature from those of the past, were continually in prospect.³⁵

However, while the signification of 'new' has unavoidable connections with temporality, it is not solely directed at the future; and in the eyes of Greeks, futurity was arguably not its central aspect. There are many ways in which the new is intimately related both to the past and the present. The way that novel events in the past are imaginatively correlated to novelty in the present is a distinctive feature of many Greek texts which treat events in the past with a vivid immediacy. The importance of this for understanding one facet of the Greek sense of the new may be demonstrated by reconsidering one of the passages that van Groningen cites in favour of his thesis. In a poem couched in characteristically personal terms, Arkhilokhos describes a character's reaction to observing an eclipse of the sun:

> There's nothing now you can't expect, nothing's against the odds,
> there are no miracles, now Zeus the father of the gods
> has turned the noonday into night and hidden the bright sun
> out of the sky, so clammy dread came over everyone.
> From now on all is credible, and like enough to be:
> let none of you now be surprised at anything you see,
> not even if land animals switch to where dolphins roam,
> and the salt sea and the crashing waves become their chosen home,
> while dolphins take a fancy to the mountains and the trees.³⁶

Van Groningen comments as follows:

From that experience, which so deeply impressed him, he draws the conclusion: 'now anything may be expected; nothing can any more be denied on oath (as improbable or impossible)'. *That which the past brought him* in that imposing eclipse bordering on the impossible, becomes an indication for the future. Naturally the idea should not be pushed in the abstract; it is a lyrical outburst; but surely *the past is felt as normative*.³⁷

The italicised passages draw attention to the tendentious nature of the interpretation. It is clear that the event can have taken place only 'in the past' for Arkhilokhos (or for the character in his poem) to refer to it as having happened. But while trivially true, the fact that the eclipse

---

[35] Cf. the formulaic coda to several Euripidean tragedies (*Alcestis, Andromache, Helena, Bacchae* and, with slight variation, *Medea*): 'Heaven's ways are many (*pollaí*), and the gods accomplish much (*pollá*) that is against our expectation (*aelptōs*). What is intended fails to come about, but god devises a way to achieve the unexpected (*adokētōn*)...'. The emphasis on the pluriform and the unexpected reflects characteristic Euripidean *kainotēs* (p. 210 below).
[36] Arkhil. fr. 122, trans. in West (1993).   [37] van Groningen (1953): 32 (italics added).

occurred before it became the subject of the speaker's comment has no bearing on the poem's meaning or effect. What is far more striking is the way Arkhilokhos constructs the experience (both for the unidentified speaker and the reader) as one that is still recent, awe-inspiring and fresh in his memory. The idea that such an event makes the future wholly unpredictable is an extravagant poetic flourish, whereby the disorienting nature of the unexpected is emphasised to humorous effect. The alarming novelty of the eclipse is precisely what makes it a worthy subject for 'a lyrical outburst' in the first place. Instead of striving to elicit from his poem a sense of the dominance of the past, we might recognise and appreciate the way Arkhilokhos is here capturing and expressing with vivid immediacy a reaction to a *new* experience.

Pindar's ninth paian, composed some two centuries later, reinforces the view that the appropriate response to a solar eclipse is not that it has either happened in or reflects on the past, but that it heralds something new. The train of thought detectable throughout the paian, together with specific word-associations within it, links the eclipse to imminent and worrying novelty:

> Beam of the sun (*aktīs āeliou*), what have you contrived, far-seeing one,
> O mother of vision, highest star,
> by being hidden in daytime? Why have you confounded
> men's strength and wisdom's way
> by hastening on a darkened path?
> Are you bringing about something quite new (*ti neōteron ē paros*)?[38]

Since the imagery of sunlight is more often equated with novelty of a desirable kind (see further Chapter 6 below), the sun's occlusion by an eclipse is naturally taken to suggest the opposite. The poet goes on to expand on how the event is likely to herald unprecedented novelty. At the end of the second verse (first antistrophe) of the paian, the chorus fearfully ask 'will you flood the land, and make new the race of men from the beginning (*andrōn neon ex arkhās genos*)?'[39] The anxiety-inducing novelty of the experience of eclipse is mapped onto the fantasy of wholesale change in the cosmic order. The portended cataclysm will, it is imagined, bring about an entirely new race (*neon genos*) of humankind, sweeping away the world as the speaker knows it to make place for a radically (*ex arkhās*) new beginning.

The verbal reminiscence of the Hesiodic catchphrase *ex arkhēs* recalls the myth of ages in Hesiod's *Works and Days*, in which a succession of

[38] Pi. *Pa.* 9.1–6.   [39] Ibid. 19–20.

'new races' of men comprise the stages of decline from a 'golden age' to the current 'age of iron'.[40] But the fresh start that a 'new race' implies is consequent on, rather than contemporaneous with, the eclipse and flood. It is what the poet or his chorus imagines *will* emerge when the flood has subsided and the sun's beam returns. Will the new race of men, we might ask, be better or worse than the current one? Unlike Hesiod, Pindar does not specify the imagined qualities of the successor race, which represents an undesired eventuality; but the idea of divine destruction of the current, flawed, world of mortals certainly allows room for the supposition that its replacement would constitute an advance rather than a regress. If the eclipse of the sun signifies some kind of ending, the expected return of the light in due course will mark a new beginning. While the portended cataclysm is not a positive prospect, the situation to which it may give rise is simply unknown; but it need not be thought of as a negative eventuality. In short, while the eclipse of the sun is Pindar's point of departure, as it was for Arkhilokhos, he is not concerned to dwell on the pastness of the event but to consider what it may mean for the future.

A continued engagement with the notion of the sun's light as portending something new (a connection explored further in Chapter 6 below) is found in the opening chorus of Sophokles' *Antigone*, which begins by quoting the opening words of Pindar's paian:

> Beam of the sun (*aktīs āeliou*), light fairer than all
> that have shone before
> for seven-gated Thebes . . . [41]

Sophokles' *aktīs āeliou* could have been expected to bring immediately to hearers' minds the scenario of eclipse painted by his lyric predecessor. But just as Pindar's paian expresses a new and dissimilar reaction from the one elaborated by Arkhilokhos, so the continuation of Sophokles' chorus immediately subverts the expectation aroused by the citation of his words:

> Finally you shone forth, eye of golden
> day, coming over the streams of Dirke.[42]

Whereas for Pindar the mention of eclipse leads to a prayer to avert calamity, in the context of the Sophoklean drama the chorus is celebrating the success

---

[40] Hes. *Op.* 109–201. What may inform Pindar's imagination, as elsewhere, is Pythagorean doctrine (Lloyd-Jones 1990: 80–109), here in regard to the notion that the cosmos undergoes recurrent destruction and is then recreated anew (see p. 113 below).
[41] Soph. *Ant.* 100–3.   [42] Ibid. 104–5.

of recent victory. The seven Argive warriors led by the renegade Polyneikes in battle against Thebes and its ruler, his twin brother Eteokles, have been defeated. The dark cloud of danger has been removed by the bright rays of sun; the eclipse itself has, as it were, been eclipsed. Towards the end of the stasimon the Chorus speaks first of Victory in the recent battle, then invokes Dionysos, the epiphanic god of Thebes, the bringer of new and joyful experiences:

> But since Victory whose name is glorious has come,
> the joy responding to the joy of Thebes with many chariots,
> after the recent wars (*polemōn tōn nūn*)
> let us be forgetful;
> and let us visit all the temples of
> the gods with all-night dances,
> and may the Bacchic god who shakes
> the land of Thebes take the lead.

The Chorus goes on to announce the entry of the city's actual 'new ruler':

> But here comes the king of the land,
> the new (*neokhmos*) ruler Kreon,
> under the new dispensations (*nearaisi suntukhiais*) of the gods.[43]

Sophokles has deliberately and almost provocatively transposed the Pindaric expression *aktīs āeliou* into a new setting. Again the sun's light heralds some kind of novelty, but here it is not one that is anticipated as bringing disaster. Rather, the chorus' introduction of the new ruler and the new political dispensation strikes a surprisingly positive note – surprising because it is common in tragedy for the notion of a 'new ruler' to be a cause for grave concern.[44] But there is an ironic twist to Sophokles' clear verbal reference to Pindar's paian. The hymn of joy and of new beginnings bids to reverse the initial expectations raised by the reminiscence of its paianic predecessor, but the audience will soon come to learn how the ascendancy of Thebes' 'new' king Kreon is itself to be terribly eclipsed by overwhelming personal tragedy.[45] This example illustrates a phenomenon that is regularly observable in the Greeks' expressions of novelty: the adaptation of these very expressions for novel purposes, to generate new meanings for new generations of readers.[46]

---

[43] Ibid. 148–57.
[44] E.g. *neos*, *neokhmos* of Zeus in [Aesch.] *PV* 96, 149, 391, *kainos* of Lykos in Eur. *Herc. Fur.* 38, 541, 779.
[45] Cf. Rutherford (1994–5) 126–7.   [46] See further Chapter 9 below.

NOVELTY AND MULTIPLICITY

The notion of novelty, distanced from a purely temporal signification, is linked to the perception of difference. If what is 'new' is 'different', the sense of novelty will be heightened as occasions to encounter or be aware of difference proliferate. Whether or not what is so identified is chronologically recent, within a matrix of diversity and plurality the identification of something as new may relate wholly to a sense of salient or unavoidable otherness. The conception of the new is in practice closely associated with circumstances of evident pluralism, profusion and polymorphism. The awareness of novelty goes hand in hand with the presence of irreducible multiplicity.

The magnitude and diversity of Homeric epic – its sheer length, large canvas, multiple characters, variety of scenes and endless scope for new interpretation – offer a fitting literary correlate to Greek views of novelty in this respect. The notion of multiplicity is personified by the figure of Odysseus. Homer introduces the hero as *polutropos*, a man 'of many turns', with reference to his mental agility and range of experiences: he wandered far and wide (*polla*), encountered many cities and the minds of many men (*pollōn*) and suffered much (*polla*) in the course of his homecoming.[47] The anaphora is insistent, and the hero's subsequent encounters with figures such as Kalypso, Kirke, Polyphemos, the Sirens and the suitors bear out his epithet *polutlās* ('much-enduring'). The sophist Alkidamas of Elea was inspired to create a novel metaphor (an unsuccessful one, in Aristotle's view) in describing the *Odyssey* as 'a beautiful mirror of human life'.[48] The tale of Odysseus' travels and sufferings was recognised as a metaphor for the variegated trajectory of an individual's life, capable of reflecting the diversity of lifeexperiences encountered by audiences and readers.

The variegation and complexity found in the Greeks' founding literary monuments are a reflection of the unceasing elaboration of their mythical and religious stories, and of their continual and productive exposure to different nations and cultures. Numerous divinities, the mass of rituals, and multiple versions of myth give Greek religion a sense of intractable plurality.[49] Some gods were age-old, others were (or, as in the case of

---

[47] Hom. *Od.* 1.1–4; in Chapter 6 I consider further connections between novelty and multiplicity.
[48] Arist. *Rhet.* 1406b12–13; Aristotle considered the metaphor contrived (*psūkhros*, literally 'frigid'). But the notion of the mirror is potentially a productive one, not least for the notion of novelty. One may see oneself reflected in a mirror; but the fact that it is not oneself, but a reflection, makes it both something familiar and something new. The 'mirror scene' in Euripides' *Bacchae* (918–70) gives concrete expression to the way the 'newly initiated' Pentheus sees the world through new eyes.
[49] Gould (2001) 226.

Dionysos, were represented as) newcomers. In addition to the Olympian pantheon, primitive 'chthonic' powers survived in Hellenic consciousness and ritual, often represented as female divinities such as Moirai, Graiai, Phorkydes and Erinyes. The plurality of gods and myths was brought into a coherent pattern by Homer and Hesiod.[50] But even these fundamental sources of Greek belief present the divine sphere as various and conflicting: the multifaceted nature of divinity offered an apt counterpart to the presence of continuing conflict and disorder in the world.[51]

Exposure to other peoples through travel and colonisation confirmed the Greeks' view of a diverse world around them. The centuries of overseas colonisation in Ionia, Italy, Africa and the shores of the Black Sea brought them into contact with a wealth of new ideas, customs, sights and objects. Nearby them in Asia Minor were the rich kingdoms of Phrygia and Lydia, on the Levantine coast the Phoenician trading-cities of Tyre and Sidon; to the west lay the inviting shores of Italy and Sicily, to the south the vast kingdom of Egypt with its manifold wonders and curiosities.[52] In cultural, ethical and literary spheres, through geographical explorations and commercial transactions, the Greeks encountered material, intellectual and ethical diversity. A sense of overwhelming plurality may have contributed to the desire of 'monistic' Presocratic thinkers such as Thales, Parmenides and Herakleitos to posit a graspable underlying unity in their physical and philosophical theories (see further Chapter 5 below). Others revelled in the multiplicity of new objects and ideas in the world around them. The sense of variety and multiplicity increased markedly during the fifth century, as Greek affairs came to be viewed in relation to the vigour and versatility of Athens (see Chapter 9).

Colourful (*poikilos*) individuality and intellectual versatility were also seen reflected in the personal attributes of innovators. Although 'polymathy' was derided by Herakleitos, popular interest was aroused by the way versatile thinkers displayed matching characteristics in their personality, life-style and appearance.[53] Thales of Miletos, the first Ionian natural philosopher, was the subject of anecdotes which portrayed him as both an absent-minded genius and a sharp businessman. He was alleged to have predicted the solar eclipse of 28 May 585 BCE, which ended a battle between Lydians and Medes.[54] He was also said to have fallen down a well when

---

[50] Hdt. 2.53.2.   [51] Gould (2001) 227.   [52] Boardman (1999); Hartog (2001) 47–63.
[53] In his *Ars Poetica* (205–301), Horace warns against the fallacy (which he attributes to Demokritos' commendation of 'native talent', *ingenium*, over skill, *ars*) of supposing that eccentric habits are necessary accoutrements of genius.
[54] Hdt. 1.74.

studying the stars, so that a slave-girl teased him with being so concerned with what was in the sky that he missed what was at his feet.[55] But he could keep his feet on the ground if necessary: he was alleged to have determined from the stars the precise time of a bumper olive harvest, and cornered the market in olive presses.[56] He became a byword for boffinry: 'The man's a Thales!' exclaims Peisetairos in Aristophanes' *Birds*, when the Athenian astronomer Meton arrives on the scene of the new foundation of Cloudcuckooland.[57] Meton himself was a versatile astronomer and inventor, credited with having observed the summer solstice of 432 BCE and introducing the controversial 'Metonic cycle' which equated 19 solar years with 235 lunar months. In the comedy he is depicted creating a novel layout for the new city in the sky:

> I'll use a ruler for measurement, in order to
> square the circle, you see, and in the centre put
> a market place, so that avenues may bear
> in straight lines to the centre-point – just like a star,
> which is a circular object from which straight beams
> radiate in all directions.[58]

The subject matter of the passage recalls the activities of Hippodamos, who had designed the layout of the Peiraieus and of the Athenian-led colony of Thourioi in South Italy (Meton's radiating circle may be a deliberate comical counterpart to the square grid layout).[59] Hippodamos' unusual appearance and habits drew comment:

In his general life, too, he was led into some eccentricity by a desire to attract attention. This made a number of people feel that he lived in too studied and artificial a manner. He wore his hair long and expensively adorned; he had flowing robes, expensively decorated, made from a cheap but warm material, which he wore in summer time as well as in winter; and he aspired to be learned about nature generally.[60]

In similar vein, the sophist Hippias of Elis was known for his practical as well as intellectual versatility; he prided himself on attending the festival at Olympia with clothes, shoes, 'Persian belt' and other accessories made by his own hands, as well as writings in a variety of prose and verse genres.[61] Accounts of these kinds testify to the continuing popular acknowledgement

---

[55] Pl. *Tht.* 174a.   [56] Arist. *Pol.* 1259a9–18.   [57] Ar. *Nub.* 1008.   [58] Ibid. 1004–8.
[59] Strabo (14.2.9) implies that Hippodamos also planned the city of Rhodes, rebuilt in 408 BCE; some accept the attribution despite the late date (see Wycherley in *CAH* 5², 204 n. 23).
[60] Arist. *Pol.* 2617b22–8.   [61] [Pl.] *Hipp. mi.* 366c–368a.

of and interest in 'innovative personalities' whose colourful appearance and habits appeared to match their reputations for thinking in novel ways.[62]

NOTHING NEW

The repetition of the old may be 'new' no less than divergence from it, if a change of time or perspective allows it to be presented in a new light. The opening scene of Aristophanes' *Frogs* of 405 BCE raises the question of novelty and repetitiveness with glittering irony. The comic figure of the god Dionysos, dressed to appear like the brawny hero Herakles, enters with his slave Xanthias carrying a mound of baggage. The audience will have seen 'porter-scenes' like this before, and will have been familiar with the scatological *double entendres* of the opening exchange:

XAN: Shall I make one of the usual cracks (*ta eiōthota*), master, that the audience always laugh at?
DION: Sure, any one you want – except 'I need to shed my load', that's just so stale.
XAN: Some other gag then?
DION: Just not 'this crap is killing me'...
XAN: So why do I have to carry all this stuff if I can't tell one of those porter jokes Phrynikhos and Lykis and Ameipsias tend (*eiōthe*) to use over and over in their comedies?[63]

Over the decade earlier in *Clouds*, Aristophanes had made a positive claim to originality: 'I'm always introducing sophisticated new ideas (*kainās ideās*), all different from each other and totally brilliant' (546–8). Here he demonstrates his claim in reverse, by repeating 'old' jokes under the guise of refusing to want to repeat them for fear of seeming unoriginal. These gags are 'the standard ones' (*eiōthota*), nothing new for Aristophanes or for his audience because, allegedly, they have been repeated *ad nauseam* by his rivals. The brazen ploy of repeating gags in the guise of criticising rivals' repetitiveness is the spur to laughter: the more they are repeated (and dismissed), the funnier the repetition seems. Accusing others of repetitiveness while exploiting the comic potential of repetition in this way may not be an original trope, but the poet goes a step further: when others tell familiar jokes they are doing nothing new, whereas his own use of old gags allows him to claim comic originality.

[62] Cf. the description of Empedokles (D.L. 8.73), and those of the painters Parrhasios and Zeuxis (below, p. 152); and Plato implicitly links Sokrates' eccentricity (*atopiā*) to his philosophical originality.
[63] Ar. *Ran.* 1–5, 12–15.

'That's nothing new' might offer a stern challenge to the practitioner seeking to claim novelty for his words, products or ideas. The denial of newness in another is an obvious tactic for putting down a rival and making one's own claim to originality. Aristophanes and the comedians of Old and Middle Comedy were happy to throw out claims and counterclaims regarding their rivals' alleged plagiarism, as did the fourth-century orators.[64] But outside these genres, emulous poets and artists keen to present themselves as innovators rarely criticise their rivals directly for lack of originality. Where the phrase *ouden kainon* is found, it tends to be when the author of a claim or proposal wishes to present what he himself is saying as being nothing untoward. *Kainotēs* is thus presented as a negative quality, which the speaker seeks to deny in his own case. In Thucydides' account, the sentiment that the desire for *kainotēs* is reprehensible in politics is stressed by the demagogue Kleon;[65] and Alkibiades flatters his Spartan audience by offering the outrageous proposition that it is nothing new to say that democracy is 'acknowledged folly'.[66] So also in the speeches of the fourth-century orators Demosthenes and Deinarkhos, the phrase 'nothing new' is aimed at providing reassurance that there is no cause for anxiety about what is being said or done.[67]

At the same time, the assertion that an idea or practice is *ouden kainon* may draw attention to the genuine novelty of the circumstances in which the words are found. The rhetoric of the phrase is brought out by the way Plato uses it in one of the most radical philosophical discussions ever penned about the political control of art. In the third book of his *Republic*, Plato has Sokrates engage in a lengthy discussion with Glaukon and Adeimantos about the kinds of music that should be allowed or forbidden in his ideal state. He insists to Adeimantos that his philosophically grounded objection to 'polyharmonic' instruments – those that do not have fixed pitches as do the strings of the lyre – means that the aulos should be banished: 'We are doing nothing new (*ouden kainon*) if we judge Apollo and his instruments to take precedence to Marsyas and his.'[68] The casual proposal that there is 'nothing new' in preferring the lyre to the aulos attracts emphatic agreement from Sokrates' interlocutor, but it conceals Plato's own innovation in the interpretation of the myth. Marsyas was the satyr who claimed to be a superior musician to Apollo, but lost to the god in a contest of musical

---

[64] See Heath, M. (1990) 151–2; Halliwell (1989).   [65] Thuc. 3.38.4–5; see p. 222 below.
[66] Thuc. 6.89.6.
[67] E.g. Dem. 15.9.1, 25.20.1, 35.1.1; Deinarkhos 5.2.1. Dem. 35 opens ironically with the assurance that the commercial dishonesty of the Phaselites is 'nothing new'.
[68] Pl. *Rep.* 399de.

skill and was flayed alive.[69] Rather than viewing the mythical contest as one of musicianship, Plato has turned it into a conflict between the two instruments, the aulos of Marsyas and the lyre of Apollo. As the instrument of drama and dithyramb, the aulos was long associated with Dionysos and with respected traditions of choral music; but on this account, the aulos is linked solely to the accursed Marsyas.

Plato has reason to gloss over the Dionysiac connection. He will in due course argue that Dionysiac genres of dithyramb, tragedy and comedy, all associated with aulos performance, should have no place in the education of citizens in his ideal political constitution. These genres were central to the new style of music of which Plato disapproved. In the early fourth century musical battle-lines had already been drawn between traditional styles of music and the 'New Music' associated with Timotheos of Miletos and Philoxenos of Kythera (see Chapter 8). The aulos with its continuous melodic range was more suited to the effects required by the new musical style than were stringed instruments with their less penetrating sound and fixed notes. Here, through exclusively associating the aulos with the hubristic Marsyas, Plato aims to downgrade the status both of the instrument and of the new music with which it was strongly associated. The innocent claim of Sokrates to be doing 'nothing new' masks, therefore, the tendentious suggestion that the fabled contest was between the two *instruments* rather than the performers: an interlocutor would be hard put to disagree that the divine Apollo should be preferred to the hubristic satyr. But although Plato's identification of the aulos as the 'instrument of Marsyas' is an implicit rejection of the new musical style, he could argue, ironically, that he himself is doing nothing new: the idea of interpreting the myth in this way could be derived from Timotheos himself, whose dithyramb *Marsyas* effectively dramatised the contest between aulete and lyrist.[70]

The rhetorical dismissal of *to kainon* is prominent in the Hippocratic treatise *On Ancient Medicine*, which launches directly into a rejection of contemporary approaches to medical theorisation:

Those who have ventured to speak or write about medicine by adopting a postulate (*hupothesis*) – hot and cold, wet and dry, or whatever else – reduce the underlying principle (*arkhē*) of causation of human disease and death to a narrow compass in postulating (*hupothemenoi*) one or two elements, and the same elements in all cases of illness.[71]

---

[69] Wilson (2004) 275–6. [70] Boardman (1956). [71] [Hp.] *VM* 1.1–6.

The author subsequently reiterates his insistence: 'in my opinion, medicine requires no new-style postulate (*kainē hupothesis*)'.[72] He does not attack any particular new *hupothesis*, but the very idea of adopting such an approach. He alludes to theories that stipulate a fixed number of elements as underlying human health, dismissing them as arbitrary and reductive. In his view the healing art is based on a long-established set of empirical practices, which should also guide future research:

> The entire field of medicine has long been in existence, and a principle and method have been found whereby numerous sound discoveries have been made over a long period (*en pollōi khronōi*). The rest will be discovered if a competent inquirer, *au fait* with past discoveries, uses these as the starting-point of his investigations.[73]

The phraseology recalls Xenophanes' progressivism (see p. 123); qualities of time, care and competence contrast with those associated with theories of healing which do not depend on observation but 'inquire into medicine in the new fashion (*ton kainon tropon*) on the basis of a *hupothesis*'.[74]

The terms in which the author rejects the value of novelty are polemical, but his insistent repudiation of *to kainon* draws attention to how intellectual innovations were popularly promoted and received. Rhetoric was inescapable, since the uses of novelty and its evaluation remained a matter of debate rather than proof. Physicians were not just practical healers; they had to be able to expound their methods in a manner that was meant to impress and persuade. They also needed to create a new technical terminology, something that seemed as reprehensible to Plato as the physical conditions described:

> When medical help is needed not for wounds or some seasonal condition but because, through idleness and the life-style we've gone through, people are filled with gas and phlegm like a swamp, so that sophisticated (*kompsoi*) Asclepiads are forced to come up with terms like 'flatulence' and 'catarrh' to describe those diseases – is that not a disgrace?
> Yes, these really are bizarre newfangled (*kaina*) terms for diseases.[75]

The author of *On Ancient Medicine* implicitly acknowledges the general principle that productive innovation may come about by transferring

---

[72] Ibid. 1.20–1: the term *hupothesis*, first attested here in this sense, signifies a theoretical underpinning or speculative foundation (from *hupo-tithēmi* 'place under'). For first-person assertion ('egotism') as a mark of innovativeness, see Lloyd (1987).
[73] Ibid. 2.1–5.   [74] Ibid. 13.1–2.   [75] Pl. *Rep.* 405c8–d6.

methods or ideas from one discipline to another. He adduces the practices of gymnastic trainers to support his empirical principles:

> At this very time, moreover, even those involved with gymnasia and exercise routines are constantly discovering new things (*prosexeuriskousin*) by pursuing this same path, investigating what is best to eat and drink to attain greater command of one's body and to become physically stronger.[76]

Gymnastics and physical exercise are appropriate spheres in which to seek new medical ideas since they are, like medicine, essentially concerned with bodily health and strength.[77] What is rejected is the application of extraneous theories to medicine, a procedure described as more suited to 'astrology and geology'. The objects of the latter pursuits are remote and less susceptible to investigation and observation.[78] Medical knowledge, which can only come about from cumulative observation of health and sickness, represents 'a substantial discovery (*heurēma*), the fruit of much investigation and skill'.[79]

Many of those whom the author is attacking self-consciously elaborated their novel theories by applying notions from natural philosophy to medical theorisation.[80] They followed the example of fifth-century thinkers such as Anaxagoras, Alkmaion and Empedokles (the only one named, at *VM* 20.4), who posited either a unitary *arkhē* or a set of fundamental elements (*stoikheia*) from which the universe was constituted. The author seeks to distance the 'founders' of his art from the speculations of such thinkers. The work of early medical practitioners must have, in his view, reflected the same empiricism he ascribes to the contemporary physician's *tekhnē*.[81] He seeks to preempt any criticism that the failure to apply new kinds of thinking might impede the development and improvement of the medical art, by reasserting medicine's empirical basis and suggesting that there is not far to go to complete the task: 'All this is proof that, using the same method of inquiry, the whole art of medicine could be discovered.'[82] The optimism of this assertion is echoed in another treatise, *Places in Man*, where we find it allied to the notion that this kind of investigation is bound to succeed because it does not rely on chance (*tukhē*):

---

[76] [Hp.] *VM* 4.6–10.
[77] It is not a coincidence that the celebrated early fifth-century physician, Demokedes, came from Kroton, a city famous for its sporting and athletic excellence.
[78] [Hp.] *VM* 1.16–17.   [79] Ibid. 4.5–6.
[80] The gnomic style and paradoxical notions used in the late treatise *Nutriment* are notably Herakleitan; cf. the 'enigmatic formulations' (Jouanna 1999: 276) of *Regimen* 10.
[81] At the same time, he recognises that his predecessors considered their art to have divine sanction: traditional religious belief is preferable to modernistic rationalism. Ibid. 14.14–20.
[82] Ibid. 8.19–20.

In my opinion, the whole of this sort of medicine that teaches about dispositions and timings has already been discovered.... Anyone who understands medicine in these terms will not rely on chance in the slightest, but would be bound to succeed whether luck were present or absent. For the whole field of medicine is based on a sound footing, and the finest and most inspired ideas are not in the slightest bit dependent on chance.[83]

The Hippocratic author provides useful insights into different mechanisms and avenues of innovation. He approves the use of cumulative inquiry to build up new ideas and techniques on the basis of earlier ones; but he also acknowledges the potential of applying principles from one domain of thinking to another, and the possibility of new discoveries occurring by chance. All of these processes were in evidence in fifth-century medicine, but Hippocratic authors were aware of the practical limitations of their *tekhnē*: 'precision (*atrekeia*) is seldom to be seen'.[84] While some make a virtue of the frank acknowledgement of fallibility, others seek to reassure their audience that obstacles would be overcome as long as medical inquiry proceeds in the right manner. The polemical thrust of the treatises adds a further dimension to their concern with *kainotēs*. Was the characterisation of the speculative method as *kainos* accepted by those who were applying abstract postulates to the medical art? It may well have been acknowledged by them in positive terms, just as Aristophanes prides himself on his own new ideas while attacking Sophistic novelties. The mark of Hippocratic empiricism is the supposition that medical knowledge can be increased only through the cumulative, painstaking investigation of disease; but the enduring application of humoral theory – the dominant model of subsequent Greek medicine and indeed of western medical thinking up to the eighteenth century – shows that the transfer of abstract patterns of thinking drawn from extraneous intellectual domains could at least lead to successful kinds of novelty, if not to genuine progress.

SONG'S NEW CHARIOT?

Khoirilos of Samos, an epic poet working at the end of the fifth and beginning of the fourth centuries, prefaces one of his poems with a lament that, in the field of epic at least, everything seems to have been done before:

> Lucky the man of those times who was skilled in song-making (*aoidē*), the Muses' servant, when the meadow was still untrodden:

---

[83] [Hp.] *Loc. Hom.* 46: p. 342, 4–9 Littré. [84] *VM* 9.21–2; cf. 12.12–13, *Morb.* 1.5, 1.9.

> But now that everything is parcelled out, and the arts have their boundaries,
> we are the last on the road, and there is nowhere for the poet,
> search as he may, to steer his freshly-yoked chariot (*neozuges harma*).[85]

This is the earliest surviving Greek text to express a sentiment of this kind, and Khoirilos' complaint is often taken at face value:[86] the poet feels unable to compose anything new, at least in the overworked field of epic verse. However, Khoirilos should be credited with more complex intentions. His complaint reads as an original trope in its own right. Rather than simply registering it as a cry of despair, it is a self-conscious bid to be original by means of deliberately *reversing* familiar epic claims made by poets such as Homer, Hesiod and Parmenides. The former bards claimed to have been blessed by the gift of song (*aoidē*): Homer's singers find (new) paths (*oimai*) of minstrelsy, Hesiod is inspired by the Muses who dance around virgin springs.[87] The philosopher uses the image of the chariot (*harma*) to convey the radical originality of the message communicated to him in the course of his uniquely personal voyage of enlightenment.[88] Khoirilos has not, in fact, refused the challenge of epic. He takes up the very images inherited from these predecessors and 'yokes' them together to make his own *neozuges harma*, the innovative vehicle for his epic poetry.

The expression of Khoirilos' preface invites comparison with that of two ancient Egyptian texts which touch on the question of the limits of art. In a composition dated to the latter part of the Sixth Dynasty (2345–2183 BCE), the Vizier Ptahhotep advises his son on the art of speaking so that he may become 'a model for the children of the great'. He aims to instruct him, he says, in 'the ways of the ancestors' by recalling 'the sayings of the past':

> Don't be proud of your knowledge,
> Consult the ignorant and the wise;
> The limits of art are not reached,
> No artist's skills are perfect.[89]

These comments lead to an exhortation to seek out the right words for the occasion, from whatever source may provide them:

> Good speech is more hidden than greenstone,
> yet may be found among maids at the grindstones.

---

[85] Khoirilos fr. 2 *PEG*.   [86] E.g. by Lesky (1966) 304–5, Hopkinson (1988) 1.
[87] Hom. *Od.* 8.74, 483, 22.347; Hes. *Thg.* 3–4, 31–2.
[88] Parm. B1.5. In *Phaedrus* 246a–254e Plato brilliantly reworks the chariot image to create an allegory of the soul pulled in different directions by spiritedness and desire.
[89] Lichtheim (1975) 63.

A second text, dating from the Middle Kingdom period (2030–1640), strikes a more fretful tone. The author presents 'the gathering of words, the heaping of sayings, the seeking of phrases by a searching heart, made by a priest of On, Seni's [son], Khakheperre-sonb, called Ankhu':

> [Would that I] had unknown phrases,
> Sayings that are strange,
> Novel, untried words,
> Free of repetition;
> Not transmitted sayings,
> Spoken by ancestors!
> I wring out my body of what it holds,
> In releasing all my words;
> For what was said is repetition,
> When what was said is said [again].
> Ancestors' words are nothing to boast of,
> They are found by those who come after.[90]

This repetitive expression of Ankhu's desire to find new words and phrases of which he can boast contrasts with Vizier Ptahhotep's calm admonition to his son not to be proud, but to seek instruction where he may. While the Vizier's maxims evince confidence in the possibility of new paths of 'good speech' being discovered even 'among maids at the grindstones', Ankhu despairs of discovering any 'novel, untried words'. His sentiment draws attention to a poetic prelude of unusual vigour and originality.

Ptahhotep's advice continues with his seeking to repeat 'the ways of the ancestors, who have listened to the gods', in order that 'strife may be banished from the people'. Ankhu's topic is more personal in nature, and he even subsequently addresses his 'heart' in a manner reminiscent of Pindar's self-address to his 'dear heart' (*philon ētor*).[91] It has been suspected that the sequel that constitutes the body of Ankhu's lament is more of a literary exercise than a tract of genuine political significance. But it is worth noting that where Ptahhotep's theme is the preservation of social stability, Ankhu's anxiety concerns changing political conditions. His lament is born of distress in the face of social turmoil that has raised his consciousness to the possibility of new and unwelcome eventualities:

> Would that I knew what others do not,
> What has not been said time and again,
> To say it and have my heart answer me:
> To tell it of my distress,

[90] Ibid. 146 (slightly modified). [91] Pi. *O.* 1.4.

> To shift onto it the load on my back –
> The things that afflict me –
> To relate to it what I suffer,
> And sigh 'Ah' with relief.
> I ponder what has happened,
> The events that occur throughout the land:
> Changes take place, this year is not like last year,
> One year is more toilsome than another.[92]

As with the preface to Ankhu's lament, Khoirilos' well-turned words preface a demonstration of his poetic originality.[93] He uses to new purpose imagery familiar from early lyric poetry, philosophical epic and the lyrics of tragic drama. In doing so he both identifies the 'problem' of his dwindling field of action and heralds his own solution – the innovative use of epic verse to narrate recent history. Biographical fiction confirms Khoirilos' literary affiliations: the Samian poet was said to have sat at the feet of Herodotos, and even to have been his lover.[94] His epic poems were entitled *Barbarika, Mēdika, Persika* – that is, 'accounts of non-Greeks, Medes and Persians', precisely the subject matter of Herodotos' prose *historiai*.[95] In a fragment of the proem, perhaps the opening, he appeals to the Muse:

> Tell me another (*allos*) tale, how from the land of Asia
> A great war came to Europe.[96]

The Homeric resonance points up the difference between the mythical war at Troy and his historical subject matter. Khoirilos is likely to have adapted the style of Homeric battle narrative for historical use, overlaid by a new self-referentiality (detectable in his surviving fragments) – something more associated with Hesiod's didactic poetry and Pindar's choral lyric (cf. the self-address noted above in relation to the use of 'heart' in Ankhu's lament). Not only, then, does Khoirilos exploit a regular mode of literary innovation by introducing novel subject matter into a traditional genre, he highlights his innovation with a prologue that constitutes (apparently for the first time) an ironic reversal of the proud self-promotion found in poetic predecessors going back to Hesiod.

Khoirilos' sentiments struck a chord with later authors. His prologue is too ingenious not to have merited emulation, and it finds a close echo in an epigram attributed to the fourth-century tragic poet, Astydamas the younger. Astydamas was the author of some much-admired tragedies

---

[92] Lichtheim (1975) 147. [93] MacFarlane (2006). [94] *Suda* s.n. Khoirilos.
[95] *P.Oxy.* 1399; Drews (1970). [96] Fr. 1 *PEG*.

including a *Parthenopaios*, an *Alkmaion* which drew praise from Aristotle, and a *Hektor* that was still being read in the third and second centuries BCE.[97] He was accorded the signal honour by his fellow Athenians of having a statue erected in the Theatre of Dionysos even before those of the three great dramatists of the earlier generation.[98] Astydamas no doubt believed that his own fame would survive alongside that of the canonical three. In this respect he may have inherited the self-assurance of his father Astydamas the elder, a nephew of Aeschylus and pupil of Isokrates, whose boastfulness gave rise to the phrase 'you praise yourself like Astydamas of old'.[99] The epigram echoes the tone of Khoirilos' prelude, in lamenting that it is impossibile for modern-day poets to match up to the 'classics':

> Would that I had been living when they were alive
> or that they were living in my time – they who are
> considered to be the first in giving pleasure through language.
> Then truly I would have been seen to be competing alongside them.
> But now they have a head start, and they are not pursued by envy (*phthonos*).[100]

The epigram may at first reading strike a note of despair. But in view of its author's public status and success, it implies a riposte to contemporary rivals: they, unlike the poets of old, are not worth competing with. Positioning himself in a diachronic, inter-generational, *agōn* with the great tragedians of old, Astydamas reprises the sentiment regarding *phthonos* of another classic poet, Pindar.[101]

CONCLUSIONS

What counts as 'new' is a subjective and cultural construction rather than an objective reality. The Greeks did not construct novelty uniformly: a wealth of passages in Greek texts can be adduced to evince antipathy to novelty, but the attitudes expressed may be those of an individual author, or even of a fictional character. To take them at face value is to overlook questions of context, authorial intent and literary or dramatic purpose. Upper-class authors will disparage the kind of sociopolitical change from which they most stand to lose. Characters in tragic drama will react negatively to 'new' revelations of disaster. A deeper analysis of poetic texts

---

[97] Garland (2004) 22: the titles alone of nineteen plays by Astydamas are known.
[98] *TGF* 1, no. 60 Tb.
[99] Suda s.v. *Sautēn*; D.L. 2.43. The attribution of works and citations to Astydamas the older and the younger (if indeed there was more than one dramatist of the name) is not definite.
[100] *TGF* 1, no. 60 T2a.   [101] Pi. *Nem.* 8.21; see p. 193.

(along the lines demonstrated above with the poem of Arkhilokhos) challenges the suppositions articulated in such stark terms by van Groningen about the Greeks' imaginative orientation to novelty and tradition, past and future.

Novelty and innovation were no less real phenomena for the Greeks than for us. In trying to pin down the disparate and diffuse conceptions of the new, some distinctions may seem over-precise, others insufficiently well-defined. 'The new' is something that constitutes a difference within a given frame of reference, temporal, stylistic or cultural. What falls outside the frame seems saliently different from what falls within it. Which frames of reference are constructed and why, and what counts as salient and to whom, are questions that raise important distinctions between different cultural perspectives and expressions of novelty.

The appeal to novelty, as we shall see particularly in the case of music (Chapter 8), is no less characteristic a trope of Greek discourse than is the appeal to tradition. This suggests the outline of a further solution to the 'paradox of innovation' in Greek culture (which may supplement rather than displace other explanations). The tendencies which van Groningen and others assert as characteristic of the Greek psyche may not simply have coexisted awkwardly with the pursuit of the new by creative individuals who contributed to the flowering of the 'Greek miracle'. Such tendencies may rather have been instrumental in allowing Greeks the psychological assurance to assimilate, adopt and, in some cases, pursue the new. A strong consciousness of the weight of tradition can, as I argue for Khoirilos' proem, be a springboard for innovative thought and expression.

Novelty in diverse areas of experience elicited a range of perceptions and attitudes to the new in Greek antiquity. The material that provides witness to these perceptions is not new. But, as in the case of the traditional mythical tales continually reinterpreted by the Attic tragedians, when viewed through a new lens it takes on a new aspect. The diverse expressions of the new that we encounter in every area of Greek life and thought, and a less restrictive analysis of the impulses that underlie them, should lead towards less reductive generalisations about Greek attitudes than has often been the case. Once the 'grip of the past' is relaxed, the variety and vigour of the Greeks' perspectives on novelty may be more fully revealed and appreciated. The sheer range of experience and expression uncovered by such an exploration undermines the proposition that the Greeks were as a rule held fast in such a grip, rather than being inspired to reach out and embrace the new. A more subtle understanding of the Greeks' imaginative explorations may overturn long-held prejudices regarding the place of novelty in the ancient Greek world. It may also, if only incidentally, throw light on the perennial question of why ancient Greece is acknowledged to have originated so many new intellectual and artistic products of enduring worth and excellence.

CHAPTER 3

The transformations of Kaineus

In nova fert animus mutatas dicere formas corpora...

Ovid

'Into new forms my spirit bids me venture, to tell of bodies changed in shape'.[1] With the programmatic opening words to his Greek-titled *Metamorphoses*, the Roman poet Ovid underscores the centrality of novelty and metamorphosis to the Greeks' mythical imagination. Innumerable Greek myths tell of literal transformations by gods, such as those undergone by Zeus in his pursuit of amours – changing into a bull to seduce Europa, a swan to seduce Leda, a shower of gold to penetrate Danae. Mortals too may be transformed – Teiresias into a woman, Kainis/Kaineus into a man, Hekabe into a she-dog, Ariadne into a constellation. In the Homeric Hymn to Dionysos, sailors are turned into dolphins; in the *Odyssey*, Odysseus' companions are changed into pigs and back again.[2] The way new things are seen to emerge is through a change in someone's, or some thing's, form or nature.

Epic poetry explores the potential of human beings to be transformed in a figurative way, through experiences, trials, the acquisition of knowledge. In real life too, an athletic victor, transformed by success, might become a 'new' person, even a demi-god and object of cult.[3] The impersonation required by drama, itself a genre that appears to have metamorphosised from ritual performances, led to the growth of the acting profession, in due course producing star performers skilled in playing new roles and characters.[4] In the performance of Mysteries, Dionysiac or Eleusinian, initiates underwent spiritual metamorphosis, seeking to gain access to new vision and to a new life beyond death by conducting secretive rituals. The plots of Aristophanes' comedies often play on the notion of such

---

[1] Ov. *Met.* 1.1. For Ovid, the literal is fused with the literary: *in nova fert animus* seems to allude to the poet's innovative treatment of the genre, and *corpora* is artfully delayed. Cf. Wheeler (1999) 11–12.
[2] See in general Forbes Irving (1990). [3] Currie (2005). [4] Csapo (2010) 83–4.

transformations: older male characters such as Trygaios in *Peace*, Philokleon in *Wasps*, Strepsiades in *Clouds* and Peisetairos in *Birds* are portrayed as being reinvigorated and rejuvenated, after undergoing trials and adventures resembling or recalling those undertaken by mystic initiands.[5] Dionysos himself, the god of theatre, is prone to metamorphic epiphanies as a bull, goat or snake. The divine embodiment of the vine and the god of masks and illusion, his transfiguring nature was transferred to the theatre, with its impersonating masks and performative transvestism, its capacity to transport its listeners to different times and places, its potentially cathartic effect on audiences.[6]

Music, particularly the music associated with Dionysos, was thought to have the ability to alter character (*ēthos*).[7] Just as the lyre of Orpheus was said to have transformed wild nature, music had the power to transform human nature. For Sokrates and Plato, philosophy was the supreme music;[8] its capacity to elicit new words and ideas (*logoi*) via dialectical interchange between active minds made it the vehicle for personal transformation. For Gorgias, Isokrates and Aristotle, rhetoric was such a tool. Both persuasion (*peithō*) and education (*paideia*) might be used to create new thoughts and new dispositions, to transform listener and student. Words and language themselves demonstrate a profuse capacity for metamorphosis, with their constant creation of novel forms, meanings, expressions and implications. Epic shows a love of puns and wordplay. Homer relishes the relationship of Odysseus' name to *odussomai* ('grudge'), and the hero's naming of himself *Outis* ('Nobody') to mock Polyphemos;[9] Hesiod plays on Aphrodite's epithet *philommeidēs*, 'laughter-loving' and indulges in kennings (riddling or oblique descriptions, such as *idris*, 'wise one', for 'ant').[10] In *Cratylus*, Plato speculates at length on etymologies and processes of word formation; in *Rhetoric*, Aristotle explores metamorphoses of discourse – the creation of metaphors, neologisms and idiosyncratic phrases (*glōttai*).

The mythical image of a physical metamorphosis converges with the development of a new word in the evolution of the word *kainos*, 'new'. The element *kain-* seems to underly the name of Kaineus, the legendary Lapith warrior who appears in Homer. The name has been taken to signify

---

[5] Bowie (1993).
[6] Dionysiac worship might also be viewed less positively, as it is by Pentheus in Euripides' *Bacchae*, as a 'novel (form of) sickness', *nosos kainē* (*Ba.* 353–4).
[7] Anderson (1966).   [8] Pl. *Phd.* 60e–61b.
[9] Odysseus/*odussomai*: *Od.*1.62, 5.339–40, 5.423, 19.275–6, 407–9. *Outis*: *Od.* 9.364–7, 399–412. Cf. the wordplay of *mē tis* / *mētis* (no one / cunning) in 414: Schein (1970) 79–80.
[10] *Idris*: Hes. *Op.* 778. Pun with *philommēdēs* (lover of genitals): Hendry (1997). Cf. Mazur (2004), West (1978) 289–90 (on 'kennings') etc.

'new man', since in the mythical account Kaineus is said to have been transformed from female to male. If the stem of *kainos* is etymologically related to that of the name 'Kaineus', what can we learn about the meaning of 'new' in Greek? A close analysis of the myth and its vicissitudes, traceable in the remains of authors and commentators spanning virtually a millennium from Homer to Apollodoros, opens up new perspectives on the significance of the name and on the etymology of *kainos*.

TWO WORDS FOR NEW

Neos, kainos: at the heart of the Greek lexical record for the notion of novelty lies a duplication, seemingly a verbal redundancy. Ancient Greek regularly uses not one word but two morphologically distinct words (along with their compounds and cognates) to denote 'new'. Both *neos* and *kainos* have been thought to derive from Indo-European roots which, though divergent in form, appear to be semantically alike, with the root meaning in both cases of 'young' or 'recent'.[11] But the two words demonstrate important differences in their usage and history; above all, it is significant that *neos* occurs in Mycenaean Greek (*ne-wo*).[12] Thereafter it is common in Greek texts from Homer onward, whereas *kainos* is not securely attested until the fifth century BCE. However, while *kainos* and cognate terms are wholly absent from Homer and Hesiod, the element *kain-* is found embedded in the songs of both poets, in the name of Kaineus.

Although *kainos* is not found in epic, there are numerous passages and contexts where we might have expected the word to be used. Homer describes, for instance, the making of a new shield and a new wagon, and in numerous verses we find mention of a new day, a new grief, or a new song. In none of these cases is *kainos* the epithet of choice. This is not because the form of the word poses any problem for the epic hexameter. *Kainos* along with its inflections, its comparative and superlative forms and a number of common compounds and cognates such as *kainotomeō*, *kainizō* and *kainopathēs*, can fit easily into the Homeric metre. The comparative form *kainoteros* is in fact found in a line of the hexameter poem *The Battle of Frogs and Mice*, a parody in epic style and metre, traditionally attributed to Homer but now dated to the Hellenistic period. In the poem we find the phrase *kainoterais tekhnais* 'by means of novel devices'; *kainoteros* is

---

[11] Chantraine (1968) s.vv. refers to the Sanskrit stem *nava-*, and reconstructs a Sanskrit adjectival form *kanīna-* from the genitive form *kanīnam*, 'girls'.

[12] Chadwick and Baumbach (1963) 224: *newo-* is used of things (oil, wool, wheels etc.) rather than persons, and its opposite term is *parajo-* (*palaios*, 'old').

here used in connection with the invention of a new and effective weapon of war (at least for the purposes of a conflict where the combatants on one side are mice) – a wooden mousetrap.[13]

The absence of *kainos* in early epic poetry may be purely a matter of chance, as may the fact that the word is not found in Apollonios of Rhodes' *Argonautica*.[14] Explanations for the word's absence from archaic epic include the possibility that it was unknown to the monumental poet, that it was not an element of the linguistic amalgam employed in traditional epic composition, or that it was known but felt to be unsuited to the linguistic register or ethical demands of heroic poetry.[15] Instead of *kainos*, Homer regularly uses *neos*, either on its own or in compound words; he also frequently uses the adverbial form *neon*, 'just now'. As the latter usage might indicate, compounds with *neo-* express newness by indicating that an action or event has taken place recently. Thus new objects, weapons and so on are commonly described with epithets such as 'recently made' and 'newly polished'. About a dozen compound epithets formed on the lines of *neoteukhēs* (new-made) and *neosmēktos* (newly polished) indicate this aspect of what may be called 'temporal' novelty.[16] Compounds with *prōtos*, 'first', serve a similar purpose. When Priam's sons build a new wagon in preparation for their father's visit to the Akhaian camp to ransom Hektor, it is new by virtue of being *prōtopagēs*, 'built for the first time'.[17] The Trojan warrior Pandaros' brand-new, unused chariots are ringingly described with the epithets *kāloi prōtopageis neoteukhees*.[18] Both compound epithets are brought to bear on the evocation of novelty. So, in a sense, is the epithet *kalos* 'beautiful', since the attribution of visual beauty (with the admiration or wonder, *thauma*, this can occasion) seems, as I shall show below (p. 143), to be a way in which Homer leads us to suppose that something is, or at least looks, new.

It is hard to determine whether any passage in epic can be found in which the implications of *neos* extend to connotations of 'new' other than purely temporal newness or recency. A few possible instances merit mention. In

---

[13] [Hom.] *Batr.* 116. 'To build a better mousetrap' has fortuitously been used in modern times (following a dictum of Ralph Waldo Emerson) to encapsulate the purpose of the inventor.
[14] The Hellenistic poet adopts the conventions of epic language and style, but with innovations of his own: Knight (1995), Fantuzzi and Hunter (2004) 94–8.
[15] Cf. Homeric anger-terms, which include *kholos*, *mēnis*, *thūmos* and *kotos* for 'anger' (Most 2003), but not *orgē*.
[16] *Il.* 5.194, 13.342. Cf. *neostrophos* for a 'newly twisted' bowstring (15.469), *neoplutos* for 'new-washed' clothing (*Od.* 6.64), *neopristos* for 'newly sawn' ivory (*Od.* 8.404) etc. For the category of 'temporal' novelty see p. 19.
[17] *Il.* 24.267. [18] Ibid. 5.194.

the *Iliad*, when the common soldier Thersites sneers at Agamemnon for coveting the spoils of battle, he does so with the words 'Maybe you need yet more gold, or *gunaika neēn* with whom to sleep.'[19] Here *gunaika neēn* might at first sight be taken to mean 'a new woman' or 'new wife'. In that case, *neos* would signify 'new' in the sense of 'another', that is an additional consort for Agamemnon, just as 'more' gold would allow him to add to his existing wealth. Such a signification, however, is unparalleled in the epic (or at least no certain parallel can be adduced); the epithet is better taken here simply to signify 'young'.[20] In another potentially ambiguous usage, where the epithet is simply *neos*, Menelaus is berated for killing Euphorbos' brother and leaving the warrior's wife bereft *mukhōi thalamoio neoio* ('in the recess of her new bedchamber').[21] In what way is the bedchamber new?[22] The implication may be that it was recently built or freshly prepared for the newly-weds, but in its immediate context, *neos* is most easily read as a transferred epithet, used to indicate simply that the bedchamber is one that the wife has recently come to occupy. It highlights the recentness of the marriage of Euphorbos' brother and the consequent prematurity of his widow's bereavement, rather than indicating any quality of newness attaching to the room's physical appearance or construction.

The *Odyssey*, a tale more self-consciously rich in instances of novelty than the *Iliad*, might be expected to have more explicit references to newness as a property of things. In the opening book, Telemakhos famously remarks that the most appealing song (*aoidē*) is the one that circulates 'newest' (*neōtatē*) among the audience (see further Chapter 8). The superlative form intensifies the meaning of *neos* to signify a song 'most recently' composed, and on that account fresh to its audience.[23] In discussing these verses, Plato insisted that they should not be taken to suggest more than a narrowly temporal significance, and on no account be understood as referring to innovation in musical style (*tropos*).[24] A similarly temporal understanding of the word may be proposed even when physical objects are identified in the *Odyssey* as 'new' by the use of unqualified and uncompounded *neos*. When Athene in the guise of Mentor exhorts Telemakhos to sail in search of Odysseus, mentioning the many ships available in Ithaca both 'new and old' (*neai ēde palaiai*), *neai* effectively signifies no more than 'recently made'.[25] The formula *neai ēde palaiai* echoes, and may be considered no more than a formulaic variant of, the Iliadic *neoi ēde gerontes*, in which

---

[19] Ibid. 2.229–33.   [20] So translated by e.g. Hammond (1987).   [21] *Il.* 17.36.
[22] This question brings to mind the memorably 'novel' bed of Odysseus and Penelope fashioned by Odysseus himself from the bole of a single ancient olive tree (*Od.* 23.184–204).
[23] *Od.* 1.351–2.   [24] See below, Chapter 8, p. 190.   [25] *Od.* 2.293.

neos has its primary meaning of 'young'.[26] Later in the tale, Odysseus is described stringing his magnificent bow like a master lyre-player who with expert ease winds a string *neōi peri kollopi*, 'around a new peg'.[27] *Neos* here does not refer to any novel quality attaching to the peg itself. As with the new bedchamber discussed above, *neos* may signify 'recently made', but is more easily taken to allude to a change of condition regarding the peg, i.e. its being re-strung. The simile draws attention to the effort and skill required to string a lyre with a cord of intractably tensile gut, a reminder to Homer's audience of the bard's own special expertise.

In short, if we judge the most natural connotations of *neos* within the contexts in which they occur, there appears to be no single instance in Homer in which a property of novelty, as opposed to the implications of 'young' or 'recent' (or at most 'additional') is explicit. In some passages a quality of newness is implicitly evoked through the ascription of attributes such as radiance and beauty. When, for instance, the women of Troy choose a new robe for Athene, taken from a pile of *peploi* woven by Sidonian women, it is described as shining 'like a star' and lying *neiatos allōn*, ('lowest of all') to ensure its protection as the most precious of the garments.[28] The appearance of the robe is primarily indicated by its stellar sheen, a peculiar lustre that recalls the Mycenaean practice of treating clothes with perfumed oil.[29] In a similar fashion, when Hephaistos is called on to forge armour for Akhilleus, we know it to be new (i.e. freshly manufactured) because we follow the account of its production in his smithy. The account of its manufacture is given in vivid detail, almost literally blow by blow.[30] We are also led to imagine that the shield possesses the quality of pristineness, i.e. that it has the appearance of being new, because what is especially emphasised is the way it shines and glistens.[31]

In none of these instances is a new *kind* of object indicated. Homer has no term for and appears to have no fully developed sense of what later Greeks called *kainotomiā*, the process of material, formal or intellectual innovation that builds on or even supersedes what is familiar, traditional or unremarkable. In the tale of Ares and Aphrodite sung by Demodokos in *Odyssey* Book 8, Hephaistos forges an invisible web to trap the illicit lovers.

---

[26] *Il.* 9.36 and 9.258. *Neos* and *palaios* meaning 'young' and 'old' are coupled elsewhere in Homer, e.g. *Il.*14.108.
[27] *Od.* 21.406–7.
[28] *Il.* 6.288–95. The phonetic similarity of *neiatos* to *neōtatos* is probably fortuitous (*neios*, 'fallow field', probably derives from a root meaning 'low-lying'), but since the choicest object would be the least used or handled, it would be in the 'newest', most pristine condition.
[29] Shelmerdine (1995). [30] *Il.* 18.468–608. [31] Ibid.18.610, 617 (etc.); see further Chapter 6.

Though undoubtedly a novel artifice, the poet never refers to it as such; it is simply a 'cunning' device (281 *doloenta*, 317 *dolos*). In the *Iliad*, although Homer has Nestor make reference to the superior valour of the heroes of old, the hero (or poet) has nothing further to say about old versus new (and perhaps less admirable) methods or styles of fighting.[32] It may be supposed that innovation of this kind is unsuited to the context of heroic action, in that it would put into question the stability and integrity of immutable, divinely sanctioned ideals of *aretē*. The heroes of epic may be permitted to boast about, and be praised for, their valour in words or deeds; if any formal innovation is acknowledged, it is in technical spheres, the province of lowly artisans and humble specialists (*dēmioergoi*) rather than heroic warriors. Even so, *dēmioergoi* lay claim to innovation only implicitly, and do not directly vaunt their claims to originality. The makers of new arms or chariots, bowls or tripods, can contribute to the *kleos* of heroes, as do creators of song *par excellence*. They themselves are not recipients of *kleos* on account of their efforts.

Moreover, achievements of *dēmioergoi*, some of which may seem to exhibit novel qualities, are not considered to be wholly self-generated. When Phemios, the representative of the bardic profession, speaks of acquiring his skill through his own efforts, he directly proceeds to attribute his gift to Apollo: 'I am self-taught (*autodidaktos*), and the god has implanted in my breast all kinds of song.'[33] Since his art depends on divine inspiration, he cannot lay claim to the kind of innovation that might in other circumstances be attributed to his personal skill and ingenuity. The fate of the mythical lyre-player Thamyras, struck blind for boasting that he could outperform the Muses, or of Ikaros flying high on the wings designed by Daidalos, served as a warning to bards and inventors not to take undue pride in their individual, all too human contribution to their art. By praising the god who grants song, and by depicting the brilliant creations of Hephaistos, Homer does indeed affirm the merits of the gods' mortal counterparts, the bard and the blacksmith. But he falls short of attributing to the productions of either gods or mortals any explicit innovation or quality of *kainotēs*.

---

[32] E.g. when Nestor reminisces in *Il*. 11.656–803, he lists Akhaian heroes wounded by missiles (*belē*, 657) and goes on to mention his own use of the javelin (*akōn*, 675). The bow is not the weapon of heroes; in the *Iliad* only Paris, Pandaros and Teukros are archers, and Diomedes disdains Paris' attempt to kill him with an arrow (*Il*. 11.384–90). Yet in the *Odyssey*, Odysseus' bow is an admired weapon, and his son is named Telemakhos ('he who fights from afar') probably in honour of his father's prowess as an archer.

[33] *Od*. 22.347.

THE EMERGENCE OF *KAINOS*

It is not only in Homeric epic that the absence of *kainos* is notable. There is no trace of the word in Hesiod's technique-conscious *Works and Days*, with its laborious instructions for making a new plough.[34] It is not found in the Homeric *Hymn to Hermes*, with its charming tale of the invention by the infant god of a new musical instrument from the shell of a tortoise, the lyre. *Kainos* appears nowhere in the Homeric Hymns or Cyclic fragments, nor in the extant verses of Kallinos, Tyrtaios and Mimnermos. Despite a continuous engagement with literary novelty in various forms, the word is not found (though in some places it has been conjectured) in the poems of Arkhilokhos, Semonides, Sappho, Alkman, Alkaios, Hipponax, Theognis or Stesikhoros. It is absent from the remains of sixth-century texts, nowhere to be found in Simonides, Ibykos and Anakreon, nor in the extant fragments of sages and philosophers such as Solon, Empedokles, Xenophanes, Parmenides and Phokylides. When Pythagoras (sixth century) is reported to have expounded the doctrine that 'nothing is really new', the testimony to his words uses not *kainos* but *neos*, just as when Herakleitos (early fifth century) remarked that 'the sun is new day by day', his expression is recorded as *neos eph' hēmerēi*.[35] While Pindar speaks of Kaineus, and although his poetry scintillates with defiantly new variants of myth, glorious new athletic victories, newly founded cities and brilliant new varieties of song, the word *kainos* is nowhere found in Pindar's extensive surviving oeuvre. Hardly reticent about laying claim to his own poetic novelty, Pindar uses only *neos*-words to vaunt his innovative *mousikē*.[36] In short, there is no certain indication of the use of *kainos* anywhere up to the end of the sixth century BCE. The earliest appearance of *kainos* comes in the scant epigraphic evidence available: on a sixth-century potsherd from the Athenian agora, new couches (?) are described with the adjective *kaino(u)s*;[37] while a *khous* (pitcher) dated to the fifth century proclaims on its surface that it is *kainē*.[38] It is significant, as I shall argue, that these are manufactured objects.

In texts that are dated to the early decades of the fifth century, *kainos* emerges into clear light, and the use of the word burgeons as the 'Athenian century' proceeds. The earliest unequivocal appearance of the word comes

---

[34] Hes. *Op.* 423–36. Equally, the succession of 'new' races of men (109–201) is indicated by *aute* (127), *allo* (143), *autis et' allo* (157), *nūn* (176) – and by a change in their metallic characteristics.
[35] Dikaiarkhos B8a, Herakleitos B6 (see further Chapter 5).
[36] *Neosīgalos* (*O.* 3.4), *neōteros* (*O.* 9.49) etc.
[37] Lang (1976) no. 1265: *kl*[*intēras*], 'couches', is a restoration. [38] Ibid. no. 21553.

in Bakkhylides' fifth Dithyramb written for the Athenians, perhaps in the decade following the Athenian victory over the Persians at Salamis in 480 BCE:

> There are countless paths
> of ambrosial verse
> for one whom the Pierian
> Muses endow with gifts,
> and whom the violet-eyed maidens,
> the garlanded Graces,
> attend, casting honour on
> his songs. Weave (*huphaine*), then,
> something brand-new (*ti kainon*)
> in lovely, blessed Athens,
> renowned genius of Keian poetry.[39]

Bakkhylides' use of *kainos* here appears to mark a departure from earlier poetry, in which *neos* and its cognates are the forms that are found to signify musico-poetic novelty of different kinds.[40] His poetic tribute to the Athenians is represented as a novel act of creation, a work of manufacture like weaving (an association reinforced by the suggested etymological connection of *humnos*, 'song', to *huphainō* 'weave').[41] Where *neon* or *neokhmon* might have implied no more than a song recently or newly composed, *kainon* draws attention to the materiality of a text that evinces a quality of novelty. The verb *kainizō* in Aeschylus' *Oresteia* (perhaps closest in time to Bakkhylides' *kainon*) supports the notion that the word's particular reference is to novelty deliberately created or brought about. 'Put on your new yoke' (*kainison zugon*), the Chorus tell Kassandra, a concrete image of her subservience as bed-slave to her new master Agamemnon. In another verse they describe how Agamemnon's killers 'devised a new kind' (*ekainisan*) of net in whose toils the king was slain.[42]

A qualitative force allied to, and perhaps arising from, the signification of humanly wrought newness, marks *kainos* semantically apart from *neos* in many of its later fifth-century occurrences. Aristophanes claims that he is always introducing '*kainās ideās*', Timotheos boasts that his '*kaina* [songs] are better', Hippias asserts that he always tries 'to say something *kainon*',

---

[39] Bakkhyl. 19.1–10.
[40] See further Chapter 8. The variant reading *ti kleinon* 'something famous' in line 9 makes less sense (Maehler ad loc. says 'kaum glaublich').
[41] Maehler (1997) 251.
[42] Aesch. *Ag.* 1071, *Cho.* 492; cf. *Ag.* 960 *pagkainiston* 'ever-renewed' (of purple dye from the sea). See below, Chapter 4, n. 14.

The emergence of kainos

Sokrates is indicted on the charge of introducing 'other *kaina* divinities'.[43] Statistics alone regarding the word's connotation cannot make the case for the qualitative force of *kainos*, since by the time it is more regularly found its meanings have become somewhat conflated with those of *neos* and vice versa. But in cases such as these, *kainos* cannot be readily replaced with *neos*, which would be felt to signify 'of recent occurrence' rather than a salient quality of created novelty.

The word *kainon* and the notion of *kainotēs* may have been especially congenial to Bakkhylides' Athenian audience. *Kainotēs* is the boast of the skilled artisan, and of a poet (*poiētēs*, literally 'maker') who here makes implicit acknowledgement of Athens' unusually positive attitude to innovation. The annual Panathenaic festival provided the context *par excellence* for the dedication of a newly woven *peplos* to Athens' patron goddess Athena, in a ceremony culminating in the ritual adornment of the goddess's image in her sacred temple on the Akropolis.[44] A land of proud 'autochthons' (Athenians supposed that they, unlike other Greek peoples, had always lived in the territory of Attica), Athens had created and continued to create their own rich traditions of innovation.[45] The 'gleaming' polis of Athena seemed *par excellence* to possess a mythical sanction for the kind of novelty designated by words such as *kainotēs* and *kainotomia*.[46] The word *kainotomeō*, 'innovate', first found in Aristophanes (*Wasps* 876), may have arisen in a peculiarly Attic context: its literal meaning 'cutting of the new' has been thought to derive from the context of opencast mining, the activity of driving new shafts into the ground to mine ores.[47] While the process was long known to Athens, the discovery of silver at Laureion in Attica was a decisive moment for Athens, which exploited the find especially in the early fifth century (on the urging of Themistokles) to create its new fleet of triremes. The association of the discovery and mining of metals with the notion of novelty, literal or metaphorical, is embedded in Greek linguistic practice and has a consistent bearing on the Greeks' conceptualisation of newness.[48]

---

[43] Ar. *Nub.* 547, Timotheos *PMG* 796.2, Xen. *Mem.* 4.4.14, ibid. 1.1.1, D.L. 2.40.7. In Chapter 4 below (p. 104) I discuss the only Herodotean passage in which *kainos* is found, where it means 'recent' in the context of an (arguably constructed) historical account of the Athenians' victory at Marathon.
[44] Parker (2007) 264–5.   [45] Loraux (1993) 3 f.
[46] See below, Chapter 6.   [47] Xen. *Vect.* 4.27–9.
[48] Cf. *metallaō* ('search for, explore'), the root of 'metal'. One talks of 'mining a new seam', and the metaphor has continuing appeal for classicists; Dodds (1973: 27) uses it in the context of the progress of classical scholarship ('[it is sometimes suggested that] the mine is approaching exhaustion'), Latacz (2004: 287) in relation to the archaeology of Troy ('every month in which new shafts are driven into the mine of mystery').

THE MYTH OF KAINEUS

The occurrences of *neos* and *kainos* that may be traced in texts from Homer to the fifth century appear to demonstrate not only the evolution of lexical usage, but a changing understanding of novelty. Detailed consideration of the Kaineus myth, to which I now turn, may offer further indications about the historical, etymological and imaginative basis of this new conceptualisation.

In early Greek myth Kaineus was a warrior from Thessaly, a leader of the legendary tribe of Lapiths, who famously fought a fierce battle against their kinsmen the Centaurs. In a well-known version of the story, Kaineus was said to have changed sex by divine fiat from a woman called Kainis or Kainē, and at the same time to have been transformed into an invincible warrior.[49] The notion of transgendering, involving a transition from a former identity to a new one, was bound to lead to the supposition that the name Kaineus derived from *kainos* and meant 'new man'.[50] The story of the sex change is given a full-blown treatment in the *Metamorphoses* of Ovid, who puts the tale into the mouth of the Homeric warrior Nestor. He reinforces the supposed derivation of Kaineus from *kainos* by punning on the name of the girl, whom he calls Caenis, as Neptune's *nova Venus* ('new love'):

Caenis, the daughter of Elatus, was famous for her beauty. She was the loveliest of all the girls in Thessaly, and roused vain hopes in the hearts of many suitors throughout all the neighbouring cities, and in those of your own land, Achilles, for she was a countrywoman of yours. Perhaps Peleus, too, would have tried to make her his bride, but already he either was married to your mother, or had the promise of her hand. Caenis refused to marry anyone, but the story spread that, as she was wandering on a lonely part of the shore, she was forcibly subjected to the embraces of the god of the sea. The same report went on to tell how Neptune, when he had enjoyed the pleasure of his new love, said to the girl: 'You may pray for anything without fear of being refused. Choose what you want.' 'The wrong I have suffered,' replied Caenis, 'evokes the fervent wish that I may never be able to undergo such an injury again. Grant that I be not a woman, and you will have given me all.' The last words were uttered in deeper tones: that voice could be taken for the voice of a man, as indeed it was. For already the god of the deep sea had granted Caenis' prayer, bestowing this further boon, that the man Caeneus should be proof against any wound, and should never be slain by the sword.[51]

---

[49] Forbes Irving (1990: 155–62) helpfully compiles the sources, but strangely concludes that 'perhaps Kaineus was never a man but a woman who was suddenly given superhuman powers'.

[50] Other interpretations relate the name to the meaning 'young (girl)' i.e. Kainis prior to transformation, and to the verb *kainō* 'kill' (Eustathius on *Il.* 1.264).

[51] Ov. *Met.* 12.189–207.

The myth of Kaineus 75

Ovid here draws on earlier sources of the myth and expands on them in a characteristically colourful and mischievous fashion. He extends the tale further by relating a final metamorphosis of Caeneus into a bird, evidently his own invention and a witty reflection on the possibilities for literary transformation of myths about transformation.[52]

The surviving Greek sources present a less eloquent narrative. The bare outline is preserved in an epitome of the *Bibliotheca* of the mythographer Apollodoros (first or second centuries CE):

> Kaineus was originally a woman; but after Poseidon had intercourse with her, she pleaded with him to turn her into an invulnerable man. As a result, he felt no anxiety about being wounded when he fought in the battle against the Centaurs, and a great number of them died at his hands. Eventually, those who remained surrounded him and battered him into the earth with the trunks of fir-trees.[53]

The rape and transformation, as recounted by Ovid and Apollodoros, appear to be central to the story of Kaineus. But it is striking that the very earliest accounts we have say nothing about them.[54] Kaineus is mentioned just once in the *Iliad*, in the course of Nestor's reminiscences of bygone heroes.[55] There he is simply a mighty Lapith warrior who fought alongside his kinsmen against the *Phēres* ('beast-men'):

> Never yet have I seen nor shall see again such men as these were, men like Peirithoös, and Dryas, shepherd of his people, Kaineus and Exadios, and godlike Polyphemos [and Theseus, Aigeus' son, like to the immortals]. These were the strongest generation of earthbound men (*epikhthonioi andres*) – the strongest, and they fought against the strongest, the Pheres living within the mountains, and mightily they destroyed them. I was in the company of the Lapiths, having journeyed a long way from distant Pylos, whence they had summoned me, and I myself did battle with the Centaurs. But against such creatures no mortal now on earth could do battle.[56]

Where Kaineus appears in Homer, then, he is one of a company of 'earthbound men' (*epikhthonioi andres*). Despite possessing exceptional prowess

---

[52] Ibid. 12.524–6; Cameron (2004) 296. [53] Apollod. *Epit.*1.22.
[54] Hesiod fr. 87 (cf. 88) is derived from Phlegon of Tralles (second century CE), whose reference (*Mir.* 5) to 'Hesiod', lumped together with later sources such as Dikaiarchos, does not reliably attest to an earlier version of the sex change story. As Forbes Irving (1990: 155) notes, 'our earliest account is that of Akousilaos' (fifth century BCE).
[55] Willcock (1964) argues that Nestor's 'mythological paradeigma' (lines 259–74), like similar passages in Homer, is the monumental composer's own invention. This view is supported by the occurrence of 'late' linguistic features in the passage, such as short-stem accusative of proper nouns in -*eus*, contracted *bouleōn* for original *bouláōn* etc.: Ingalls (1976) 203–4.
[56] Hom. *Il.* 1.262–72 (line 265 is an interpolation: West (2001) 186).

in battle, he is presented as no more than a mortal man, and immutably male.

The pseudo-Hesiodic *Shield*, probably composed around the end of the seventh century or the early sixth, likewise shows no awareness of 'Kainis' having been transformed into Kaineus. The poet describes the battle between Lapiths and Centaurs by means of an ekphrasis, a literary description of a scene depicted on an *objet d'art*. In this case the scene is described as being inlaid in silver and gold on the shield of Herakles:

> On it was depicted the battle of the Lapith spearmen, gathered around the prince Kaineus and Dryas and Peirithoös, together with Hopleus, Exadios, Phaleros and Prolokhos, Mopsos son of Ampyke of Titaresia, scion of Ares, and Theseus son of Aigeus, like to the immortal gods. Their figures were wrought in silver, with armour of gold upon their bodies. The Centaurs were gathered against them on the other side: Petraios and Asbolos the diviner, Arktos, Oureios and black-haired Mimas, and the two sons of Peukeus, Perimedes and Dryalos; these were fashioned from silver, wielding fir-trees (*elatai*) of gold in their hands. The two sides were rushing into the fray in a way that made them seem alive, and assailing one another in hand-to-hand combat with spears and with fir-trees.[57]

Here the Lapiths are introduced as 'spearmen' (*aikhmētai*), and they are pictured as wielding spears against the pinetrees of their opponents. The names borne by some of the Lapiths – Dryas 'oak-(shaft)', Hopleus 'weapon-man' (or 'shield-man') – reinforce their association with man-made, manufactured weaponry. By contrast, the half-beast Centaurs who wield pine-trunks (*elatai*) are given names that evoke wild nature – Petraios 'rocky', Peukeus 'fir-tree', Arktos 'bear'.

In the Iliadic account, the summoning of Nestor from faraway Pylos to bring aid to the Lapith warriors suggests that the conflict was an extended one which came to a head in a final pitched battle. Later versions make the battle a more impromptu affair, originating in a fight that breaks out when the Centaurs become drunk and violent at the celebration of the wedding of Peirithoös and Hippodameia. The earliest testimony to this version of the story is a fragment of Pindar:

> When the Pheres discovered the overpowering blast of honey-sweet wine, they roughly flung the white milk off the tables with their hands and, drinking uninvited from the silver drinking-horns, began to lose control of their faculties.[58]

Another passage, from a Pindaric *thrēnos* (dirge), relates the manner of Kaineus' death:

---

[57] [Hes.] *Scut.* 178–90. [58] Pi. fr. 166.

Struck by green fir-trees Kaineus passed down below, splitting open (*skhisais*) the earth with his outstretched foot (*orthōi podi*).[59]

Plutarch cites this passage with the accompanying comment:

Pindar's Kaineus was criticised as an implausible creation – unbreakable by iron, unsuffering in body, and finally sinking unwounded below the ground 'splitting open the earth with his outstretched foot'.[60]

The phrase *orthōi podi*, which in some contexts appears to mean no more than 'standing upright', here seems to bear a more literal meaning as translated above – the warrior's leg is fixed straight, down to the end of his foot. It assimilates the image of the Lapith's final posture to the spearman's deadly weapon. By splitting the earth with his unbending foot at the point, the impervious Kaineus invites identification with a spear or sword-tip of hard iron.

The Pindaric fragment describing Kaineus' eventual demise is preserved for us by a scholiast commenting on a passage from the *Argonautica* of Apollonios of Rhodes, who strongly reinforces the impression of spear-like hardness attributed to the Lapith warrior:

Poets celebrate how Kaineus was destroyed by the Centaurs while he was still alive, when he took them on single-handed in his warrior might. They rushed upon him from every side, but they could not bend or penetrate him. Unbroken and unbending he sank beneath the earth, battered by the hammering of massive firs (*elatēisin*).[61]

Pictorial representations of Kaineus from the sixth century on depict the battle and the distinctive manner of Kaineus' downfall at the hands of the Centaurs.[62] Kaineus is imagined in the poetry and art of this period not just as an exceptionally strong hero of human stock, but as something more ominous. He is someone who cannot be killed in any normal fashion, but only through living inhumation. His invulnerability makes him unsettling and alien. He represents in effect a dangerous weapon that can only be disposed of, like nuclear waste, by being thoroughly submerged beneath the earth.[63] The fact that Kaineus' threatening presence is ultimately neutralised by his being bludgeoned into the ground makes him more akin to an iron weapon than a human being. Herein, perhaps, lies the essence of his nature; but Kaineus' spear-like persona has been obscured by the fact that, by the later stages of the mythographical tradition, his liminal status

---

[59] Pi. fr. 128f. [60] Plut. *De absurd. Stoic. opin.* p.1057D. [61] A.R. *Arg.* 1.59–64.
[62] Schefold (1992) 168–9. [63] For parallels in other Indo-European myths, see West (2007) 445.

as an 'impenetrable' mortal is more strongly associated with the story of his sex change than with his quasi-metallic characteristics.

Just as Kaineus meets his end not by dying but by being buried alive, 'Kainis' too does not die, but instead undergoes metamorphosis into a man. The invulnerability bestowed by Poseidon (perhaps a double-edged gift, like so many divine benefactions) ensures that Kainis will remain *atrōtos*, 'impervious to penetration'. The clear sexual symbolism in this version of the story is reinforced by the violated maiden's transformation into a man, and might be further linked to the phallic imagery of Kaineus' standing 'erect' (*orthōi podi*) and splitting open the 'female' earth.

The sex change story, with all its drama and pathos, has been taken by many to be the kernel of the myth.[64] But it is first found in the fifth-century mythographer Akousilaos of Argos (Pindar's contemporary and an important source of Apollodoros' *Bibliotheca*) who gives the name of Kaineus' earlier female incarnation as Kainē.[65] Akousilaos, part of whose account survives in a third-century CE papyrus fragment, preserves a detail of the myth that may have been known to Ovid and Apollodoros, but which they choose not to repeat. Kaineus, we read, '[set up his] spear-head (*akontion*) [in the middle of] the agora [to be worshipped as] a god'.[66] This incongruous feature of the story is likely to be a survival from an early version of the Kaineus myth.[67] It has been thought on account of its phallic implications to relate once again to the change of gender. It seems, however, in the light of the above analysis, that it is a further crucial indicator of the way Kaineus is to be identified with his spear, i.e. in a literal fashion, rather than simply via narcissistic self-identification. In his very person he possesses the features of the iron weapon, which resists penetration and destruction, which can be disposed of only by being buried, and which, when hammered upright into the ground with mallets consisting of the trunks of fir-trees (*elatai*), splits the earth asunder.

The warrior may have inherited something of his nature from his father: Kaineus' patronymic Elatides (i.e. son of Elatos, i.e. 'fir-tree') is found in a fragment of Stesikhoros.[68] The fir-trees (*elatai*) with which Kaineus is eventually overpowered not only recall his ancestry, but suggest a symbolic succession from old to new in the form of weaponry, from wooden clubs and stakes to swords and iron-tipped spears. The occasion of Kaineus'

---

[64] E.g. by Kirk (1970). [65] Akousilaos fr. 22 Fowler.
[66] The fragment is restored, but its content can be derived from later evidence (sch. Ap. Rhod. 1.57–64a, sch.D *Il.* 1.264).
[67] There are other instances of spear-worship in Indo-European myth: West (2007: 464).
[68] *PMGF* 222 i.9; the father was the eponym of Elateia (West 1985: 71).

bludgeoning, which ends with the defeat of the Centaurs by the Lapiths, is the wedding of the Lapith Peirithoös, the 'very swift' (rider) with Hippodameia, 'horse-tamer'.[69] In this scenario, organic nature is seen as subjugated: the horse has become an adjunct to human combat, and tree-wielding Centaurs ultimately yield to men wielding the weapons of human artifice. Ultimately, but not immediately: the end of Kaineus must first be accomplished. Kaineus' defeat and burial in myth psychologically represent an attempt to allay intolerable anxiety; an invulnerable killer is (as modern films such as *Terminator* demonstrate) a nightmarish fantasy. But although this monstrous living weapon is ultimately neutralised, it is horrifyingly effective while it is alive, and in the event the Lapiths go on to win the battle against the Centaurs. The mythico-historical symbolism of the tale is that henceforth iron weaponry, not wooden clubs, will be the preeminent resource of the victorious warrior.

The evolution of horsemanship, in combination with the discovery and use of sophisticated iron weapons, mark the triumph of civilisation over brute nature. These developments recall an age when the recently introduced iron armour and weaponry may have seemed to possess quasi-magical attributes of hardness and indestructibility, properties which will have had a profound impact on iron's beneficiaries and victims. The ancient production of hardened iron is associated with metallurgical techniques developed in the Near East in the second millennium BCE; the earliest known manufacture of iron weaponry took place in the Hittite empire of Asia Minor.[70] A figure in the shape of a sword carved in relief on the Hittite rock fortress of Yazilikaya, perhaps based on a metal prototype, has been identified as a 'Sword God'.[71] Such a figure, the symbolic personification of iron weaponry, seems to lurk in the background of the story of Kaineus.

THE MARK OF *QĀYIN*

The identification of Kaineus with his spear demands recognition of a linguistic fact that is hard to attribute to mere coincidence. The Hebrew word *qāyin*, the name borne by the biblical character Cain, means 'spear'.[72] In the second Book of Samuel it is used to designate the weapon of a Philistine giant (not the famous Goliath, but one Ishbi-Benob) who is described as 'armed with a new spear'.[73] Semitic words and roots underlie

---

[69] The etymology of the name Peirithoös indicates 'ultra-fast' (from *peri-thoos with metrical lengthening of the first element).
[70] Muhly *et al.* (1985). [71] Yener (1995).
[72] Hess (1993) 24–7. [73] 2 Samuel 21.16. Cf. Wyatt (1986) 89–90.

the names of a number of figures of Greek myth, whose connections to Near Eastern contexts and counterparts have long been recognised and explored. Thus the name of Kadmos is derived from Phoenician *qedem* ('east'), Adonis from *'adōn* ('lord'), Nereus perhaps from a word for 'river' (Akkadian *nāru*, Hebrew *nahar*). Kinyras is the personification of *kinnōr* ('lyre'), Erebos may derive from *'ereb* ('west'), and the name of Prometheus' father Iapetos is the counterpart of biblical Japheth, son of Noah.[74] If *qāyin* is at the root of the name Kaineus, the onomastic origins of the Lapith warrior make him literally a *spear man*. It would be only the later assumption that his name was based on *kainos*, 'new', and that the name 'Kaineus' signified 'newly made a man', that led to the invention of a feminine counterpart called Kainis or Kainē.[75]

If this newly proposed etymology is valid for 'Kaineus', how might the name be connected, if at all, to the word *kainos*? Indo-European philology, which standardly derives *kainos* from a lexical root related to *kanyā* ('young woman' in Sanskrit), does not explain the semantic characteristics of *kainos*, namely its tendency to mean 'new' rather than 'young', and the fact that, to a greater extent than *neos*, it is used with the ambivalent associations related to novelty rather than youth. Moreover, there seems little reason why a word with an unimpeachable Indo-European pedigree should not have been used interchangeably with *neos* from early times. Yet, as we have seen, one of the most striking facts about the distribution of *kainos* is that, in contrast to *neos*, there is no firm attestation to the word in our corpus of Greek texts until the beginning of the fifth century BCE. Kaineus thus appears in Homer some three centuries before the adjective *kainos* is found in Greek.

The evidence marshalled above suggests that a gradual reconceptualisation of novelty took place over the centuries in question, involving a movement from the essentially temporal understanding of *neos* as 'young' or 'recent' to a notion of novelty as a quality of recently manufactured objects. *Neos* is the appropriate word to signify organic, natural and recurrent kinds of novelty. But the property of newness signified by *kainotēs* is not an organic property like youthfulness, nor even a temporal one like recency. *Kainos* is more readily suggestive of modern, artificially created and

---

[74] Cf. Burkert (1992) 33–40, who notes the problem that in Greek 'there can be no method to discover borrowed words. They imitate and go into hiding, adapting themselves to the roots and suffixes of native Greek.'

[75] The instability of the feminine version of the name may be an indication that the creation of an earlier female identity was simply extrapolated backwards from 'Kaineus' on the supposition that the name signified 'new (as a) man'.

potentially disruptive kinds of novelty. These notions are often represented in Greek literature by images that relate to the visual impact of brightness or fire (see Chapter 6), and the prime candidates in this period for exhibiting such qualities were new objects wrought in metal. Metal weapons, utensils and *objets d'art* emerge from the fire and the forge 'brand-new'.[76] The English term presents a telling analogy: 'brand-new' originally signified 'newly forged' or 'new from the fire' (the spelling 'bran-new' and the term 'fire-new' are also found).[77]

From this perspective, it is hard not to find significance in the fact that *qāyin*, 'spear', arises from the Semitic verbal root *qyn*, which means 'to work metal'. A nexus of *qyn*-words related to metalworking extends across the Near East, Hittite Asia Minor, Arabia and Mesopotamia. In South Arabian inscriptions of the first millennium BCE a noun form of *qyn* is found with the meaning 'smith'. The biblical tribe of Kenites (not to be confused with Canaanites, whose name derives from the unrelated root *kn'n*) are also called *qāyin* in Hebrew (i.e. 'Cainites', with the singular form *qaynī* or *qēnī*). Originally the appellation 'Kenites' simply meant 'metalworkers', *qāyin* being a generic term applied to the nomadic tribes of smiths operating in copper-rich southern Palestine. In Genesis, one of the descendants of Cain is named as Tubal-Cain, 'Tubal the smith', reputed to be the ancestor of artisans and the founder of metalworking (Gen. 4.22, Gen. 10.2).[78]

The expertise of the Kenites was matched by that of ancient peoples from lands further to the north. In Greek lore and experience, the tribes inhabiting the southern shores of the Black Sea had a long-standing association with metalworking.[79] This was the land of the legendary ironworkers the Khalubes (*khalups* and *khalubos* are Greek words for hardened iron). To their west in Asia Minor was the home of the Idaian Daktuloi (the name means 'fingers', and the epithet refers to the mountain range of Ida in the Troad); these dwarfish metalworkers were credited, in the earliest known

---

[76] *OED*² s.v. 'brand-new'. It was partly on the strength of this analogy that I proposed (1998) that *kainos* was etymologically related to *kaiō*, 'burn'; but the morphology is dubious, since the root *kaw-* with adjectival suffix *-nos* should make *kaunos.

[77] Cf. the phrase 'spick and span' (also found in the form 'spick and span new') which originates in the context of naval construction and refers to the visual impact of a ship gleaming with new 'spicks' (i.e. spikes, nails) and 'spans' (wooden boards).

[78] Tubal came from an inventive family: musical instruments were said to have originated with his brother Jubal (whence the word 'jubilee' etc.): Gen. 4.20–1. North (1964) explores the connection of music making and metallurgy with the Kenites.

[79] Drews (1976).

mention of 'first discoverers', with the invention of the blacksmith's skill.[80] They were also associated with other fabulous metallurgists, the Kabeiroi of Samothrace and the Telkhines of Rhodes.[81] Historically attested indigenous groups included the Moskhoi and Tibarenoi:[82] renowned as metalworkers, they appear in the Bible as the tribes of Meshech and Tubal.[83] Between the ninth and the seventh centuries BCE artisans from among these tribes, travelling from bases in central Asia Minor and Cappadocia, were noted suppliers to the metalware trade throughout the Mediterranean. Ezekiel (27.13) brackets them together with Ionian Greeks, *Yawan*, as suppliers of 'slaves and vessels of brass' to the markets of Tyre. Scholars have documented how, during Greece's orientalising period of the eighth to sixth centuries BCE, Phoenician traders, whose mercantile activities extended east and north into the Caspian region and west and south into Egypt and Arabia, exported finely made metal objects westwards as far as Spain in increasing quantities, along with materials and technologies of metalworking.[84]

These considerations do not require us to posit any direct etymological genealogy of *kainos* from Kaineus, of the kind that relates, say, the adjective 'Semitic' directly to the biblical name Shem. But what may reasonably be postulated is that both Kaineus and *kainos*-words are derived, via diverging and ultimately untraceable paths, from a common root related to the Semitic triliteral *qyn*. We may speculate, for instance, that a word based on *qyn* (perhaps *qaynī*) may have been used to describe the wares of *qāyin*, metalworkers. Signifying '*newly* wrought in metal', such a word will originally have evolved in the Near Eastern sphere of production and sale as a term used by Phoenician traders to designate a range of metal products. It would subsequently have been adopted by Greeks trading with Phoenicians, an interchange already well known in Homer's time and familiar to Greeks of the archaic period.[85] In the opening paragraphs of his *Histories*, Herodotos alludes to Phoenician merchants voyaging to Greek shores for purposes of trade:

---

[80] The epic poem *Phoronis* (fr. 4 West), dated to the early sixth century and probably the source of the pseudo-Hesiodic *On the Idaian Daktyloi* (fr. 282), calls them 'Phrygian sorcerers': Zhmud (2001). On 'first discoverers' see further p. 132.
[81] Hemberg (1950). Various roots have been suggested for *Kabeiroi*, most obviously Semitic *kabbīr* 'great' (cf. the appellation *Megaloi Theoi*); the name of one of the Kabeiroi, Atabyros, has been compared to Hebrew Tabor, a mountain in northern Israel. Burkert (1985: 282) cites a suggestion by Dossin (1953) that the name is related to *kabar*, allegedly Sumerian for 'copper'.
[82] Hdt. 3.94, Strabo 11.14.5.
[83] Gen. 10.2; thus the Hebrew name Tubal-Cain signifies 'the Tibarenian metalworker'.
[84] Burkert (1992) 14–33.   [85] Winter (1995) 253–5.

They carried Egyptian and Assyrian merchandise, arriving among other places at Argos, which was at that time preeminent in every way among the people of what is now called Hellas. The Phoenicians came to Argos, and set out their wares.[86]

By the end of the sixth century, the Greeks' own maritime and mercantile networks in the Aegean and Mediterranean had overtaken those of the Phoenicians. But the semi-mythical status of the episode related by Herodotos is grounded in the reality of Phoenician imports into Greece, amply attested by archaeology.[87] The wares that would have seemed most strikingly 'new' to the Greeks were those wrought in metal, whether homegrown or of diverse non-Greek origin: objects such as metal bowls, cymbals, figurines, as well as spears, swords, shields and greaves. In the sixth century, gleaming coins struck from various metals in imitation of the electrum (silver-gold) coinage originally minted in Lydia would represent a novel addition to this list. The attribution of a distinct property of 'newness' to the shining products of metal manufacture coincided with ideal conditions for the dissemination of a new word for 'new'.[88]

'Kaineus' and *kainos* may thus ultimately stem from the same verbal root *qyn*, with the proper name and adjective achieving their specific connotations in different ways and in different periods. Whereas the mythical Kaineus derived his name and nature by the end of the first millennium from the personification of an iron spear (*qāyin*), with its apparently indestructible nature, the emergence of the adjective *kainos* will have been related to the reception and description of a wide variety of metal objects perceived as 'shining new', whether in iron, copper, brass, silver or gold, over the course of the eighth to sixth centuries BCE. The word may even have been known and commonly used by Greeks throughout these latter centuries, but if so, its use remained latent for the purposes of poetry and literature. As an Ionian Greek, Homer was well placed to encounter Phoenician imports of both material and intellectual kinds.[89] But while the epic bard may well have known and encountered the word *kainos*, the notion of 'brand-new' products, the work of artisans (foreign or local) designed for commercial exchange or barter, may have seemed foreign to and insufficiently admirable for his traditional heroic subjects.[90]

The distinctly non-heroic associations of trade and manufacture associated with *kainos* may help to account for its absence in the epic and in

---

[86] Hdt.1.1. [87] Boardman (1999) 210–16; Sherratt and Sherratt (1993).
[88] On the associations of brightness to novelty see Chapter 6 below. [89] Winter (1995) 261.
[90] In the world of epic, the central mechanism for the transfer of value is gift exchange: von Reden (1995) 13–37.

religious and aristocratic texts from the archaic age. The non-appearance of *kainos* in Homer and early Greek hexameter poetry will also have contributed to its being avoided by subsequent Greek poets and thinkers who looked to the epic for inspiration, example and modes of expression. However, during the centuries of oriental influence, *kainos* will gradually have become established as an alternative word to *neos*, signifying a new kind of newness.[91] The greater status accorded to the profession of the metalsmith, abetted by the rise of monetary exchange and indicated by such phenomena as the increasingly conspicuous worship (particularly in Athens) of craft gods such as Hephaistos and Athena, will have allowed a word used primarily in 'banausic' and mercantile circles to signify 'new-made in metal' to rise in register and become a respectable and commonly used word for 'new'. In due course, as the word's connotations converged with those of *neos* (though this convergence was never wholesale), *kainos* came to mean 'young' as well.

[91] It may be significant that *arkhaios* is not attested earlier than the fifth century, and may have arisen partly out of a sense of the need for an antonym to *kainos* with similarly 'qualitative' connotations (rather than the temporal *palaios*, as found from Homer onwards).

CHAPTER 4

Old and new

> Ring out the old, ring in the new.
>
> Alfred Lord Tennyson

The aim of this chapter is to throw the notion of the new into sharper relief through consideration of its relationship to its antonym, 'old'. The sense that old and new are opposite rather than complementary terms may seem self-evident in a post-industrial world, where the old is constantly superseded by the new, where new developments are invariably associated with progress, and where new styles and technologies readily adopted by the younger generation present a stark contrast to those familiar to the older. Some ancient equivalents of such technologisation – the introduction of writing, the spread of money, the development of specialised skills – may have aroused in Greek minds similar associations to 'new' and 'old'; but the cultural context and far slower pace of technological change are bound to have affected the way the opposition operated. Below I shall consider the opposition with reference to a list of explicit oppositions preserved by Aristotle, the so-called Pythagorean Table. While this list does not include the terms 'old' and 'new' – an absence for which some explanation is sought – it provides a useful starting-point for thinking about the nature of opposition in general in Hellenic thought. In the remainder of the chapter I consider passages in Greek writings which show how the opposition of 'old' and 'new' functioned in different contexts, genres and environments.

What is new is not old, what is old is not new. While the habit of defining a quality through its negative relation to an opposite is universal, it occurs with particular insistence in Greek thought and discourse. Polarities and oppositions of various other kinds are regularly found in Greek texts, whether as unselfconscious patterns of speech or in quasi-formal attempts to articulate definitions.[1] In due course, the underlying logic of binarism

[1] Lloyd (1966).

came to be formalised in Aristotle's 'law of non-contradiction' (A ≠ not-A).[2] In practice, however, opposites (or notionally opposing qualities) have more complicated relations to each other than the simple negation of one by the other; and imagination and discourse can blur, whether unconsciously or with express intent, qualities, conditions or entities that are generally supposed to be mutually exclusive.[3]

In the case of 'new' and 'old', there are many ways in which the supposed opposition may function in everyday speech. The new may be thought of as something that wholly replaces the old, like the skin of a snake; or the old may remain part of the new, as when a new house is built around existing structures or on old foundations. Things may present themselves for identification as in some way new and in other ways not – a new text inscribed on an ancient papyrus, an old story presented in a new translation. Depending on the kind of thing of which 'old' is predicated, the word may signify 'used' or 'obsolete', 'traditional' or 'established'; the latter terms offer more precise or appropriate ways of describing new artefacts, ideas or institutions in opposition to old ones. It may be no more obvious to us, however, than it was to the Greeks whether a new law might be thought to supersede or to complement an established one (Greek *kathestōs*), whether a new joke might be funnier or more effective than a familiar one (*eiōthos*), or whether a newly minted expression is heard as being genuinely fresh or merely contrived (the Greek term *psūkhros* literally signifies 'frigid').

Nor can we expect representations of the opposition of 'old' and 'new' in Greek thought and discourse to map precisely on to those of the modern world. In deriding old-fashioned behaviour, the Worse Argument in Aristophanes' *Clouds* associates it with musty religious festivals, outmoded music and antiquated cicada-brooches.[4] These would not be our associations, but the implication is clear: 'old' suggests that something has been around for a long time, evidently too long, while 'new' indicates that it is of recent creation, use, or application. In some cases, English usage makes the distinction more clearly than Greek, in others it presents similar ambiguities. Thus we can clearly distinguish the meaning of a 'new leader' from a 'young leader', but the opposite in both cases is the potentially ambiguous

---

[2] Arist. *Met.* 1011b13–14 (cf. 1005b19–20, 23–24); the principle is earlier stated by Plato (Sokrates at *Rep.* 436b6–437a).
[3] 'Who knows whether living is really dying?' ask characters in Euripides' *Polyeidos* (fr. 638) and *Phrixos* (fr. 833), a question subjected to gleeful parody in Aristophanes' *Frogs* 1477–8 (cf. 1082).
[4] Ar. *Nub.* 984–5, *Eq.* 1331. Cf. *Nub.* 398, where Strepsiades is called *Kroniōn ozōn*, 'smelling of the Kronia' (an ancient festival for Kronos), and in *Vesp.* 1480 antiquated tragedians are called '*Kronoi*'. The 'age of Kronos' was opposed to the present 'age of Zeus' (cf. p. 96 below, and Timotheos' boast, p. 201).

'old leader', which may refer to a past holder of the office or to the advanced age of the incumbent. Greek has terms for 'old' which are regularly used for things, e.g. *arkhaios*, *palaios* (cf. Latin *vetus*, *antiquus*), and other terms that refer primarily to persons or living creatures e.g. *gerōn*, *graus*, *presbus* (cf. Latin *senex*, *anus*); we too would reserve 'senior' and 'elderly' for persons, and find them inappropriate epithets for things or ideas. While 'old' may be applied with equal propriety to an ancient edifice as to an octogenarian, near-synonyms such as 'ancient' or 'antiquated' would, if applied to people, appear somewhat eccentric or used for effect (humorous, insulting and so on).

These considerations point to the way the temporal attributes of artefacts and inorganic objects are conceived differently from those of people or living organisms. While the notions of youth and newness overlap, 'young' and its synonyms (youthful, recent etc.) primarily express a relationship to age and time. 'New' more often denotes a perceived quality, which may be only incidentally connected to temporality. Insofar as the term implies succession from some earlier state, eventuality or location, the passage of time is a feature of its connotations, but is not felt as its primary aspect. One may read a new book or face a new challenge; but the simple fact that these succeed an earlier book or challenge need not be the most salient aspect of their being 'new'. The narrative of ageing assigned to living things allows 'young' or 'old' to describe a relative position on the path of their expected lifespan. In speaking, like Lewis Carroll's Walrus, of shoes and ships and sealing-wax, 'new' and 'old' may seem straightforwardly to be the appropriate contrary epithets; in the case of cabbages or kings, 'young' may be considered the more appropriate opposition, and to signify a different kind of contrast. 'Young' indicates that a living thing or creature will have aged, if only to a relatively minor degree. 'New' is in a different descriptive category, indicating a quality that falls outside the framework of biological age. A woman may marry a new husband who need not be a young husband; a mother will give birth to a new baby, but hardly to a young baby.[5]

Ancient Greek perspectives on the dichotomy will have been affected by the fact that the words for 'young' and 'new' are not linguistically distinguished as sharply as they are in other languages. In ancient and modern Indo-European languages, the words for 'new' (Latin *novus*, French *nouveau*, German *neu* etc.) and for 'young' (Latin *iuvenis*, *iunior*, French *jeune*, German *jung* etc.) are phonetically if not wholly semantically distinct.

---

[5] A god or goddess may, however, be born 'young': see Chapter 6 below.

They derive from different lexical roots; the one that gives rise to *young* and related words has no obvious cognates in Greek. Instead, *neos*, which is found as Mycenaean Greek in the syllabic spelling *ne-wo*, is the word most frequently attested in Greek texts as denoting both 'young' and 'new'. When *kainos* emerges at a much later stage in the lexical record, we find it used with both connotations: and although its earliest attested use is with the meaning 'novel' (in Bakkhylides' dithyramb, p. 72 above), in its earliest prose attestation, in a passage of Herodotos discussed below, it signifies 'recent'.

In everyday thought and discourse, the new requires or assumes the old. Novelty can be recognised and asserted only against a pre-existent background, be it of tradition, of the past, or of the obsolete. The contraries may be expressed in explicit relationship, as when one speaks of old heads on young shoulders, or old wine in new bottles. But even the apparently straightforward temporal opposition – what is old is past, what is new is present or to come – is open to contestation. One may look to the past to observe something new, one may await the future for something to be old. The birth of the cosmos is an event in the remote past; but in imagining it one may conceive oneself as present at the birth of a 'new' world. The oldest events of history lie far in the past; but for a newborn infant, old age lies far in the future. Where young and old, recent and past, are located on a continuous temporal spectrum, they presuppose rather than oppose each other. What is old will once have been young; what is past survives (as a tradition, a vestige, or only a memory) to exist in the present. Fashions and styles change, and may (at least in some respect) revert to those of a former age: 'with the passage of time, the old becomes new' runs a verse attributed to the comedian Nikostratos.[6]

The status of the perceiver is often key to the attribution of newness. Even if an object's identity is stable, in a changed context or in altered surroundings it may seem to be something new. Whether seen through new eyes or deliberately presented in a new light, the old can appear new, the new old. The rhetorical and literary potential of creating the new by presenting a change in perspective was relished and exploited by the Greeks. The orators Teisias and Gorgias, for instance, were said to be capable of 'presenting through the power of language new things in old ways and old things in new ways (*kaina te arkhaiōs ta t' enantia kainōs*)'.[7] The rhetoric

---

[6] Nikostratos fr. 30. The comedian was one of Aristophanes' three sons, so the official revival of Old Comedy at the City Dionysia (recorded first for 339 BCE) lends a certain piquancy to the sentiment.
[7] Pl. *Phdr.* 267b1.

of novelty – identifying something as new in order either to endorse it or condemn it – is a noteworthy element of the discourse of innovation. It is found, on the one hand, in Greek music and literature, and, on the other, in Greek medical and political discourse. The idea that old and new could apparently be conflated or confused also finds various kinds of expression, not least when subjected to the logic of comedy. In Aristophanes' *Clouds*, Strepsiades fears the so-called 'Old and New day', the last day of the month when creditors would apply to prosecute debtors to make good their debts.[8] His newly sophisticated son assures him that he has nothing to fear:

PHEIDIPPIDES: Now what are you afraid of?
STREP: The Old and New Day.
PHEID: So there is a day that is old and also new?
STREP: Yes, the day they declare they will file their suits against me.
PHEID: Then those who file will lose. There's no way that one day could become two.
STREP: Couldn't it?
PHEID: How? Unless it were equally possible for the same person to be an old woman and a young girl![9]

The rhetorical conflation of old and new has a practical counterpart in the use of deliberate archaism to create something new in artistic and verbal contexts. In the sixth century BCE, the Athenians revived the manufacture of large amphorae for olive oil, with a distinctive new shape, to serve as prizes for events in the new Panathenaic festival;[10] deliberate archaism is detectable in the work of the sculptor Alkamenes, Pheidias' pupil;[11] and in the fourth century amphorae are found with representations that reprise earlier, archaic, styles.[12] When a slave in the third-century comedy *Phoinikides* by Straton uses old Homeric vocabulary, the account given by his master plays on the perception that antiquated terms seem new (*kaina*) in their unfamiliar context:

> It's a male sphinx, not a cook, that
> I've brought home. By heavens, I simply don't
> understand a word he says. He's come equipped
> with a load of new (*kaina*) words. When he came in,
> he looked at me haughtily and asked 'Tell me,
> how many wights (*meropes*) have you invited to dinner?'
> 'Me, invited wights to dinner?' I said. 'You're crazy.' ...

---

[8] The naming of the 'Old and New Day' was attributed to Solon: Plut. *Solon* 25.3.
[9] Ar. *Nub.* 1178–84.   [10] Davison (1958) 26–7.   [11] Robertson (1981) 119–20.
[12] Pollitt (1986) 180–1; archaism is also detectable in vase-painting and the designs on coins.

> I reckon that the wretch had been the slave
> from childhood of one of those rhapsode fellows,
> and got stuffed full of Homeric phrases.[13]

Kaina in this passage signifies 'new', with the undertone of 'strange' or 'unusual', which some have supposed to be the word's original signification.[14] *Neos* and *kainos* in Greek are regularly used with more clearly evaluative overtones – 'original, therefore good' or 'newfangled, therefore bad'. In extant Greek literature, negative associations to the notion of newness are more numerous than positive ones, but the latter are far from absent. Similarly, 'old' and related terms such as the adverb *palai* ('of old') may be found laden with emotional associations, favourable or unfavourable, in addition to the temporal qualities associated with biological or chronological ageing. *Arkhaios* is used, for instance, to imply 'familiar', 'traditional' and 'old', often with neutral or positive significance, but also with the negative implications of 'stale' or '*passé*' (as almost always in Aristophanes' comedies). Overtones of these kinds can seem intrinsic to the words' signification, but they are not invariably or necessarily so. They are usually dependent on the point of view from which particular objects, events and experiences are perceived, so more correctly attributable to the outlook of an individual percipient than to any objective property attaching to novelty or age. Moreover, as I have noted before, the literal meaning of the commonly used comparative forms *neōteron* and *kainoteron*, 'more new', carries the implication 'newer than might be expected or desired'.[15]

THE PYTHAGOREAN TABLE

The student of ancient Greek language and idiom rapidly becomes familiar with the particles *men* and *de*, conventionally translated 'on the one hand', 'on the other hand', which are used even when no real opposition is present

---

[13] Straton 1.1–7, 48–50. In a scene in Aristophanes' earliest (now lost) play *Banqueters*, a father and son challenge one another to expound unfamiliar expressions (*glōttai*), including Homeric words (*Daitaleis* frr. 205, 233); the fragments are cited by Galen to demonstrate how 'the ancients used to invent words for themselves' (*Glosses on Hippokrates* 19 p. 65 K, 1–2).

[14] E.g. Hose (2000: 8 n. 29), who cites the use of *kainizō* at Aesch. *Ag.* 1071 and (following Fraenkel (1950), ad loc.) refers to Wackernagel (1953: 799) to suggest strangely that the original meaning of the word is 'unusual' or 'out of the ordinary'. In neither passage in which some form of the word is used elsewhere in the *Oresteia* (*Ag.* 960 *pagkainiston* 'ever-renewed', *Cho.* 492 *ekainisan* 'they devised a new [kind of net]') can any signification be extracted other than that of newness, innovation, or renewal.

[15] E.g in Ar. *Eccl.* 338, with sinister overtones; but *neōtera* in Ar. *Av.* 252 has a more neutral connotation (cf. Dunbar ad loc.).

The Pythagorean table

or intended. A polarity may often be asserted for rhetorical emphasis, with or without *men* and *de*. The Homeric expression *palai ou ti neon ge*, for instance, emphasises the idea of 'in the past' (*palai*) by the apparently redundant addition of *ou ti neon ge* 'not recent(ly) at all'.[16] Many facets of Greek thinking reflect a tendency to polar expressions and to thinking in terms of oppositions. More generally, Greek history and thought lend themselves to being elaborated through a series of binary terms: the understanding of the world in terms of divine and human, Greek and barbarian, slave and free, male and female, may be felt to structure not only the Greeks' linguistic and literary perspectives but their social and political relationships as well.[17]

Thinking in polar terms is sometimes considered to characterise a specifically western mode of reasoning. But the cultural specificity should not be exaggerated, since the listing of binary categories is widely found in non-western cultures as well.[18] Opposite terms reflect something fundamental about the way human beings perceive the world – black is not white, tall is not short, here is not there. However, the polar opposites of attributes and objects are not always straightforwardly determinable. Even where the denotations of words in different languages appear to coincide, their opposite terms are not always self-evident across different linguistic or culturally diverse communities. There may, for instance, be common assent about the opposites of the notions of 'big', 'dark' and 'male', but the same cannot be said for 'gold', 'earth' and 'blue' (for which, moreover, the Japanese colour-name *aoi* denotes both 'blue' and 'green'). What are assumed to be appropriate oppositions may often be specific to a particular linguistic or social group, a matter of cultural convention rather than one of intrinsic or essential 'nature'.

The list of oppositions (*sustoikhiā*) attributed by Aristotle to 'some Pythagoreans' contains the ten terms shown in Figure 2.[19] Significantly, the table includes the fundamental moral terms 'good' and 'bad'. Aristotle's reference to the list as a column of 'goods' (*agatha*) suggests that some moral or ethical weighting could be attached to all the items listed.[20] Words in the left-hand column, such as *limit* and *male*, would have positive associations in this respect, while attributes on the right such as *unlimited* and *female* would have negative ones. The particular items included are indicative of the context of the table's compilation. The oppositions *odd / even, unity /*

---

[16] *Il.* 9.527.
[17] Cf. Vidal-Naquet (1981) 175: 'these and other pairs may be considered to constitute the framework of the discourse of the Greeks'. Cartledge (2002) gives practical effect to this structuring principle.
[18] Lloyd (1966) 32–3.   [19] Arist. *Met.* 986a22–6.   [20] Arist. *EN* 1096b6; Burkert (1972) 51–2.

limited	unlimited
odd	even
unity	plurality
right	left
male	female
at rest	in motion
straight	crooked
light	darkness
good	bad
square	oblong

Figure 2 Pythagorean table of oppositions

plurality and *square / oblong* reflect the Pythagoreans' interest in the notions of number and geometry, and their application of numerical and geometrical doctrines to everyday reality. The blending of mathematical notions with ethical and religious doctrines is characteristically Pythagorean. Even so, the preferred weighting might not always be obvious, and the rationale for the placing of particular terms in one or other column might be open to question on a variety of grounds.

The oppositions whose positive associations are least easily accounted for in terms of specific Pythagorean doctrines might be thought more representative of Greek attitudes generally. The value attached to right-handedness, for instance, and disavowal of the left is not specifically Pythagorean, but reflects a universal prejudice, lexically enshrined in numerous languages.[21] In the case of *male* and *female*, Pythagorean practice is known to have been unconventional, in that women were accorded an unusual measure of

---

[21] E.g. Latin *sinister/dexter*, Greek *skaios/dexios* and the euphemistic *aristeros* ('the better side') etc. Russian *pravda* 'truth' is connected to *prav* 'right' (hand, etc.). Vidal-Naquet (1986: 61–82) suggests that later Pythagoreans, in particular Philolaos, challenged the norm by acknowledging that 'right' and 'left' are relative concepts; but it is doubtful that Epaminondas' 'skewed phalanx' (see p. 176) was born from his Pythagorean studies.

equality with men.[22] As regards other oppositions, the priority implicitly accorded in the table can generally be explained with recourse to common-sense arguments and analyses.[23] But any definitive prioritisation, temporal or otherwise, of old over new (or vice versa) would be as arbitrary as prioritising the proverbial chicken over the egg.

More significantly, the theoretical privileging of one side of an opposition over the other was bound to be confounded in practice. For instance, the attribution of positive status to *motion* over *rest*, or *straight* over *crooked*, might be readily challenged or countermanded by philosophical arguments, medical considerations, or the inventive scenarios with which myth and literature abound. Greek writers and thinkers were also prepared to reverse natural or culturally approved categorisations to accord with their personal outlook and experience, imaginative inclinations, or their particular brand of intellectual or social critique. Even with regard to the initial priority assumed in the table, the dialectic between successive Presocratic philosophers regarding the priority of One or Many indicates a continuing atmosphere of intellectual dissent about the fundamental nature of the universe.

A more everyday example of the unsustainability of a stated opposition is that of *male/female*. The general view that the masculine is superior to the feminine is supported by the disposition of these terms on either side of the table. But positive representations of the feminine often weighed against any male-centred assumptions evident in Greek social practice. Qualities such as intelligence, wisdom, toughness, beauty and creativity were represented by female divinities – Metis and Athena, Aphrodite and the Graces, the Muses, Artemis and Demeter, the Great Mother and Gaia.[24] Linguistic features themselves posed a challenge to sexist assumptions: abstractions such as fortune (*tukhē*), knowledge (*epistēmē*), force (*biā*) and wisdom (*sophiā*) are feminine in gender, as are powerful personifications such as Justice (*Dikē*), Peace (*Eirēnē*) and Victory (*Nīkē*). Even if men were considered physically and intellectually superior to women, the fantasy of women's potentially alarming capacity for strength and intelligence

---

[22] Dikaiarkhos F33, D.L. 8.41–2; Iamblichus (*VP* 267) lists seventeen notable Pythagorean women.
[23] In giving *unity* precedence over *plurality* or *rest* over *motion*, it could be supposed that the former term in each case appears to present a precondition of the latter: *unity* is numerically prior to *plurality*, *at rest* is empirically prior to *in motion*. On similar lines, *old* could be considered prior to *new* from genealogical and historical perspectives: the old produce the young, so must 'precede' them, and older events are temporally anterior to (and may be determinants of) newer ones.
[24] This is not to deny that the femininity of such divinities was (often) an idealised, 'pure', projection of such qualities, as argued by Loraux (1992); but the fact remains that the attributes are attached to female figures.

is attested to by the powerful, eloquent women of Greek literature and drama – Homer's Penelope and Helen, Aeschylus' Klytaimestra, Euripides' Elektra and Medea and many others.[25] Greek women, though often constrained and politically disadvantaged, assumed dominant roles in certain religious and domestic contexts. 'Women are better than men, and I shall prove it' says Euripides' Melanippe, 'they manage the house and guard within the home goods brought from over the sea. No house is clean and prosperous without a wife. And in dealings with the gods – I judge these of prime importance – we play the greatest part.'[26]

Euripides was even inclined, if somewhat provocatively, to suggest women's special capacity for innovative thinking. In *Medea*, the dangers of appearing too clever are clear-sightedly observed by Medea herself:

> If you bring new kinds of cleverness (*kaina sopha*) before foolish men,
> you will be considered useless, not clever (*sophos*);
> and if you are regarded as better than people who are supposed to
>   know a clever thing or two (*ti poikilon*),
> you will seem offensive to the city.[27]

In *Iphigenia among the Taurians*, Iphigenia's resourcefulness in the face of Orestes' despair is characterised by words indicating cleverness and invention:

ORESTES: Ah, we are done for. How can we be saved?
IPHIGENIA: I think I have hit on a new plan (*kainon exeurēma ti*).
ORESTES: What plan? Share your idea with me.
IPHIGENIA: I shall employ your troubles as a cunning ruse (*sophismasin*).
ORESTES: You see, women are clever (*deinai*) at inventing devices (*heuriskein tekhnās*).[28]

With more obvious irony, the brilliantly resourceful Praxagora in Aristophanes' *Ecclesiazusae* uses the nine-times repeated refrain of 'just like in the old days' (*hōsper kai pro tou*) to stress supposed female traditionalism, even as (in the guise of a man) she makes a radically novel political proposal on women's behalf:

> I say that we should hand over the city
> to the women. After all, we already employ them
> as managers and stewards of our households...

---

[25] Cf. Gould (1980).
[26] Eur. *Melanippe Captive* (fr. 494). Buxton (1994: 114–17) stresses how mythical representations of women highlight their role as providers of continuity to the community.
[27] Eur. *Med.* 298–301.   [28] Eur. *IT* 1028–32.

> I will also show that they have better qualities
> than we do. First of all, they maintain their
> ancient (*arkhaion*) custom of dyeing wool in hot water,
> one and all, and you would never see them
> trying anything different; whereas the city of Athens,
> if that was working, wouldn't leave well alone,
> but would busy itself doing something else new (*kainon allo ti*).
> When women roast corn they squat, just like in the old days.
> They carry things on their heads, just like in the old days.
> They observe the Thesmophoria, just like in the old days.
> They bake their cakes, just like in the old days.
> They wear away their husbands, just like in the old days.
> They bring lovers home, just like in the old days.
> They squirrel away food for themselves, just like in the old days.
> They enjoy strong wine, just like in the old days.
> They love getting screwed, just like in the old days.[29]

Old and *new* pose to us a contrast no less self-evident than *male/female*. If no particular positive or negative charge were thought intrinsic to the words' connotations, their distribution in a 'column of goods' might not be obvious. However, indeterminable weighting in this respect could be said with equal force to apply to listed contraries such as *square* and *oblong*, *unity* and *plurality*. In contrast to these, 'old' and 'new' did have, as mentioned earlier, regular if not wholly consistent affective associations for the Greeks.

A measure of evidence for how the old might generally be evaluated relative to the new in contexts of social traditionalism can be derived from findings in comparative anthropology. A table of oppositions compiled by members of the Amboyna tribe of Indonesia, in which the opposition *old/new* is included, disposes the antithesis so that the terms tally with *right/left* and *male/female*.[30] In accord, therefore, with the evaluations indicated by the Pythagorean table, *old* receives a favourable evaluation in contrast to *new*. The opposition may, however, have been less easy to assert for the Greeks because of the fact that *neos* and *kainos* denote both 'young' and 'new'. The possibility that one might perceive the contrast as holding between 'old' and 'young' considerably complicates the nature of the opposition. A new (*neos*) law or newfangled (*kainos*) argument might have some claim to be viewed in negative terms, but a youngster (*neos*, *kainos*) could not be similarly evaluated without qualification. Secondly, the fact that the same word might signify both 'new' and 'young' creates

---

[29] Ar. *Eccl.* 209–11, 214–28; line 214 seems deliberately reminiscent of the introductory line to the praise of women in Euripides' *Melanippe* fr. 494, quoted above.
[30] Lloyd (1966) 33.

potential ambiguities: a new (*neos*) ruler might be an old man (*geraios*), an old (*arkhaion*) institution might be called 'new' (*kainon*).[31] Such ambiguities could be resolved, but not without more, and more advanced kinds of, explanation than would be called for by other oppositions in the table.[32]

Additionally, any a priori assignment by the Greeks of *old* and *new* to positive and negative categories would be susceptible (as with *male/female*) to being undermined by experience. Even in areas of religious and social institutions, where we might expect the old to be respected and the new abjured, the latter might be favoured. Greek societies were constantly changing, and along with new social and intellectual conditions there inevitably evolved new forms of social and cultic interaction. New political circumstances demanded revision and rethinking of constitutional principles, just as correct celebration of gods required the performance of 'fresh' songs to honour the gods fittingly. 'New' codes of law needed to be devised and drafted to ensure the correct, up-to-date, observance of law and ritual.[33] Greek myth and literature provided well-known models for how the creation of a 'new order' might supersede an older one. In Hesiod's 'myth of ages' there is a narrative of regress, in Aeschylus' *Oresteia* one of progress; but in both cases what emerges is 'new'. The grim Erinyes in the final play of the latter trilogy initially represent the old divine order, and assert their ancient privilege and wisdom vis-à-vis younger divinities such as Apollo and Athena.[34] When they accept in the end their new status as Semnai ('Revered Goddesses'), they call on Athens the blessings provided by the 'bright gleam of the sun' (*phaidron hāliou selas*).[35]

In myth the 'new' god Zeus' forceful supplanting of his father Kronos and the violent displacement of Titans by the current order of Olympians might be considered positive developments; but in the classical polis, the notions of political revolution (*neōtera prāgmata*) and civil strife (*stasis*) aroused fear and disapproval. In late fifth-century Athens, 'introducing new divinities' (*eisagōn kaina daimonia*), the charge on which Sokrates was indicted and condemned to death in lieu of a more overtly political indictment, was

---

[31] Cf. *to Kainon*, the 'New Court'; p. 23 above.
[32] Discomfort with this kind of apparent contradiction leads Plato to posit the notion of eternal, unchanging 'Forms' which cannot, like everyday things, be both A and not-A.
[33] E.g. the 'thoroughly conservative' commission to draft a new law code for Athens was entrusted to Nikomakhos, who (like Sokrates) was prosecuted in 399: Parker (1996) 218–19.
[34] Aesch. *Eum.* 394 (*geras palaion*), 838, 871 (*palaiophrona*); frequent attention is drawn to the contrast between the 'younger' and the 'older' gods (150, 163, 172, 721, 727, 778, 808, 848, 882).
[35] Ibid. 926; earlier the chorus have sung of 'sunless gloom' (*kai dusālion knephas*, 396), in words of identical metre but opposite import: Sommerstein (1989) ad loc. The transformation of Erinyes into Semnai (Eumenides, 'Kindly Ones', is only found in the title) seems to be an Aeschylean innovation: ibid. 11–12.

The Pythagorean table

calculated to arouse superstitious anxieties.[36] But new religious forms were being constantly introduced: at the start of the *Republic* Plato reminds his readers (with latent irony) of the popular celebrations of exciting new equestrian rites in honour of the Thracian goddess Bendis.[37] During these years the cult of Phrygian Sabazios had been enthusiastically received by Athenians (though not formally incorporated into state religion), and the new cult of the healer-god Asklepios – to whom Sokrates' enigmatic last words as reported in Plato's *Phaedo* allude – had been introduced at the behest of the aged Sophokles.[38] Not all 'new' divinities were equally to be condemned.

In circumstances where stability and permanence are more highly valued by the prevailing culture than movement and change, 'new' will tend to carry less appeal than 'old'. The latter accords with what is known and trusted, while the former is unfamiliar and therefore suspect. 'New (*neai*) friendships are necessary, old friendships are more binding' runs a fragment of Antiphon.[39] Thrasymakhos of Khalkedon, a grammarian and orator active in the 430s, begins a speech by drawing the contrast between 'then' and 'now' and the different dispositions of the old and the young:

> I would have wished, Athenians, to be alive in the days of old (*tou khronou tou palaiou*), when the younger men (*neōteroi*) were content to remain silent because political affairs did not urge them to speak, and the older men (*presbuteroi*) were guiding the state properly . . . But farewell to all that, since now we have exchanged peace for war and approach this period beset with dangers, recalling the bygone day with affection and greeting the coming one with fear.[40]

Even if *palai/neon* ('of old' and 'recent') were thought a suitable opposition for the Pythagorean table, the signification 'recent' raises considerations that obscure the determination of positive or negative weighting no less than in the case of *old/young*. Just as no consistent ethical priority is

---

[36] Garland (1992) 144–5, Parker (1996) 202–5.
[37] Pl. *Rep.* 328a: 'A race on horseback? Well, that's a novelty (*kainon ge touto*).' Further Platonic irony in relation to the charges against Sokrates appears in the subsequent exchange (328de), when in response to Kephalos' exhortation 'go ahead, hang around with the youngsters (*neāniskoi*)' Sokrates replies 'But Kephalos, I actually enjoy talking to terribly *old* people! (*tois sphodra presbutais*).'
[38] 'We owe a rooster to Asklepios' (*Phd.* 118a6). Whatever the true implication of these words (for a summary of suggestions and a novel proposal, see Most 1993), we might detect more Platonic irony at work in Sokrates' invocation of this old-new god; Asklepios was hardly a 'new god', even if he was new to Athens: Parker (1996) 176–85. Women played a prominent part in Sabazios' cult: Dillon (2002) 158–60.
[39] Antiphon B64; my translations 'necessary' and 'more binding' bring out the force of the contrast, though the same adjective is used in Greek (*anagkaiai* and *anagkaioterai*).
[40] Thrasymakhos B1. Aristotle (*Soph. El.* 183b29–33) lists the orator among those who advanced the art; according to the Suda 'he was the first to discover the period and the colon, and he introduced the modern kind of rhetoric (*ton nūn tēs rhētorikēs tropon*)'.

attributable to one side of youth and old age, so one might find as many reasons to prefer recent times to olden times as to privilege ancient over modern. Patently verifiable recent history might, for instance, be thought better because it was less uncertain and more instructive (*sumpheron, ōphelimon*) than that of olden times. 'Ancient history', whether sanctified by tradition or bardic inspiration, might be approved as being more impressive (*thōmaston, axiologon*). Where olden days provide stories of wonderful or monstrous deeds, recent ages present vivid monuments to human genius and folly. In a speech reported by Herodotos (9.26, discussed below), the Tegeans argue for martial priority over the Athenians. They begin with ancient deeds (*palaia*), in the historian's account of the debate, before proceeding to recent ones (*kaina*), a prioritisation apparently according with traditional evaluations about the primacy of the old over the young, of the time-honoured over the recent. The Athenians, claiming a more lately won repute and speaking second, win the argument. In the later context of the Peloponnesian War, Aristophanes coins an extended metaphor on contemporary Athenians' attitudes to their political leaders:

Many times we've thought the city behaves the same way towards its decent citizens as it does towards the old coinage (*arkhaion nomisma*) and the new gold (*kainon khrūsion*). Those currencies – not counterfeit but considered the finest of all, the only ones honestly struck, tested and proved among Greeks and non-Greeks alike everywhere – we make no use of, but we use these base bronze coins, struck only yesterday and the day before, the worst of coinage. So with our citizens: those we know as noble, sensible, honest, decent men, reared in wrestling-schools and choruses and culture, we reject, while for all purposes we make use of those of base metal, aliens, redheads, scoundrels born of scoundrels, the latest arrivals, who formerly the city would not have easily used even as scapegoats.[41]

Here the issue is not the contrast of old and new; both the reputable old (*arkhaion*) silver currency of Athens and the new (*kainon*) gold coinage are considered exemplary by contrast to the base bronze coinage. Ultimately, a simple binarism cannot be sustained. The opposition of new and old unravels in multiple ways as we have seen, and any assignment of ethical or even logical priority is problematic and elusive.

OLD AND YOUNG

The notion that old age merits respect is found in Greek literature from Homer onward. In common with all traditional societies, the older generation was considered more worthy of respect than the young.[42] But even

---

[41] Ar. *Ran.* 718–33.   [42] Falkner (1995) 24–7.

if 'old' was on these grounds considered superior to young, logical and practical considerations rapidly confuse the picture regarding the relative position they might be assigned, were they included in the Pythagorean scheme. Within an individual's lifespan, youth precedes old age: things both organic and manufactured must be young (fresh, new) before they become old (mature, obsolete). Commonplace in Greek thought, moreover, is the sentiment that youth is desirable, whether in the service of love or war. Epithets for old age in epic are mostly uncomplimentary: it is miserable (*lūgron*) and hateful (*stugeron*), in it 'strength has dissolved'.[43] The seventh-century poet Mimnermos of Kolophon lamented:

> The ripeness of youth's fruit is short,
> short as the sunlight on the earth,
> and once this season of perfection's past,
> it's better to be dead than stay alive.[44]

The Greeks expressed their clear-sighted recognition that although the young may lack wisdom and experience, they have compensating qualities.[45] Old age can mean greater knowledge and authority, but it can also mean senility and decrepitude. 'It's an old saying', says a character in Euripides, 'that the young have command in action, the old in counsel'.[46] In the words of Demokritos, 'strength and beauty are the good things of youth, good sense is the flower of age'.[47] The passage of time brings about loss as well as gain, suggesting an ironic paradox to the philosopher: 'Old age is complete – it is complete debility: it possesses everything, but everything is deficient.'[48] A man or woman, boy or girl, must be young before growing old. While the old were necessarily young once, the young might never live to be old – a palpable asymmetry in a society where death in infancy was not uncommon, and the battlefield was a place from which young men did not return.[49] Demokritos observed that at least the good elements of the past are determinable, unlike those that are to come:

---

[43] *Il.* 8.103; *lūgron*, *Il.* 10.79, 18.434 etc; *stugeron*, *Il.* 19.336. Falkner (1995) 9–10.
[44] Mimn. 2.7–10, trans. in West (1993). Cf. Thgn. 527–8, Sem. 1.11–12 etc.
[45] Cf. Epicurus at the start of the *Letter to Menoikeus*: 'both the young and the old should practise philosophy, so that when old, one may still be young with gratitude from all past joys, and when young, one may at the same time be old through fearlessness of what the future has in store'.
[46] Eur. fr. 508, cf. *Phoen.* 528–30, fr. 291, etc.; but note also fr. 509 'an old man is but voice and shadow'.
[47] Demok. B294.   [48] Demok. B296.
[49] In *Virginibus Puerisque* (1881) Robert Louis Stevenson writes: 'It is customary to say that age should be considered, because it comes last. It seems just as much to the point that youth comes first. And the scale fairly kicks the beam, if you go on to add that age, in a majority of cases, never comes at all. Disease and accident make short work of even the most prosperous persons; death costs nothing, and the expense of a headstone is an inconsiderable trifle to the happy heir' (Stevenson 2006: 28).

The old man was born a young one, but whether the young man will reach old age is unclear. So the good that is accomplished is better than the future that is still uncertain.[50]

The pursuit of the new and dismissal of the old are often considered particularly characteristic of youth. If the young find novelty more appealing and more easily assimilable than do the older generation, it may be partly because, in their inexperience, many things seem new; so to them one novelty may not be uncomfortably 'newer' than another. With less familiarity with the status quo, the young have less to lose from upsetting it; less invested in the past, they have less to mourn at its passing. Youth tends to be more resilient in the face of loss, and more excited by the prospect that the future will be bright – a brightness located for many older people in fantasies of a former 'golden' age. With less long-established reputation and wealth, young men are more often inclined to experiment and take risks; lacking in knowledge and experience, they incorporate, through learning, observation and participation, traditions that are initially new to them. But not only will they learn what they are instructed, they will criticise and challenge elements of tradition that seem outdated, in obedience to a generational imperative to reject the experience of older members of society in pursuit of authentically new experience.[51] The new politicians of the late fifth century were, or were felt to be, young politicians.[52] Youthful venturesomeness was embodied by the flamboyant figure of Alkibiades;[53] and the political tensions of the period may partly be explained in terms of a growing 'generation gap'.[54]

The Greeks did not speculate about how growing minds evolve in response to stimuli, or about the way young people's outlook on novelty will differ from that of the older generation simply because of the difference in their knowledge and experience.[55] Plato's discussion of children's toys in

---

[50] Demok. B295. The humorist Saki (H.H. Munro) notes more poignantly that 'the young have aspirations that never come to pass, the old have reminiscences of what never happened'; the words are put into the mouth of the Duchess in Saki's short story 'Reginald at the Carlton': Munro (1993 [1904]) 20–1.
[51] Arendt (1990: 28) argues that the Greeks (in contrast to the Romans) recognised the inevitability of generational change because 'the young, who at the same time were "new ones", were constantly invading the stability of the *status quo*'.
[52] Connor (1971); Strauss (1993) 139–43.
[53] Alkibiades was archetypally the 'youth' corrupted by Sokrates: Gribble (1999) 216; Strauss (1993) 4, 176.
[54] Forrest (1975).
[55] Speculations about the mental processes at work in infant, child or adolescent development are rare, partly because the use of reason and intelligent discourse (*logismos*, *logos*) was considered to be

Laws comes closest to a sociological perspective on the influence of novel stimuli in early youth:

> What are we to make of change and innovation in toys, and variation and constant fluctuation in the tastes of the young? A situation where there is no fixed standard of what is good and what not in their bearing, dress and other accoutrements, where the innovator who introduces new patterns, colours, and so on is specially honoured? It would be right to say that nothing could be worse for a society.[56]

The young, *neoi*, are at the same time 'new ones', who embody a potential challenge to the status quo. The Greeks recognised that as a people they were *neoi* compared with other nations. Their cultural traditions were relatively recent, particularly vis-à-vis Egypt. Plato imagined an aged priest of Sais speaking to Solon in these words:

> 'Ah Solon, Solon, you Greeks are always children (*paides*), there is no old man (*gerōn*) among you.' On hearing this, Solon said 'What do you mean?' 'You are young (*neoi*),' replied the old priest, 'young in your souls, all of you, because you do not have in them any age-old opinion about anything handed down by ancient tradition, nor any learning made grey by time.[57]

While Homer and Herodotos tended to treat the antiquity of Egypt with curiosity and wonder, Plato was impressed by the stability of its traditions. The Egyptians' unchanging laws and practices, their static artistic and literary forms, seemed to him to offer an appealing contrast to the changeability of contemporary Athens.[58]

The Greeks' sense of their relative youthfulness as a 'race' may have afforded some psychological licence for them to act in the manner of *neoi* – to innovate and to feel excited by novelty. In a fragmentary satyr-play by Aeschylus entitled *Theōroi* ('The Ambassadors') or *Isthmiastai* ('Celebrants at the Isthmian Games'), the satyr-chorus is presented as a group of creatures who personify childish attitudes. In a surviving passage, the satyrs are depicted deserting their duties out of a desire to participate in athletic events, whereupon they are upbraided for 'playing at being Isthmian and learning new (*kainous*) habits' (34). They are subsequently presented with athletic 'novelties', javelins or the like:

> Since you like to learn these new (*kaina*) ways
> I'm bringing you some novel toys (*neokhma athurmata*),

---

the province of adults rather than children (as well as free men rather than slaves, and men rather than women).

[56] Pl. *Leg.* 7.797bc; Gouldner (1965) 45–7.   [57] Pl. *Tim.* 22b4–8.
[58] Plato's invention of 'new' myths (such as those of Er and Atlantis) have been seen as an attempt to compensate for the fact that Greeks could not boast traditions of similar age to those of Egypt.

freshly fashioned (*neoktita*) with adze and anvil.
Here, take the first of the toys (*paignia*)...
It suits the skill (*tekhnē*) you've taken up.[59]

The associations here of youthfulness, novelty, physical playthings and *tekhnē* are noteworthy. The kind of novelty enjoyed by Aeschylus' Athenian audience raises a nexus of notions which insistently affirm the connection of newness with youth.

OLD VERSUS NEW

In his ninth Olympian Ode, Pindar gives a brief account of the myth of the 'new' human race created by Deukalion and Pyrrha after the flood. He rounds off the tale with a reference to the originality of his own composition: 'Praise wine that is old, but the blooms of songs that are new' (*ainei palaion men oinon, anthea d' humnōn neōterōn*).[60] Although the formula suggests that opposite qualities are praiseworthy in different things, here as elsewhere the poet is concerned to promote his own work, with the emphasis falling on the value of his newly composed songs.[61]

According to a scholiast, Pindar's words were written as a response to verses composed by his older contemporary Simonides:

When Simonides lost in a contest with Pindar, Simonides levelled abuse at the judge [Agathonidas], writing 'Not yet does new wine outclass last year's gift of the vine; this is the thinking of vain-minded youngsters.' That is why Pindar sings the praises of old wine.[62]

Pindar's dictum is taken to allude to the verses of Simonides. Even if the commentator has imagined the scene, such a reconstruction would not be entirely fanciful; formal competition was a common context of Greek poetic production and contestation.[63] The scene envisaged in this case is a contest of poetic skill between the older and the younger poet, in which Pindar emerged the winner; evidently his 'new wine' was approved by

---

[59] Aesch. fr. 78c, 85–8, 92 (Sommerstein); Henry (2001) argues that the speaker here is unlikely to be Dionysos.
[60] Pi. *O*. 9.48–9.
[61] Cf. Hesiod's 'praise a small boat, but put your cargo in a big one' (*Op.* 643), where the emphasis is on the latter.
[62] Sim. fr. 602. 'Agathonidas' is a reconstruction; *keneophronōn* (amended from *keneophrōn*) is used by Pindar (fr. 212) for competitive envy. The phrasing is reminiscent of Simonides' comment (fr. 581 *PMG*) on a dictum of Kleoboulos, one of the Seven Sages: 'this is the saying of a fool'.
[63] An epigram (27.792–5 *FGE*) recorded Simonides' 'fifty-six victories' in earlier dithyrambic competitions, and an anecdote (Ar. *Vesp.* 1410) told how he had once defeated Lasos of Hermione, who was allegedly Pindar's teacher, in such a competition.

the judge as more palatable than the Simonidean vintage. The old poet makes the supposition that the 'young and foolish' are not good judges of quality because they are drawn to novelty. Simonides uses 'wine' as a metaphor for song and poetry, but in this game of wits Pindar takes his rival literally to score his own point. We may indeed accept that the bouquet of old wine is better than that of new wine, but just as flowers (*anthea*) are more fragrant when fresh, so songs may be more appealing when new.[64]

Whether or not his point of departure was Simonides' phrase, Pindar's words appear to constitute a more general observation about old and new. The Pindaric dictum demonstrates how the evaluative force of 'old' and 'new/young' varies depending on the object qualified. An old king may be preferable to a young one, an old law more venerable than a more recent one; but new shoes may be better than old ones, and a new song more entertaining than a familiar one. The fourth-century comic poet Euboulos offered a ribald perspective on the opposition:

> It's an odd thing that courtesans always approve
> of *old* wine, but when it comes to a man
> it's not an old one they want but a *young* (*neōteron*) one![65]

Old and new, and old and young, need not always exclude one another, but may combine in productive ways. In his fragmentary eighth paian, possibly written to celebrate the new temple at Delphi built at the end of the sixth century, Pindar recounts the myth of the construction of four earlier Delphic temples. The latest temple had been built with stone by the sons of Erginos, the architects Agamedes and his brother Trophonios (a figure of oracular cult at Lebadeia in Boiotia).[66] In his old age Erginos, king of the Minyai, lacking wife or child, had consulted the Delphic oracle and received the response:

> Erginos, son of Klumenos son of Presbōn,
> you have come seeking offspring; but even now (*eti kai nūn*)
> put a new (*neēn*) tip on the old (*geronti*) plough.[67]

---

[64] The Greek adjective for wine with a fine bouquet was *anthosmiās*, 'flower-smelling': see Ar. *Ran.* 1150 with Sommerstein's note (1996, ad loc.).
[65] Euboulos fr. 122 (cf. Alexis fr. 284). The verses are preserved by Athenaeus (1.25f–26a) in a discussion that starts with a citation of the Pindaric fragment.
[66] The theme of the 'origins of temples' may be a Pindaric innovation; but there are parallels in Near Eastern and Egyptian literature (see Rutherford (2001), ad loc.).
[67] Paus. 9.37.4.

The words used show that the picturesque phrase is an instruction to 'old' Erginos (*geronti*) to take, despite his advanced age (*eti kai nūn*), a 'young' (*neēn*) wife. In due course he was said to have fathered Agamedes and Trophonios, the architects who built the Delphic temple. They were told that, as their reward, after six days they would be granted their 'dearest wish'; and on the seventh day they died.[68] The story is reminiscent of Herodotos' account of Kleobis and Biton, whom Solon praised to Kroisos as the most fortunate of men, because they died young after performing a deed of heroic and pious duty.[69] Such stories illustrate the sentiment encapsulated by the verse from Menander's *Double Deceiver*, 'those whom the gods love die young'.[70] Within the comedy, the context is that of a slave ironically commending the notion to his unhappy master; the age-old sentiment of melancholy wisdom is repeated, but the poet of New Comedy has given it a new twist. An old plough can be renovated with a new blade, an old man can take a new wife, an old theme may reappear in fresh form, and an old literary trope will take on new meaning in a new context.

KAINA KAI PALAIA

At the battle of Plataiai in 479 BCE, the Hellenic alliance memorably defeated the army of king Xerxes, putting an end to the second Persian incursion into the Greek mainland. Herodotos gives a detailed account of the preliminaries to the fighting and of the positions taken by the various Greek contingents in the order of battle. The Spartans, as leaders of the alliance and the strongest fighting force, assumed the traditional place of honour on the right flank. The second largest contingent, that of Athens, took their place on the left. Herodotos records that a curious episode took place in the run-up to battle, before the troop dispositions were finally settled. A debate was alleged to have arisen between the Athenians, who had fielded a force of 8,000, and the Tegeans who numbered 1,500:

> During the drawing up of battle order, a fierce quarrel flared up between the Tegeans and the Athenians. Each side claimed that they should hold the second wing, citing deeds new and old (*kaina kai palaia*) in support of their claim. The Tegeans spoke first: 'We among all the allies have always claimed the prerogative to hold this position in the campaigns of the combined Peloponnesian armies, both of old and in recent times (*kai to palaion kai to neon*), from the time that the sons of Herakles sought to return to the Peloponnese after the death of Eurystheus... Accordingly we and not the Athenians should hold the second

[68] Paus. 10.5.13, Pi. fr.3.   [69] Hdt. 1.31.1.   [70] Men. fr.125.

[left] wing. They have not achieved such feats of arms as we have, neither recently nor of old (*out' ōn kaina oute palaia*).'

To this the Athenians replied: 'We know that we are here to fight the barbarian, not to give speeches. But since the Tegeans propose to speak of all the noble deeds, old and new (*palaia kai kaina*), that each of us has achieved in all time, we must show you why we rather than the Arkadians have on account of our valour inherited the right to occupy the place of honour.'[71]

Commentators have reasonably doubted the historical validity of this account.[72] The Tegeans were far fewer in number than the Athenians, and their claim to outrank the Athenians seems far-fetched. Moreover, had there been a debate over fighting positions it seems unlikely that it would have been held so soon before the battle rather than much earlier on. We subsequently learn that the Tegeans distinguished themselves at Plataiai. The first contingent to break through enemy lines, they pressed on and sacked the Persian encampment. It has accordingly been suggested that the story of the debate was relayed to Herodotos by an informant who wished to stress the Athenians' contribution to the battle, and to belittle that of the Tegeans by way of contrast.[73]

This suggestion gains support from a linguistic peculiarity of Herodotos' account. This is the earliest passage of Greek prose in which the adjective *kainos* is found, and the only place in all of the *Histories*. One earlier instance of the verb *kainoō* refers to the inauguration of a new underground chamber by the Egyptian queen Nitokris, a performative use of the word that relates its connotation to the deliberate assignation of newness.[74] It is somewhat surprising that *kainos* is not used more often by Herodotos, given his insistent fascination with novelties and 'wonders' (*thōmata*) which, even if not new in temporal terms, are intimately related to the experience of the new (see Chapter 6). Here, in the space of two paragraphs, *kainos* is found three times, each time coupled with its opposite term *palaios*. If the phraseology is not the historian's but the informant's, it makes contextual and linguistic sense that the latter should be an Athenian seeking to undermine Tegea's claim to honour vis-à-vis that of his own city.[75]

---

[71] Hdt. 9.26.
[72] The order of speeches follows a standard pattern whereby the eventual winners speak second, but need not impugn their historicity. Herodotos even insists on the historicity of the 'constitutional debate' (Hdt. 3.80–3) in which the winner speaks last, though it can hardly have taken place in the form in which it is presented: Cartledge (2009) 73–5.
[73] Woodhouse (1898); *contra* Hignett (1963: 311–12), who defends the episode's historicity.
[74] Hdt. 2.100.3.
[75] Plutarch (*Aristeides* 12) specifies the speaker on the Athenian side as Aristeides 'the Just', named as the Athenian general by Herodotos (9.28.6); but his abbreviated account of the speech makes no mention of *kaina*.

Both the use of *kainos* and the tendency to evaluate *kaina* (new things or events) positively suggest an Athenian dimension. As previously noted, the earliest secure attestation of *kainos* occurs in Bakkhylides' dithyramb for the Athenians: its use may have been more prevalent in the Attic dialect, and perhaps had an unusually positive resonance for his addressees. The insistent juxtaposition of *palaia* and *kaina* also seems to prefigure the 'Gorgianic' verbal tropes that particularly appealed to Athenians such as the orator Antiphon and the tragedian Agathon. In the context of the alleged debate, it would be to the Athenians' advantage to draw attention to their recent accomplishments. The legendary account on which the Tegeans base their claim, that of the defeat of the Heraklid Hyllos by their former king Ekhemos, could not stand easy comparison with the Athenians' status as the almost single-handed victors over the Persians at Marathon.

In this passage *kainos* is synonymous with *neos*, as found in the subsequent phrase *kai to palaion kai to neon*. It connotes 'recent', with perhaps an underlying sense that *kainotēs* has been assigned by human decision to the accounts of recent deeds, but does not carry the negative connotations that attach to *kainos* and its compounds (e.g. *kainopēgēs*, *kainopathēs*) in early fifth-century tragedy.[76] Here, the *erga* described as *kaina* are to be commended no less than those that are *palaia*. The negative associations of *kainos* found in the tragic context have shifted in the historiographical account to neutral if not positive ones. The appeal to recent history is put on a par with the recalling of ancient mythical traditions, rather than the latter being privileged by virtue of their age. The fact that *kainos* here is evenly balanced with *palaios* anticipates subsequent occurrences in which *to kainon* is accorded, without any sense of paradox or inappropriateness, an equal or even superior evaluation to *to palaion*. In Euripides' *Orestes* of 408 BCE, the use of the word explicitly intimates a prospect that may be positive no less than negative:

> ORESTES: You are about to tell me some new thing (*ti kainon*);
> if good, you have my thanks.
> If it tends to harm, I have had enough of misfortune.[77]

The notion that what is new need not on that account be feared may be related to the increasingly positive view of 'modern' modes and techniques of evaluation in the course of the fifth century. Accuracy (*akrībeia*,

---

[76] Aesch. *Sept.* 642, Soph. *Tr.* 1277.
[77] Eur. *Or.* 239–40. At 790 the more traditional negative association is found, when Pylades reacts to Orestes' expression of worry by asking *ti tode kainon au legeis*? Cf. the Messenger's *ti kainon Argei*? (875).

saphēneia) becomes a watchword for sophists, medical writers, historians and artists.[78] The author of the Hippocratic treatise *On Ancient Medicine* sees 'precision' (*atrekeia*) as a desideratum.[79] Herodotos' own innovative historical methodology demonstrates his attempt to select the correct account from among those presented to him by different sources and experts. Thucydides' rationale for composing his history includes an explicit rejection of *to muthōdes*, the 'story-tale' element, in favour of 'the clear truth' (*to saphes*).[80]

Qualities of clarity and accuracy are less applicable to orally transmitted tales and traditional myths than to written arguments and accounts, which offer factual 'truths' and may attract criticism and contestation. In Sophokles' *Oedipus Tyrannus*, when the Chorus seek to discount the rumours they have heard of the killing of Laios, they call them *kōpha kai palai' epē*, 'vague (literally 'mute') and antiquated tales'.[81] What is *palaion* cannot speak with a clear voice. Earlier, the chorus have addressed a two-pronged question to the oracle, invoking the language of debt (*khreos*) to speak of what is owed by Fate:

> What, I wonder, is the kind of settlement (*khreos*) you will exact?
> perhaps a new (*neon*) one or perhaps one
> that comes round again as the seasons turn?[82]

The former kind of 'news', unforeseen and unprecedented, is destined to bring a dreadful kind of enlightenment to Oedipus. In his final words before he puts his eyes out, he invokes the light which illuminates a new truth for him, one from which his vision has hitherto been occluded:

> Oh, oh! All is now clear!
> O light, may this be the last time I look on you,
> I who am revealed as cursed in my birth,
> cursed in my bed-mate, cursed in the man I killed.[83]

The illumination of the new is not always to be welcomed. For Oedipus it cannot be resisted, though its effect will be to dazzle and literally, in the end, to blind him.

---

[78] For *akrībeia* used in art criticism, see Pollitt (1974) 117–25, 351–7, and below, p. 153.
[79] [Hp.] *VM* 9.21–2, 12.12–13.   [80] Thuc. 1.22.4.   [81] Soph. *OT* 290.
[82] Ibid. 155–7.   [83] Soph. *OT* 1182–5.

CHAPTER 5

Nothing new under the sun

There's nothing new except what has been forgotten.
                                                Marie Antoinette

It is not surprising that the Greeks should have been inclined, given the overwhelmingly agrarian context of their lives, to hold cyclical views of life and time. Despite the increasing urbanisation and interchange between city centres over the classical period, ancient thinkers appear to have been slow to embrace the possibility of radical, non-temporal novelty. Over this period, however, the notion that something may exceed natural, observable processes of change or recurrence, something that cannot be contained by or entertained in terms of what has gone before, is increasingly detectable in Greek thinking. In this chapter, I argue that some of the earliest occurrences of 'new' indicating 'saliently different' appear to be transmitted in observations by the philosophers Pythagoras and Herakleitos. The fragmentary remains of other early Presocratic thinkers yield few explicit references to the new; but their doctrines suggest an engagement with the idea of newness, and give pointers to how they thought about it. The eagerness of natural philosophers (*phusikoi*), for instance, to identify cosmic first principles (*arkhai*) points less to a preoccupation with the remote past than with the way new things may be imagined to emerge into being. At the same time, the challenge to the very possibility of newness from theories such as that of Parmenides demands a more complex perspective on early Greek views of novelty and their relationship to cyclical views of time.

The writings of later Presocratics (amongst whom are commonly included younger contemporaries of Sokrates such as Demokritos of Abdera, Hippias of Elis and Arkhytas of Taras) raise questions about the way new knowledge is thought to arise. '[People] thinking new thoughts day by day', a tantalising quotation from Demokritos, appears to locate novelty and its generation within individual human minds rather than as emanating from some 'outside' source.[1] At the same time, the notion that new ideas might be adopted from external sources, whether from beyond the human sphere or from outside the Hellenic context, is a recurrent theme in classical texts. By the fourth century, authors of heurematographic treatises were compiling lists of 'first inventors' and seeking to attribute a range of cultural innovations to divine beings or culture heroes of superhuman status. Foreign peoples with developed cultures were, or were thought to be, a fertile source of such novelty, a recognition summed up in the truncated proverb derived from the fourth-century comic poet Anaxilas, 'Libya is always begetting some new thing.'[2] The most momentous contribution from the East was one of undisputed provenance: the Greek alphabet, derived from Phoenician script, became a uniquely successful and economical means of recording and transmitting Greek writings. The spread of written documents raised the stakes for those who might set out or claim to say something new. One could generate new ideas through observing, criticising and contesting established theories and practices; but at the same time, the accumulated record of thoughts and experiences might make it harder for something incontestably new to be found or created.

WHAT'S NEW UNDER THE SUN

My point of departure, 'there's nothing new under the sun', suggests that in principle everything has already happened or been done. The proverbial phrase is uttered with surprise, chagrin or resignation, usually when something hitherto thought to be new is found to have existed previously. Central heating, thought of as a nineteenth-century invention, is found to have been installed at ancient Ephesos and Sybaris; atomic theory, the pinnacle of modern physics, appears to be anticipated by the ideas of Demokritos and Epicurus; school massacres at Dunblane (1996), Columbine (1999) and Beslan (2004) bring to mind the slaughter perpetrated by Kleomedes of Astypalaia (Paus. 6.9.6) or the atrocity at Mykalessos in 413 BCE (Thuc. 7.29–30); the credit crisis in Rome in 88 BCE prefigured the 'credit crunch' of 2008. It can seem that there's nothing new under the sun.

---

[1] Demok. B158.
[2] Anaxilas (*apud* Athenaeus 14.18.10–12) compares the diverse novelties of *mousikē* to those of Libya (used metonymously for both Eastern and Southerly regions): 'the arts, like Libya, produce some new beast (*thērion*) every year'. Aristotle, *De. Gen. Anim.* 746b7–8, quotes *aei ti pherei Libuē kainon* as referring to 'the tendency of even heterogeneous creatures to interbreed there': Romm (1992) 88–91. For the vicissitudes of the proverb (e.g. Zenob. 2.51, Livy's *ex Africa semper aliquid novi*, etc.), see Feinberg and Solodow (2002).

The idea that days of old might provide an inexhaustible repository of matters and events that prefigure the future chimes readily with the supposition that the Greeks' mental compass was directed towards the past. But although the sentiment may be timeless, the expression itself, with its undertones of world-weary resignation in the face of apparent novelty and change, was itself once new. The phrase seems to demand a classical pedigree, but it is not attested in Homer or Hesiod, nor anywhere else in classical Greek poetry, philosophy, drama or prose literature. This form of words occurs first and most insistently in the biblical book of Ecclesiastes (Greek for Hebrew *Qoheleth*, 'preacher'), traditionally thought to represent the wisdom of Solomon, king of Israel in the tenth century BCE, but datable to within the period 400–200.[3] In the opening chapter of Ecclesiastes, the author introduces his central contention that 'all is vanity' with the following reflections:

3 What does a man gain by all the toil at which he toils under the sun?
4 One generation goes, and a generation comes, but the earth remains forever.
5 The sun rises, and the sun goes down, and hastens to its place where it rises.
6 The wind blows to the south and goes around to the north; around and around goes the wind, and on its circuits the wind returns.
7 All streams run to the sea, but the sea is not full; to the place where the streams flow, there they flow again.
8 All things are full of weariness; a man cannot utter it; the eye is not satisfied with seeing, nor the ear filled with hearing.
9 What has been is what will be, and what has been done is what will be done, and there is nothing new under the sun.
10 Is there a thing of which it is said, 'See, this is new'? It has been already, in the ages before us.
11 There is no remembrance of former things, nor will there be any remembrance of later things yet to be among those who come after.[4]

The phrase 'under the sun', which runs like a refrain through the book of Ecclesiastes, may simply be a synonym for 'on earth'.[5] However, rather than limiting the frame of reference (i.e. *only* on earth), it implies universality: what happens 'under the sun' is *everything* that transpires,

---

[3] Most commentators suppose a date around the mid to late third century, but earlier and later datings have been proposed on linguistic grounds.
[4] *Ecclesiastes* 1.3–11 (English Standard Version).
[5] The phrase occurs twenty-nine times in all, and 'under heaven' also occurs three times (1.13, 2.3, 3.1).

actually or potentially, in the world.[6] The phrase further evokes toil undertaken literally under the sun, in the heat of the day: the physical discomfort of human effort exacerbates its futility. In addition to the topographical relationship signified by 'under the sun', the fact that the presence of the sun is coterminous with daytime gives a temporal connotation of 'as each day passes'. The resulting image is one of a continual cycle of successive days filled with futile labour, yielding the further sense for the phrase of 'in the course of a person's lifetime'.

The meaning of 'under the sun' thus exceeds its prima facie implication of place. It evokes the brief and effortful span of life granted to mortals for their earthly existence. The author goes on to contrast human life, the discrete period on earth bounded by the termini of birth and death, with the underlying permanence and continuity of the earth itself. The emphasis lies not on the endings brought about by time and circumstance, but on the changelessness that underlies the cyclical recurrence of birth and death: 'one generation goes, and another generation comes, but the earth remains forever'. There is an air of paradox about this assertion: in the face of the phenomena of change and death (generations 'come and go'), in spite of the motion and haste of solar revolutions (the sun 'hurries back' to where it rises), nothing really changes. *Plus ça change*: the more things (appear to) change, the more they stay the same. The circuits of winds and rivers instantiate perceptible natural cycles. Their return to their starting-points affirms the author's contention that, despite the appearance of ceaseless motion and change, the underlying principle of the universe is homeostasis. In verses 7–8 the notion of cyclicality, as demonstrated by the image of waters constantly circulating, is aligned to endlessness – there is no limit to what can be uttered, seen, or heard. That this should arouse a sense of futility (rather than, say, a hope or expectation of future good) is assumed. It is connected somewhat obscurely to the eventual conclusion that 'nothing is really new'. The argument is not that nothing is new because nothing has ever changed nor can ever change in future, but because everything *has* happened before – and will happen again in the same way.

Why should the proposition that 'nothing is new' follow from the assertion of cosmic stability and earthly permanence? Whatever the original source of Ecclesiastes' ideas, the pattern of thought closely parallels

---

[6] This recalls the image found in early Greek poetry of the Sun as 'all-seeing' (e.g. *Od.* 8.271).

philosophical formulations in Greek antiquity.[7] In particular, the notion that the regular cycle of the sun with its daily recurrence in identical form sets the pattern for all other events in the universe is familiar from Presocratic thought. It recalls the principle of 'eternal recurrence', the earliest Greek formulation of which is traceable to the doctrines of Pythagoras. According to Aristotle's learned pupil Dikaiarkhos of Messana, in whose native Sicily followers of Pythagoras had settled following their expulsion from the gulf of Tarentum, the teaching of Pythagoras on the matter was that 'whatever comes into being recurs again in the revolutions (*periodoi*) of time, and nothing is unqualifiedly new (*haplōs neon*)'.[8]

The attribution to Pythagoras himself of any particular doctrine associated with his name cannot be assured.[9] But if the use of *neon* in this expression preserves a genuine element of the sage's original formulation, it ranks as one of the first attestations of the word with the unmistakable meaning of 'new', as distinct from 'young' or 'recent'. The predicate *neon* in this phrase signifies the kind of novelty that makes an event qualitatively different from another, rather than describing an event as merely 'recent' or as following another in due sequence. The addition of *haplōs* to *neon* does not produce this qualitative, as opposed to temporal, connotation, but emphasises it.[10] The conceptualisation of 'new' envisaged by the Pythagorean statement may accordingly be novel for its time. It is therefore somewhat ironic that the doctrine goes on to dismiss novelty of this kind as being in the last resort illusory. Nothing, we are told, may be called 'new' without qualification, nothing is *wholly* 'new'. At the very point at which we encounter *neos* used with the signification of qualitative novelty, the reality of what is signified by the word is denied.

CYCLES OF NOVELTY

The rationale behind the Pythagorean assertion that nothing is *haplōs neon* is not simply the supposition that what has occurred previously will occur again in a more or less similar way, but that it will recur in exactly the

---

[7] The structure of antitheses in Eccl. 3.1–8 ('to everything there is a season..., a time for A, a time for not-A'), is related by Albright (1972: 238) to the Pythagorean *sustoikhiā* (p. 92 above); but the trope is too universal for influence in either direction to be supposed.

[8] Dikaiarkhos A8 (ap. Porph. *Vit. Pyth.* 19).

[9] Later Pythagoreans notoriously used the phrase *autos ephā* ('Himself said it', *ipse dixit*) to father their own ideas on the Master: Burkert (1972) 91 n. 36.

[10] As I note in Chapter 3 above, the explicit articulation of such a conception of novelty emerges relatively late in the lexical record, and tends subsequently to become associated more with *kainos* than *neos*.

Cycles of novelty 113

form it did before. The former, less demanding, assertion was to be made in the late fifth or early fourth century by Thucydides, who claims that his *Histories* are a 'possession for all time' (*ktēma es aiei*), intended to be of use to those who seek 'the clear truth of what happened and of things that will, given human nature, happen sometime again in the same or nearly the same way'.[11] For the first 'scientific' historian, it is a crucial qualification that events are likely to recur in a general rather than identical way. But the fragment in question proposes a much more specific and radical doctrine. The Pythagoreans held that the universe undergoes recurrent destructions, whereafter it is reborn again in such a way that events proceed to take place in an *identical* fashion to the previous cycle.[12] Adherents of such a doctrine would naturally suppose that the memory of past cycles would be lost (cf. Ecclesiastes 1.11, 'there is no remembrance of former things'): it is evident that observers and agents do not, on the whole, know or even sense that current events are identical repetitions of events that occurred in a previous cosmic cycle. Equally, those destined to experience the selfsame events in future cycles cannot be presumed to retain any memory of their having occurred in the current round, or in a previous cycle.

The period of cosmic existence between the birth and destruction of the universe was named, in Pythagorean parlance, the Great Year, *megas eniautos*.[13] This period, within which happenings were said to take place in an identical way to those in previous cycles, was accorded (on some reckonings) a duration of 10,800 solar years.[14] What such a doctrine allows for is that people may reasonably suppose that events and objects that are new in their everyday experience are indeed describable as 'new'. The ascription of novelty to events is no less reasonable for someone ignorant of their supposed occurrence in a former cycle than for someone who perceives events as unique and unrepeatable. As the qualification *haplōs* indicates, the impossibility in question is that of novelty being an objective property of events, not of the way events are experienced. Concern with the precise numerical determination of the cycle's duration distinguishes the philosophical doctrines of Pythagoras and Herakleitos from more generally

---

[11] Thuc. 1.22.
[12] Plato apparently alludes to the Pythagorean notion of recurrent cosmic destruction in *Timaeus*, *Statesman* and *Laws*. The related idea of a recurrent universal conflagration (*ekpurōsis*) is ascribed to Herakleitos, and has been connected to the latter's conception of fire as a symbol of cosmic justice: Finkelberg, A. (1998).
[13] Folk etymology linked *eniautos* with *en heautōi* on the basis that the cosmic period contains all things 'within itself' (Hermippos fr. 4, Eur. fr. 862, Pl. *Crat.* 410cd).
[14] Herakleitos A13; it is not clear whether this represents his own opinion or is a mocking allusion to Pythagorean doctrine.

held assumptions of cyclicality in Hellenic life and thought. The majority of Greeks took for granted the visible facts of seasonal and annual recurrence, and celebrated them in their myths and festivals in order to ensure their continuation. They will have been less engaged in speculation about the length of the fixed cycle of cosmic rebirth than with the vital benefits and demands of seasonality.

When Plato raises the theory of recurrent cosmic conflagrations in *Laws*, the interlocutors (the Athenian and Kleinias) agree that loss of earlier knowledge in such destructions accounts for the notion that inventions or discoveries might be described as 'new':

ATHENIAN: So shall we say that all their tools were lost, and any important discoveries they may have made in politics or other fields perished at that time? For if things had remained throughout just as they are today, how, sir, could anything new (*kainon*) have ever been invented?
KLEINIAS: Yes, we must suppose that the men of those days knew nothing of these techniques for tens of thousands of years. Only one or two thousand years ago Daidalos, Orpheus, and Palamedes made their various discoveries, Marsyas and Olympos invented the art of music, Amphion invented the lyre, and various other discoveries were made by others. All this happened, so to speak, yesterday and the day before yesterday.[15]

The doctrine allows that new events, even if they are known to be recurrent elements in an endlessly repeated cycle, may still be experienced as new. Pythagoreans who supposed that they knew all events to be merely repetitions were not insusceptible to wonder or surprise in the face of new phenomena (the significance of such responses for identifying what may be called 'new' is explored in Chapter 6). Some people, however, who were endowed with exceptional abilities, could vouch for cyclicality directly: knowledge of earlier events and existences was ascribed to the Master himself, and to a handful of similarly enlightened, godlike individuals.[16] Pythagoras was said to have recalled his own previous incarnation as Euphorbos (the Trojan warrior responsible in concert with Apollo and Hektor for Patroklos' death in the *Iliad*) when he recognised Euphorbos' shield, hanging on the wall of Hera's temple at Argos, as his own.[17] Strictly speaking, this 'memory' entails only that Euphorbos lived at a period earlier than Pythagoras within the *current* world cycle. But other wondrous capacities, such as an aptitude for being in two places at the same time ('bilocation'), secured the sage's reputation for operating outside

[15] Pl. *Leg.* 677cd. [16] 'There are mortals, gods, and beings like Pythagoras': Iambl. *VP* 31.
[17] See Burkert (1972) 138–9.

normal temporal constraints, and will have helped to establish his claim to knowledge of previous and future cycles.

The idea of an eternally recurrent period, whatever its form or duration, implies that all events might be characterised as in some way a repetition of the past rather than as happening 'new' for the first time. But even if the observable cycles of nature are felt to entail some such restriction of the view that completely new or unprecedented things might happen, there is scope for events within each cycle being viewed and experienced as new – that is, as the kind of singular, contingent, constantly new events of which history consists.[18] The Pythagorean belief that nothing is 'absolutely' (*haplōs*) new lays constraints on the scope of novelty: the qualification requires that 'new' could only signify the first time *ever* that an event could be said uniquely to have occurred, its 'original' occurrence. Such an occurrence would have to have taken place within the period of the 'original' cycle, if such a cycle could be identified. A supposed archetypal (and so incontrovertibly new) event could be thought to serve as the model which any subsequent event of the kind recapitulated.[19] But if world cycles were thought to stretch back indefinitely into the past and forward into the future, there can be no archetypal cycle, only an infinite series of cycles.

The Pythagoreans supposed the cosmos to be structured so that certain qualities are superior to and prevail over their opposites – limited over unlimited, male over female, light over dark and so on.[20] Imbalance is therefore characteristic of the Pythagoreans' outlook; and a similar asymmetry could be posited for their understanding of the relationship between new and old. Rather than a seamless interchange of old and new, or the movement of new into old and vice versa according to cosmic demands for balance and reciprocity, the idea that that the old might be wholly superseded by the new, or that the new might give way entirely to the old, is implied by Pythagorean doctrine.[21] The Pythagorean belief in cycles of identical recurrence thus 'saves the phenomena' in that it allows for things and events to appear and to be called 'new' even if from a deeper metaphysical perspective they are no more than repetitions and recurrences that will return in identical form. The notion that the new supersedes rather than recapitulates the old also suits the newly historical

---

[18] Cf. Paul Valéry's dictum (1938: 142) 'L'Histoire est la science des choses qui ne se répètent pas ('History is the science of things that do not repeat themselves').'
[19] Eliade (1971) ch. 1.
[20] See p. 91 above. By contrast, Herakleitan thought constantly reiterates the view that opposites coexist in tension.
[21] Seaford (2003) 158–60.

sense of time as unidirectional rather than recurrent, linear rather than cyclical.

The empirical recognition that the world is replete with novelty of diverse kinds is philosophically undermined if, at some more profound metaphysical level, all novelty is to be dismissed as appearance rather than reality. This opposition is related to the familiar tension between the ideal and the observable found in many areas of Greek thought; the drive towards an all-encompassing ideal is characteristic of Greek philosophical thinkers, who in many cases end up expressly disputing, by means of logical or conceptual analysis, popular and everyday views of how the world works. But the naive understanding of phenomena needs to be taken into account in considering the character of Greek thinking about the new. It is clear that Greeks did not suppose that everyday forms of novelty were a phantom or fantasy, or that the new had no real existence or instantiation on the earthly plane. Phrases like 'nothing is completely new' and 'there is nothing new under the sun' draw attention to the way that thinkers strove to formulate the contradiction between the real and observable fact of novelty and the underlying uniformity or changelessness which logical or philosophical considerations compelled them to posit. A clear intimation of a shift in thinking towards the view that genuine novelty might unfold sequentially in the course of time, albeit that the underlying pattern of events might still evince some kind of recurrence, is the development of historiography, and with it the idea of history as we know it. The unfolding of events in a linear fashion is how historical time is presented by Herodotos and Thucydides, regardless of their belief that history demonstrates, to a greater or lesser degree, recurring broad patterns of human behaviour.[22]

CYCLES OF NATURE

In his battlefield encounter with Diomedes in Book 6 of the *Iliad*, the Trojan warrior Glaukos memorably compares men's life and death of men with seasons of natural growth and decline:

> As are the generations of leaves, so are the generations of men;
> The wind scatters one year's leaves to the ground, but the forest
> bursts into bud and puts out new leaves when the spring comes round.
> Just so does one generation of men flourish while another declines.[23]

[22] Cf. Csapo and Miller (1998) 112–13.   [23] *Il.*6.146–9.

The image of recurrent cycles of life and death accords with other indications of cyclicality within the epic. The passage of time is regulated by the rising and setting of the sun, by the waxing and waning of the moon, and by the cycle of seasons and years. The start of a new day is signalled by the evocative formula 'when the early-rising (*ērigeneia*) rose-fingered dawn appeared'.²⁴ The advent of a new period of time is referred to by the rising of the new moon and the subsiding of the old. The passage of the seasons and the rolling by of the years are indicated by the changing positions of the stars. Newness, like life and death, presents itself as part of the natural order. New living things constantly take the place of earlier ones, new phases of life follow older ones and are succeeded in their turn. We find *neomai* and its cognates, 'to return, come round', used for the turning of the seasons, the flowing of rivers and the return (*nostos*) of heroes to their homeland.²⁵

The everyday world of the Greek farmer and artisan, depicted in Homeric similes and elaborated by Hesiod, is constructed around seasonality, the stable, predictable patterns of farming and ploughing, work and weather. Within a cyclic world-view, what is repeated may yet be thought of as 'new'. The turning year brings new seasons of sun and rain, heat and cold, sowing and harvest: the advent and passage of the new are inevitable and regular. From the perspective of the *longue durée*, the new is less a manifestation of change than of reassuring seasonality and vital continuity, represented by the new year, the new plough and the new crop. Inscribed in Greek myth and legend, such novelty was also rooted in religion and ritual. The Greeks welcomed the newness of the natural order in celebrations of birth and seasons, in rites of passage and in the complex series of festivals with which they greeted the new year and new moon.²⁶

While there is comfort in repetition, nature evolves, and what is alive is apt to alter. What is *neos* is transient, since in time youth gives way to age, in its turn new becomes old. The new dawn announced by the Homeric formula does not only herald the repetition of familiar actions and events, but holds out the promise of new ones. With respect to the narrative of events in human life, the expectation of novelty is ever-present. When Glaukos aligns human life with the natural cycle of growth and decline, the main implication is that the lives of individuals are insignificant; but the comparison also serves to emphasise how heroic valour can make the

---

[24] *Il.*1.477, 24.788; *Od.*2.1, 3.404 etc.
[25] Despite these connections, *neomai* (< *nes-*) is not etymologically related to *neos* (< *newo-*).
[26] Burkert (1985) 227–34.

individual stand out against the background of nature's regularity. The turning year for Hesiod brings the possibility of accumulation, and with it a change of status for the hard-working peasant. Although the cosmos may display unceasing regularity, although the stars and planets may appear to follow their orbits without deviation, nature is not predictable. Earthquakes, floods, disease and other natural disasters threaten the regularity of human life.

Demokritos supposed that fear of celestial phenomena was the root of religion.[27] By attributing fearsome eventualities to gods, human beings could hope to exert some measure of control through prayer, piety and sacrifice; but the divine sphere itself is, as Solon in Herodotos observes, 'jealous and disruptive' (*phthoneron te kai tarakhōdes*).[28] Human beings too behave in a conspicuously irregular and unseasonable manner. In the *Iliad*, Agamemnon offends the only warrior strong enough to defeat Hector; Akhilleus withdraws in pique, leaving his beloved Patroklos to die in battle. In the *Odyssey*, the companions of Odysseus sabotage their *nostos* by slaughtering the cattle of the Sun; the suitors bring about their own deaths 'through their own foolishness' (1.34). In *Works and Days*, the judges against whom Hesiod rails fail to observe justice, as does his brother Perses. The hero of Sophokles' *Ajax* is a figure taken from the age of epic. He is made to express a cyclical perspective on the inevitability of change:

> All things long and countless time
> brings to birth in darkness and covers after they have been revealed.
> Nothing is beyond expectation; the dread oath and
> unflinching purpose can be overcome...
> After all, the most powerful of things
> bow to office; winter's snowy storms
> make way before summer with its fruits,
> and night's dread circle moves aside for day
> drawn by white horses to make her lights blaze;
> and the blast of fearful winds lulls to rest
> the groaning sea, and all-powerful Sleep
> releases those whom he has bound, nor does he hold them for ever.
> So how shall we not come to know sense?[29]

In the drama recounted by Sophokles, the hero is faced with an *impasse*. He cannot and will not change, despite his recognition that change is a principle of human life as well as nature. His solution is to embrace the

---

[27] Demok. A75 (Sext. Emp. *Math.* 9.24). Similar ideas are expressed in verses ascribed to Kritias (B25), and by Prodikos of Keos: Henrichs (1975).
[28] Hdt. 1.32.   [29] Soph. *Aj.* 646–9, 669–77.

only kind of change he can: death. People will act in similar ways, observes Thucydides, so long as human nature remains the same. But the vicissitudes of human nature create ever new initiatives, circumstances, and outcomes. While, on one view, the reduction of events to a repeated cycle bids to make the world uniform and controlled, on another view multiplicity and alterability are irreducible aspects of the cosmos.

EX ARKHĒS

In a spurious fragment attributed to Epikharmos, the Sicilian comic poet of the late sixth and early fifth centuries BCE, two characters argue about the logic of a primal element, alluding to the Hesiodic Khaos:

> A: The gods were always there, they were never absent; and these things always existed just as they are and forever will be.
> B: But they say Khaos was the first god to be born.
> A: How could that be? He had nothing to come from and nowhere to go to, in the beginning.
> A: Then didn't anything come first?
> B: No, nor anything second, by Zeus, of the things we're now talking about – they existed always.[30]

The new must arise from the old; but at what point does the process begin? The notion of birth as a genetic principle of cosmic significance raises the questions of ultimate origins. If whatever gives birth must itself have been born, this seems to require an endless series of forebears stretching back into the past. Rather than adopt a notion of infinite regress, a number of early Greek thinkers responded to the question of origins by positing a permanent, eternal ground of being. While some posited an unchanging principle out of which emerges the perceptible variety of the phenomenal world, others sought to reduce the multiplicity of the world into a singularity. Where the former principle allows for the generation of new things in the course of time, the latter seems to exclude the possibility of 'genuine' novelty.

Aristotle traces the birth of this kind of philosophical thinking to natural philosophers (*phusikoi*) in sixth-century Miletos. Miletos was a neighbour and subject of Kroisos' Lydia, a realm of proverbial wealth whence the Greeks had first adopted the practice of minting coins. A thriving commercial centre and mother-city of numerous colonies around the Black

---

[30] Epikharmos 23B1 (275 KA).

Sea, the city was constantly exposed to new ideas, artefacts and stimuli.[31] Against this variegated backdrop, the early *phusikoi* sought to identify a single fundamental substance as underlying the multiplicity of the perceptible world. Thales supposed this to be water, Anaximenes air; from these elements every 'new' substance was thought to have arisen, or to have the potential to come into being through processes such as rarefaction and condensation. Anaximander, to whom the first use of the term *arkhē* is attributed, broadened the conceptual arena by positing as first cause an abstraction to which he gave the name of 'the Limitless' (*to apeiron*). These speculations need not indicate a desire to deny the reality of change and multiplicity. New things can come into being even if they depend on an original element that is eternal and universal. To characterise the work of the *phusikoi* and their successors as simply looking 'back into the past' for origins misrepresents their imaginative procedure. The object of their search and the manner in which they pursued it, their speculative energy in pursuit of new candidates for *arkhai* and exhaustive argumentation in support of their ideas, indicate that the process was intimately related to the experiences of novelty in which they were immersed.

The notion that some kind of elemental stability underlies the appearance of change has ambiguous implications for the notion of novelty. The rejection of the possibility of novelty appears in its most radical and sophisticated form in the arguments of Parmenides of Elea. According to the vision of Being which he claims to have had imparted to him by the goddess, no development or change at all can logically take place:

> There still remains just one account of a way,
> that *it is*. On this way there are many signs,
> that being uncreated it is imperishable,
> whole and of a single kind and unshaken and perfect.
> It never was nor will be, since it *is* now, all together,
> one, continuous. For what birth will you seek for it?
> How and whence did it grow?[32]

For Parmenides, the true 'way of Being', as opposed to the false but commonly accepted 'way of Seeming', logically cannot admit coming-to-be or ending. What-is, Parmenides asserts, is all there is. Change would involve what-was and what-will-be, hence is impossible. Novelty must be an illusion. In arguing for the impossibility of change, the Eleatic philosopher rules out the possibility of the new.

---

[31] Pliny the Elder records (*N.H.* 5.112) that Miletos founded ninety colonies.
[32] Parm. B8.1–7 (trans. *KRS* 259, 296, slightly modified).

On the surface, Herakleitos of Ephesos appears to take a diametrically opposite stance to Parmenides in positing not the absence of change but a world of ceaseless change. 'Everything is in process and nothing stays still' (*panta khōrei kai ouden menei*), he is quoted as saying.[33] For Herakleitos, however, the idea of observable plurality, rather than conflicting with that of fundamental unity, is in harmony with it:

> Things taken together are wholes and not wholes, something which is being brought together and brought apart, which is in tune and out of tune; out of all things arises a unity, and out of a unity all things.[34]
>
> People don't realise how what differs with itself is in agreement: harmony consists of opposing tension, like that of the bow and the lyre.[35]

The cosmos, with all its appearance of multiplicity and changeability, is thus conceived of as a unified whole, but a *dynamic* unity. However, if everything were new all the time, nothing could stand out as being newer than anything else. This recognition would impel Herakleitos to arrive at a similar conclusion regarding novelty to that of Parmenides: the salience that is the distinguishing aspect of novelty is obliterated by the constancy of change.

The thinkers who attempted to address the question of change have been broadly divided into monists and pluralists. Monistic thinkers who sought to 'preserve the phenomena' needed to take account of observable multiplicity in their metaphysical notions. In the early fifth century, the philosopher-poet Empedokles of Akragas proposed a new and influential doctrine of cosmic genesis. He theorised that four ultimate, unchanging 'roots', the elements of fire, air, water and earth, combined in myriad ways to create all the structures in the universe. Different kinds of matter emerge according to the different proportions in which these elements are combined. While the aggregation and segregation of the original elements correspond to processes of change, the continuous exchange between unity and multiplicity amounts to a kind of changelessness:

> In that the elements of matter tend to become one out of many
> and multiplicity occurs through the separating out of that unity,
> things come into being and have no stable existence.
> But in that they never cease this continual interchange,
> they remain in this way always unchanged (*akīnētoi*) within the cycle (*kata kuklon*).[36]

---

[33] Pl. *Crat.* 402a.   [34] Herakleitos B10.   [35] Herakleitos B51.
[36] Emped. B17.10–13; cf. B17.31–5 and B26. Plato conceives of time as a cycle, stable and infinite (*Timaeus* 37c6–38b5).

Although Empedokles suggests that there may be changes in the way elements combine, the constant return to 'roots' leaves no room for the persistence of anything new. However, in positing that the four basic elements combine in different proportions (to create, say, recognisable matter such as wood and hair) Empedokles does not wholly eliminate the possibility of the birth of novel forms. Things that emerge from the combination of original elements might reasonably be called 'new'.

The ideas of Anaxagoras of Klazomenai, a younger contemporary of Empedokles, appear more inimical to the notion that anything emerges wholly new:

The Greeks are wrong to recognize coming into being and perishing; for nothing comes into being nor perishes, but is rather compounded or dissolved from things that are.[37]

Anaxagoras rejects Empedokles' notion of the creation of matter through the intermingling of elements, and instead posits that, since nothing can come from nothing, there must exist in everything a tiny portion of everything else that might emerge from it. Since a portion of every natural substance, as well as its opposite element, must be supposed to be present in the original mixture and in every constituent part of matter, matter such as wood and hair can be generated from the elements that form them without their emergence indicating the genesis of something new.[38]

THINKING NEW THOUGHTS (1)

The forum for the exchange of ideas in the sixth century centred on the Ionian seaboard. The encouragement of commercial activity by tyrants in mainland Greek cities such as Corinth and Sikyon provided new opportunities for the exchange of goods as well as ideas, leading to materialistic excesses that were condemned by Xenophanes of Kolophon.[39] Where other thinkers engaged in the contestation of doctrines about cosmic origins, Xenophanes' novel stance on religious and social practices indicates that criticism itself could constitute a productive form of intellectual innovation.[40] His strictures extended to the religious beliefs and cultural values espoused by the Greeks, and had a humanistic bent. Countering the Hesiodic verse 'the gods keep hidden from men their means of living' (*Works and Days* 42), he proposed that human beings encounter new notions and make discoveries through their own efforts:

---

[37] *KRS* 469 (1–3).   [38] Ibid. 370.   [39] Xenoph. B3.   [40] Cf. Edelstein (1967) 11–15.

> In no way did gods reveal everything to mortals from the beginning,
> but in time, through their seeking, men discover what is better.[41]

Xenophanes criticised Homer and Hesiod on moral grounds, but he himself came in for criticism from Herakleitos of Ephesos as someone whose intellectual versatility detracted from true profundity: 'Much learning (*polumathiē*) does not teach thought, else it would have taught Hesiod and Pythagoras, Xenophanes and Hekataios.'[42]

Herakleitos' profundity, however, often descends into obscurity. His oracular prose style was as novel as his doctrines, but he had little time for the kind of engagement with diversity enjoyed by the polymaths he criticised. In a number of fragments he appears to advocate that the truth, though veiled, may be elicited by systematic introspection and analysis of empirical data:

> Let us not conjecture at random about the most important things.
> I inquired into myself.
> The things we learn via sight and hearing are what I commend.
> Thinking is common to all.[43]

Another, characteristically paradoxical, Herakleitan maxim is usually taken to stress the need for intellectual persistence: 'If one does not expect (*elpētai*) the unexpected (*anelpiston*) one will not discover it, since it cannot be tracked down and has no path.'[44] On one analysis, this observation suggests a curious angle on the question of how human beings are to think of novelty: what is new is unexpected, but can be discovered only if one expects in principle to encounter it. In psychological terms, this suggests that a readiness to accept the new *as* new is the only way novelty can arise and be recognised as such in an individual's experience. Although one cannot determine in advance what form such novelty will take, the anticipation of the new means that nothing will on that account be wholly or 'radically' new.

This paradoxical understanding of novelty as something graspable only if it is both new and not new may be brought to bear on the truncated utterance attributed to Herakleitos that the sun is *neos eph' hēmerēi*, 'new every day'.[45] As in the case of the Pythagorean citation, the Herakleitan fragment uses *neos* with the unmistakable sense of 'new' rather than 'young'. The sun is not just a 'recent' or 'early-born' phenomenon that recurs from

---

[41] Xenoph. B18.   [42] Herakleitos B40.   [43] Herakleitos B40, B47, B101, B55, B113.
[44] Herakleitos B18.   [45] Herakleitos B6.

day to day, it is in some way *made* new on a daily basis.[46] By calling the sun 'new', Herakleitos invokes, in a manner similar to Ecclesiastes, an implicit opposition to the unchanged and unchanging subsolar world. While for the biblical author the permanence and stability of the earth is both opposed to and reflected in the 'hurried' regularity of the sun's rising and setting, by contrast, Herakleitos' overall metaphysical conception invariably emphasises the unity of such opposites as movement and stillness, change and constancy. A number of Herakleitan fragments equate the underlying principle (*logos*) of the cosmos to fire, the sun's component matter. Fire is thought to animate and unify the universe by continuous reciprocal interaction with other elements:

> The lightning-bolt (fire) steers the cosmos.
> No god or man made this cosmos, but it always was and is and shall be, an eternal fire that is kindled and extinguished in equal measures.
> Fire lives the death of earth, and air lives the death of fire; water lives the death of air, earth of water.
> All things are an equal exchange for fire and fire for all things, as goods are for gold and gold for goods.[47]

Consistently with these propositions, 'the sun is new every day' proposes that the sun's fire is constantly renewed by the utilisation and consumption of other elements (such as air).[48] This is a very different kind of explanation from traditional mythical accounts. Mimnermos of Kolophon, for instance, speaks of the sun (the 'son of Hyperion') mounting 'a new (*heteros*) chariot' after travelling overnight from the westernmost Hesperides to the eastern shores of the world.[49] The popular supposition that the sun is extinguished in the Ocean at night and reborn anew would entail that today's sun was a wholly new entity, constituted of entirely different elements of matter from yesterday's sun. It is more in tune with the ideas of Herakleitos (whose notion of elemental reciprocity prefigures the Newtonian principle of the conservation of matter) to suppose that the disappearance of the sun at night is to be explained by its 'exchanging its fire' for other elements such

---

[46] By contrast, the Homeric epithet *ērigeneia* might suggest that Dawn (Eos) is 'young' since she is newborn at break of day.
[47] Herakleitos B64, B30, B76, B90. The authenticity of B76 has been doubted, but as Kahn (1979: 153–5) argues, while in form it is open to suspicion, its content has much in common with other expressions of Herakleitan thought on cyclicality (e.g. B36).
[48] The full citation by Aristotle (*Meteorology* 355a13–15) reads '*The sun* is not only, as Herakleitos says, *new each day*, but always new continually', and the whole sentence rather than just the italicised words could be taken as Herakleitos' words: Graham (2010) 192. The notion is fortuitously similar to the modern scientific account of the exchange of gases that takes place within the sun.
[49] Mimn. fr. 12; cf. the sun's cup in Stesikhoros S17. West (2007: 203–7) cites Indo-European parallels.

as water and air during the hours of darkness. The sun's reappearance at daybreak results from the recreation of its fiery imago 'by exchange' with those same elements.

Accordingly, the Herakleitan fragment that alludes to the idea that the sun is a fiery disk 'the breadth of a man's foot' can best be interpreted as a comment on the erroneous nature of human perception.[50] The understanding of perspective demonstrated in vase-paintings of the period refutes the persistence of such a naive view; and moreover, Anaxagoras supposed the sun to be a burning rock of molten lava larger than the Peloponnese.[51] 'The sun is new every day' might accordingly refer to the way the sun is *incorrectly* perceived as a 'new' object when it rises at dawn. What rises for Herakleitos could be thought of both as a 'new' sun and as the same sun, since the sun that people see is both the same and not the same object (hence 'new') as yesterday's.[52] A solution to this apparent contradiction was in due course articulated by Aristotle, with his distinction between formal and material causes: the sun is formally the same object, even if its material constituents are different. For Herakleitos, however, the constant flow and exchange of elements that constitute the sun's fire ultimately preserves the unity of apparent opposites, such as darkness and light, or night and day.[53] Such a collapse of oppositions yields the kind of paradox for which Herakleitos finds universal application:

What is in us is the same thing: living and dead, awake and sleeping, as well as young and old (*neon kai gēraion*); for the latter changes and becomes the former, and this again changes and becomes the latter.[54]

The use of *gēraion* here shows that Herakleitos is thinking of the opposition of *young* and old. On similar lines, however, *new* and old may be allowed

---

[50] Herakleitos B3; cf. *P.Derv.* col. 4.7 (Betegh 2004: 10–11).
[51] D.L. 2.8. According to Plutarch (*Lysander* 12), Anaxagoras foretold the fall of a meteorite at Aigospotamoi in 467 BCE (*DK* 59A12); in fact, this event could not have been predicted, but may have prompted his theorising about the nature of the sun. Cf. Bicknell (1968).
[52] In his *Carmen Saeculare* of 17 BCE, Horace skilfully combines the traditional image of the sun with this philosophical notion (vv. 9–11): *alme Sol, curru nitido diem qui / promis et celas aliusque et idem / nasceris...* ('Kind Sun, in your shining chariot you bring and hide the daytime, and are born new and the same...').
[53] Cf. Herakleitos B7: 'Hesiod is the teacher of very many, but he did not understand that day and night are one.'
[54] Herakleitos B88. Kahn argues (1979: 221) that Herakleitos generalises the notion of death to encompass 'any change of state in which something old gives way before something radically new'. Cf. B62: 'immortals are mortal, mortals immortal, living the others' death, dead in the others' life', on which Kahn notes (1979: 220) that Herakleitos' mystic language suggests 'the drastic novelty of his own insight into the unity of life and death, the radical, "unexpected" truth that awaits men beyond the grave'.

to collapse into one another and become 'the same thing'. What is new changes and becomes old, while what is old is in time replaced by the new. Taken to its logical conclusion, the denial that anything new can persist for an appreciable length of time, or for any time at all, means that nothing new can emerge into existence. We come full circle back to the conception expressed by Ecclesiastes that 'there is nothing new under the sun'.

THINKING NEW THOUGHTS (2)

In the opening scene of the *Odyssey*, Zeus complains that human beings are responsible for their misfortunes 'because of their own foolishness'.[55] The ultimate initiative may rest with the gods, but the multiple determination of events at least allows the perspective to shift between the divine sphere and the human. However, the generation of novelty from within is largely (though not wholly) precluded by the overarching theological perspective of archaic poets and thinkers.[56] The implication that the proper locus of new ideas is the individual's mind, independent of external sources of knowledge, is more regularly implied in the thought of Presocratic philosophers. Although some thinkers such as Thales and Pythagoras were said to have travelled widely to obtain knowledge of the advanced intellectual traditions of the Egyptians, Babylonians or even Indians, others were more culturally and intellectually hermetic.

A fragment of Demokritos speaks about 'people thinking new thoughts day by day' (*nea eph' hēmerēi phroneontes anthrōpoi*).[57] Where Herakleitos' 'day' evokes for him a principle of the reciprocal self-sufficiency of matter, that of Demokritos seems to raise the notion that time brings about genuine novelty, through the operation of individual minds generating 'new thoughts' on a daily basis. This would be at variance with the Herakleitan proposition that the reciprocal action of change and conflict results in a kind of changelessness and harmony of opposites.[58] Given Demokritos' own intellectual breadth and originality, one might suppose that he would view 'new thoughts' with approval.[59] Here he seems to be positively commending the notion that new ideas are continuously emerging in people's minds, in the way that Xenophanes had proposed that 'in time human beings think up improvements'. The notion of the daily production of new

---

[55] *Od*. 1.32–4. [56] Cf. Thales' dictum (A22) 'all things are full of gods'.
[57] Demok. B158. [58] Cf. Herakleitos B84a '[Fire] rests from change.'
[59] As Cartledge (1998a: 47) suggests, Demokritos' philosophical originality 'consists not only and not so much in novelty, but rather in powerful generalization and the fruitful interrelation of ideas'. Cf. the philosopher's express disapproval of *epikainourgein* (Chapter 2, n. 14).

thoughts ties in with the increasing recognition of unprecedented intellectual progress in Greek texts of the late fifth century. The *locus classicus* is the so-called 'ode to man' in Sophokles' *Antigone*:

> Many things are formidable, but none more formidable than man.
> He crosses the grey sea, driven by the wintry wind,
>   leaving his wake in the surge that would engulf him.
> He wears away the highest of gods, Earth, immortal and unwearying,
>   as year upon year his ploughs go to and fro, turning the soil with horses.
> He traps birds who fly free of care, and wild animals and the fish that teem in
>   the sea;
>   catching them in the woven coils of his net, man who excels in skill.
> By his arts he has subdued the mountain beast whose home is in the wilds,
>   and he tames the rough-maned horse and tireless mountain bull,
>   and puts a yoke on their necks.
> He has developed language, and thought swift as wind, and the tempers that
>   rule cities,
>   and how to escape the exposure of inhospitable hills and the arrows of rain.
> Resourceful in all things, he goes to meet nothing in the future without
>   resource.
> Only from Hades he has no means of escape, though for sicknesses without
>   cure he has devised relief.
> Wise beyond hope is the contrivance of his skill, that brings him sometimes
>   to evil, sometimes to good.[60]

That human beings might arrive at new knowledge from 'outside' or from within their own minds was explicitly noted by Arkhytas of Taras, the early fourth-century Pythagorean statesman and inventor:

> In subjects of which one has no knowledge, one must obtain knowledge either by learning (*mathonta*) it from someone else, or by discovering (*exeuronta*) it oneself. What is learned comes from someone else, with external assistance. What is discovered comes through one's own efforts, independently. To make a discovery without undertaking research (*zātounta*) is difficult and seldom happens, but with research it is possible and easily accomplished (though for one who does not know how to research, it is impossible).[61]

Arkhytas passes over the external mode of knowledge acquisition and goes on to comment further on 'research'. As an original thinker and inventor, he would have aligned himself less with those who could be credited with generating novel ideas for themselves. Personal experience will have underpinned his insistence on research (his dismissal of 'pure' thinking has a polemical ring). His theories of sound and hearing were derived

[60] Soph. *Ant.* 332–68.   [61] Arkhytas B3.

from empirical investigations, such as the observation of the way 'whirlers' (*rhomboi*) at the Mysteries emit different kinds of sound.[62] Research of this kind is almost wholly absent until the time of Arkhytas. The medical theorist Alkmaion of Kroton, around a century earlier, may have used dissection to inform his physiological views, and in the late fifth century Aristophanes' *Clouds* offers some ingenious comic instances;[63] but practical experimentation was still a rare and unsystematic phenomenon.

While the notion that new knowledge might be acquired through thinking for oneself without the benefit of research is not wholly dismissed by Arkhytas, he suggests that it is a rare and unlikely occurrence. He might have considered such 'knowledge' to include the kind of theories proposed by Presocratic philosophers about the material basis of the universe or the origins of human culture: inspired speculations, largely devoid of sound empirical foundations. Herakleitos' view that introspection is the right method for arriving at the truth is congruent with his disparagement of 'polymathy', with its implication of the promiscuous acquisition of ideas from disparate sources, including those outside the Hellenic sphere. The notion that one mind may engage with another to come up with a new idea is evident in practice by the sixth century. Successive Presocratic philosophers take up the challenge set by Thales in seeking new foundations for existence through competitive intellectual engagement with predecessors and contemporaries, a philosophical dialectic that demonstrates the continual search for new explanations and meanings.[64]

The Greeks recognised that many familiar things and ideas that came new to them had previously been known to others. Their origins were often forgotten or obliterated; but names and words of foreign sound and flavour, accounts of advent and alien intrusions, tales of exotic characters and remote places, presented clues that many cherished Hellenic traditions were not autochthonous or home-grown. For the most part, debts to external sources were absorbed, unacknowledged, into the mainstream of Greek culture and expression. Spheres of knowledge and expertise such as mathematics, sculpture, philosophy and architecture were transformed to become peculiarly and identifiably Greek in their style and presentation: 'whatever Greeks acquire from foreigners they eventually bring to a finer perfection' claims the Athenian in the pseudo-Platonic dialogue *Epinomis*.[65] In countless cases where the influence of external sources is presumed, the

---

[62] Arkhytas B1.   [63] Alkmaion: Guthrie (1962) 349. On *Clouds* see p. 213 below.
[64] In his revisionistic account of the Ionian philosophical tradition, Graham (2006) argues that 'it is unified historically as a series of connected explorations, and pragmatically as a series of contributions to a common program' (298).
[65] [Pl.] *Epin*. 987d.

Greeks appear to have suffered a wholesale cultural amnesia (the striking counter-example is the alphabet, discussed below). Early Greek poetry and literature in particular give no explicit indication of their debt to the Near East and Mesopotamia. Their roots in local and Indo-European traditions are no less passed over; rather than recognising Homer and Hesiod as inheritors and adapters of age-old traditions, Greeks accorded them quasi-divine status as supreme originals, constructing an imaginary template for a continuing tradition of musico-literary innovation. Forgetfulness, whether unintended or deliberate, has vital implications for the new. Since the identification of what is new or old is dependent on memory, ignorance of the past opens up new vistas for innovation.[66]

Novelty from 'outside' is not necessarily to be thought of literally. Taken to refer to the space beyond one's frame of knowledge or matrix of cultural experience, or located in supernatural realms beyond human reach, what is outside presents a potentially limitless source of novelty. By contrast to novelty that originates from within one's own mental and physical environment, the idea of new things coming 'from without' seems to compel a new perspective on one's place in the world. What is new in this way is a change of circumstances that seems to arrive from 'out there', a movement of difference that forces itself on one's attention, something that happens *to* an experiencing subject. It may be an unheralded visitation, an adventitious event, an unprecedented vision. Such novelty may arise as an unanticipated consequence of one's own efforts and actions, or in defiance of any prior action and expectation. It may be absorbed into one's identity and outlook, or remain immutably alien. The reaction to extraneous novelty may be pleasurable anticipation or discomfited rejection; the new may be perceived as an opportunity to be grasped or a monster to be tamed. Recognition of an external sphere highlights the existence of phenomena beyond one's acquaintance and control. To adopt, possess and transform the new into one's own creation is one form of innovation. Whether spurned or welcomed, novelty that comes from without seems to testify to the operation of independent forces, external agencies, factors beyond an individual's normal confines of awareness or attention.

EX ORIENTE NOVITAS

As the sun rising in the East brings a new day, so the 'orient' was viewed as a source of endless novelty. Substantial elements of Greek myth and religious

---

[66] Conte (1986) 70 n. 35 quotes Byron's mischievous comment regarding literary innovation, 'it is a bad thing to have too good a memory'.

practice, poetry and literature, art and architecture, music and science, demonstrate the debt. The earliest Greek mythology and wisdom literature have close parallels in Hittite, Sumerian and Akkadian traditions;[67] we can trace features of Greek temple construction to Syria and Palestine, the use of couches to Assyria, styles of monumental statuary to Egypt, and items such as the parasol to Asia Minor.[68] The origins of Greek science, mathematics and philosophy may also be traced to Babylonia, Egypt and Persia.[69] The Phoenicians were the immediate sources of contact and the most familiar go-betweens. From them the Greeks adopted new techniques of cloth-dyeing and metalwork; the latter may even underlie, as I have argued in Chapter 3 above, the development of the Greek word *kainos* (with its implication of metal artefacts emerging 'new from the fire'). Above all, Phoenicia imparted to Greece the technology of alphabetic script. The letter names, meaningless in Greek, unmistakably preserved its Phoenician heritage. In crediting the introduction of the alphabet to Phoenician Kadmos, Herodotos acknowledges genuine intercultural indebtedness, unlike his almost indiscriminate attribution to Egypt of many other elements of Greek culture.[70]

The myths that surround Kadmos carry a range of associations to novelty, reflecting different domains of innovation (cultural, historical, religious) and diverse mechanisms such as borrowing, metamorphosis and birth. He sowed the dragon's teeth from which sprang the Spartoi ('sown men'), and founded the city of Thebes. His daughter Semele, inseminated in unprecedented fashion by Zeus' thunderbolt, bore the 'twice-born' god Dionysos, the 'new' deity whose cult brought the Greeks face to face with new forms of otherness and initiatory transformation. Expelled from Thebes, he underwent metamorphosis into a serpent. His name, from Semitic *qedem* ('the orient'), proclaims his origins from Tyre in Phoenicia. The alphabet that Kadmos brought was adapted for Greek use from the Phoenician script, crucially supplemented by home-grown modifications (above all the use of symbols for vowels) but still called 'Phoenician letters', *Phoinikēia grammata*. As Herodotos recognised, this type of script was a new phenomenon in Greek culture:

The Phoenicians who came with Kadmos, of whom the Gephyraians were a part, settled this land and brought to the Hellenes many kinds of learning, and in particular taught them the alphabet which, I believe, the Hellenes did not have

---

[67] West (1978) 3–15; West (1997). [68] Burkert (1992); Miller, M. (1997) 193–4.
[69] West (1971); Heath, T. (1981[1921]) 8–9, Hodgkin (2005) 14–17; Lindberg (2007) 12–15.
[70] Hartog (2001) 50–4.

previously, but which was originally used by all Phoenicians. As time went on the sound and form of the letters were changed. At this time it was mainly Ionians who lived around the Phoenicians, and they were the ones first instructed in the use of the alphabet by them. After making a few changes to the form of the letters, they put them to good use, but when they spoke of them, they called them 'Phoenician' letters, as was only reasonable since the Phoenicians had introduced them to Hellas.[71]

The adoption of Phoenician letters was not the end of the story; to become the world's first alphabet, what was required was the creation of true vowel-signs. The names of those responsible are unrecorded, but additional refinements were credited to individuals: the invention of the supplementary letters *phi, khi, psi* and *ōmega*, used in the Ionic version of the alphabet, was attributed variously to Palamedes, Pythagoras and Simonides.[72] But despite such Hellenic innovations, the alphabet's eastern origins were not forgotten, its provenance indelibly stamped on it by the Semitic letter-names.

Travel, colonisation and warfare brought a vista of novel influences from foreign cultures. Herodotos tells how Solon of Athens, after instituting new laws for Athens, embarked on a ten-year journey to 'see the world' (*theōriēs heineken*).[73] In Lydia, his host Kroisos sought his advice on account of the wisdom (*sophiē*) he had acquired from his experience. 'As I grow older I am constantly learning many [new] things (*polla didaskomenos*)' are the words of Solon himself.[74] A traveller no less than Solon, Herodotos could identify with the sage and pride himself on the wealth of new knowledge and experience that might be acquired by years of travel and observation. While travellers experienced at first hand the wonders of the exotic and the unfamiliar, those at home could encounter novelty through imaginative engagement with the accounts of adventurers, historical figures and persuasive fictions. These were not only a source of new ideas and knowledge; authors such as Herodotos evince an enjoyment of difference and otherness for their own sake. In the *Odyssey*, the hero and others react in new ways to new experiences, encouraging hearers and readers to undertake their own voyages of discovery, physical or intellectual. Odysseus' journey reflects and symbolises the universality of change, inner and outer, in human life.

---

[71] Hdt. 5.58.
[72] Powell, B. (1991); the Ionic alphabet was officially adopted by Athens in 403 BCE (D'Angour 1999a).
[73] Hdt. 1.30.1.
[74] Solon fr. 18; my adaptation of Solon's words for this book's dedicatory epigram draws attention to the connection between the many (*polla*) and the new (*kaina*).

Odysseus is *polutropos*, 'versatile', on account of his character as well as his experiences.[75] While he does not set out to encounter monsters and marvels, his response to them tests and forms his character. His voyaging enables him 'to see the cities of men and know their thinking': the sheer multiplicity of sights, places and people is something to be celebrated. Greeks relished Homer's depiction and learned lessons of life through the constant rehearsal of the hero's adventures.

As well as seeking the origins of culture outside the Hellenic realm, the Greeks attributed inventions and discoveries (*heurēmata*) to gods, semi-divine benefactors and inspired individuals. Once a narrative of human evolution had arisen, it was assumed that the most important elements of human life had at one stage been new, so suitable founders needed to be found or invented. From the seventh century on, Greek literature contains scattered and unsystematic references to gods, peoples and characters credited with notably innovative achievements. Most of the necessities of human existence were on the whole considered by the Greeks to have been bestowed on mortals by gods. The results of human inventiveness, the legacy of what has been called the 'Neolithic revolution', were projected onto deities, semi-divine characters and 'culture-heroes', whose benefactions were enshrined in numerous popular myths and tales.[76] On these accounts, fire was not a human discovery, but a gift from the Titan Prometheus to humankind, grain was the benefaction of Demeter, wine of Dionysos. These attributions were perhaps an inevitable consequence of the ritual associations and identification of these substances with gods. The accoutrements of civilised life were also ascribed to divinities: the lyre was devised by Hermes, the chariot along with horse-taming by Athena, cheese-making and bee-keeping by Aristaios, son of Apollo and Kyrene. In the age of the sophists, these stories were subjected to rationalising explanations.[77]

By the fourth century, traditions were being compiled in heuremato-graphic treatises.[78] The Daktuloi ('Fingers') of Mount Ida in Crete are alleged to have invented ironwork, the Thebans are credited with constructing the first chariots; the Lydians are recognised as the creators of coinage and culture-heroes legendary and historical such as Palamedes and Pheidon of Argos are praised as the inventors of weights and measures. The desire to record 'discoveries' and 'inventions' (*heurēmata* covers both)

---

[75] Hartog (2001) 15–21.   [76] Burkert (1997) 22.
[77] E.g. by Prodikos, who argues (B5) that the human discoverers were elevated to the status of divinities.
[78] Kleingünther (1933).

points to a new interest in the inventive consciousness that might lead to things being brought into existence, usually through a recognition of some human need. Accounts of *heurēmata* not only documented past inventiveness, but served to promote the very notion of invention. The notion of initial discovery has peculiar force, and the impulse to determine who did what first, to identify a starting-point, requires an imaginative projection into the past. The praise and repute accorded to inventors offered a new kind of inducement to those capable of producing new ideas, objects and techniques for their own times and circumstances.

CHAPTER 6

The birth of Athena

All wonder is the effect of novelty upon ignorance.
            Samuel Johnson

Birth, wonder, light: the Greeks persistently associate these notions (and related images and narratives) with novelty. Ideas of origination are regularly accompanied by images of light, and both birth and light evoke responses of wonder and bedazzlement. Birth, the moment at which a new life is seen to begin, the visible entry into a world of change, is at the heart of a host of images of novelty; it is a frequent metaphor for origins and coming-to-be, natural or otherwise. Subjects both animate and inanimate, real and imaginary, young creatures and manufactured products, emerge into existence through the process of *genesis*. The notion gives central expression to the symbolic representation of the new in philosophical, historical and religious contexts; forms of *gignesthai* (to become, to be born) abound in writings that deal with origins and beginnings. In Greek poetry and prose, birth is equated with coming into the light (*es phaos*). That light is virtually synonymous with life: it is both a starting-point for new events, and a marker of continuity with old ones. Euripides' tragedy *Danae* begins with the heroine's father connecting the beauty of sunlight with the 'bright' birth of children:

My wife, this light (*pheggos*) of the sun is beautiful – just as it is beautiful to behold the sea when calm, the earth flowering in spring, the water teeming with riches – and I can tell the praise of many beautiful things: but nothing is so brilliant (*lampron*) or beautiful to behold, for the childless and those bitten by longing, as the light (*phaos*) of newborn children.[1]

In due season, departure from the light will constitute death, a passing back to the dark and the unknown. Only initiates of the Mysteries, 'knowing'

---

[1] Eur. *Danae* fr. 316.

ones (*eidotes*) enlightened with a vision of life beyond death, may hope to enjoy the prospect of renewed access to light.

Observation and contemplation of the way things have come into being – the birth of worlds, elements, gods, people or other creatures – are apt to inspire imaginative visualisations in the present and of the future. Early thinkers, I have suggested, continually raised the question of origins and causes (*arkhai, aitiai*), not because they were doggedly retrospective, as has sometimes been argued, but so that they might achieve fresher and truer insights into the nature of things. Speculation about *arkhai* prompted continual creative revisions of philosophical constructions regarding the way things had come into existence in the past, and might likewise arise in the future. The multiple guises and manifestations in which things are seen to arise offer a guide and template for how they will continue to emerge. That is why starting-points and beginnings, within the diverse milieus in which they occur, are seldom to be thought of merely as matters of ancient history. Even originary events are not located only in the remote past: far from being dead and buried, beginnings and origins are repeatedly renewed by Greeks in their solemn rites and seasonal practices. Through ritual iteration, divinised archetypes of primal moments and occasions are constantly relived and recreated.[2] Light is frequently found both as a sacral image and a practical adjunct to ritual.[3]

In addition to theories of cosmic origins, the Greeks readily projected the notion of birth onto the emergence of anthropomorphised objects such as planets and stars, natural elements such as seas and winds, and abstract phenomena such as love and thought. A novel idea might be 'conceived' by the mind, and, by a natural extension of the metaphor, a period of gestation could be expected to bring it to birth. In *Clouds*, Aristophanes plays on this imagery: a student in the Thinkery describes how a new thought conceived by Sokrates is prevented from coming to birth, literally 'aborted' (*exēmblōmenon*), by an unexpected interruption.[4] Sokrates likened his aim of bringing new ideas to birth to the task of a midwife;[5] and in Plato's *Symposium*, he defines love itself as birth-giving in relation to a beautiful object (*tokos en kalōi*).[6] Just as insemination may lead to the literal birth of a new child, so the philosophical engagement with the mind of another allows for the figurative birth of new ideas (*logoi*). The enhancement of the

---

[2] Cf. Eliade (1971).
[3] Parisinou (2000) explores the role of light and light-bearing utensils in cult practice and in contexts relating to rites of passage.
[4] Ar. *Nub.* 139. [5] Pl. *Tht.* 149ad; Sokrates' mother Phainarete was allegedly a midwife.
[6] Pl. *Symp.* 206b, 206e.

psyche by these means is, for Plato, not just a process of instruction by a teacher, but an act of love through which new knowledge can be brought to take root in the learner's mind. By means of this act, the true lover (*erastēs*) helps to turn the object of his love (*erōmenos*) into a new, and in principle better, person.[7]

In the lived experience of human beings, the event of birth is the first vital encounter with the new. It initiates the chance of a life in which change, novelty and eventually death are assured. The first of life's new experiences, though rarely if ever remembered as a sensation, may be reconstituted through subsequent thought or observation. It provides a latent, unconscious, template for the perception and representation of later encounters with new things. Revelatory events, changes of form, spiritual regeneration, transformations of identity – all draw on the imagery of birth and hark back to the sensation, real or imagined, of the birth-process. As the ground and condition of existential vicissitudes to come, both positive and negative, the event of birth carries an inevitable ambivalence. It means loss as well as gain: the initial separation of self from other that wrenches the neonate from the comfort of the womb is at the same time the gain of individuation.[8]

The advent of light is generally conceived of in positive terms, but the sudden, dazzling shock of luminosity which greets the newborn child is not always something to be welcomed. The irruption of light at the moment of birth, the first new experience of the newborn infant, may be associated with trauma no less than with pleasure.[9] In Greek, none of the earliest attested compounds with *neo-* and *kaino-* have positive associations. Adjectives such as *neokēdēs* in Hesiod, *neopenthēs* in Homer and *kainopathēs* in Sophokles juxtapose the notion of the new with worry, pain and suffering. In Greek tragedy, the metaphorical use of light and of coming-to-be often signals the disclosure of a hidden truth, or the unhappy revelation of bad news. In Euripides' *Hippolytus*, when the chorus learn that Phaidra has conceived a terrible passion for her stepson, they describe the discovery as a bringing of calamitous events (*kaka*) into the light, and express foreboding about what the revelation portends for Theseus' household:

---

[7] The *Symposium* arguably illustrates the failure of this ideal in the case of Alkibiades, perhaps reflecting Plato's own sense of failure regarding the philosophical education of the Syracusan tyrant Dionysios (Denyer 2001: 13–14).

[8] Caldwell (1993: 23–4, 132–42) explores the notion of psychological individuation in relation to the Hesiodic narrative of the birth of the gods.

[9] Otto Rank's theory that states of anxiety might be traced to 'birth trauma' was rejected by Freud (1926) on empirical grounds. The association of light with different types of newness is discussed further below, and see also p. 47 above.

Oh, the burdens that beset mortals!
You are undone, you have brought disaster into the light (*es phaos*).
What lies ahead for you in the hours of this full day?
There will come to pass some new state of affairs (*ti kainon*) for the house.[10]

The natural corollaries of birth are growth and ageing. What is 'new' at birth (*neognos*, new-born) is by the same token 'young', *neos*; and youth (*neotēs, to neon*) itself, though it may initially be distanced from the pains and sorrows that crowd in as life progresses, is destined for loss. Genetic novelty heralds its own eventual decline and reversal. What was once young will age and in due course die, and the natural cycle will come round anew.

The coming to fruition of calamitous events can lead to a desire to reject birth itself. The certainty of suffering in life prompts the melancholic view that it is best not to be born. In contemplation of the fate of Oedipus, the chorus in Sophokles' *Oedipus at Colonus* cites with approval the proverbial phrase:

> 'Not to be born' comes first on any
> reckoning; and once one has appeared,
> to go back to whence one came
> as soon as possible is the next best thing.
> For even while youth (*to neon*) is present,
> and with it light-headed freedom from care,
> what agonising blow of fate is far away?
> What suffering is not nearby –
> murders, civil strife, contention, battles
> and envy? And the next stage, the last, is despised old age,
> powerless, unsociable, and friendless, where all
> the worst of sufferings are close at hand.[11]

As so often, a trope that has a bearing on some aspect of novelty is itself apt to be reframed in a novel fashion. The provocative maxim 'best not to be born' was prone to literary palingenesis, and cited in different contexts as a gloomy, proverbial comment on the sorrows of the human condition.[12] It was also subjected to comic reversal and reinterpretation. 'I'd rather be alive again!' exclaims the corpse in Aristophanes' *Frogs*, disgusted at being offered an insufficient fee to transport Dionysos' baggage through the Underworld.[13] In a fragment of the fourth-century comic poet Alexis,

---

[10] Eur. *Hipp.* 368. [11] Soph. *OC* 1224–38.
[12] The sentiment is found in Theognis (425–428), Bakkhylides (5.160–2), and Euripides (fr. 285.1–2), and reappears in the fourth-century *Contest of Homer and Hesiod* (Alkidamas ap. Stob. 4.52.22).
[13] Ar. *Ran.* 177.

the maxim is used to cap, with humorous extravagance, a harangue against the petty inconsistencies of taste:

> We chill our drinks by adding snow,
> but complain when a starter isn't piping hot.
> We spit out wine that's too tart,
> but go into Bacchic ecstasy over sour pickles.
> So, as so many men of wisdom have said –
> *It's far better never to have been born,*
> *And once you're born, to end it as soon as possible.*[14]

THE BRAINCHILD OF ZEUS

The mythical and symbolic narratives that surround the birth and career of Athena demonstrate many common ancient perspectives on the notion of newness. Stesikhoros provides the first mention of how 'shining (*lampomenā*) in armour, Pallas sprang down to the broad earth'.[15] As described by the Homeric Hymn, the event of Athena's birth was itself a novelty, making a spectacular visual impact on the inhabitants of Olympos. Zeus had been warned that his offspring by Metis ('wisdom') would be greater than himself, and to foil the prediction had swallowed Metis when she was pregnant with Athena. In due course the divine child issued from her father's head, resplendent in armour:

> Zeus himself begot her
> from his divine head, holding weapons of war,
> golden and wide-gleaming; and awe (*sebas*)
> seized all who were watching, immortal as they were.[16]

The scene, depicted on Greek vases from the seventh century on, often shows Zeus accompanied at the birth of the goddess by the figure of the craftsman-god Hephaistos.[17] For such a novel form of birth, the attendance of the divine technician and blacksmith was required. Hephaistos is made to stand nearby, an obliging if ungentle midwife, holding an axe ready to split open the head of his immortal father so as to release the warrior goddess into the world.

Athena's association with Hephaistos as a fellow patron of *tekhnē* is already indicated in the *Odyssey*.[18] Both gods represent the range of skills

---

[14] Alexis fr. 145; Dobrov (1995) 72.
[15] Stes. fr. 233; a scholiast on Apollonios of Rhodes (4.1310) states that 'Stesikhoros was the first to say that Athena sprang in armour from Zeus' head.'
[16] *H. Hom. Ath.* 28.4–7.   [17] Schefold (1992) 7–15.   [18] *Od.* 6.233–4, 23.160–1.

required to make 'brand-new' objects, ranging from items of clothing to weapons of battle. In what may be the earliest of Homeric Hymns, that to Aphrodite, Athena is said to be concerned with 'splendid work' (*aglaa erga*):[19] 'she was first to teach mortal craftsmen to make carriages and chariots worked with bronze, and she taught splendid work to soft-skinned girls in their homes, instilling it into their minds'.[20] The god and goddess were jointly honoured in the Hephaisteion, the Athenian Temple of Hephaistos and Athena built in 449 BCE at the foot of the Akropolis, and at the Athenian festival of Khalkeia ('bronze-working'). Endowed with the epithet *Erganē* ('worker-woman'), Athena was the patron of wagon-wrights and shipbuilders, metalsmiths and potters.[21] In Arkadia there was a sanctuary to Athena the Contriver (*Mēkhanītis*), the inventor of ideas and devices.[22] An Orphic verse, 'when hands perish, resourceful Athena absents herself', equated the goddess allegorically with *tekhnē*.[23] The cunning wisdom (*mētis*) derived from her mother, together with the range of her functions and abilities, associates Athena with novelty of ideas as well as objects. 'I am preeminent among the gods' she declares in the *Odyssey*, 'for invention (*mētis*) and resource.'[24] Her favoured mortal hero is Odysseus who, with his epithets *polutropos* and *polumētis*, reflects and emulates the manifold resourcefulness of his divine patron.[25]

In the case of gods, the natural narrative of human origins and infancy is itself prone to dramatic revision and innovation. Events in the divine sphere do not accord with the laws of terrestrial nature. Apollo, whose birth was delayed due to Hera's hostility until he could be born on floating Delos, kills the Python while still a child and establishes his cult at Delphi.[26] Hermes too is no sooner born than he embarks on his inventive career, creating the lyre from a tortoise's shell, plaiting sandals with twigs, and displaying his cunning by dragging Apollo's cattle backwards into a cave so that the direction of their tracks would conceal the theft.[27] Dionysos was said to be born not just once but twice, the first time from his mother Semele's womb after her fatal impregnation by Zeus' thunderbolt, the second time from Zeus' thigh wherein he was concealed from Hera. The *di-* element

---

[19] H. Hom. Aph. 5.11: the root *ag-* connotes 'wonder' at something fine or bright.
[20] Ibid.12–15. [21] Paus. 5.14.5, 1.24.3. [22] Ibid. 8.36.5. [23] PEG 856F. [24] Od. 13.298–9.
[25] Detienne and Vernant (1978: 18–21) trace the Homeric associations of *mētis* to multiplicity, *poikiliā*, and shifting brilliance, qualities that give mastery in domains 'where each new trial demands the invention of new ploys' (21).
[26] Zeitlin (2002).
[27] H. Hom. Herm. 20–78. The newly invented lyre is described as a 'delightful plaything', *erateinon athurma* (40, 52), the sandals as *thaumata erga* (80). Subsequently the infant Hermes is credited with first producing fire from firesticks (111).

in the name of Dionysos and in his cult hymn *dīthurambos* seemed to offer confirmation of his double birth, and might also have suggested the possibility of a 'second birth' for those initiated into his cult.

In some versions of Athena's birth no mother is involved. Her emergence from the head of Zeus without any matrilineal aspect could serve to reinforce the fantasy of the self-sufficiency of fatherhood and the masculine intellect. In Aeschylus' *Eumenides*, the goddess votes to acquit Orestes of matricide after approving the idea that she herself was born of a father alone, as proposed by Apollo:

> The mother is not parent of the child,
> Only the nurse of what she has conceived.
> The parent is the father, who commits
> His seed to her, a stranger, to be held
> With God's help in safe keeping. In proof of this,
> Father there might be and no mother: see
> A witness here, child of Olympian Zeus,
> Begotten not in wedlock neither bred
> In darkness of the womb, a goddess whom
> No other goddess could have brought to birth.[28]

The story of Athena's birth offered a fertile source for literary adaptation. The comedy *Birth of Athena* (*Athēnās gonē*) by the late fifth-century poet Hermippos spawned a subgenre of *theōn gonai* ('births of gods') in the lost works of comedians of the late fifth and early fourth century such as Alexis, Antiphanes, Nikophon and Philiskos.[29] In adapting the traditional tales of divine births to the comic stage, they were able to add modernistic, rationalising twists. Rape, illegitimate births and the concealment of children – themes that had been from time immemorial projected onto the careers of Olympian gods – were elaborated for comic purposes. Subsequently, these motifs regularly reappear in the domestic dramas penned by poets of New Comedy. Athena was also subject to symbolic analysis and allegorical interpretation. Since she was literally Zeus' 'brain-child', the Stoic philosopher Khrysippos of Soloi (second century BCE) interpreted the story of her birth as symbolic of the fact that wisdom originates in the head.[30] The manner of the goddess's emergence suggests an understanding not explicitly proposed in ancient sources. Springing into existence fully formed, resplendent in her metal panoply, Athena undergoes no developmental stages requiring growth and learning (Hermes likewise is born with the ready-made traits

---

[28] Aesch. *Eum.* 658–66, trans. Thomson (2004). [29] Nesselrath (1995) 11–12.
[30] Struck (2004) 119.

of inventor and trickster). The eponymous goddess of Athens is an appropriate enough figure to patronise the Athenians' vaunted *kainotēs*. What she will become, she is from the start: Athena emerges at birth not just young, but new.

THE RADIANCE OF THE NEW

Newness, so hard to define as a quality in descriptive terms, may be more readily indicated by images. Metaphorical applications of qualities such as brightness and freshness are involved in our own constructions of the new no less than those of the Greeks. When we distinguish something as new by virtue of its looking, feeling, sounding or tasting different from something old, we regularly use epithets and criteria which may be independent of temporal attributes. 'Fresh' may be literally predicated of newly baked bread or recently obtained milk; but a quality of 'freshness' may equally be attributed to a classic poem, a philosophical argument, or a finely sculpted statue, all of which are far from young or recently produced.[31] Metaphorical descriptors of this kind defy the purely temporal attributes associated with novelty, and elide distinctions between age and youth. Eros is oldest of the gods because Love was present at the birth of the world;[32] but he was born a youth and is forever young, since love is the province of youth. The epics of Homer are the oldest known and were the most revered songs of the Greeks; but they sprang into birth at the 'dawn' of literature, and remain eternally 'fresh'. The statue of Aphrodite of Knidos with its unprecedented nudity seeks to provoke the 'shock of the new' in long retrospect, no less than at the time of its production; and Aristophanes' 'new ideas' (*kainai ideai*) are millennia old, but his inventiveness still 'sparkles'.

All that glisters is not gold, nor all that sparkles new. But what is new frequently manifests itself, literally or figuratively, as bright or radiant. Light is a metaphor for new experience, in the form of athletic success, intellectual illumination, moral enlightenment, or the reception of news. New religious insights and phenomena, experiences of revelation and epiphany, are described in terms of light. The advent of new knowledge or information can bring illumination or enlightenment, and may be likened to light piercing the veil of darkness. While the image of light does not invariably represent novelty, brightness is persistently linked to newness, notably

---

[31] Demosthenes speaks of witnesses being tried when 'fresh' (*prosphatos*) rather than after their crimes have become 'stale and cold' (*Against Meidias* 112).
[32] Cf. Pl. *Symp.*178a5–c2.

newness of an artful and manufactured kind. 'News' is literally communicated in the form of lit fires, torches or beacon-flares.[33] New objects and artefacts, whether metalware extracted new from the fire, new-minted gold and silver coins, cloth or wood glistening with fresh manufacture, radiate a visible newness.[34] A new sword gleams, a new jewel glitters.[35] Even if what makes such objects properly describable as 'new' or 'old' is a temporal attribute unrelated to their appearance – their having been recently, only just, manufactured or polished – they seem to possess in addition a more timeless quality of novelty.

Light out of darkness evokes the idea of novelty as *ex nihilo* emergence. This is philosophically problematic. Nothing comes from nothing, and in particular darkness and nothingness seem incapable of containing within themselves the light that is said to emerge from them. In some cases an external, divine, agency must be posited, as in the biblical story of creation. Operating outside human time and logic, God causes the appearance of light in or from the darkness: 'Let there be light' (*Gen.* 1.3) is the instruction that brings about the first 'new' event in the cosmos. In Hellenic thought too, the newness of creation may be all but identified with brightness. In Orphic doctrine, Time (*Khronos*) generates a 'bright white egg', from which the First-born (*Prōtogonos*) hatches:

> His most distinctive name is Phanes, 'the one who makes (or is) Manifest'. When he came forth the Aither and the misty Chasm were split open, and the gods were amazed at the unimagined light that irradiated the air from his dazzling, unseen body. In the *Hymns* he is addressed as the one 'who cleared the dark fog from before (our) eyes', as he flew about the cosmos, and 'brought the bright holy light, wherefore I call thee Phanes'.[36]

Because the advent of the light signals a new day, the light of dawn and the coming of day are intimately linked to newness. In Herakleitos' gnomic observation that the sun is 'new every day' and in Demokritos' reference to 'people thinking new thoughts day by day' (above, pp. 108, 126), newness is associated with the coming of day or with the novelty brought about by its advent. For Herakleitos, night and day, dark and light, form a continuum in such a way that he can designate them as 'the same thing', different

---

[33] Lewis (1996). [34] Cf. p. 83.
[35] Cf. Poseidippos' recently discovered *Lithika* (Austin and Bastianini 2002, epigrs. 1-20), a collection of epigrams about jewellery noted for its beauty and sparkle. Novelty as such is rarely explicit (e.g. 1.24–9 describes a glittering (*marmairon*) beryl necklace, but the reconstruction [*kharis kain*]*ē* is dubious; in. 2.28 *glumma ?n*[*eon*] of a 'newly incised' stone is more likely).
[36] West (1983) 203–4, referring to Orphic fragments 72 and 86. West goes on to cite in comparison an Egyptian hymn to the sun-god Reʿ (*ANET* 365f.).

The radiance of the new

aspects of an underlying unity (see p. 121). But for most observers, the contrast of night and day is exemplary and proverbial. Darkness can hardly be 'the same thing' as light. In common discourse it is constructed as its precise opposite – 'as different as night and day'. Darkness is the obscure, undifferentiated background against which emerging light appears, the source of new forms of existence and the basis of all further differentiation.

Episodes in Greek poetry from Homer onward use the imagery of light, brightness and 'wondrous' beauty in relation to newness, whether that newness is owed to deliberate human contrivance or thought to emanate from a divine source. We find elements of both divine origination and artisanship in, for instance, the description of Athena's immortal, ever-new, chariot in the fifth book of the *Iliad*.[37] These attributes are strikingly manifest in the detailed narrative of the fashioning of Akhilleus' new armour by the blacksmith-god Hephaistos in the eighteenth book.[38] In the latter passage the craftsman-god creates the artefacts in response to Thetis' request to replace the old armour of Akhilleus in which Patroklos fought and died. No word for 'new' is found throughout the long description, but the newness of the god's creation is pervasively indicated with a variety of epithets indicating radiance and intricate workmanship. What Hephaistos promises to provide for Akhilleus are 'beautiful' (*kāla*, 466) arms that anyone who beholds 'will be amazed by' (*thaumassetai*, 467). He proceeds to create the shield by 'adorning it (*daidallōn*, 479) all over' and surrounding it with a 'shining' (*phaeinēn*, 479) rim, threefold and 'glittering' (*marmareēn*, 480). On it he depicts cities that are 'beautiful' (*kālās*, 491), armies 'gleaming' (*lampomenoi*, 510) in armour, a field which, though chased in gold, causes 'amazement' (*thauma*, 549) by the way it turns dark where it is ploughed, and a vineyard 'beautiful and golden' (*kālēn khruseiēn*, 562). The shield is accompanied by a breastplate 'brighter' (*phaeinoteron*) than blazing fire (610) and a helmet 'beautiful and finely wrought' (*kālēn daidaleēn*, 612) with a golden crest. Thetis leaves Olympos with the 'glittering' (*marmaironta*, 617) armour for her son. Not once do we read of a 'new' shield or 'new' armour; but epithets and images signifying beauty, wonder and brightness are insistent and cumulative.

When Alkaios, the soldier-poet (seventh to sixth centuries BCE) from Mytilene on Lesbos, describes the radiance of a room hung with weaponry and armour, the explicit epithet *neos* is used just once. It appears alongside a

---

[37] *Il.* 5.722–31. In *Od.* 6.74, Nausikaa's linen may be imagined as new, though soiled, since it is described as *phaeinē* yet requires washing; this need not be incompatible with the oralist analysis of Homer's use of the epithet (Parry, M. 1971: 121).
[38] *Il.* 18. 462–617.

series of words that describe the light and glitter that emanate from shining artefacts, the proud products of human handiwork:

> The great house glitters (*marmairei*)
> with bronze. The entire ceiling is dressed for Ares
> with shining (*lampraisin*) helmets, down
> from which white plumes of horsehair
> nod, adornments (*agalmata*) for
> men's heads. Greaves of bronze
> cover the pegs on which they hang,
> brightly shining (*lamprai*), a means of defence against strong arrows,
> while corselets of new (*neō*) linen,
> and hollow shields, lie scattered about.[39]

The notion of beauty, the attribute of youth (*neotēs*) *par excellence*, is itself associated with what is bright and new; what is lovely 'shines'.[40] In the *Odyssey*, when heroes or heroines are 'renewed' by the action of gods or goddesses, the process is invariably indicated by the qualities of youthful radiance and beauty with which they are endowed, to the astonishment (*thauma*) of bystanders and observers. When Odysseus in Book 6 washes and dresses himself at Nausikaa's behest, Athena intervenes to give him an added sheen of miraculous beauty. Her action is compared in a simile to that of a craftsman in metal 'finishing' an artefact with gold:

Just as a skilled craftsman to whom Hephaistos and Pallas Athene have taught all manner of art puts a fine finish to his work by overlaying silver with gold, she finished now by pouring a sheen (*kharis*) over his head and shoulders. Odysseus went to sit down by himself on the sea-shore, radiant with beauty (*kallei stilbōn*) and grace, and the young woman gazed (*thēeito*) at him.[41]

Nausikaa's womanly gaze at Odysseus has a counterpart in the arguably erotic gaze of Herakles at the beautiful Meleagros, as described in Bakkhylides' fifth Ode. In admiration of Meleagros' appearance and stature, Herakles offers an oblique compliment by asking him if he has an unmarried sister whom he might make his wife. Such a girl is anticipated by Herakles to be 'radiant' (*liparā*), an epithet that indicates both her virgin youthfulness and her beauty:

'Is there in the palace of Oineus loved of Ares an untamed (*admēta*) daughter like you in stature? I should willingly make her my radiant (*liparān*) wife.'[42]

---

[39] Alkaios fr. 140.
[40] The etymology of *kalos* (from earlier **kalwos*) may be related to words indicating 'shining' such as Latin *calvus*, 'bald' (German 'kahl'), and perhaps Greek *kel-ainos*, '(shiny) black'.
[41] *Od.* 6.232–7.   [42] Bakkhyl. 5.169.

The new state that a woman enters into by marriage also evokes the imagery of light.[43] In Euripides' *Suppliant Women*, Evadne on the point of suicide recalls her wedding night with these words:

> What light (*pheggos*), what gleam (*aiglān*)
> did the sun bear forth on its chariot,
> and the moon across the sky as she rode
> swiftly accompanying my bridal celebrations
> through the darkness with her fast-moving torches?[44]

In the Victory Odes of Pindar and Bakkhylides, the success of the victorious athlete itself constitutes a new and noteworthy event. The triumph of the contestant brings 'sweet news' (*glukeian angeliān*); it is a 'victory which occasions new applause' (*neokroton nīkān*).[45] Pindar represents the salient juncture of victory with the imagery of light. The newly won success in the Games is likened to a shaft of radiance sent by Zeus. The divine gleam elevates and enriches, if only for a brief but glorious moment, the insubstantiality of human life:

> What is a someone, what is no one? A dream of a shadow
> is man; but whenever a Zeus-given gleam (*diosdotos aiglā*) appears,
> a brilliant light (*lampron pheggos*) falls on men, and life is sweet.[46]

With his new victory come to birth, the athlete returns to his community, a figure of radiance whose return rekindles the hearth of his *oikos*. The *oikos* of the athlete has sent out its 'shoot' to compete in the games, in the hope that it will be invigorated by new light on his victorious return: the imagery of light restored to the hearth is also applicable to the birth of an heir.[47] The return of the victor is assimilated to a new birth in, or a rebirth of, his household.

The recurrent event of the Games itself brings about the opportunity for regular new celebrations of victory. The opening of Pindar's fourth Olympian Ode invokes Zeus as the creator of the 'circling seasons':

Supreme charioteer of thunder with untiring feet, Zeus, I invoke you because
    your Seasons,
circling round to the lyre's varied tones, have sent me
as a witness of the greatest games.[48]

---

[43] Insofar as marriage is a change of state, it is akin to death; on the 'marriage-to-death' motif in tragedy, see Swift (2010) 250–5.
[44] Eur. *Supp.* 990–4.   [45] Pi. *O.* 4.5, Bakkhyl. 5.48–9.   [46] Pi. *P.* 8.95–7.
[47] Kurke (1991) 80–1. Cf. Eur. *Ion* 475–7: youths 'gleam' (*lampōsin*) in an ancestral home.
[48] Pi. *O.* 4.1–2.

Pindar goes on to welcome the news of the victory of his friend Psaumis of Kamarina:

> When guest-friends achieve success,
> good men right away rejoice at the happy news (*angeliā*).
> Come, son of Kronos, you who rule Aitna,
> windswept weight that presses down mighty hundred-headed Typhos,
> receive this Olympic victor
> and, for the sake of the Graces, welcome this celebratory procession,
> a most enduring light (*phaos*) for achievements of great strength.[49]

The poet has composed his song (dated to 452 BCE) for a celebratory procession (*kōmos*) which he designates as a 'light' (*phaos*, 10). The light of praise is here afforded by Pindar's own poetic craft (*sophiā*, *tekhnā*). The choral performance is the visible and resplendent marker of praise, one that will aim to lastingly commemorate the victor's achievement.

The association with light or brightness of things 'newly created' by virtue of human skill persists. Aeschylus' *Oresteia* trilogy begins with a series of symbolic equations of light with the advent of the new. The *Agamemnon* opens with the scene of the Watchman on the roof, who has been waiting for a signal, in the form of a lit beacon, that Troy has at long last been taken. His prefatory words allude to the absence of novelty: of the kind of novelty, that is, that might counteract the monotonous regularity of the cycles of day and night which he has had to endure:

> I beg the gods for release from these toils –
> from my year-long watch, during which I have lain
> on the roof of the Atreidai, resting on my elbows dog-wise,
> and come to know well the throng of stars of the night,
> and also those brilliant potentates, conspicuous in the sky,
> which bring winter and summer to mortals,
> observing them as they set and others rise.[50]

The shining constellations provide a light that is intimately connected to the cycle of night and day. The stars are manifestations of unchanging nature, the visible witness, as it were, of the continuing darkness that is unbroken night. For the Watchman, the new that is desired is *news*, which is not a function of nature but of human action and perception. Unlike the stars, the lamp that will break the endless cycle of nights by bringing news

---

[49] Ibid. 4–10. The invocation of Zeus as 'ruler of Aitna', the mountain under which Typhos is buried, recalls Pindar's earlier Pythian 1 (dated to 470), with its reference to the new foundation of the city of that name by its tyrant Hieron.

[50] Aesch. *Ag.* 1–7 (reading Campbell's *tērōn* in line 7).

of Troy's destruction is man-made. When the news comes, it is literally as well as figuratively in the form of light out of darkness:

> But now at last may good news in a flash
> Scatter the darkness and deliver us.
> (*The beacon flashes*).
> Hail, lamp of joy, whose gleam turns night to day![51]

The torches that provide such welcome news to Aeschylus' Watchman have a deadly counterpart, those of the Akhaian army that have recently set Troy ablaze. This side of the picture is painted by Euripides in his tragedy *Trojan Woman*. A series of references in the tragedy make the associations of *to kainon* inescapably malign. At the first entrance of Agamemnon's herald Talthybios, the Chorus describe him with dread as a 'dispenser of new reports' (231, *neokhmōn muthōn tamiās*). He confirms their fears, saying he has come to bring new instructions (238, *kainon angelōn logon*) that they are to be separated and assigned individually to serve Greek masters. When Kassandra emerges with a burning torch, the gleam (298, *selas*) immediately alarms Talthybios, who wonders if the Trojan women are planning to set themselves alight. Kassandra, however, sings with irony of her marriage to Apollo (308–41), prompting Hekabe to draw a bitter contrast between the happy torches that accompany a new bride and those that now presage sorrow (343–52). Subsequently the Chorus call on the Muse to sing a new mourning-song (513–14, *kainōn humnōn ōidān epikēdeion*) on the theme of Troy's destruction.[52] When Talthybios returns, Hekabe anticipates with dread the 'new plans' (708, *kaina bouleumata*) he will announce: what transpires is the horrifying proclamation that her grandson Astyanax will be thrown from the battlements. All that remains to Hekabe is to pray that the hateful Helen, the cause of Troy's downfall, will be duly punished according to divine justice. Her invocation to Zeus is couched in novel terms, reminiscent of the kind of fifth-century philosophical 'kainotheism' which was popularly equated with atheism:[53]

> Vehicle of Earth, you who have your seat thereon,
> Whoever you may be, so hard for conjecture to discover,
> Zeus, whether you are nature's necessity or the intelligence of mortals...[54]

'How newfangled your prayers to the gods are' (889, *eukhās hōs ekainisas*, literally 'how you have innovated your prayers'), responds Menelaos.

---

[51] Ibid. 20–2. [52] On this 'new hymn', see p. 194 below.
[53] '"Kainotheism" is not an alternative to atheism but the form it takes': Parker (1996) 204–5.
[54] Eur. *Tro.* 884–6.

Hekabe's novel style of prayer will fall on deaf ears. Finally, when Talthybios enters to announce the order for the city's destruction, the Trojan women anticipate their city's fate. The gleaming fires of destruction are immediately associated with the fearful nexus of *kainotēs* that has afflicted their city:

> Ah, ah! Who are these men I see on Troy's heights
> with gleaming torches waving
> in their hands? To Troy's woes
> some new horror (*kainon ti kakon*) is about to be added.[55]

NOVELTY AND WONDER

Things may arouse surprise or admiration because they are new. Equally, they may be experienced as 'new' because they are objects of awe or wonder. When Sokrates asks Euthyphro, in the Platonic dialogue named after him, whether he really believes the shocking things said about the gods' behaviour are true, the brash young soothsayer replies: 'Yes, Sokrates, and so are even more surprising things (*thaumasiōtera*), about which most people are ignorant.' When Sokrates suggests that these things include 'theomachies, myths elaborated by painters and stories embroidered on the *peplos* of Athena', Euthyphro agrees, adding that there are many other things that he knows Sokrates 'would be astounded (*ekplagēsēi*) to hear'. Such stories would indeed be new to Sokrates, and his reply to Euthyphro's claim to esoteric knowledge is suitably double-edged: 'I should not be surprised (*ouk an thaumazoimi*).'[56] Similar connections of thought are regularly found in Attic drama. In Euripides' *Iphigeneia among the Taurians*, for instance, when a herdsman arrives claiming to bring 'new reports' (*kaina kērugmata*), Iphigeneia asks 'What is startling (*ekplēsson*) about your announcement?'; and after the herdsman tells his tale, the Chorus exclaim 'Wondrous (*thaumasta*) are the things you have said.'[57] Towards the end of Aristophanes' *Birds*, the chorus ringingly declare 'Many (*polla*) and novel (*kaina*) and wondrous (*thaumasta*) things have we flown high above, and many strange things (*deina*) seen!'[58]

The memorialisation of phenomena that arouse wonder (*thōma* in the Ionic dialect) is part of the programmatic declaration of the opening paragraph of Herodotos' *Histories*:

---

[55] Ibid. 1256–9. [56] Pl. *Euthyphro* 6bc. [57] Eur. *IT* 239–40, 340.
[58] Dunbar (1995: 689) rightly doubts that these words are intended as a parody of Sophokles' *polla ta deina* etc. in *Antigone* 332; *contra* Segal (2001) 509 n. 95.

The inquiries of Herodotos of Halikarnēssos are presented here, to preserve the memory of the past by putting on record the important and astonishing achievements (*erga megala te kai thōmasta*) of Greeks and non-Greeks, and in particular to show how they came into conflict.[59]

The wonders recorded by Herodotos notably include unprecedented feats of engineering such as those he describes on the island of Samos: the temple of Hera, the harbour mole and the tunnel of Eupalinos.[60] These constructions were not recent, but the brilliance of their accomplishment and their capacity to evoke awe and admiration made them 'news' to the historian and his audience.

Awe, wonder and astonishment (*sebas, thauma, thambos*) involve a reawakening of the senses. This is often expressed in visual terms, as the dazzling experience of being in the presence of exceptional beauty, youth, wisdom or strength. The awe, *sebas*, that seizes the immortal observers of Athena's birth is a reaction to the radiance of the goddess's epiphany, and to the unprecedented novelty of her manner of birth. In the epic, *sebas* is what Nestor feels when he sees young Telemakhos in Pylos, the image of his father, and what Odysseus admits to feeling at the sight of Nausikaa's grace and youthfulness.[61] In the Homeric Hymn to Demeter, *sebas* and *thambos* describe the reaction of Persephone to the ensnaring 'wonderfully gleaming' narcissus.[62] *Thambos* is Akhilleus' response to the epiphany of Athene when she appears to him as he ponders drawing his sword to strike Agamemnon for the insult he has suffered; it seizes Telemakhos when the goddess, having appeared to him in the guise of Mentes, takes her leave.[63] *Thambos* is the stupefaction that assails Helen when she is confronted by Aphrodite 'of the flashing eyes', and that besets Aiolos' household when Odysseus returns unexpectedly and inopportunely to the palace of the winds.[64] *Thauma* is the imagined response of the viewer to Akhilleus' magnificent new shield, and of Priam when he first sees Akhilleus at close quarters.[65]

Even if an object of wonder is familiar, the experience of *thauma* may create a new perspective which transports the observer into new realms of emotion, thought or feeling. As in the case of Akhilleus' shield, *thauma* is an appropriate response to works of notable skill and inventiveness. 'The

---

[59] Hdt. 1.1.1.   [60] Ibid. 3.60; on the tunnel of Eupalinos, see Rihll and Tucker (1995).
[61] *Od.* 3.123, 6.161.
[62] H. Hom. Dem. 10, *thaumaston ganoōnta, sebas to ge pāsin idesthai*; 15 *thambēsāsa*; In Soph. *El.* 685, Orestes is described as *lampros* and attracts *sebas*.
[63] *Il.* 1.199, *Od.* 1.323. cf. H. Hom. Dem. 187–90, 275–83.   [64] *Il.* 3.397–8, *Od.* 10.63.
[65] *Il.* 18.467, 24.629.

wondrous works (*thaumata (w)erga*) shone bright' writes pseudo-Hesiod, describing the jaw-gnashing snakes on the shield of Herakles.[66] Objects of art, particularly representative images and sculpted figures, could seem to have quasi-magical qualities. The term for these were *agalmata*, literally 'things that give rise to wonder/delight'. In the case of legendary Daidalos, supposedly the originator of realistic figurative sculpture, statues seemed literally to come alive;[67] and earlier wooden statues that could be found in shrines and temples were felt to lack their human appeal (*kharis*).[68] While lacking in sophisticated technical skill, however, the older statues could still be revered for their aura of sacredness, as might an ancient hymn:

> They say that Aeschylus, when asked by the Delphians to write a paian for the god, replied that the best paian had been written by Tynnikhos. He said that if his own composition were compared to the latter's, it would be like comparing new statues with old. The old, though simply made, are felt to be divine. The new ones arouse admiration for their elaborate workmanship, but give less of an impression of holiness.[69]

THE SHOCK OF THE NEW

A different kind of *thauma* could be experienced in response to works of art that displayed the naturalism which visual depictions increasingly strove to attain. The illusionistic goal of art is a theme which runs throughout ancient literary appreciations of representational art, which are mainly preserved in much later sources such as Pausanias' *Description of Greece* (second century CE) and the *Natural History* of the first century CE Roman polymath Pliny the Elder.[70] These authors were, however, to some extent compilers of artistic traditions dating to at least the fourth century BCE.[71] The judgements Pliny expresses reflect the views of these earlier commentators, which may in turn have derived from contemporary and near-contemporary artistic evaluation and criticism. Responses to innovation in art may also be inferred from allusions in literary sources, and from passages in later writers such as Diodorus, Plutarch and Lucian, who occasionally offer explicit

---

[66] [Hes.] *Scut.* 165; Pollitt (1974) 189–90.   [67] Zenob. 1.14; Morris (1991) 215–37.
[68] [Pl.] *Hipp. ma.* 282a. It was commonplace that sculptors of *kolossoi* used illusionistic techniques which involved some understanding of perspective effects, and the criteria for judging a painting for its ability to present a realistic depiction could be quite demanding: Pl. *Soph.* 236a, *Crit.* 107d.
[69] Porph. *De abst.* 2.18. The 'ancient image' (*palaion bretas*) of Athena is reverently mentioned in Aesch. *Eum.* 80; cf. Paus. 1.27.1, 2.4.5.
[70] The relevant chapters (36–9) are compiled and annotated by Jex-Blake and Sellers (1896).
[71] Pliny, for instance, cites Douris of Samos (*c.*340–260) as a source, as well as third-century BCE authorities Xenokrates of Sikyon and Antigonos of Karystos: Tanner (2006) 212–14.

accounts of artists considered to be conspicuously innovative by ancient viewers.

Surviving ancient artworks can aid the evaluation of Greek artistic experience, but cannot tell us how contemporaries themselves viewed the innovative features which we may ascribe to them.[72] Without written testimonies, for instance, it would be hard to imagine that Praxiteles' 'Aphrodite of Knidos' (*c*.340 BCE, known from a Roman copy) was to become the focus of unprecedented admiration in its time.[73] The recognition of artistic innovation also depends on what different artistic genres signified to its viewers: the aesthetic appeal of art was rarely its sole or primary function. As the words *tekhnē* and *ergon* imply, art was primarily something that required skill and labour, the product of which might be tangible and utilitarian, but might also partake of the sacral dimension accorded to culturally significant activities. This significance may itself have been shifting, just as intellectual innovations in the increasingly secular atmosphere of the late fifth century were affecting the connotations of words such as 'nature', 'soul' and 'god'.

The naturalistic revolution in Greek visual art is standardly thought to fall at the boundary between the archaic and classical periods.[74] According to Pliny, the Athenian painter Apollodoros (active at the end of the fifth century) 'was the first to represent realistic figures, and was the first to confer glory justly on the paintbrush'.[75] For Plutarch, Apollodoros symbolised Athens' claim to artistic excellence:

This city has been the mother and kind nurse of many other arts, some of which she was the first to discover and bring to light, while to others she added strength and honour and advancement. Not least, the art of painting was by her enhanced and embellished. Apollodoros the painter, the first man to discover the art of creating depth with light and shade, was an Athenian. Regarding his works the following verse was composed: 'Easy to deprecate, harder to emulate'.[76]

The idea of painting's power to deceive was traditional; as with sculpture, it was largely judged according to its success in presenting a realistic

---

[72] Cf. Tanner (2006) 116–17.
[73] Pliny *N.H.* 36.20–1. In a society long familiar with lifelike portrayals of men but not women, the sensuous portrayal of a nude female body in the guise of Aphrodite may have seemed both exciting and novel: the response to Praxiteles' Aphrodite suggests an ancient approximation to the 'shock of the new': Spivey (1996) 178–86, Havelock, C. (1995).
[74] Gombrich (1960) 99–125; Tanner (2006) 31–2 considers change in the visual arts in relation to developments of Greek religious and social attitudes.
[75] Pliny *N.H.* 35.60: the judgement derives from Xenokrates.
[76] Plut. *Glor. Ath.* 2 (*Mor.* 346a): Pliny ascribes the verse to Zeuxis (*N.H.* 35.62).

depiction.[77] An anonymous sophistic writer notes that 'in tragedy and in painting, whoever is most deceptive in making things like the truth is the best';[78] and Empedokles cautioned against the deceptions presented by temple-paintings.[79] Gorgias, however, stresses the delight afforded by artistic multiplicity:

> When painters create a single figure and image out of many colours and forms, they give delight to the sight; and the creation of sculptures and the fashioning of statues affords a divine pleasure to vision. In this way it can make eyes grieve or make them yearn. A profusion (*polla*) of images engenders in many people (*pollois*) a love of diverse (*pollōn*) actions and figures.[80]

Pliny's anecdote about the two most celebrated late fifth-century painters, Parrhasios of Ephesos and Zeuxis of Herakleia, makes naturalism the sole canon of artistic value judgement:

> Parrhasios is said to have embarked on a contest with Zeuxis, who produced a picture of grapes so successfully that birds flew up to the stage buildings. Parrhasios then painted a curtain with consummate realism. Zeuxis, full of pride at the birds' testimony to his skill, eventually requested that the curtain be drawn and his picture shown. When he realised his error, he conceded defeat with a modesty that did him honour, saying that while he himself had only deceived the birds, Parrhasios had succeeded in deceiving him, though he was himself an artist.[81]

Parrhasios was also highly praised for a public depiction of *Demos*, which was thought to capture the mercurial nature of the Athenian *dēmos* as 'fickle, irascible, unjust, at the same time merciful, gentle and compassionate, boastful and proud yet humble, bold yet timid, and all equally'.[82] The painting was emulated by Euphranor of Corinth (mid fourth century);[83] the latter drew attention to his use of *chiaroscuro* (the use of highlights and shading to give the illusion of depth) in commenting that Parrhasios' Theseus was fed on roses, his on beef.[84]

---

[77] Pl. *Soph.* 236a, *Crit.* 107d. Myron's sculpture of a heifer (early fifth century) is extensively praised for its realism in numerous epigrams that are preserved (*Anth. Gr.* 9.713–42).
[78] *Diss. Log.* 3.10 (2.410.30–411.1 *DK*). The moral aspect of the question was to exercise Plato, who censured painting as a *mimēsis* at a remove yet further from reality than the object itself: Pl. *Rep.* 596e–597e.
[79] Emped. B23. [80] Gorg. *Helen* 18.
[81] Pliny *N.H.* 35.64–5; another story records Parrhasios being worsted in a competition at Samos with Timanthes of Kythnos (*N.H.* 35.72). A verse is preserved in which Parrhasios boasts of 'having revealed (*heurēsthai*) the limits of art': Athenaeus 12.543e.
[82] Pliny *N.H.* 35.69. [83] Paus. 1.3.3.
[84] Pliny *N.H.* 35. 129, Plut. *Mor.* 346a. Parrhasios' Theseus may have been included in the same composition (in the Stoa Eleutherios) as his *Demos*: Robertson (1981)152.

The shock of the new

In discussing parallels between rhetoric and painting, Lucian suggests that there was a self-conscious pursuit of innovation by fifth-century artists:

> Zeuxis, the most excellent of painters, avoided as far as possible painting popular and hackneyed subjects like heroes, gods and battles. He was always trying to be novel (*kainopoiein*), and whenever he thought up something unusual (*allokoton*) and strange (*xenon*) he demonstrated the precision of his artistry (*akrībeian tēs tekhnēs*) in its depiction.[85]

An example of the artist's provocatively novel approach was his depiction of a female centaur nursing twin centaur babies.[86] But the impression of novelty-seeking may have been more in the minds of the viewers than in that of the artist, whose primary aim may have been to achieve greater *akrībeia*. Zeuxis himself was said to have repudiated popular applause as insufficiently discriminating:

> When Zeuxis saw that the novelty of the subject was the focus of their attention and distracted them from the technique of the work so that its accuracy of detail was a side-issue, 'Come, now', he said ... 'these people are praising the mere clay of my craft. They're not interested whether it is finely and skilfully executed in terms of light and shade: the novelty (*kainotomiā*) of the subject counts for more than precision of workmanship.'[87]

However, the attribution to Zeuxis of a conscious attempt to be original is in keeping with the competitive spirit of the age. Both he and Parrhasios were remembered as 'innovative personalities' in their lifestyle and couture;[88] but Zeuxis' imaginative sensationalism distinguished him from his rival, whose sober images set a standard for later representations.[89]

The story of the *agōn* between Parrhasios and Zeuxis highlights recurrent themes in the Greeks' cultural imagination: competitiveness, deceitfulness and breaching the limits of *tekhnē*. An explicit indication of the first of these is apparent in the comment written on an early fifth-century Greek vase, which seems to point to the use of foreshortening in the artist's depiction of the symposiasts; its creator Euthymides boasts 'Painted by the son of Polios, as never Euphronios did' (*hōs oudepot' Euphronios*).[90] Artists,

---

[85] Lucian, *Zeuxis* 3.
[86] Tanner (2006) 179–80; such bizarre novelties might 'attract the crowd's applause' (the disparaging phrase of the Hippocratic author ([Hp.] *Art.* 4.182.15–20) in relation to the 'succussion-ladder' used to shake patients with physical deformities such as hunchback). Pretzler (2009: 163–9) cautions that the picture may be Lucian's own invention.
[87] Lucian, *Zeuxis* 7; the rejection of popular taste as a way of highlighting the artist's quality becomes a literary trope, e.g. in Call. *Ep.* 28.4 (cf. Hor. *Odes* 3.1.1, *odi profanum vulgus et arceo*).
[88] Athenaeus 12.543, Pliny *N.H.* 35.62: cf. Tanner (2006) 175, who suggests that 'they were seeking to redefine the role of visual artist by personifying it in a fundamentally new way'.
[89] Quint. *Inst. Or.* 12.10.5–6.   [90] Robertson (1981) 64–5.

as well as rhetoricians, musicians and physicians, might seek to outdo their fellows in technical and imaginative inventiveness.[91] Art historians detect in the refined and fussy style of the sculpture produced towards the end of the century, exemplified by the wind-blown drapery on the reliefs on the temple of Athena Nike on the Akropolis, a retreat from the loftier artistic ideals of the High Classical era. The pursuit of formal detail, masking the absence of a confident artistic statement, has been compared to the rhetorical gestures of Gorgianic prose.[92] Some of these developments, occasionally discernible from the archaeological record, may have been presented by the sculptors as technical and stylistic innovations; an example may be the Corinthian capital, which first occurs in the temple of Apollo Epikourios ('the Helper') at Bassai, its invention attributed to the sculptor Kallimakhos of Athens.[93] The temple itself is notable for its novelty of design and other unusual features (such as its north-south orientation).[94] While the essentially Doric structure lacks such refinements as the Parthenon's subtle horizontal curvature, other features, such as the ornamental interior columns and the theatrical poses of figures on the frieze, seem to anticipate the styles of the fourth century.[95]

The novel features of the Bassai temple may perhaps be connected with a new, theoretically informed critique of prevailing architectural and artistic canons. The advent of more widespread literacy and increased communications throughout the Greek world will have had an incalculable effect on the understanding of artistic accomplishment and on self-conscious attempts to innovate. Polykleitos' *Kanōn*, the first attested professional treatise on sculpture, applied mathematics and geometry to determine the principles of *summetriā* and proportions of the human figure.[96] Beauty, Polykleitos wrote, arises 'in minute details through complex mathematical calculations'.[97] Polykleitos' *Doryphoros* (spear-bearer), constructed according to these principles, demonstrated his artistry in practice; 'he is the only man', writes Pliny, 'who is thought to have embodied the principles of his art in a work of art'.[98] Artistic production of a high order could be viewed

---

[91] However, the notion that painting contests took place at the Isthmian and Pythian festivals (Pliny *N.H.* 35.58) appears to be a fantasy: Jex-Blake and Sellers (1896) lxiv.
[92] Pollitt (1972) 123–5; this view is contested by Hallett (1986).   [93] Vitr. 4.1.9–10.
[94] Cooper (1968); Stewart (2008) 214–18.   [95] Pedley (1992) 278–80.
[96] Cf. Stewart (2008) 144–7.
[97] Philo Mech. 4.1, p. 49: 20, cf. Plut. *Mor.* 45c. On Polykleitos' interest in precision in practice, cf. his statement that 'the work is hardest when the clay comes to the nail' (*eis onukha*), a notion that I have argued is at the root of Horatian *ad unguem* ('to a nicety'): D'Angour (1999b).
[98] Pliny *N.H.* 34.55, quoting Varro whose source was Xenokrates (cf. Jex-Blake and Sellers (1896) on *N.H.* 34.56.9).

as a *tekhnē* worthy of respectful consideration and intellectual analysis. A Hippocratic author casually illustrates the tendency to draw notions from one field to invigorate another when he writes 'In my opinion, whatever some expert or physician says or writes about "nature" is less suited to medicine than to painting (*graphikē*).'[99] Physicians who proposed 'novel hypotheses' about humours were (illegitimately, in his view) applying the painter's technique of combining different pigments to depict a human figure.[100]

The newly vigorous debate about the relationship of *nomos* and *phusis* will have encouraged artists to experiment with ways in which the *phusis* of a sculpted object or painted scene might be represented through the application of artistic *nomoi*.[101] Conversely, philosophers whose physical theories led them to examine the nature of perception may have been inspired by new graphic techniques. The treatise by Agatharkhos of Samos on his use of perspective (*skēnographia*, which he was said to have invented) was known to Anaxagoras and Demokritos.[102] As a physical atomist, Demokritos held that the true nature of an object was distinct from the way it was seen. 'Colour exists by convention', he writes, and sight, along with the other elements of perception, is not a genuine but an 'obscure' (*skotiē*) kind of knowledge.[103] If vision was an illusion, art was a fortiori illusory, and innovation in art might be theorised as progress in the creation of just such an illusion. A noteworthy use of foreshortening may be seen in vase-paintings of the 420s by the Eretria Painter and the Meidias Painter.[104] The technique was also used with considerable effect by the painter Timanthes of Kythnos, a contemporary of Parrhasios:

Wanting to emphasise, within the small frame of a picture, the size of a sleeping Cyclops, he painted some satyrs nearby, using a ruler to make them the same size as the Cyclops' thumb. He is the only artist whose works always suggest more than is in the picture, and while his technique is consummate, his imagination (*ingenium*) surpasses it.[105]

---

[99] [Hp.] *VM* 20.8–11 (Loeb). [100] Pl. *Crat.* 424de.
[101] On the *nomos/phusis* controversy see Heinimann (1987 [1945]), Kerferd (1981) 111–30.
[102] Vitr. 7 *praef.* 11. The technical connotation of *skēnographia* may be distinguished from its literal meaning 'scene-painting', the invention of which was attributed to Sophokles (Arist. *Poet.* 1449a18); cf. Padel (1990) 347–52.
[103] Demok. B9, B10b, B11. Surviving titles of works by Demokritos include *On Colours, On Disproportionate Lines and Solids* and *On Painting*: A5h, A11p, A28a.
[104] Pollitt (1974) 240–7.
[105] Pliny *N.H.* 35.74. Plato considered such techniques akin to conjuring tricks which aim to deceive by taking advantage of some weakness in human nature: *Rep.* 602cd.

Although explicit attributions of stylistic newness are sparse, some ancient judgements on what was thought to distinguish older styles of art from newer styles accord with modern views about the development of the Greek artistic vision. The Hellenistic literary critic Demetrios, in seeking to contrast the simple style of early orators with the greater complexity of their successors, drew a parallel with the contrast that archaic statuary presented to the works of Pheidias and his successors:

> The earlier rhetorical style is well-polished and neat, rather like ancient statues whose art seemed to lie in their compactness and economy. Their successors' style is like the sculpture of Pheidias, in having a quality of grandeur combined with precision (*akrībes*) in detail.[106]

Demetrios here offers Pheidias as a chronological marker separating old from modern works; but the attribution of qualities such as grandeur and precision shows that distinction of old from new could be a matter of style as much as chronology. Pausanias uses *arkhaios* with similar stylistic connotations to describe the properties characteristic of art of the Archaic period (i.e. before 480 BCE).[107] Works of this kind might be identifiable as 'old-fashioned' both in their composition and by the comparative simplicity of their workmanship; and we might concur with judgements of this kind in comparing, say, the static, impassive *kouroi* of the early Archaic period with the more lively and fluid creations of the High Classical and Hellenistic periods.

The modernistic desire to achieve greater *akrībeia* could lead to over-elaboration. Kallimakhos, the reputed author of the Corinthian column, was, according to Pliny, both tireless in the execution of his art and his own harshest critic in this regard: 'from this he received the nickname *Katatēxitekhnos* ('Pernickety'), a noteworthy warning that even diligence has its limits. His *Spartan Girls Dancing* is a work of consummate technique which has lost all charm through fussiness.'[108] The pursuit of originality put pressure on artists to seek undesirable effects to impress their viewers and peers, but new elements of technical mastery in art and sculpture were to culminate in the achievements of fourth-century painters such as Euphranor of Corinth and Apelles of Kos, and heralded the sculptural masterpieces of Praxiteles of Athens and Lysippos of Sikyon.[109]

---

[106] Demetr. *Eloc.* 14.   [107] E.g. Paus. 10.38.7, 8.40.1.
[108] Pliny *N.H.* 34.92; Pausanias (1.26.7) and Vitruvius (4.1.10) give a more favourable view of the artist.
[109] Stewart (2008) 230, 310; 257–64, 285–90.

BIRTH INTO THE NEW

'I am come, the son of Zeus' (*hēkō Dios pais*) announces Dionysos at the beginning of Euripides' *Bacchae*. The opening scene brings the god onto the stage in the guise of a mortal 'stranger'. Having travelled from Phrygia to Thrace, he arrives in Greece accompanied by a band of raving devotees, the maenads, and the womenfolk of Thebes are roused from their homes and hearths into joining the ecstatic bacchants on the slopes of Mount Kithairon. The joy with which the women greet the introduction of Dionysos is matched by the anger and alarm of their menfolk, as represented by Pentheus, Dionysos' cousin and the ruler of Thebes. Pentheus' father Kadmos and the aged prophet Teiresias are wiser, and don the apparel and accoutrements associated with Dionysiac cult, claiming to be beneficiaries of a miraculous rejuvenation:

> KAD: I wouldn't tire night or day from striking the earth with the thyrsus. In our joy we have forgotten our old age.
> TEIR: Then you're experiencing the same things as I. I too feel young and in a mood to dance.[110]

Kadmos views Pentheus' furious agitation as he approaches, and asks Teiresias with a familiar expression of apprehensiveness: 'What will he say now?', *ti pot' erei neōteron* (lit. 'what will he say that is newer?').[111] Pentheus' opening words pick up on the notion that the recent, destabilising, events are a cause for alarm:

> I happened to be absent from this land,
> and I've heard of the troubles newly come (*neokhma kaka*) to this city:
> that our womenfolk have deserted their homes
> in fake Bacchic revels, and are darting around
> in the thickly wooded mountains, honouring this parvenu god (*ton neōsti daimona*)
> Dionysos, whoever he is, with dances.[112]

Pentheus goes on to reject Dionysiac cult with scorn as a pretext for sexual licence. He accuses Teiresias of 'introducing this new god to mankind' (*ton daimon' anthrōpoisin espherōn neon*, 256) so that he may benefit from the extra fees he can earn as a diviner.

While the use of *neos* in this sentence straddles the meanings of 'young', 'additional' and 'recently come', the more colourful term *neōsti* (219) is both more pejorative and less ambiguous. For Pentheus, Dionysos is an upstart

[110] Eur. *Ba.* 188–90. [111] Ibid. 214. [112] Ibid. 215–20.

and represents an unwelcome religious innovation; everything he stands for is unacceptably novel. This view is in clear opposition to what the chorus of maenads has been at pains to stress from the first stanza of the opening chorus, the *parodos* during which the chorus enters the *orkhēstra*. There the chorus sings 'I will hymn Dionysos with songs that are established for all time (*aei*).'[113] While Teiresias remonstrates with Pentheus' stance, he agrees that this 'new/young god' (*houtos ho daimōn ho neos*, 272), will in the future be (*estai*, 274) the recipient of unprecedented worship throughout Greece as Zeus' son, bringer of wine, spur to prophecy, provider of ecstasy, and rouser of war-frenzy.

It was long assumed that Dionysos was, in historical terms, a genuine newcomer to the Greek pantheon, an exotic young divinity who entered Greece from the eastern lands, as dramatically related in the prologue of the *Bacchae*. The discovery of Dionysos' name incised on tablets from Pylos in Linear B script overturned this assumption.[114] The new god turned out to be an age-old object of worship, and the foreignness, exoticism and 'outsider' aspects of Dionysos were quickly reframed as metaphorical attributes.[115] Like his eternal youthfulness, the sense of novelty attaching to his worship may be interpreted as emanating from his nature as a god of advent and epiphany, madness, ecstasy and inventiveness, and from aspects of his cult worship that reinforce a sense of that novelty. The newness ascribed to Dionysos is manifest in different ways. It is present in the change of identity, the sense of rejuvenation, experienced by candidates in Dionysiac *teletai* (initiations). It is related to the unusual and alarming *maniā* (frenzy) aroused by the god in his worshippers. It is evident in the ecstatic new songs, the innovative performances, and the exotic and mysterious cult objects attached to Dionysiac worship.[116] The shifting complexities and stylistic extravagances of the dithyramb, originally a responsional song for 'twice-born' Dionysos, reflects the god's own multifariousness (*poikiliā*). Dionysiac multiplicity and changeability are also consistent with the mingling of dithyramb and other ritual genres in tragedy (a form allegedly derived from the dithyramb, but historically coexistent with dithyrambic performance).[117]

---

[113] Ibid. 70–1.
[114] Chadwick (1985) 194. A Dionysos cult may have existed on the island of Keos (at Ayia Irini) as early as the third millennium BCE: Caskey and Caskey (1986) 39–43.
[115] Walter Otto (1933) had previously characterised Dionysos as the god of advent ('*der kommende Gott*').
[116] 'You're always coming up with novel things to say (*kainous logous*)' says Pentheus to the god (Eur. *Ba.* 650); it is hard not to detect some metapoetic irony.
[117] Swift (2010) 23–6.

In Pindar's Dithyramb for the Thebans, the poet represents his singer-dancers as the possessors of arcane knowledge, 'knowing well' (*eu eidotes*) how the initiation-rites (*teletai*) of Bromios are performed on Olympus. He himself is the 'choice herald of clever words', able to impart to his performers and audience the secrets he has obtained from a communion with the Muses that has endowed him with a special vision.[118] A grander scene is described in a Christian context by John of the Revelation:

1 Then I saw a new heaven and a new earth, for the first heaven and the first earth had passed away, and the sea was no more.
2 And I saw the holy city, new Jerusalem, coming down out of heaven from God, prepared as a bride adorned for her husband.
3 And I heard a loud voice from the throne saying, 'Behold, the dwelling place of God is with man. He will dwell with them, and they will be his people, and God himself will be with them as their God.
4 He will wipe away every tear from their eyes, and death shall be no more, neither shall there be mourning, nor crying, nor pain anymore, for the former things have passed away.'
5 And he who was seated on the throne said, 'Behold, I am making all things new.'[119]

In the Dionysiac mysteries, the process of initiation, *teletē*, centrally involved the initiands in activities directed at giving them an experience of 'a new heaven and a new earth'. The experience of a change of identity, whether accomplished through the operation of a regular *rite de passage* or brought about by the passing of time and changes of place, represents an important mechanism of novelty. The new emerges if the perceiver changes in such a way that the object of perception appears in a new light. The possibility of such a change in perception and identity is a key element in different facets of Greek religion, but nowhere more than in the Mysteries.

One of the characteristic activities of Dionysiac initiation rituals may have been transvestism, which stripped the male initiand of his previous identity in preparation for his assumption of a new one.[120] The process seems to be described in symbolic, dramatised form in Euripides' *Bacchae*, where Pentheus undergoes a change of personality as well as outward appearance when he takes on the garb of a maenad at Dionysos' suggestion: 'Now (*nūn*) you see what you should see.'[121] Equally, the disorientation effected by Dionysos on the women of Thebes – their frenzied departure from their homes and hearths – may relate to the disorientation of the

---

[118] Pi. fr. 70b.23; see below, p. 198. [119] Revelation 21.1–5 (English Standard Version).
[120] Seaford (1994) 272–3; the evidence is slim. [121] Eur. *Ba.* 924.

initiand in Dionysiac initiations (*teletai*), used as a means of detaching them from their previous identities in preparation for a new one. Such practices and secret rituals (*orgia*) included the use of clappers, drums, mirrors and fire, and possibly mock sacrifices of the initiand, who would bid to 'become temporarily like an animal in order to become permanently like a god'.[122] The experience was aimed at making the initiand see the world through new eyes: one cannot return from a vision of one's own death without such a change in perspective.

The blessings of initiation held out the promise for human beings to bypass the normal process of mortality. Immortalisation, however, was granted only to a few, select mortals, and in poetry and myth was more often than not a cause for discomfort.[123] The fate of Tithonos, whose immortalisation resulted in his growing older for ever, was apt to cause concern about the perils of immortality:

> Rosy-armed Dawn, they said, aglow with love
> once bore Tithonos to the world's end,
> lovely and young (*kalon kai neon*) as he was; yet grey old age
> in due course afflicted him, the husband of an immortal wife.[124]

For those who did not take part in initiations, the theatre itself, a Dionysiac forum (at least in Athens), might be the source of transforming experience. This was to be identified by Aristotle by the vexed term *katharsis* (purgation), which has been compared with the psychotherapeutic concept of 'working through':

The psychotherapeutic expression *working through* is a perspicuous translation of many aspects of the classical notion of catharsis. In *working through* his emotions, a person realizes the proper objects of otherwise diffuse and sometimes misdirected passions. Like a therapeutic *working through*, catharsis occurs at the experienced sense of closure. In recognizing and re-cognizing the real directions of their attitudes, the members of an audience are able to feel them appropriately; and by experiencing them in their clarified and purified forms, in a ritually defined and bounded setting, they are able to experience, however briefly, the kind of psychological functioning, the balance and harmony that self-knowledge can bring to action.[125]

The sophist Antiphon is said to have set up a kind of 'talking cure' in Corinth, to offer relief from mental distress by using the consoling power

---

[122] Seaford (1994) 288.
[123] Horace draws this moral from the fates of Tantalos and Tithonos: D'Angour (2003).
[124] *P.Köln* 21351; 'aglow' translates James Diggle's unpublished conjecture *ph[lege]thoisan*. Cf. *H. Hom. Aphr.* 218–38, Ibykos 286.
[125] Rorty (1992) 15.

of words.¹²⁶ Although this is the only hint that the Greeks might have developed their psychological insights into formal therapeutic methods, many of their words and practices indicate their awareness that the experience of novelty might be related as much to processes of internal change and rebirth as to any external stimulus.¹²⁷

[126] Antiphon A6.
[127] On equivalents of the notion of 'psychotherapy' in the ancient context, see Gill (1985).

CHAPTER 7

Inventions of Eris

He that will not apply new remedies must expect new evils; for time is the greatest innovator.

Francis Bacon

'Innovation' in the modern world is primarily associated with the products of technology and consumerism. The design and development of new goods and services, the constant evolution of new technologies of production and delivery, are crucial to the success of corporations large and small. While the drive to innovate may arise from necessity, individual impulse or pure experimentalism, corporate innovation is most commonly linked to the demands of competition: 'radical innovation is *the* competitive advantage for the new millennium'.[1] In science, medicine and the arts, innovation is intensified and encouraged by public incentives and private rewards. The imperative extends across fields both popular and esoteric – fashion design no less than military and information technology, popular music and media, education and academia. Born of ceaseless competition, innovative products and inventions impinge on the lives and consciousness of individuals with relentless rapidity. The idea that inventions come 'out of the blue' is a persistent myth; innovation in most areas tends to owe less to inspirational genius than to small, painstaking improvements in products, designs and techniques.[2] But although novelties generally arise from deliberate, controlled processes and incremental advances, to the observer and consumer they can seem radical and sometimes epiphanic.

The ethos of competition in ancient Greece led Jakob Burckhardt to characterise the archaic epoch as 'agonal'.[3] Notions of competitiveness are prominent in the foundational texts of Greek literature. In Homer, warriors compete in excellence (*aretē*) and for commemorative glory (*kleos*)

---

[1] Hamel (2000) 62; the classic work on 'competitive advantage' for business is Porter, M. (1985).
[2] Berkun (2007) 1–15.   [3] Burckhardt (1998 [1872]) 162–213.

on the battlefield and in athletic events, gods compete for honour (*timē*) and gratification (*kharis*), rivals strive to outdo each other in strength, speech and cunning. Competition is not only the prerogative of emulous heroes and contentious divinities; dancers, craftsmen and bards also seek to impress and win rewards for their skills. Hesiod explicitly recognises competition to be a primary motive force of human life, presenting the personified figure of Eris ('strife' or 'contention') in dual guise. The two Erides symbolise the competitive impulse in both negative and positive forms, destructive warfare and beneficial rivalry:

> There was never just one Eris, then, but on the earth
> there are two. One you would welcome when you come across her,
> the other is hateful; the two Erides are opposite in nature.
> One promotes hateful war and slaughter;
> she is harsh and loved by no one, but by compulsion
> and the will of the gods, men honour this destructive Eris.
> The other is the first-born daughter of dark Night.
> High-throned Zeus who lives in heaven
> placed her, a far kindlier Eris, in the roots of the earth and among men.
> She spurs the lazy man to work, for all his indolence.
> A man is roused to labour when he views his rich neighbour
> pressing on with his ploughing and planting
> and ordering his estate; thus neighbour contends with neighbour
> in keenness to acquire wealth. This Eris is a good friend to mortals:
> potter competes with potter and carpenter with carpenter,
> beggar with beggar and bard with bard.[4]

Competition for honour (*philotīmiā*) and victory (*philonīkiā*) was deeply embedded in classical Greek culture.[5] But to what extent was competitiveness of this kind directed at doing or producing something *new*? The most common and explicit goals of action, such as excellence, fame and financial gain (*kerdos*), might be achieved without innovation. But modern assumptions may not be wholly anachronistic. In some areas (such as *mousikē*, considered in Chapter 8 below) we appear to find explicit recognition of an essential link between novelty and success from the earliest times; in others, such factors as monetisation, increasing commercialisation, and the disruption of old social hierarchies in the Greek world are likely to have affected attitudes to competitive innovation.

---

[4] Hes. *Op.* 11–26. Hesiod also implies that legal disputes such as that between himself and Perses are a destructive kind of *eris*.
[5] Dover (1974) 229–34.

Homer himself appeared to promote musico-poetic novelty, and his musical and literary successors took up the challenge with vocal enthusiasm (see pp. 190–5). But many of the earliest traditional forms of musical and verbal creativity – epic song being the prime example – were of an improvisational or semi-improvisational nature. This leads one to ask what might count as novelty in a largely oral context of competitive production and performance, something I shall consider below in connection to some of the earliest written evidence for extemporised song and dance. Apart from *mousikē*, two of the most prominent manifestations of Greek competitiveness were warfare and athletics. The direct evidence for innovation in these areas is remarkably slight, though we may find different kinds of 'newness' indicated by the texts (see pp. 102–5 above on Herodotean and Pindaric passages). The invention of artillery devices in fourth-century Sicily, often seen as a clear instance of innovation arising from deliberate competition, does not, as I shall discuss, demonstrate an unassailable connection, since we are told about efforts made to build the weapons but not to design them.[6] But the 'skewed phalanx' deployed by the Theban general Epameinondas demonstrates the benefits of contrarian thinking in a manner that makes it paradigmatic of that approach to innovation.

Little explicit evidence survives for the classical period regarding the kind of competitive innovation which we might most readily associate with commercial activities, such as innovation in everyday goods and products or in mechanical and engineering techniques.[7] The growth of trade and advent of monetisation from the seventh century on, in conjunction with the inroads of secular thinking, would seem to provide a promising background for a focus on innovative efforts in practical, everyday crafts and 'banausic' *tekhnai*. Surviving material evidence, ranging from the design and decoration of pots to forms of large-scale architecture, suggests deliberate efforts at innovation: the red-figure style of vase painting succeeds the black-figure, the Corinthian and Ionic orders supersede the simpler Doric figuration of column capitals, and we find striking (if unrepeated) design experiments such as the female figures (*korai*) used as columns in

---

[6] Artillery devices were also developed in fourth-century Macedonia, but the only explicit evidence that internal competition spurred the design of such weapons is in Diodorus' account of Sicily under Dionysios I.

[7] More study is needed of devices used in public entertainment (to which Eric Csapo draws my attention), such as the giant mechanical snail which propelled itself (and left a trail of slime) at the *Pompē* of the Athenian Dionysia organised by the regent Demetrios of Phaleron (Polyb. 12.13.11); other similar automata are attested in the Hellenistic period.

the Karyatid porch of the Erekhtheion.⁸ On the whole, however, the claim that such innovations were the goal or consequence of competitive striving can only be a reasonable surmise, since few explicit claims are to be found. As we have seen (p. 37), Hippodamos' proposal, mentioned by Aristotle in *Politics*, to reward 'any who should make an invention of benefit to the state' is not directed at inventors of socially useful artefacts or designs, but at progressive acts of legislation and politically beneficial proposals.⁹

Even if the same psychological impulses evident in such spheres operated in matters of sculptural technique or practical inventiveness, prevailing elite attitudes debarred the latter from enjoying the whole-hearted admiration accorded to more 'serious' (*spoudaia*) accomplishments. Writing many centuries later in the first century CE, Plutarch sums up the attitude held even towards the production of sculpture and poetry:¹⁰

No gifted youngster, on seeing the Zeus at Olympia or the Hera at Argos, ever longed to be Pheidias or Polykleitos, or felt induced by pleasure in their poetry to be an Anakreon, Philetas or Arkhilokhos. If a work pleases us for its beauty, it does not follow that the man who made it is worthy of serious regard (*spoudē*).¹¹

Lucian recounts a dream he had when contemplating a career as a sculptor, in which *Paideia* (education personified as a woman) warns him:

Were you to become even a Pheidias or Polykleitos and produce many marvellous works, everyone would praise your craftsmanship, but none of those who saw it, if they had sense, would pray to be like you. For whatever you were, you would be considered a *banausos*, a manual worker who lives by his hands.¹²

The low esteem in which artists were traditionally held, stemming largely from elite perceptions of their social class and origins, may have acted as a spur for Polykleitos and others (such as Iktinos, designer of the Parthenon) to provide, in the newly burgeoning book-culture of fifth-century Greece, an intellectual analysis of their *tekhnai* in published treatises which are now

---

⁸ Stewart (2008) 210–12. Giant male statues (called *telamōnes* or *atlantes*) served as columns in the temple of Zeus in Akragas, and a portico of defeated 'Persians' is reported from Sparta (Vitr. 4.1.6, Paus.3.11.3), but the Karyatids are unusual in being both female and apparently not slaves: Rykwert (1996) 129–38.
⁹ Arist. *Pol.* 1268a6–8; see p. 37 above. Xenophon similarly promoted public incentives: 'if it were clear that innovations in any area of life will not go unrewarded, this too would encourage large numbers of people to make it their business to try to discover something useful' (*Hiero* 9.10). This assertion may tacitly refer to the innovative economic proposals Xenophon presented in *Ways and Means*.
¹⁰ Pheidias, Zeuxis and Parrhasios were cited as admired exemplars in the fourth century, e.g. Isok. *Antid.* 2, Pl. *Meno* 91d.
¹¹ Plut. *Per.* 2.1.   ¹² Lucian, *Somn.* 9.

SERIOUS PLAY

'Potter competes with potter and bard with bard', says Hesiod. His choice of practitioners embraces both the notion of everyday competitiveness and the kind of competition promoted in formal *agōnes*. Little specific can be said about competition between ancient potters, although emulation between painters for illusionistic accuracy was the subject of anecdotes (see p. 152 above). Specific occasions of bardic rivalry are far better attested. Hesiod himself was thought to have competed directly against Homer in song contests;[15] and his *Theogony*, which combined existing material from oral wisdom poetry with numerous poetic innovations, may have been composed for and performed at a song contest (at the funeral games for Amphidamas of Khalkis).[16] Later tradition revelled in the picture of Homer and Hesiod competing for the highest prize of poetic repute: the *Contest of Homer and Hesiod*, a hexameter poem which may derive from the *Mouseion* of the fourth-century sophist Alkidamas of Elea, pits the two bards against each other in a capping competition, of which Hesiod is judged the winner.[17] Originality was not (at least explicitly) a criterion in the adjudication. Hesiod was judged superior on ethical criteria (though Homer won the popular vote), as the singer of peace rather than war. This judgement, however, may carry some further implication that (in the eyes of later commentators at least) to sing of the arts of peace was a novel use of *epos*, the traditional 'heroic' verse form.

At local and Panhellenic *agōnes* from the seventh century on, notable instances of musical innovation are recorded; a contest between bards fits into a broader picture of competitive events staged at such festivals. In addition to public contests of musical skill, rhetorical show-pieces (*epideixeis*) were subject to competitive assessment, in parallel with the more informal competitions in verbal creation (as well as *mousikē*) displayed in elite symposia.[18] The latter expressions of impromptu creativity seem

---

[13] Iktinos co-authored a treatise on the Parthenon with Karpion (otherwise unknown): Vitr. 7 *praef.* 12 (Vitruvius here lists a number of other authors of architectural treatises).
[14] Métraux (1995). [15] [Hes.] fr. 357 (see p. 191). [16] Hes. *Op.* 650–62; West (1966) 43–5.
[17] For the contest as Alkidamas' invention, see West (1967); *contra*, Richardson (1981).
[18] Murray (1990).

more analogous to the kind of innovations introduced by epic singers than the more studied originality of later written compositions. In oral contexts, repetition rather than innovation is paramount: memory is aided by constant refamiliarisation, whether with proverbial instructions, performances of ritual songs, or verse formulae in sympotic entertainment. To what extent was there a pressure or expectation for something *new* to be generated in such contests, and what would novelty in such cases have comprised? Can the kind of novelty produced by improvisation and extemporisation be compared with that of a finished literary product? These questions raise issues of how musico-poetic novelty may have differed in contexts of orality versus literacy; and they touch on concepts central to the psychology of innovation, those of the role of play and creativity.[19]

In oral composition, a degree of novelty may arise from the introduction of new elements into existing genres, the adaptation of traditional song structures for new occasions of performance and so on. By contrast, a written text pins down the utterances of memory and creates a record of thought, allowing subsequent readers and hearers to examine, criticise, dispute and reinterpret the products of other minds with greater certainty and precision. Although oral tradition subsisted side by side with growing literacy for centuries after the alphabet's adoption, the continuous accumulation and accretion of words in writing were soon bound to outstrip the most capacious powers of memory; the introduction of writing clearly impelled new forms of literary innovation.[20] The more permanent and reliable record of thought permitted by the use of script had momentous consequences for the generation of new ideas and texts. Preservation in writing meant that the old could be distinguished from the new, allowing authors scope for individuality and the confidence to take credit for novel thoughts and compositions. At the same time, both oral and written preservation encouraged the reiteration of words and song in private and public contexts, leading to the development of a canon of classics; reperformance

---

[19] 'Play often involves symbolic transformations in which objects and actions are used in new and unusual ways. These transformations are similar to the novel, imaginative combination of ideas, which are the product of creative thinking': Christie and Johnsen (1983) 96. Psychological and clinical approaches draw on the work of Piaget and Winnicott, e.g. Piaget (1999 [1951]), Winnicott (1982 [1971]); Huizinga (1971 [1938]) is the classic socio-historical approach. For a general overview see Storr (1972) 147–62.

[20] Thomas (1992) 27–8. Cf. Eisenstein's observation in discussion with Hall *et al.* (1975) 325: 'the modern concept of innovation is the offspring of preservation after printing. You can see more clearly where you are innovating because previous steps are more permanently fixed and also made more visible.'

becomes increasingly important (particularly in the case of drama) in the late fifth century.[21]

Two surviving examples of the earliest inscribed hexameter verses indicate a connection between the playfulness of *mousikē* and competition, and demonstrate the impulse to record in more permanent form a memorably original end-product or performance. The Dipylon *oinokhoē*, an Attic wine-jug of Late Geometric style dated *c*.740–730 BCE, carries a fragmentary couplet beginning with a complete hexameter verse, 'Whoever of all the dancers now dances most energetically (*atalōtata*) . . .'; the missing verse may have added something to the effect 'let him take the prize for his skill'. The scenario is one of competitive challenge, and *atalo-* in the compound *atalophrōn* carries associations of youthfulness similar to *neos*. The gist of the activity suggested by the verses may be compared to a scene in the *Odyssey* of dancing in the court of the Phaeacians, where we are told how Odysseus sat marvelling (*thaumaze*) at the young dancers' 'twinkling feet'.[22] The stars of the show, the youths Halios and Laodamas, are described as presenting a tumbling act, which included throwing a ball in the air to be caught in mid leap.[23] Odysseus' *thauma* is an indication that the spectacle was impressive for its skill, and also perhaps for qualities that to him seemed novel (see p. 148).

Competitive creativity also seems to underlie the hexameter inscription incised on the so-called 'Cup of Nestor' from Pithekoussai, the city on the island in the bay of Naples founded by the earliest Greek colonists from Euboia:

> I'm Nestor's worthy drinking cup:
> Whoever from this drinks will straight away
> Fall under fair-crowned Aphrodite's sway.[24]

The opening line makes a humorous identification of a simple *skyphos* or drinking-cup on which the verses are inscribed with the elaborately wrought flagon described by Nestor in *Iliad* 11.[25] The subsequent verses, a hexameter couplet, may be the result of impromptu versification by two or more participants capping one another's invention in a symposium.[26] The first hexameter line sets up the expectation of a threat or curse of the formulaic type 'whoever does *a* will suffer *b*'. This is turned in an unexpected direction by the following verse: 'fair-crowned Aphrodite' indicates sexual arousal,

---

[21] Herington (1985) 48 f.; Csapo and Slater (1994) 2–5; cf. (on Pindaric reperformance) Currie (2004).
[22] *Od.* 8.265.   [23] Ibid. 370–80.
[24] Powell, B. (1991: 163 n. 110) gives references to publications and discussions.
[25] *Il.* 11.632–7.   [26] Powell, B. (1991) 165–7.

which is here juxtaposed with the image of aged Nestor to humorous effect (it may be that Nestor was also the name of the cup's owner). While the authors of this creative *jeu d'esprit* produced it extempore, they were keen to create a more permanent record of their ingenuity.[27] The kind of impromptu creativity that led to original poetic expressions could be thought of as the work – or rather play – of inspiration, rather than simply of skill: the earliest productions of epic song are not presented as the product of *tekhnē*.[28]

In the Homeric Hymn to Hermes, a hexameter poem probably to be dated to the early fifth century, the action of the new-born god is compared to that of participants trading playful insults in symposia:

> The god sang beautifully in accompaniment
> Trying out the lyre in improvisatory fashion (*ex autoskhediēs*),
> in the way young men at feasts hurl taunts at one another.[29]

The kind of novelty produced by improvised 'flyting' (the exchange of insults, often in verse) may perhaps be compared with that of an instrumentalist who seeks to interpret existing music anew in performance (e.g. to 'play' a Beethoven sonata), rather than that of a composer who aims to create a new piece of music. In Plato's *Ion*, when the rhapsode Ion tells of his victory at a contest in Epidauros, he is presented as recreating (literally 'adorning', *kosmein*) the Homeric text in an individualised performance which has a marked impact on his audience:[30]

> I look down at them every time from up on the rostrum, and they are crying and looking terrified, and as the stories are recounted they are filled with amazement.[31]

Creativity of this kind may be of a high order, and can attain heights of professional virtuosity; but its 'product' tends to be transient and secondary to the creations of authors or composers. Just as a recording of a modern musical performance may, however, serve to preserve and enhance the reputation of the interpreter no less than the composer, so the written record of extemporised verse could allow its composer-performers to acquire a degree

---

[27] D'Angour (2005) 92.
[28] Finkelberg, M. (1998); in Chapter 8 I argue that musico-poetic claims to producing something 'new' demonstrate different aspects of originality (and different purposes in claiming it), which change over the archaic and classical periods.
[29] H. Hom. Herm. 54–6.
[30] Pl. *Ion* 530d6 (*kekosmēka*); according to Collins (2004: 220) *kosmein* here 'is to be interpreted broadly to include the range of rhapsodic performance techniques: mimetic and gestural elements, vocal range, and especially improvisation and modification of verses'.
[31] Pl. *Ion* 535e1–3.

of stature for speaking in accomplished original voices. In an anonymous elegiac fragment from the fifth century, exhortation to symposiastic 'play' (*paizein*) is related to both excellence (*aretē*) and seriousness (*spoudē*):

> Hail, fellow drinkers, agemates: starting from the good
>   I'll end my speech with the good.
> When we friends gather for such a purpose
>   We should laugh and play (*paizein*) in fine style (*aretēi*),
> Enjoy each other's company, make repartee with one another
>   And banter in such a way that makes us laugh.
> Then let the serious (*spoudē*) take over, and let us listen
>   To each speaker in turn; this is the symposium's excellence (*aretē*).[32]

The competitive capping that took place in such symposia is illustrated by the scene of the '*skolion* game' in Aristophanes' *Wasps*.[33] Its form has been related to traditions of contests using riddles (*ainigma, grīphos*), rhapsodic contests, and to such literary tropes as dramatic stichomythia (verse-by-verse exchange between speakers).[34] In Plato's *Symposium*, participants speak in succession, aiming to add something new and different to what has preceded them in an agonistic display reminiscent of the pattern of events at the Dionysiac festival.[35] Although such literary expressions of verbal contestation are presented as secondary descriptions of such events, they display a similar playfulness and creative virtuosity in their own right.[36]

THE GLEAM OF GLORY

'Always to excel and to be superior to others' (*aien aristeuein kai hupeirokhon emmenai allōn*) was the counsel given to Akhilleus by his teachers, and subsequently adopted by Alexander the Great as his motto.[37] The sentiment was valid both in fighting and in the Panhellenic games, whose importance is underlined by their choice for the Greek dating system starting with the traditional year of the first Olympic Games in 776 BCE. The enormous prestige of the games throughout the Greek world made them prime competitive events, through which individual victors could achieve extraordinary levels of fame, material success, and in some cases become

---

[32] *Eleg. adesp.* 27 West, 1–8.   [33] Ar. *Vesp.* 1222–49; cf. 1299–1325.
[34] Collins (2004) 99–110.   [35] Biles (2007) 24.
[36] Agathon draws attention to the semi-playfulness of his own speech on Love (*Symp.* 197e). Cole (1991: 78–9) connects the metaphor to the use of writing, belittled by Sokrates as mere play in *Phaedrus* 277b–278a. Cf. Ford (2002) 185–6.
[37] *Il.* 6.208, 11.784.

the recipients of hero-cult worship.[38] But athletes compete to win, not to innovate. New victories were the aim, not new ways of winning. If the strong desire for victory spurred innovative approaches to enhancing athletic performance, little evidence survives. Participants are likely to have sought out performance-enhancing foods, followed special diets and undertaken rigorous training, but there is no indication of a systematic search for techniques for enhancing athletic performance or for acquiring an edge in speed, strength and so on.[39] Moreover, no accurate measurement was made, and few records kept, of such goals as the time taken to complete the footrace or the distance achieved in long jump.[40] The achievements of earlier victors could be praised, but the only basis for superseding their record of athletic excellence was to win a greater number of victories.

A competitive purpose was retrospectively accorded to the origin of the tradition that the games were performed in the nude. According to Thucydides,

> the Spartans were the first to play games naked, to take off their clothes openly and to rub themselves down with olive oil after their exercise. In ancient times even at the Olympic Games the athletes used to wear coverings for their loins and indeed this practice was still in existence not very many years ago.[41]

While Thucydides gives no rationale for the change, later authors ascribed to it a competitive aim. Pausanias tells how Orsippos of Megara, winner of the footrace at the Olympics of 720 BCE, realised that he could run faster by abandoning his loincloth (elsewhere the innovation is attributed to Akanthos of Sparta).[42] The purpose of improving performance has also been attributed to the use of weights (*haltēres*), perhaps during training, in the standing or running long jump.[43] But there is no certainty that any such 'innovations' were made by individual athletes seeking a competitive advantage.[44] Additions to the programme of events, introduced over the

---

[38] Currie (2005) 120–57.
[39] Galen, *On the Powers of Foods*, trans. Grant (2000). Incidents of cheating are recorded, mainly involving the bribing of athletes: Forbes (1952).
[40] Only three distance records are preserved by late sources: those achieved in the pentathlon jump (*halma*) by Phaÿllos of Kroton (early fifth century BCE, 55 feet) and Khionis of Sparta (seventh century BCE, 52 feet), and by Phaÿllos in the discus throw (95 feet). The distances are too large to be credible for the long jump, but Hyde (1938) argues from a passage in Themistius' paraphrase of Aristotle's *Physics* that the Greeks practised the triple jump.
[41] Thuc. 1.6.5–6.   [42] Paus. 1.44, D.H. 7.72.2–3.
[43] Blau (2003); Lampis of Lakonia is named as the first winner of the long jump in 708 BCE, but the earliest *haltēres* found date to around 600 BCE.
[44] Jeanmaire (1939: 413–18) argues for ritual origins to athletic nudity.

course of centuries, show a recognition of the need to update the Games so as to vary the fare of what had once been no more than a running contest, the *stadion*. The augmentation of the Games over the centuries by such events as the *hoplītodromiā* (race in armour) and the four-horse chariot race was symptomatic of changing tastes and resources.

In general, the notion of a goal of performance which competitors strive to attain seems incompatible with innovation. As early as the funeral games for Patroklos described in *Iliad* 23, aristocratic contests of physical prowess require a display of individual *aretē* in traditional modes of competition; innovation has no place. The most copious witnesses to the prestige and ethos of athletics, the *epinikia* of Pindar, say nothing about athletic innovations; although we hear about 'new' victories won by athletes and patrons, there is no mention of new ways of winning. In Pindar's poems, victories are ascribed to skill (*aretē*) and innate talent (*phuā*), fortune (*tukhē*) and divine beneficence (*kharis*). The word *kainos* is found nowhere in Pindar's oeuvre; victories can only be *nea* (in some form), new eventualities ascribed ultimately to divine dispensation and favour. The novelty attaching to the Games was the acquisition of new markers of repute (*kleos*) for new winners, the kind of novelty afforded by chance and the ability to seize the moment (*kairos*). Victory afforded individuals both famous and obscure the chance to attain, with divine aid, greater recognition and reward. Winners who commissioned *epinikia* might be celebrated by the likes of Bakkhylides and Pindar, the novelty of whose songs was acclaimed as a counterpart to their patrons' virtues.[45]

Losers remained inglorious and unsung, their toil undertaken in vain and their efforts seldom appreciated.[46] On the rare occasions that Pindar speaks of the losers, he simply inverts the picture of the victor's expected reception. Thus the situation of the unsuccessful challengers in the boys' wrestling provides a foil to the triumph of Aristomenes of Aigina, who is the addressee of a striking passage in Pindar's eighth Pythian ode:

> On four bodies you launched yourself from high up,
> intent on doing them harm.
> To them no joyful homecoming like yours
> has the Pythian festival afforded.
> On their return to their mothers no happy laughter

---

[45] E.g. the opening of Pi. *O.* 3; see p. 193 below.
[46] The fact that more than one prize is awarded in the funeral games for Patroklos appears to be an unusual feature; but these are Games as depicted in an epic story, and there are other exceptions: Crowther (1992). An inscription (*IG* II².2311) confirms the award of lower prizes in the fourth-century Panathenaic Games: Shear (2003).

is raised about them; keeping clear of their enemies, they slink down alleyways, bitten by failure.[47]

By contrast, the new victor is imagined 'flying high' in his pride and pleasure at achieving success 'superior to wealth', though that delight is always tempered by the short-lived nature of all such experience:

> But he who has achieved a new success (*kalon ti neon*)
> basking in great splendour
> soars (*petatai*) from hope to hope
> on the wings of his manly deeds, dwelling on
> thoughts superior to wealth.
> But short-lived is the delight of mortals, which flowers then falls to the ground,
> shaken by the shifting breeze of purpose.[48]

There follows the famous expression of human ephemerality ('creature of a day', *epāmeros*), and the accompanying image of the shaft of light which irradiates the victor when a new moment of success relieves the shadows of mortality (see above, p. 145).

INNOVATION IN BATTLE

Classical Greek warfare is usually taken to begin with the development of new weaponry during the eighth or seventh centuries to create the hoplite phalanx. Citizens wealthy enough to provide their own panoply of heavy arms and armour – double-grip shield, double-pointed spear, 'Corinthian' helmet and bell-shape breastplate – gathered to fight together in close-knit formations for which orderliness and solidarity were the key to success.[49] The collective fighting style is associated with the development of poleis, and has been linked to the increasing agrarian wealth of citizens:

> Gradually the spread of diversified, intensified farming created a shared ideology of new landowners, men in the ranks who no doubt had begun to accumulate capital from their farming success. With the same ingenuity by which they devised new approaches to traditional land use, the planters of trees and vines began to fabricate bronze weapons to improve their performance in the traditional mêlée of Greek battle.... In the period innovative agricultural strategies were gaining momentum – tree and vine grafting, homestead residence, slave labor, diversified crops, incorporation of marginal land, on-the-farm storage and

---

[47] Pi. *P.* 8.81–7. Cf. fr. 229 'those who lose are bound with a gag of silence, unable to face their friends'. In *O.* 8.69, the victor projects onto the losers 'a most hateful homecoming, words less honouring, an obscure path'.
[48] Pi. *P.* 8.88–94.   [49] Hanson (1995) 224–5.

processing – farmers also sought to consolidate, reaffirm, and accelerate their efforts at agrarian government through a radical remaking of traditional Greek mass warfare.[50]

Little further change appears to have taken place in weaponry or fighting methods for centuries. Although outright victory was the aim of battle, methods of winning and battlefield behaviour were required to accord with notions of honour. 'Helping friends and harming enemies' may offer a rule of thumb for Greek ethical assumptions;[51] but in military actions as in athletics, ritualistic behaviours prevailed. One aspect of hoplite tactics, the traditional placing of the best fighters on the right wing of the phalanx (see p. 104), demonstrates this with particular force. With the shield held on the left arm, the right arm was free to attack; but the consequence was that the formation had a tendency to veer to the right during battle, 'because fear makes each man do his best to shelter his unarmed side with the shield of the man next him on the right'.[52] It was important for the best troops stationed on the right flank to hold firm so that the line should not be exended to allow the enemy to break through at any point. A battle might be decided when the stronger of the two right wings broke through the opposing ranks and 'rolled up' their adversaries. The disposition of troops may have led to a rather formulaic style of fighting, with the success of the elite fighters tending to decide the battle and leading to the other side's surrender; but in this way the outright slaughter of vanquished opponents might be prevented.

This honourable pitched battle between hoplites was to some extent an 'invention of tradition', a wishful retrojection by Greek authors looking back from the perspective of the Peloponnesian War and thereafter, when styles of fighting were more varied and instrumental.[53] Tactical innovations were made, such as that remarked on by Herodotos at the battle of Marathon (490 BCE), where the Athenians 'were the first of all Hellenes we know of to use the running charge against their enemies'.[54] Waging war against non-Greek forces was a special spur to rethinking traditional modes of fighting, not least in relation to naval manoeuvres such as the *diekplous* ('sailing through and out') and *periplous* ('sailing around').[55] In fifth-century naval warfare, competition between captains for honour was strong, but again it was competition for success rather than novelty.[56] But there is greater urgency in the recognition that no quarter could be given to

---

[50] Ibid. 238–9.   [51] Blundell (1989).   [52] Thuc. 5.71.   [53] van Wees (2004) 115–17.
[54] Hdt. 6.112. 'At a run' (*dromōi*) occurs four times in the paragraph, but the notion that the Athenians ran the eight stades (just under a mile) separating them from the Persians is untenable; Donlan and Thompson (1976) argue that the 'run' covered the last 200 yards.
[55] These may have been two stages of a single manoeuvre: van Wees (2004) 228.   [56] Ibid. 229.

the Persian invaders: 'now all is at stake in this contest' (*nūn huper pantōn agōn*) arose the cry at Salamis (480 BCE), according to the Aeschylean Messenger-speech in *The Persians*.[57]

New methods of combat and technical innovations emerge more regularly in the course of the Peloponnesian War. The prolonged fighting was the stimulus to crucial changes in the development of naval tactics, the use of light-armed troops and mercenaries, methods of training and a general turn towards military professionalism.[58] At the second sea-battle of the siege of Syracuse in 413, the Syracusans and their allies modified their triremes with reinforced rams that could attack the Athenian ships head-on.[59] While naval training was long-standing Athenian tradition, military training on land was considered, somewhat disdainfully, to be confined to Sparta.[60] It gradually became more widespread, and Aristotle was unequivocal about its importance in a world of professional armies:

> Even the Spartans themselves, as we know from experience, were superior to others only so long as they alone trained assiduously. Nowadays they are beaten both in athletic contests and in actual war. Their previous superiority was not due to the particular training they gave to their youth: it was simply and solely due to their having some form of training when their opponents had none at all.[61]

The Athenian general Demosthenes' defeat in Aitolia in 426 was a turning-point for the introduction of light-armed troops on the battlefield. He learned the lesson well, and applied it subsequently to obtain victory against the Spartans on Sphakteria.[62] Battlefield novelties were also tested at Delion in 424, when the Boiotian general Pagondas employed unprecedented operations against the Athenians, drawing up his phalanxes twenty-five deep instead of the usual eight to twelve. He also innovated in his employment of cavalry and reserve formations, and in his exploitation of tactical shifts during the battle.[63] The siege of Delion also saw the use of a novel artillery device, a flame-thrower, for the first time.[64] The tactical conduct of siege warfare was a constant military concern.[65] The following decades were to see further notable changes in the conduct of siege warfare, largely as a result of the development of offensive artillery. The claim of sophists such

---

[57] Aesch. *Pers.* 405.
[58] Hornblower (2002) 194–7. Ober (1996: 64–9) argues that the Athenians' democratic political culture was a particularly potent factor in the erosion of the Greeks' 'rules of war'.
[59] Thuc. 7.36. [60] Thuc. 2.84–5, 2.38–9. [61] Arist. *Pol.* 1338b24–9 (trans. Barker, adapted).
[62] Thuc. 3.94–8, 4.33–6. [63] Ibid. 4.90–6.
[64] Ibid. 4.100.2–4. The Spartans did something similar in creating a 'sheet of flame' at the siege of Plataiai in 429 BCE: Thuc. 2.77.
[65] In Aristophanes' *Clouds*, Strepsiades initially misinterprets Sokrates' *kainās mēkhanās* (new techniques of examination), and asks if he is literally about to be besieged: Ar. *Nub.* 476–80.

as Euthydemos and Dionysodoros to teach the art of war (*polemikē tekhnē*) could be dismissed: Plato makes Euthydemos admit that their instruction in that regard was not for serious ends.[66] Written works on military matters began to appear: the earliest extant treatise on siegecraft, the *Siegecraft* (*Poliorkētika*) of Aeneas 'the Tactician', dates from the mid fourth century. Xenophon's *Cyropaedia* ('Education of Cyrus') reads like an informal handbook of strategy and military training, and in later times fulfilled that role.[67]

The organised use of peltasts by Iphikrates at the battle of Lekhaion in 390 suggested new freedom from conventional restraints:[68]

Warfare had emerged from the realm of morality and honour. It had become something more than a way of life to be conducted according to ancestral expectations of 'men of honour'. As the Greeks moved rapidly towards the creation of integrated armies, they began to view warfare as a complicated social activity. Warfare had become innovative rather than traditional.[69]

The Thebans pursued further novelties in the fourth century; and the tactics employed by Epameinondas against the Spartans at the battle of Leuktra in 371 have become a case study in the use of 'contrarian' thinking as a mechanism of innovation.[70] At Leuktra, the Spartan general Kleombrotos had drawn up his elite Spartiate forces in their usual place on the right wing, placing the weaker Peloponnesian allies on the left. Epameinondas, however, whose forces numbered 9,000 to the Spartans' 12,000, reversed the expected disposition of his army. He heavily reinforced the left wing of the Theban battle line, placing his strongest fighters there to a depth of fifty ranks; the far left was manned by the Thebans' most indomitable troops, the Sacred Band, commanded by the Theban Pelopidas.[71] Epameinondas instructed the weaker troops on the right to avoid battle and to withdraw gradually before the Spartan advance. The reinforced Theban left flank attacked at double speed, so that the opposing Spartans gave way under the impetus, and Kleombrotos was killed. The Theban cavalry, which was superior to that of Sparta, was brought in to disrupt the enemy lines, and the Peloponnesian allies broke and ran. The battle shook the foundations of Spartan military dominance. Epameinondas used similar tactics at the battle of Mantinea in 362, and although he himself was killed in the engagement, the 'skewed phalanx' gave the Thebans

---

[66] *Outoi tauta . . . spoudazomen*: Pl. *Euthyd.* 273d3.
[67] Scipio Africanus used it as such: Cic. *Tusc. Disp.* 2.62.
[68] Xen. *Hell.* 4.5.10–16, 6.4.12; Ferrill (1985) 157–62, 166–70.   [69] Ferrill (1985) 165.
[70] E.g. Kirton (2003) 342–3.   [71] D.S. 15.55; Plut. *Pelop.* 23.1; Xen. *Hell.* 6.4.8–15.

a decisive victory over the combined forces of Sparta, Athens, Elis and Arkadia.

The contrarian tactics employed by Epameinondas required a psychological shift of consequence. They signalled a battle ethos that matched, and may to some degree have been a consequence of, the yielding of traditional religious perspectives to rational and instrumental attitudes during the previous half century, to which authors such as Thucydides and Aristophanes bear witness. What had come to matter in battle was victory by whatever means were needed, not by fighting according to 'the rules'. By the fourth century these means embraced the use of surprise tactics, light-armed troops, forced marches, foreign mercenaries and the outright bribery of one's opponents. Demosthenes, speaking in the summer of 341 BCE in the shadow of the advance of Philip II of Macedon, identified warfare in retrospect as the paramount sphere of innovation in his time:

> In my own opinion, while virtually all the arts have made a great advance and we are living today in a very different world from the old days, nothing has been more revolutionised and advanced than the art of war. First I know that in former times the Spartans, like everyone else, would spend the four or five months of the summer season invading and laying waste enemy territory with heavy infantry and citizen levies, and would then return home. They were so old-fashioned, or rather such good citizens, that they never used money to buy an advantage from anyone, but their fighting was fair and open. Now you will find that most disasters are due to treachery, not the result of a regular pitched battle. You hear that Philip marches unchecked, not because he leads a phalanx of heavy infantry, but because he is accompanied by skirmishers, cavalry, archers, mercenaries, and similar troops. Relying on these forces, he attacks people that are divided against each other, and when through mutual distrust no one fights for his country, he brings up his artillery and lays siege. I need hardly tell you that he makes no difference between summer and winter, and sets no season apart for inaction.[72]

INVENTIONS OF WAR

The account of the invention of new weapons of war in early fourth-century Sicily appears to provide a paradigmatic instance of the connection between competition and technological innovation in the ancient world. In the course of a long conflict with Carthage, the wealthy and powerful city of Syracuse developed new kinds of artillery weapons and ships of unprecedented size. These were to contribute to a marked change in the nature of warfare for the Greeks, and would in due course be exploited

---

[72] Dem. 9.48–51.

to even greater effect by their Roman successors. The initiative for their invention was alleged to have come directly from the tyrant of Syracuse, Dionysios I. Diodorus Siculus, the Sicilian historian of the first century BCE, drawing on authoritative fourth-century authors, paints a detailed picture of the unprecedented war effort orchestrated by Dionysios in 399 BCE:

> He gathered together skilled workmen from the cities under his control and enticed them with high pay from Italy and Greece as well as from Carthaginian territories. His aim was to produce weapons and missiles of all kinds in vast quantities, and ships with four and five hulls, larger than had ever been constructed. He divided the workmen into teams according to their skills, headed by the leading citizens, and offered them large rewards to produce arms...
>
> The Syracusans took up Dionysios' project with enthusiasm, and they competed strenuously to manufacture weapons. All available spaces, from the porticoes and back rooms of temples to gymnasia and the colonnades in the agora, were crowded with workmen. In addition to public spaces, the most opulent private houses were used for the production of huge quantities of armaments. And in fact (*kai gar*) it was at this period, with the most skilled craftsmen being concentrated in one place, that the catapult was invented in Syracuse. The efforts of the workmen were encouraged by high pay and by the numerous rewards offered to those who were adjudged the best. In addition, Dionysios circulated daily among the workers and chatted amicably to them, rewarding the most hard-working with gifts and inviting them to dine with him. Consequently the craftsmen applied themselves wholeheartedly to devising outlandish (*xena*) missiles and military machines that might be able to provide great services (*megalās khreiās*).[73]

While this passage might at first sight be taken as evidence for the link between competition and innovation, on closer analysis it defies such a straightforward interpretation.[74] Initially, competition and rewards are mentioned solely in relation to the pace of production and accumulation of weapons, not the creation of new designs of weaponry. Prizes and prestige are bestowed, we are told, not on the most inventive but on the most industrious and productive craftsmen. Diodorus finally introduces the invention of a supposedly new weapon of war, the catapult, with the words *kai gar*, 'and indeed', which suggests that this was the goal of Syracusan

---

[73] D.S. 14.41–2. Xenophon (*Ages*. 1.25–8; cf. *Hell*. 3.4.16–19) gives a curiously similar description of the effort of the Spartan king Agesilaos to motivate his forces when on campaign in Ionia in 395 BCE. We read (1.26) that 'the city square was so filled with all kinds of armour and horses for sale, and every single bronze-smith, carpenter, ironsmith, leather-worker and engraver was so busy working on weapons of war, that you would literally have thought the city a workshop of war'.

[74] Cuomo (2007: 43–6) raises the question of how 'new' a weapon the catapult could be thought to have been.

efforts. But he goes on to relate its invention to the sheer number of skilled technicians present in Syracuse, rather than to the pressures or incentives provided by the competition. As a result, he appears to suggest that the invention was the result of the preponderance of expertise rather than a competitive desire on the part of technicians to outdo each other in inventiveness.

Nor is it clear, when the historian goes on to speak of novel or 'outlandish' (*xena*) missiles and machines, whether their devising was the aim or just the lucky outcome of the craftsmen's intensive efforts. In a coda to the passage cited above, Diodorus gives a comparable rationale for the construction of exceptionally large new warships:

> Dionysios also initiated the construction of four- and five-hulled ships, the first person to entertain the creation of vessels like this. As the ruler of a city originally settled by Corinthians, and knowing that triremes had first been built in Corinth, he was eager to build ships of yet greater dimensions.[75]

Even in this case, then, the design and construction of these outsize ships is not related to the notion that craftsmen were competing for financial rewards or even for honour. Instead, Diodorus explicitly attributes the initiative solely to Dionysios' personal zeal to surpass the invention of the trireme by Syracuse's mother-city – an example of the diachronic competitiveness to innovate of the kind we have encountered in accounts of Presocratic philosophers and successive 'first inventors' (pp. 128, 133).

On this analysis, then, Diodorus' account does not live up to the promise of tying competition firmly to innovation in the context of warfare. While it suggests that the Greeks may have recognised some natural connection between competitive incentives and innovation, it is more congruent with the Greek notion that novelty emerges in contexts of multiplicity (see p. 49). The invention of new types of artefacts, whether the catapults and warships mentioned by Diodorus or other novel devices on a smaller scale, though undoubtedly stimulated by a need or desire to compete for military advantage, cannot unequivocally be attributed to competition on an individual level.

INVENTIONS OF PEACE

The 'great services' provided by Dionysios' war machines reflects a recognition of the potential for competition to further practical ends. 'He is wise

[75] D.S. 14.43.

who knows what is useful (*khrēsima*), not who knows many things', reads a fragment of Aeschylus.[76] The creation of new objects or methods will sometimes have brought a degree of repute to their inventors, as indicated by anecdotes about them and the fact that individuals' names were remembered. In Xenophon's *Memoirs of Sokrates*, Sokrates is depicted questioning an armourer called Pistias about his procedures. The fact that the superior proportions of Pistias' breastplates allows him to charge more for them indicates the potential benefits of innovation for profitability:

On visiting Pistias the armourer, who showed him some finely made breastplates, Sokrates exclaimed 'Heavens, Pistias, what a fine design (*heurēma*) – the breastplate covers the parts that need protection without impeding the use of the hands. Tell me,' he added, 'why do you charge more for your breastplates than other makers, even though they are no stronger and cost no more to make?' Pistias replied 'Because the proportions of mine are better, Sokrates.'[77]

In the matter of innovation of small-scale technical and domestic, rather than military, products, evidence for the connection is less explicit. Herodotos records the names of some individual inventors of specific techniques or artefacts which in his view deserve mention. Iron soldering (*sidērou kollēsis*), for instance, is credited to Glaukos of Chios; but it may simply be that Herodotos had noted the application of the technique in works ascribed to Glaukos that he observed.[78] The craftsmanship of Theodoros of Samos, creator of the cauldron dedicated by Kroisos at Delphi and of Polykrates' seal-ring, is admired, but his reputation as an architect and inventor of architectural tools goes unmentioned.[79]

When other small-scale inventions occasionally crop up in the sources, a connection with competition is obscure. The sophist Protagoras of Abdera was credited with inventing a kind of shoulder-pad to help with carrying heavy loads; the attribution may simply preserve the memory of an item of this kind associated with the appearance of the travelling teacher.[80] Equally impressive is the mention of the invention of a water alarm clock, by none other than Plato.[81] The philosopher's friend, the statesman and inventor Arkhytas of Taras, was better known for creating ingenious mechanical

---

[76] Aesch. fr. 390. [77] Xen. *Mem.* 3.10.9–10. [78] Hdt. 1.25.
[79] Ibid. 1.51.3, 3.41.1. According to Pliny (*N.H.* 7.198), Theodoros invented the architect's square, the level and the lathe (or possibly compass: Munn 2006: 201) and planned the foundations of the temple of Artemis at Ephesos (D.L. 2.103). Hahn (2001) connects the ideas of Anaximander with the work of Theodoros and other Ionian architects.
[80] D.L. 9.53, 4.2.
[81] Athenaeus 4.174c; the anecdote may be related to Plato's disapproval of excessive sleep as indicated in *Leg.* 807e–808c: Riginos (1976) 188–9.

products. The account by the Hadrianic polymath Favorinus of Arelate records his invention of a child's rattle, which may perhaps be related to Arkhytas' acoustic theories. More spectacular was a steam-powered mechanical bird, which was said to have flown.[82] All these thinkers were famed for their intellectual contributions to Greek culture, rather than their invention of ingenious artefacts. It may have seemed appropriate for men of evident intellectual creativity (as with those demonstrating 'creative personalities', p. 51) to have displayed a related capacity for invention.

CONCLUSIONS

Classical Greek society lacked the economic imperatives of the modern world – large-scale market forces, consumerist pressures and motives of corporate profit – which drive the supply of and demand for new consumer products. The development of gadgets and devices that might be considered useful belongs to a post-industrial mindset, and seems to have had little purchase on the Greek imagination. The widespread and largely unquestioned use of slaves for physical, menial and mechanical tasks will in any case have removed much of the incentive to practical inventiveness in commercial and technological arenas. Equally significant was the weight of elite cultural expectation that, at least in the early classical period, meant that the pursuit of such objectives was considered trivial and unworthy.[83] Even in cases where minor inventions were attributed to or fathered on individuals known and admired for qualities other than practical ingenuity, there is no association either with a formal contest of skill or with the urge to compete.

In line with the aristocratic values espoused by our sources, winning in formal competitive events or *agōnes* was principally considered of value for its own sake. Such victories brought prestige to the individual victor and to the wider community with which he was associated.[84] In the crown ('stephanitic') Games, the prizes for winning were symbolic – an olive-wreath for the Olympic victor, laurel for the Pythian etc., but more tangible rewards, sometimes of great monetary value, invariably followed. Money prizes were were common and substantial in other ('chrematitic') Games.[85] But the material benefits that winning or participating in a competition might offer, directly or indirectly, were never proclaimed as reasons for

---

[82] Athenaeus 4.75; Arkhytas A10.   [83] Finley (1981), 176–95; Austin and Vidal-Naquet (1977) 11–18.
[84] Cf. Douglas (2007). It was taken for granted that physical fitness was required for effectiveness on the battlefield.
[85] Miller, S.G. (2004) 129–49.

competing. In formal artistic contests such as those held at the Pythian games some emphasis was placed on originality, but this was not regarded as the basis of success; in the *Contest of Homer and Hesiod*, as mentioned above, the prize goes to Hesiod on the basis of a moralising judgement.

In general, the production of novelty as such was prized more in intellectual and artistic spheres rather than in practical ones. Accounts of Greek innovations in music, mathematics, astronomy or rhetoric are more frequent and conspicuous than reports of novelties in trade and commerce, carpentry and building construction, or sundry everyday skills. Competition to come up with new ideas and artefacts was not related to formal contest, and in many areas where innovations are recorded, a diachronic perspective on competition seems more evident than a synchronic one: Anaximander's invention of the map, the celestial globe and the *gnōmōn* (sundial), for instance, may be viewed as a practical response to geographical and cosmological views held by his predecessors.[86] Innovations in the dithyramb, the circular dance and hymn in honour of Dionysos, were variously ascribed to Arion of Methymna and to Lasos of Hermione; since the former was active around 585 in Corinth, the latter around 510 at Athens, there was no direct competition between them to innovate in the genre. Their contributions to it were successive and perhaps complementary, with the result that later writers were content to credit both as 'first inventors'.[87] Inventors such as Arkhytas may have felt themselves to be in competition with forerunners in their field as much as with their contemporaries.

Practical innovations were admired for their ingenuity as much as their usefulness. Where we have no written evidence, we can only conjecture about the impulses underlying the invention of objects that may in their time have been held in considerable regard. The *klērōtērion*, for instance, the machine for selecting jurors at random for Athenian lawsuits in the fifth century, was a significant symbolic and practical adjunct to legal practice; but no written account of its designer or the path to its invention survives.[88] By contrast, we learn that some time in the mid fifth century, one Pythagoras of Zakynthos invented a musical instrument called the *tripous* ('tripod'). This was not (so far as we know) the outcome of competition with other contemporary inventors or musicians. The instrument, a combination of three kitharas set up with different tunings on a revolving base, was designed to facilitate the performance of music which modulated

---

[86] D.L. 1–2.
[87] The innovations relate to different aspects of the dithyramb: D'Angour (1996) 346–50, and see below p. 196.
[88] Dow (1939).

between different modes, an increasingly popular feature of melodic composition in the late fifth century. Lyre-players and kitharists were already emulating the range of the auloi by performing multimodal music on a single instrument; the *tripous* 'had brief vogue in Pythagoras' lifetime, but thereafter fell into disuse'.[89] No invention of similar stature is recorded until the creation of the *hydraulis* (water organ) by the versatile engineer Ktesibios of Alexandria in the third century BCE.[90] While we hear little about the development of such artefacts in the classical period, it is hard not to suppose that the seeds were being sown for the work of brilliant Hellenistic inventors such as Heron of Alexandria and Arkhimedes of Syracuse, and for mute marvels of practical ingenuity such as the calendrical mechanism (dated to the Hellenistic era) found off the coast of Antikythera.[91]

---

[89] Artemon ap. Athenaeus 14.637cf; D'Angour (2006).
[90] Vitr. 10.8; in 1992 the earliest remains of a hydraulis, made in bronze in the first century BCE, were excavated at Dion in Macedonia: Harrington (1996).
[91] Research into the Antikythera mechanism continues; its design suggests it was intended for predicting the dates of eclipses and of Panhellenic games: Freeth *et al.* (2008), Hannah (2009) 49–67.

CHAPTER 8

The newest song

> I feel free to cleave the ether on a new-found path to novel spheres of pure activity.
>
> <div align="right">Goethe, <i>Faust</i>, Part I</div>

Mousikē provides the most explicit and enduring examples of innovationist discourse in any sphere of Greek cultural activity. The significance and function of that discourse vary, reflecting both the variety of the domain of *mousikē* and the different ways things can be called 'new'. The rhetoric of innovation often elides such distinctions, intentionally or otherwise; but the mass of verbal indications of innovationism in Greek musico-poetic texts, combined with the ubiquity and popularity of Greek musical activity, leaves little room for doubt that the idea of the new played a vital role.

Testimony to the place of novelty in music begins with the songs of Homer. In the first book of the *Odyssey*, Homer depicts the bard Phemios entertaining suitors in Odysseus' palace with a song about the return of the heroes from Troy (*nostos Akhaiōn*). The song distresses Penelope, who bursts into tears and asks the minstrel to change his tune:

> Phemios, you know many other pieces to enchant mortals,
> deeds of men and gods that bards celebrate (*kleiousi*) in song.
> Sing one of those as you sit among these men, and let them
> drink their wine in peace. But stop singing this
> distressing song – it always breaks my heart,
> since I, more than any, am constantly racked by grief.
> I pine for my dear husband and am constantly reminded
> of him, whose fame (*kleos*) is wide throughout Hellas and in the
>   heart of Argos.[1]

---

[1] *Od.* 1.337–44.

Telemakhos intervenes:

Don't scold Phemios for singing of the Danaans' tragic fate:
People give greater acclaim (*epikleiousi*) to the newest (*neōtatē*) song that attends their ears.[2]

Telemakhos' forthright statement makes him 'the poet's spokesman in his plea for artistic freedom and his emphasis on the importance of poetic novelty'.[3]

While the words appear to offer explicit justification for novelty in song, what exactly is meant by 'the newest song'? Although the earliest uses of *neos* generally have temporal significance, *neōtatē* here cannot indicate simply the latest song to be sung; a song without substantial qualities could not be supposed to be worthy of acclaim merely on account of its recency. In the context of the narrative, what readers and hearers take Telemakhos' words to mean is likely to differ from the significance attached to them out of context. Here, within the narrative situation Homer has depicted, the reader may discern various latent motives for Telemakhos to intervene in support of the bard's song. The recent visit to him of Athene in the guise of Odysseus' guest-friend Mentes has quickened his interest in *nostos Akhaiōn*. He will know that Phemios' song raises the prospect of Odysseus' return, not just for him and for Penelope, but for the suitors as well. And since the song will remind them, just as it does Penelope, that Odysseus' fate is not settled, their presumed discomfort at the thought may afford Telemakhos a certain relish.[4] This also accounts for Telemakhos' suggestion that his mother should be consoled by the knowledge that 'many others also died at Troy' (354–5). This seems unduly harsh, given that he himself has grounds for hope; but for the moment it may serve to deflect suspicion that he has reason to think Odysseus is alive.

The terms in which Telemakhos defends Phemios are unique to this passage. No similar rationale is offered in Book 8, for instance, on behalf of Demodokos, when king Alkinoös stops the bard singing in order to curtail the distress it causes Odysseus.[5] Telemakhos contradicts Penelope in an apparent display of indignation in support of the bard's pursuit of professional acclaim. While Penelope finds the song only distressing (*lūgrē*), Telemakhos identifies its claim to novelty. One may perhaps expect a young man (*neos*) to be naturally disposed to hear the latest (*neōtatē*)

---

[2] Ibid. 350–2.   [3] West, in Heubeck *et al.* (1988) 119.
[4] His anger towards the suitors becomes evident in his subsequent speech: *Od.* 1.368–98.
[5] *Od.* 8.536–43.

song; in Aristophanes' *Clouds* father and son come to blows over the issue.[6] In this case, the appeal to the demands of novelty in bardic performance allows Telemakhos to begin asserting his authority, both over his mother and vis-à-vis the suitors.[7]

The remark Homer puts into Telemakhos' mouth includes an undoubted element of bardic self-advertisement. Homer's identification with his bardic characters is evident. His depiction of minstrels, whether Phemios in Ithaka or Demodokos on Skheriē, is self-reflexive and arguably self-interested. The figures of the bards attract epithets such as 'blameless' and 'divine', their singing is described as 'heavenly' and 'enchanting', they are accorded the power to delight and to draw tears. Demodokos' impressive performance merits a special reward from Odysseus, and Phemios' successful plea to Odysseus to spare his life is supported by his claim to divine inspiration.[8] Homer projects his own interests and assumptions onto the figure of the bard. Here Phemios' innovative *aoidē* is to be identified with his own, the newest song that listeners more readily acclaim (*epikleiousi*). Literally, 'they attach more *kleos*' to it: the word resonates with a central motif in heroic song, and echoes Penelope's claim (344) that Odysseus' *kleos* is celebrated throughout the land. *Kleos* is the goal of the epic hero, the recognition and celebration of his excellence (*aretē*). The bard's own virtuosity in *aoidē* attracts a portion of the *kleos* sought by and invested in the heroes of his song.[9] The originality of the singer, be he Phemios or Homer, is assimilated to the heroic virtue of his subject.[10] Through the mouth of Telemakhos, the composer draws attention to his own choice of theme and its original treatment.

Homer's commendation of the 'newest song' may be considered alongside other indications of the poet's attitude to the new. The positive evaluation of novelty is demonstrated by the way new objects, as well as newly invigorated characters and newly epiphanic divinities, are invested by Homer with qualities of beauty and radiance (see Chapter 6). As we have seen, when Homer wants to describe a ship, shield or shin-plate as

---

[6] Ar. *Nub.* 1353–76.
[7] Ford (2002) 5: 'the most basic issue at stake in Book 1 is who shall call the tune'. In a wide-ranging discussion Pucci (1987: 196–208) calls Telemakhos' reaction 'oedipal'.
[8] *Od.* 8.477–83, 22.347–57. The latter passage is a reminder of Telemakhos' intervention, since Phemios (implicitly) invokes his protection as witness to the fact that he performed under duress.
[9] Cf. Goldhill (1990: 69–166): 'the notion of *kleos* is linked in a fundamental way to the poet's voice'.
[10] Cf. the Pindaric notion that *kleos* (often accompanied by epithets indicating brightness) renews an athletic victor (Chapter 6, p. 145 above). Pucci (1987: 202) observes the reversal implied by *epikleiousin* whereby 'the center of the song is no longer the hero and his *kleos*, "glory", but the poet and the fascination he exercises over his listeners'.

new, he uses *neos* or compounds such as *neoteukhēs*, 'lately fashioned' or *prōtopagēs*, 'constructed for the first time'. Within the spectrum of signification of 'new', these epithets are of essentially temporal character. Such objects are 'new' because, at the moment of description, they have not had time to become old, used or obsolete. What is recent may be welcome in its unfamiliarity, or unwelcome in its strangeness; but the kind of newness indicated by *neos*, whether applied to people or things, generally has positive overtones and associations for Homer. The young wife sought by Agamemnon, the new shield fashioned by Hephaistos, the new wagon driven by Priam – all are the more desirable in respect of their being young or new. The evaluation of a new song may have little in common with that of a new sword; but the distinction between intellectual and material culture is not absolute for Homer, whose list of *dēmioergoi* ('masters of public craft') includes builders as well as seers, physicians and bards.[11] One might suppose that all have the opportunity to be acclaimed for producing something new.

An organic or generational metaphor, one of growth and development over time, is inherent in *neos*. Evaluatively, this cuts both ways: what is young may be appreciated for its freshness, strength and purity, or deprecated for frailness, insufficiency and immaturity. In what specific way might the bard suppose his audience to understand song to be *neōtatē*? The modern critic recognises Homer's innovative genius in the original fashioning of inherited material, in his complex plot-structures and varied similes, in his well-developed characters and verbal inventiveness. Phemios' listeners are not invited to analyse the minstrel's novelty in these respects, only to admire and applaud his performance. *Aoidē* also includes the singing itself, that is the melodic contours of voice and instrument; musical sound was long associated almost exclusively with the words for which it was the vehicle.[12] But the melodic and instrumental elements of epic seem far less susceptible to variation and novelty than its narrative style or subject matter.[13] What may be inferred about the melic practice of epic suggests little scope for expressive variety (the limited melodic compass of Serbian oral song may be comparable in this respect).[14] Furthermore, by the sixth

---

[11] *Od.* 17.381–5. [12] Havelock, E. (1963), reaffirmed by Ford (2003) 8–9.
[13] The *phorminx* or four-stringed lyre that accompanied epic singing was tuned to fixed pitches (perhaps the four notes conventionally transcribed into the modern pitch-names *e f a d*, found in the gapped structures of most later Greek modes). The natural pitch profiles of Greek words, which are preserved for us by the accent-marks invented by the Alexandrians, may have guided the singer to produce a fitting melodic line: West (1981).
[14] E.g. those recorded by Parry and Lord, some of which are now available on CD with Lord (2000). I use the term 'melic' rather than 'musical' as a counterpart to 'rhythmic', i.e. to embrace all

century epic performance had shifted to non-melodic (or semi-melodic) recitation by rhapsodes, and the absence of 'music' was evidently not accounted much of a loss.

In view of these considerations, Telemakhos' 'newest song' should be taken as referring not to the sound of Phemios' song, but at least principally to narrative novelty. Penelope's words show that Phemios' song is not a wholesale departure in tone or content, let alone in melodic form, from other items in the bard's repertoire of *thelktēria*.[15] In extempore oral composition of the kind that epic composition comprises, various kinds of verbal innovation are possible. New words and names must be adapted to the metre of the hexameter; new epithets and formulae may be created and manipulated; new stories and characters are invented and elaborated. But Homer is not advertising either Phemios' or his own mastery of bardic technique. What is praised as novel is not the creative process but the particular product of that skill, the song that 'circulates' (*amphipelētai*) on the occasion of performance. The newness of Phemios' 'newest song' is imagined from the viewpoint not of the bard, but of the listeners (*akouontessi*): the focus is on the way they are affected by the song, not on any appreciation of how it is composed.[16]

In accordance with the temporal signification of *neos*, the effect of novelty may seem to arise when a song is 'young' – that is, when its narratives, themes and characters have not circulated long enough to be familiar to its audience. Insofar as the newest song must be one which deals with, relatively speaking, the most recent events, it is likely to include incidents and depictions previously unheard by its listeners, and to present them in a novel form and manner. The *nostoi* of heroes returning from a war that ended some ten years earlier will not be supposed to constitute an entirely new theme for Phemios or his audience. In the scheme of things they count as recent: they are not of an age with the long-past voyage of Argo 'enthralling to all' (*pāsi melousa*), the campaign of the Seven against Thebes, the gigantomachies and theogonies set close to the dawn of time.[17] Phemios' *nostoi* tell of the deeds and adventures of warriors who are notionally the

---

the elements that may have contributed to the melodic realisation of song (such as instrumental accompaniment, the use of 'harmonic' scale structures, heterophony etc.).

[15] Powell, B. (2002) 141: 'The Homeric *aoidos* was an oral poet, a *guslar*, who made new songs every time he sang, depending on traditional stories, traditional themes, and traditional language, but always adjusting his story to his audience and the needs of the moment.'

[16] Plato's citation of these verses with the variant *aeidontessi* (singers) is discussed below (p. 190).

[17] *Pāsi melousa* is literally 'of concern/interest to all'. I have suggested (2005: 99, with n. 5) some underlying wordplay with *melos* ('song'), a word not used by Homer (though *melpō* is).

audience's own contemporaries, some of whose returns have not yet been sung or even, as in Odysseus' case, not yet accomplished.[18]

The audience will be more appreciative of Phemios' song not only because it is new, but because it is news. Elements of subject matter will be new simply because they tell of recent events, and all the more painful for Penelope because of her preoccupation with Odysseus' failure to return home. But for Phemios and his listeners there remains in the background a song that is yet to be sung, the *nostos* of Odysseus. Homer's audience may be expected to recognise that the very song they are listening to would be, for Phemios' listeners, the newest and most glorious of all.[19] The newness of Phemios' song reflects on Homer's status no less than it captivates the listeners who are said to acclaim it. The Muse communicates to the minstrel new information about people and events, and about divine motives and actions. This material, arising from singers' artistic elaboration and drawing on his imaginative and technical resources, is presented by bards themselves as Muse-inspired 'fictions resembling the truth' (*pseudē etumoisin homoia*). While the verisimilitude of Phemios' song makes it distressing to Penelope, its novelty does not preclude her previously having heard similar *nostoi*, the kind of songs that always give her pain because they make her think of Odysseus.

The scene in the palace at Ithaka is a reminder that novelty is not simply a formal attribute of poetry. Not only may the reworking of a familiar theme to embrace relatively recent and unsung events exhibit novel focus and structure, it can arouse new kinds of emotional response in its listeners, as well as responses that feel 'new' because they are largely indefinable. Phemios' song is both truth and fiction, both distressing and a *thelktērion*: the potential for arousing a mixed response may be part of why it is felt to be novel. Moved in different directions, listeners feel pity, fear and pleasure in different degrees, successively and simultaneously.[20] The effect of Phemios' tragic song in some way prefigures Aristotle's identification of *katharsis* as the 'proper pleasure' (*oikeiā hēdonē*) of tragedy. The qualities initially attached to the song yield to the emotions of the listener, whose sense of personal renewal through engagement with a work of art validates the attribution of novelty to it.

---

[18] Scodel (2002: 53–4) notes that Homer 'powerfully underscores the traditionality of his material ... the *Odyssey* is new in part because it so boldly assimilates other returns'.
[19] Cf. Nagy (1990) 69: '[Odysseus'] *nostos* is literally in the making, which is precisely the subject of the singer.'
[20] In *Ion* 535be Plato describes the intense physical effects that recitation of Homer could have on both rhapsode and listener, to the extent that they can no longer be thought 'in their senses' (*emphrones*).

THE DISCOURSE OF NOVELTY

Telemakhos' dictum, repeated and debated in later centuries, presented itself as a challenge and an invitation to poets and musicians in search of artistic excellence and acclaim. The divine poet, it appeared, had not only sanctioned the pursuit of musico-poetic novelty, but demanded it. Plato was concerned that the 'newest song' had the imprimatur of Homer himself, and makes Sokrates insist that the verses should be interpreted strictly as not sanctioning any fundamental innovation in music:

Whenever it is said that the music people most approve of is 'what circulates newest for singers (*aeidontessi*)', the poet should not be taken to mean a new kind (*tropos*) of singing, but only to be recommending new songs.[21]

By quoting the verse with *aeidontessi* rather than *akouontessi* ('for listeners'), Plato appears to be raising the stakes for his desired interpretation. As I have argued, the Homeric phrase is most likely to have referred to narrative rather than melic features. However, while a new story might satisfy an audience's desire for novelty, practitioners of music could be expected to have a professional inclination to develop new *kinds* of song, not just to sing new songs. Plato did indeed have the professionals in his sights – those virtuoso singer-performers of his own and an earlier generation whose efforts had revolutionised the nature of music, in his view, in a wholly detrimental fashion. Those selfsame professionals will have preferred to cite, and may even have been responsible for, the more tendentiously 'technical' variant of the Homeric line.

The modification of tradition, by means of the variation, revision or embellishment of myths, tropes, themes and so on, is recognised as the principal mechanism of Greek literary innovation. Since *mousikē* embraced both words and the music, practitioners might seek to do something novel and untried in either or both spheres. Accordingly, claims to be doing something new might point to departures in narrative or myth, to verbal dexterity, melodic variety, structural ingenuity or even ethical originality. The discourse of novelty that recurs insistently in Greek song and poetry raises the question of the extent to which 'music' and 'poetry' are separate spheres, and whether particular elements of novelty in poetry and music may be identified in each case.

Equally, the purpose of those who claim to be doing something new will vary. Some may wish to draw attention to genuine innovations; others will seek to impress or persuade their audiences or fellow professionals by such

[21] Pl. *Rep.* 424bc.

claims. Poets may be demonstrably innovative, or may appear to be doing little more than paying lip-service to the trope of novelty. The context may be that of a new tune composed for an existing text, or an existing melody that is being repeated on a new occasion. Each passage containing such a claim must be considered on its own terms; a bald compilation of assertions of novelty in Greek poetic texts is apt to conceal a wide variation of the kind of novelty to which appeal is made.[22]

No verses of Hesiod's survive to confirm that his view of musico-poetic novelty accorded with that of Homer. However, the supposition that Hesiod was no less in favour of bardic innovation is supported by whoever composed these words in Hesiod's name:[23]

> In Delos, then for the first time, did I and Homer, the bards, raise our songs,
> stitching them in new hymns (*nearois humnois rhapsantes aoidēn*),
> to Phoibos Apollo of the golden sword, child of Leto.[24]

These verses reflect an archaic context of competition and religious worship for the generation of musical novelty; gods and festival audiences demand *nearoi humnoi*.[25] Hellenic bards might in similar vein be called upon, and in turn call upon their Muse, to create new compositions to honour their gods. However, rhapsodes whose profession involved the performance of established texts were not expected to innovate.[26] In the pseudo-Hesiodic fragment, the honorific naming of Apollo with cultic epithets and genealogy is reminiscent of Homeric Hymns, in which inherited, formular elements of epic song were used to create new narratives of worship. 'Stitching minstrel-song' seems to refer to the creation of *nearoi humnoi* on these lines.

The composition of a hymn could make various demands on a poet's skill and originality. In a chant of unknown date ascribed to 'phallos-carriers' (*phallophoroi*) performing in honour of Dionysos, what is emphasised are melodic originality and complexity (*poikiliā*):

> For you, Bakkhos, we adorn this music,
> pouring forth a simple rhythm in varied song (*poikilōi melei*),
> a Muse fresh (*kainān*) and maiden, never used before
> in previous songs; but virgin-pure
> is the hymn that we strike up.[27]

---

[22] E.g. Lavecchia (2000) 134.
[23] Janko (1982: 113–15) plausibly suggests that the author was a rhapsode.   [24] [Hes]. fr. 357.
[25] The Hebrew exhortation to 'sing to the Lord a new song' occurs in *Isaiah* 42.10, with similar expressions in *Psalms* 96.1, 98.1, and 149.1.
[26] Graziosi (2002) 33–4.   [27] *PMG* 851b.

In this instance, as in pseudo-Hesiod, an exemplary inventiveness seems to be claimed by or for the singer-poets.[28] By contrast, when Alkman invokes the Muses in a partially reconstructed maiden-song (*partheneion*), he appeals to novelty of a less ambitious kind:

> Olympian Muses, [fill my] heart with
> desire for [new] singing ([*neā*]*s aoidās*):
> [I am keen] to hear
> [the maiden] voices
> of girls singing a lovely melody [to the skies].[29]

Alkman dwells less on the novelty of his '[new] song' than on the beauty of the sound he anticipates emanating from the voices of young girls.[30] In the opening of another *partheneion*, he appeals to the Muse on similar lines:[31]

> Come, Muse, clear-voiced Muse of many tunes and everlasting song,
> begin a new song (*melos neokhmon*) for girls to sing.[32]

Melos neokhmon here, like the *neā aiodā* earlier, seems to signify no more than 'another' tune.[33] The 'Muse of many tunes' may be presumed to have a wide repertoire from which a new melody may be drawn, but she need not demand anything particularly innovative in that regard. In later times Alkman had a reputation for being an innovator, but one who, commendably, innovated within tasteful bounds.[34] It was claimed that he was the first poet to set lyric (i.e. non-hexameter) poetry to music; and the *kainotomiā* of his rhythmical structures was noted. There may have been no independent grounds for such assertions other than the poet's frequent allusion to 'new songs', which were perhaps taken over-literally by later commentators to constitute a claim to his being the originator of certain features instantiated in his songs.

Pindar's Muse exercised a more demanding role than Alkman's. In his third Olympian ode, composed for Theron of Akragas in honour of a chariot victory, the poet invokes the tangible presence of the goddess. Theron's divine supporters, the heavenly twins Kastor and Polydeukes, are

---

[28] For 'exemplary' inventiveness see Attridge (2004) 36, and below, p. 210.
[29] Alkman fr. 3 *PMG* (the papyrus fragment as reconstructed by D.L. Page).
[30] For beauty as an index of newness, see above, Chapter 6.
[31] Cf. Horace *Odes* 3.1.2–4 *carmina non prius / audita Musarum sacerdos / virginibus puerisque canto* ('I, the priest of the Muses, sing songs not hitherto heard to girls and boys').
[32] Alkman fr. 30.
[33] Alternatively, from the listener's viewpoint, a song as yet unheard; cf. fr. 14c, 'strike up a new (*neokhmon*) song for maidens to sing'.
[34] [Plut.] *Mus.* 1135c; Stesikhoros too is here commended for innovating in a way that preserves *to kalon*.

imagined to have accompanied the victor as he yoked his horses to the chariot. In similar fashion, the Muse's proximity to the poet is an assurance of his successful originality:

> Just so, I believe, the Muse stood beside me
> as I found (*heuronti*) a brilliantly shining new style (*neosīgalon tropon*)
> for yoking to the Dorian sandal a splendid voice of celebration.[35]

The poet's relationship to the Muse is here aligned with that of the victorious chariot-owner to his divine patrons: the 'brilliantly shining new style' of song and dance reflects the brilliance of the tyrant's 'new' victory.[36] Newness in this case is related to the new style (*tropos*) of song, which Pindar proceeds to describe. His task, he says, is 'to combine in fitting manner the variegated strains (*poikilogārun*) of the *phorminx*, the drone of pipes and the setting of words'.[37] The combination of lyre and auloi is a standard pairing in Pindar;[38] and the 'Dorian sandal' refers to the ode's dactylo-epitrite metre, which will have presented no particular novelty in itself (it is used by Simonides, though in less complex form). But the use of dactylo-epitrites in praise poetry ('the splendid voice of celebration'), in combination with its rich instrumental accompaniment, appears to be the innovation to which Pindar is drawing attention.

By contrast, Pindar's claim to 'coin novelties' in his eighth Nemean ode relates solely to the content of the story. The poet suggests that his creative skill in refiguring ancient myth risks attracting envy (*phthonos*):

> Many a tale has been told in many a way;
> but for one who discovers novelties (*neara d' exeuronta*) and tests them on the touchstone,
> danger abounds. Words are a bait for envy . . .[39]

Fear of *phthonos* does not appear to limit the kind of innovation Pindar considers possible and desirable. Elsewhere he observes that, in poetry, novelty may be valued over age: 'praise wine that is old, but the bloom of new songs' (see p. 102 above). Pindar's poetic contemporary and rival,

---

[35] Pi. *O.* 3.4–6.
[36] For the victory as a new event, cf. p. 172 above; for the association of brightness with novelty, p. 145.
[37] Pi. *O.* 3.9–11.
[38] Mixed instrumentation: cf. Pi. *O.* 7.11–12, 10.93–4, *Nem.* 9.8 etc. The instruments are often treated in tragedy as being at odds (though less so in Euripides); cf. Prauscello (forthcoming).
[39] Pi. *Nem.* 8.20–1; an innovative praise song may have been thought worthy of greater remuneration in underscoring the strikingness of the new victory it celebrated.

Bakkhylides, acknowledges more directly the pressure of balancing tradition against innovation. In one of his paians he formulates the nature of poetic skill with the image of a relay race:

> One poet takes the cue for skill from another,
> both in days of old (*palai*) and now (*nūn*).
> [for it is no easy matter]
> to discover (*exeurein*) gates of words hitherto unsaid (*arrhētōn epeōn*).[40]

Bakkhylides here alludes to narrative content (*epē*) rather than to music or to performance. Elsewhere Pindar similarly bids to be a 'word-finder' (*heurēsiepēs*);[41] and Bakkhylides' exhortation to himself in his fifth dithyramb to 'weave something new' for Athens, the first attestation of *kainon* in Greek (see p. 72), refers primarily to the verbal content of his dithyramb.

Over half a century later, the chorus of Euripides' *Trojan Women* (413 BCE) are made to sing of Troy's fall:

> Regarding Ilion, O
> Muse, sing a song of novel strains (*kainōn humnōn*),
> a mourning-song
> accompanied by tears;
> for now I shall utter a song (*melos*) for Troy . . .[42]

The novelty here may lie both in the retelling of the story of the fall of Troy from the perspective of the defeated women, and in the fact that their *humnoi* are couched in lyric rather than epic rhythms.[43] Given the reference to *melos*, we may speculate that melic novelty was also an issue. In the decades that separate Bakkhylides from Euripides, a musical revolution was thought by ancient commentators to have taken place (see below, p. 202). By the mid fifth century, melodic and instrumental innovation was a *cause célèbre*; Euripides was notorious for the novelty of his melodic style, and was associated in this respect with the avant-garde musician Timotheos of Miletos, whose mentor and friend he was alleged to be.[44] Their novel style may have been in evidence here, and gives added point to the choral reference to *kainotēs* if the choral mourning-song was reminiscent of other 'New Musical' compositions, with their tendency to exhibit a profusion of references to novelty. Innovative effects, whether

---

[40] Bakkhyl. fr. 5; the words are taken by some to allude to Pindar's statement in *O.* 2.86–8 that 'the skilled poet is he who knows much by nature, whereas those who have learned their trade are like noisy crows whose harsh croak is pointless in the face of the divine eagle of Zeus'.
[41] Pi. *O.* 9.80.   [42] Eur. *Tro.* 511–15.   [43] Sansone (2009).
[44] Sat. *Vita* 22. On Timotheos and the New Music see Csapo and Wilson (2009).

in vocabulary, content, language, or melody, were particularly associated with the genre of dithyramb in this period (though even earlier, as we have seen, the Bakkhylidean exhortation to 'weave *ti kainon*' occurs in a dithyramb). The point was laboured in an exchange in Aristophanes' *Birds* of 414 BCE between the fictional hero Peisetairos and the real-life dithyrambist Kinesias, who speaks of the genre as literally inspiring novel 'flights':

KIN: 'I soar towards heaven on pinions light'.
  I fly here and there, along the paths of song –
PEI: We shall need a cartload of wings.
KIN: Intrepid in mind and body, ever charting a new course (*neān* sc. *hodon*)! ...
PEI: Stop your singing and tell me what you mean.
KIN: Give me wings with which to float
  high in the air, to use the clouds to make
  new (*kainous*) air-whirled, snow-clad, dithyrambic preludes.
PEI: So preludes can be plucked from the clouds?
KIN: My very art (*tekhnē*) depends upon the clouds:
  the brightest parts (*lampra*) of dithyrambs are born
  as vaporous, dusky things, streaked with bluish light, borne on the wind.[45]

In this passage the dithyramb appears to be envisaged as a virtuoso solo performance rather than the circular dance that more often characterises it. This was not the only metamorphosis the genre had undergone. The dithyrambic 'circular chorus', performed competitively at Athenian festivals through the fifth century and beyond, appears to have adopted its shape thanks to a deliberate reform of its manner of performance, to which I now turn.

PRIN AND NŪN – THEN AND NOW

The dithyramb was originally a cult-song in honour of Dionysos. After an obscure history from the time of its first mention by Arkhilokhos, it emerged as a genre of central importance in fifth-century Athens, where dithyrambic competitions held at the annual Great Dionysia preceded the inter-tribal contests for tragedy, comedy and satyr-drama. On these occasions, newly composed dithyrambs were performed by *khoroi* consisting of fifty men or boys arranged in a large circle, a structure so intimately associated with the dithyramb that it was generally called the 'circular dance',

---

[45] Ar. *Av.* 1373–6, 1382–90: the first line is a quotation from Anakreon (*PMG* 378).

kuklios khoros.⁴⁶ It had not always been so; evidence points to archaic dithyrambs being sung by a *kōmos*, a group of revellers in procession, which remained a feature of Dionysiac worship and ritual.⁴⁷ The earliest attestation to the dithyramb is a fragment of Arkhilokhos, 'I know how to give the lead (*exarxai*) to the song of lord Dionysos, the dithyramb, when my wits are lightning-struck with wine.'⁴⁸ These words could themselves have constituted part of a performance of dithyramb, in which the leader (*exarkhōn*) of a group of revellers exchanges verses with an informal chorus.⁴⁹

The indications, then, are that the dithyramb in its early manifestations was performed by a processional dance-line rather than by choreuts arrayed in a circle.⁵⁰ It follows that at some stage the circular form of the classical dithyramb was an innovation. If so, it was such a successful one that the fact of and rationale for the change were largely forgotten; but fragments of evidence have been pieced together to provide a solution to why and when the dithyramb was reformed.⁵¹ The main clue comes in Pindar's dithyramb entitled *Herakles* or *Kerberos*, written for the Thebans in the early decades of the fifth century. The riddling verses that introduce the song indicate that its dancers are modelling a new style of circular dithyrambic *khoros*:

> In former times (*prin men*) the singing of dithyrambs came
> stretched out like a measuring line,
> and the *s*-sound emerged base-born to people from singers' mouths.
> But now (*nūn*) young men are spread out wide
> in well-centred circles, well acquainted ([*eu*] *eidotes*) with
> how the Olympians too in the presence of Zeus' sceptre
> celebrate the rite of Bromios in their halls.⁵²

The dithyramb's opening words *prin men*, followed shortly by *nūn* (4, as restored), clearly indicates that a contrast is being drawn between an earlier style of performance and a newer one. The performers here are claimed to be in the know (*eu eidotes*), like initiates of Dionysiac cult;⁵³ specifically, they are *au fait* with the true form and character of this dance-genre. The 'before' and 'after' refer inescapably to dance-form: the straight-line

---

⁴⁶ In official Athenian documents of classical times references are made to 'boys' and men's [choruses]' rather than 'dithyramb' or even 'circular chorus', reflecting a perceived disjunction between the cultic functions of dithyramb and their competitive performances in the theatre.
⁴⁷ E.g. Pi. *O*.13.18–19, 'the ox-driven (*boēlatās*) dithyramb'.
⁴⁸ Arkhil. fr. 120.   ⁴⁹ D'Angour (forthcoming).
⁵⁰ Hedreen (2007: 166–8) usefully scrutinises vase-paintings for indications of dance-forms.
⁵¹ The following section essentially follows my argument for 'how the dithyramb got its shape' (1996).
⁵² Pi. fr. 70b.1–8, with my reconstructions.   ⁵³ Cf. Hardie (2000).

performance (2, 'stretched out like a measuring line') has been replaced by 'well-centred circles' (5). The reason for the change is suggested in the parenthetical third line: something relating to the sound of the *s*, connected to the earlier formation, is apparently no longer an issue.

Ancient scholarly testimonies fill in the picture. Pindar's remark about the sibilant is connected to the fact that Lasos of Hermione had composed 'as a kind of poetic riddle (*grīphos*)' an 'asigmatic song' i.e. one that did not make use of *s* at all.[54] Lasos was a highly regarded musician and *khorodidaskalos*, and was alleged to have been Pindar's teacher (though this may be a biographical connection that reflects an association of their musical styles). Lasos was invited to Athens by the tyrant Hipparkhos, where he established dithyrambic competitions. A number of stories told about him depict him as a man with a penchant for riddles, and a keen ear for words and music.[55] In particular, he was said to have taken objection, as did other *mousikoi*, to the sound of 's' in combination with the aulos.[56] Such discomfort would have been intensified if the sibilant was untidily enunciated by the large number of singers required for the performance of dithyrambs in his day. While his 'riddle' – composing a song without 's's – was an ingenious and striking means to protest against such sibilance, his more lasting solution to the problem was more practical: in place of the 'linear' dance, his performers were arrayed in a circle or concentric circles, allowing the aulos-player to stand in the middle of the 'well-centred circle(s)' so as to co-ordinate the voices of the performers and ensure that undue sibilance was controlled.

The continuation of Pindar's dithyramb (the text is incompletely preserved on a papyrus first published in 1919) depicts a scene on Olympos of wild dancing reminiscent of the ecstatic Dionysiac worship described in Euripides' *Bacchae*. There is no shortage of sibilants in the Greek, but we may suppose that the perspicuous new formation introduced by Lasos helped to mitigate any untoward effect:

> In the presence of the reverend
> > Great Mother, the whirling of tambourines strikes up,
> among them crackle castanets and torches, blazing
> > beneath the tawny pines.
> There too arise the strident cries
> > and manic shrieking of the Naiads,
> > their heads flung back in ecstasy.

---

[54] Athenaeus 10.455bc, D.H. *Comp.* 14.87–91, Aristox. fr. 87 Wehrli. J. Porter (2007)shows that Lasos' ode itself constituted the 'riddle in lyric poetry' (*grīphos en melopoiiāi*).
[55] Privitera (1965) 53.   [56] Athenaeus 11.467 (Aristox. fr 87 Wehrli).

> There too the omnipotent fire-belching thunderbolt
> is brandished, and the War-god's
> spear, and the mighty aegis of Pallas
> rings with the hissing of countless serpents.[57]

The adoption of a new form or institution quickly dulls or obliterates the memory of an older one. The purpose of Lasos' innovation may have been sufficiently well known to Pindar's generation for the riddling allusion to be understood, but it rapidly became obscured. This was helped by the fact that the innovation was made within a sphere of activity which constituted, as did the performance of other Greek ritual songs, a regularly observed routine. In this case, the effect of the change was so wholesale that the term *kuklios khoros*, 'circular dance', became (in the context of theatrical performances) synonymous with 'dithyramb'.[58]

We may be fortunate in this case to be able to discern the outline of events from surviving testimonies. There will have been countless cases of equally significant innovations in this and other spheres of activity whose introduction or implementation have left no trace at all on the historical record. Pindar adds an interesting twist in this case by attributing the new dance form only implicitly (by mentioning the *grīphos*) to Lasos' initiative, but more explicitly to the gods on Olympos. The novelty of the Theban god's circular dance is validated by appeal, not (as in many cases) to a remote tradition of mortal ingenuity nor to a recent one of non-Theban provenance.[59] It is referred to a divine model, knowledge of which is uniquely available to a poet who claims himself to be the 'choice herald of clever words' (23, *exaireton kāruka sophōn epeōn*), and through him to his chorus. Novelty and inspired *sophiā* are, as we find elsewhere, intimately connected.

A TRADITION OF INNOVATION

Pseudo-Plutarch's *On Music*, probably a third-century CE compilation of sources on Greek music, presents a narrative of more or less continual innovation in the development of the elements of musical sound – its rhythms, melodies and instrumental resources. A book of similar date, Athenaios' *Learned Banqueters*, devotes long passages of Books 4 and 14 to

---

[57] Pi. fr. 70b.9–18.
[58] This may account for why a later source (Clement of Alexandria, *Strom.* 1.18) claims that Lasos 'thought up (*epenoēse*)' the *dithyramb* rather than the 'circular chorus'.
[59] Elsewhere Pindar is happy to credit the origins of the genre to cities of which his patrons are native, such as Corinth (*O.* 13.18–19) and Naxos (sch. in *O.* 13.25).

music, presenting a similar picture mainly in relation to the development of musical instruments. The approach of both authors reflects the work of heurematographers from the late fifth century BCE.[60] Musical innovators are identified and praised for their roles, starting from the art's obscure beginnings in the activities of semi-mythical figures such as Amphion of Thebes, Thamyras and Orpheus of Thrace, and Olympos of Phrygia. These and a succession of subsequent 'first discoverers' are credited with originating the melodic and rhythmical techniques familiar to Greeks of historical times.

The perspective from which these innovations are viewed is that of the late fifth and early fourth century BCE, when critics of new musical styles became alarmed about the nature and pace of musical innovation. Aristotle observed that the new social context in Athens after the Persian Wars encouraged the growth of musical exploration and accomplishment.[61] The commentators note that in earlier times, 'while new discoveries were made, they were discoveries that conformed with dignity and propriety'. Musicians of the fifth century appeared to have betrayed the canons of their art for the sake of money and popularity:

Krexos, Timotheos and Philoxenos, and other poets of the same period, displayed more vulgarity and a passion for novelty, and pursued the popular and what is now called the 'commercial' style. The result was that music limited to a few strings and simple and dignified in character went quite out of fashion.[62]

It was supposed that before these developments, specific modes had tended to be used exclusively in association with certain genres and occasions. Aristotle relays an anecdote suggesting that a properly trained composer would have found it hard to breach the appropriate conventions:

For example, the dithyramb is by general admission a genre that requires the Phrygian mode. Musical experts adduce many instances to prove this, especially how when Philoxenos attempted to compose his dithyramb *The Mysians* in the Dorian mode he could not, but lapsed back naturally into the appropriate Phrygian.[63]

The new musical innovations paralleled the growth of technical specialisation and the mood of exploration detectable in other areas of fifth-century

---

[60] E.g. Glaukos of Rhegion's *On Ancient Poets and Musicians* (a primary source for Ps.-Plutarch), Damastes of Sigeion's *On Poets and sophists*. Glaukos' title has been taken to indicate that poetry and music had become distinguishable: Pfeiffer (1968) 53 n. 5.
[61] Arist. *Pol.* 1341a24–32. Cf. Horace's *positis bellis* ('once the wars were ended', *AP* 93).
[62] [Plut.] *Mus.* 1135cd.
[63] Arist. *Pol.* 1342b; the description of Philoxenos' *Mysians* (probably from Aristoxenos) indicates that the piece modulated away from and eventually back to the Phrygian *harmoniā*; see West (1992) 371–2.

artistic and intellectual activity. There was a brief vogue for technical innovation in musical instruments: a certain Pythagoras of Zakynthos designed a composite instrument of three lyres (the 'tripod'), and the famous aulete Pronomos of Thebes invented a rotating collar for the auloi which allowed the piper to play in different modes.[64] In both cases the aim appears to have been to exploit the possibilities of modulation (*metabolē*) which was considered a prominent feature of the new musical style. Such modulations were a natural development of musical style and technique, but were viewed by conservatives as an unwelcome innovation.[65]

The indignation aroused by the professionals seems to have been partly due to the spirit of commercialism that had entered many kinds of social interaction, creating a shift in traditional hierarchies. Novel procedures of payment reinforced the position of auletes as star performers:

> Aulos-playing changed from a simple style to the more elaborate kind of music we find today. In the old days, up to the time of Melanippides the dithyrambist, it was customary for auletes to receive their fee from the poets, since obviously the poetry came first and the auletes were subordinate to them as *khoros*-trainers. At a later date this arrangement too became corrupted.[66]

In a passage rife with sexual innuendo from Pherekrates' *Kheiron*, a comedy written in the late fifth century, the Muse identifies Melanippides of Melos as the originator of outrageous new practices and the first of a succession of Muse-violators:

> Melanippides was the beginning of my troubles;
> he was the first to grab hold of me and to loosen
> me up, with those twelve strings of his.
> But in the end he turned out good enough
> to me [as regards his art], compared to my present troubles.
> That damned Kinesias of Attica has done me such damage
> with his exharmonic twists inside the strophes,
> so that in the composition of his dithyrambs
> right and left are confused like a reflection in a shield –
> But still, I could put up with him.
> Then Phrynis assaulted me with his 'pine-cone',
> and ravaged me completely with his bending and twisting,

---

[64] Paus. 9.12.5–6; cf. Athenaeus 631e: 'Pronomos of Thebes first played all the *harmoniai* on the same *auloi*.' For Pythagoras' tripod (Athenaeus 637b) see D'Angour (2006).

[65] [Plut.] *Mus.* 1133b. The sense of 'political revolution' signified by the technical term *metabolē* (combined with the democratic associations of *polu-* words attached to this kind of music) may have contributed to its unwelcome associations: cf. Csapo (2004).

[66] [Plut.] *Mus.* 1141cd. The significance of the 'voluble' aulos for the New Music is stressed by Csapo (2004) 216–22; cf. Wilson (1999).

> getting a dozen modes out of five strings.
> All the same, he too proved acceptable:
> he went off the rails, he got back on again.[67]

Melanippides, a musician skilled in both lyre and aulos, was said to have changed the nature of the dithyramb by abandoning strophic responsion for a freer style of virtuoso performance.[68] The 'loosening up' of the Muse refers to techniques that increased the range of melodic expression. The broader ambit of notes employed by New Musicians may underlie various accounts that tell of Timotheos' 'adding new strings' to the lyre.[69]

'Without Phrynis there would have been no Timotheos', writes Aristotle.[70] Phrynis of Mytilene was the most renowned kitharist of the mid fifth century, against whom Timotheos (as he tells us) won a competitive victory around 415 BCE.[71] 'Right Argument' in Aristophanes' *Clouds*, recalling practices of lyre-playing by young pupils in the old days, says 'If one of them played the fool or did a turn like those stomach-turning Phrynis bends we hear nowadays, he'd get a good thrashing for blotting out the Muses.'[72] 'Bends' (*kampai*) must again refer to modulation between modes. But if Phrynis laid the groundwork for musical innovation, his successor Timotheos paraded his own novelty and *poikilia* loudly and with relish. His dithyrambs and *nomoi* (solo pieces with fixed melodies) were markedly variegated and sensationalistic in their exploitation of the possibilities of musical onomatopoeia and dynamic contrast: he was said to have imitated a storm in his *Nauplios* and Semele's cries in his *Birthpangs of Semele*.[73] He declared a self-conscious disregard of traditional music with the notorious verses:

> I don't sing the old songs,
> my new (*kaina*) ones are better.
> Now young (*neos*) Zeus is king:
> In the old days Kronos held sway.
> Get lost, ancient Muse![74]

---

[67] [Plut.] *Mus.* 1141df.
[68] Arist. *Rhet.* 1409b26. Another Melanippides, perhaps this one's grandfather, won a dithyrambic victory at Athens in 493. The dates of the younger Melanippides are uncertain: West (1992: 357) places his period of activity as 440–415.
[69] Timotheos' own words in *Persians* (*PMG* 791.230) referring to his 'eleven-noted metres and rhythms' on the kithara may have encouraged such stories: Csapo and Wilson (2009: 283).
[70] Arist. *Meta.* 993b15.   [71] Plut. *Mor.* 539c (Timoth. *PMG* 802).   [72] Ar. *Nub.* 969–72.
[73] Athenaeus 8.337f, 352a; on Timotheos' *poikilia* cf. Csapo and Wilson (2009) 283.   [74] *PMG* 796.

Elsewhere he defends himself against 'Spartan' hostility to his 'new hymns' (*neois humnois*).[75] His words introduce a note of defiant modernism into the rhetoric of musical innovation. For Timotheos – and for both his critics and for his admirers – *to kainon* was decisively more revolutionary than the newness extolled by Pindar and Bakkhylides.[76]

As we have seen, the new musical expressiveness spilled over into the melic component of tragedy, particularly that of Euripides. Both men represented artistic iconoclasm for Athenians. The tragedian could be accused, with comic extravagance, of combining musical styles indiscriminately, and introducing low genres into high art: Aristophanes lists 'whores' songs, Meletos' drinking-songs, Karian pipings, dirges and dances'.[77] Euripides' extension of the first syllable of *heilissō* over several notes was also sufficiently avant-garde to evoke satire.[78] The norm had once been a single note per syllable, but in this respect, as in others, Euripides was a modernist.[79]

NEW MUSIC, NEW SOUNDS

The New Music was both a social and technical phenomenon.[80] The former aspect has been considered in depth, but the scope of the latter is harder to gauge, and requires more general consideration about the place of *melos* in Greek culture. The Greek language has its own music and a melodic shape, involving syllable lengths, verbal rhythms and distinctive word-accents. Aristoxenos notes 'we actually talk about speech-melody too, which consists of the tonal inflections inherent in words'.[81] The latter, according to Dionysios of Halikarnassos, altered the pitch of a syllable by roughly a musical fifth.[82] Musical forms of song are likely to have developed from or alongside the spoken 'music' of the language, which helps explain why the sound of music could be considered as late as Plato to be inseparable from the *logos* for which it was the vehicle. By the end of the fifth century, however, the connection had been severed for most listeners, not least by generations of analytical scrutiny of both language and melody. When Gorgias defined poetry as *logon ekhonta metron*, 'words

---

[75] *PMG* 791.211–12; he also draws metapoetic attention to the newness of his golden lyre (791.202–3, *khrūseokitharin . . . neoteukhē*). 'Spartan' need not have been intended literally, but used as a term to indicate musical conservatism (Csapo and Wilson 2009: 284).
[76] Cf. Csapo and Wilson (2009) 281 n. 28.   [77] Ar. *Ran.* 1301–3.
[78] Ar. *Ran.* 1314, 1348.   [79] On Euripidean *kainotēs* cf. Chapter 9, n. 12 below.
[80] The classic discussion is Csapo (2004).   [81] Aristox. *Harm.* 1.18.
[82] D.H. *Comp.* 11.29–32; Devine and Stephens (1994: 171–2) suggest that Dionysios meant up and down a fifth from a midline, but this cannot be extracted from the Greek and it seems better to suppose that the interval was an impressionistic assessment: Probert (2003) 6.

in metre', the absence of *melos* is telling.[83] Although his purpose is to draw the connection between poetry and rhetoric (as the latter was not sung), the fact that he could overlook the demands of *melos* shows the extent to which poetic texts could be considered separate from their melodic realisation.[84]

Separate notations for vocal and instrumental use are thought to have developed around the fifth century, but an agreed system is attested only from the mid third century, the date of the earliest surviving fragments. In the absence of musical notation, the composition of melody will most often have been semi-improvisatory, within certain formulaic conventions and constraints. The tonal properties of spoken Greek and the rhythms inherent in the metrical quantities of syllables provide the only natural and memorable basis for creating the shape of the melody. The introduction of strophic forms of verse, perhaps first in the sixth century BCE, may have hastened the need for melody to diverge from the natural pitch-accent of words; but it is not clear that lines of the same metrical form needed to be melodically identical, at least not in the note-for-note manner that we understand the notion of melodic identity.[85]

Scholars have often supposed that in responsional verse word-pitch could not be taken into account in melodisation. The earliest, and only substantial, evidence for this practice is a fragment of a strophic lyric from Euripides' *Orestes* in which the melodic line pays no heed to word-pitch.[86] The fixed melody would have created a uniform melodic line between responsional verses, but at the expense of a more 'fitting' correlation with word-pitches, which, arguably, would have been more readily intelligible to a Greek audience. We are bound to wonder (and there are some suggestive fragments of evidence) whether the use of a fixed melody in these circumstances was not the rule, but a Euripidean innovation. Such an innovation would fit with Euripides' modernistic inclinations and his reputation for unconventionality. The absence of pitch correspondence may have been felt as a startling and unnatural development of traditional melodisation.[87]

Later musical fragments show a significant degree of correspondence between melody and word-accent. But the New Music initiated a split between the music composed to be performed by amateur choruses and music requiring advanced professional skills. Demands on choruses became

---

[83] Gorg. *Helen* 9.
[84] Glaukos' title *On Ancient Poets and Musicians* (see n. 60 above) has been taken to indicate that poetry and music had become distinct: Pfeiffer (1968) 53 n. 5.
[85] I argue this thesis in D'Angour (2006).   [86] Pöhlmann and West (2001) 16–17.
[87] The new musical sounds were part of a more general atmosphere of auditory novelty in late fifth-century Athens: D'Angour (2007).

increasingly technical.[88] Authors like Euripides may have sought to compensate for a decline in the skills required of choral performers by providing a fixed melody (as well as set rhythm and movement) for *khoroi* that would have been distinguishable from the more complex musicianship required of his lead soloists. The triumph of the new professionalism is indicated by the increasing popularity of complex kitharodic pieces such as Timotheos' *Persai*.[89] The new-style dithyrambs, the fashionable vehicles of musical display in late fifth-century Athens, exhibited rhythmic, melodic and dramatic complexity that required high professional skills in performance.

The decline of amateur musical skills was irreversible. While dithyrambs continued to require formal choric performances (as pictured on the 'Phrynikhos' crater of *c*.425), the term 'dithyrambic' came to be applied to virtuoso solo songs (kitharodic *nomoi*) sung to lyre accompaniment. The new musical idioms were increasingly the preserve of star performers, excluding the wider public from traditional modes of civic participation in music and turning them into musical consumers. Plato inveighs against *theatrokratiā*, 'the tyranny of the theatre audience', and censures musicians for pandering to popular taste at the expense of quality.[90] His complaints echo those levelled at popular music in other contexts and periods: Aristotle's pupil Aristoxenos deplored the desire to abandon older musical styles in order to make music more accessible to the uninitiated.[91] The difficulty of mastering the performance of more complex modern styles and the move away from improvised music towards spectacular set-piece compositions encouraged the formation of a repertoire of 'classics'. Playing the works of composers of a bygone age became customary, and heralded the increasing prominence of instrumentalists. Even old-established customs are at one stage new; but once controversial musical innovations were rapidly absorbed into the mainstream.

The new musical styles that became popular in Athens in these decades were associated by conservative thinkers with educational laxness, sexual permissiveness and antisocial individualism, attributes inevitably attached to the rebellious 'younger generation'. For the musicians themselves, they resulted from the freedom to experiment with the possibilities of their art and to acquire unprecedented popularity with audiences who, in a climate of widespread innovation, were no longer interested in musical styles which were perceived to be old-fashioned and technically unchallenging. The growing separation of musical practices from social rituals seemed to reflect a new emphasis on individual gratification at the expense of the values of

---

[88] [Arist.] *Pr.* 19.918b.   [89] *PMG* 788–91.   [90] Pl. *Leg.* 700a–701a.   [91] Aristox. *Harm.* 1.123.

community extolled in the Periklean funeral speech. The rapidity of change in musical practices seemed to contravene and belie deeply held ideas of ethos in music. In the second half of the fifth century, musical novelty had been linked by the musician and political theorist Damon of Oa to sociopolitical upheaval: 'a change to a new type of music is something to beware of as a danger to society as a whole'.[92] In the later decades, his words may have seemed to have a prophetic ring.

The problem of musical novelty exercised fifth- and fourth-century thinkers to a degree that cannot simply be put down to reactionary tendencies. One explanation is the widening of the deep-seated ambivalence in Greek culture regarding the pursuit of artistic originality as a function of the vitality of *mousikē*. Originality was admired and sought after insofar as it could be accommodated within traditions that were understood, acknowledged and revered. Plato's distaste for innovation in music was such that he wanted to turn the clock back to a period which had never existed in reality. He was inclined to dismiss the aulos wholesale, along with triangles, harps (*pēktides*) and other *polukhorda kai poluharmonia*.[93] For him, music for unaccompanied kithara was tasteless and meaningless, aiming to 'cause amazement for speed and virtuosity and through the production of animal-like sounds'.[94] Traditional Greek music required a degree of improvisation, but this meant a limited kind of innovation within a fixed framework. In citing Homer's well-known verses about musical 'novelty', Plato did not rule out variation within melodies employing conventional and respectable modes: he accepts that a limited sort of *kainotēs* is needed to forestall boredom. He speaks with admiration about the static musical traditions of Egypt, which he believed were mirrored in their political stability. Their *nomoi*, in both senses, remained in his view happily unaltered over the centuries.[95]

The other side to the conservative, backward-looking reaction to musical innovation uncompromisingly expressed by Plato was the pleasure and pride with which the new professionals like Timotheos and Philoxenos grasped the opportunity to extend the bounds of their *tekhnē*. The broadening range of musical possibilities, eschewed by the older generation, was welcomed by innovative performers keen to find new styles with which to rival their classic forerunners and to defeat their contemporaries in competitive events (cf. p. 166 above). Their controversial innovations made their music conspicuously popular in its own time, and renowned in the

---

[92] 'So says Damon, and I agree', says Sokrates (Pl. *Rep.* 424c); see Wallace (2004).
[93] Pl. *Rep.* 399de.   [94] Pl. *Leg.* 669e–670a.   [95] Pl. *Leg.* 665c.

ears of a posterity that absorbed its once radical novelty more readily than nostalgia-prone critics.[96] A character in a comedy by Antiphanes singles out the daring musicianship of Philoxenos for the highest praise, contrasting it with that of musicians who clung to traditional canons:

> Philoxenos stands head and shoulders above
> other poets. First of all he uses new (*kaina*) words
> of his own invention everywhere;
> secondly, see how well his music combines modulations
> and key-changes. He was a god among men,
> for he knew what true music meant.
> The poets of today produce only ivy-wreathed, spring-pure,
> flower-suckled poetry, dreadful stuff,
> and set others' tunes (*allotria melē*) to their wretched words.[97]

The rhetoric of reaction is reversed: here Philoxenos' adventurous words and music are praised, while the melodic traditionalism of lesser poets is condemned. Real innovations undoubtedly happened in the course of Greek musical history. But the fact that it is not easy to separate out what is new from the rhetoric of innovation, or to distinguish which elements of *mousikē* were considered new, reinforces the inextricability of the new from the vagaries of its perception and reception.

---

[96] On the lasting popularity of Timotheos see Csapo and Wilson (2009) 279–80.
[97] Antiph. fr. 207 (Athenaeus 14.643d). Some prefer to understand *allotria* as 'unfitting', but my translation seems to make better sense in the context of accusing poets of a want of inventiveness.

CHAPTER 9

Constructions of novelty

Make it new.

Ezra Pound

A recurrent theme of the foregoing chapters has been the way that the processes and products of writing and literary composition are implicated with the Greeks' constructions of novelty. Words are not simply neutral tools that symbolise an external reality. By articulating varied social expectations and viewpoints, discourses incorporate unspoken assumptions and create varied versions of the world.[1] Consequently, one might suppose that nothing is good or bad – or new or old – but thinking and speaking make it so.[2] The beginnings of critical understanding of discourse (*logos*) along these lines is evident in the relativistic doctrines of early sophists such as Protagoras and Prodikos, whose thinking influenced tragedy and comedy, Herodotean and Thucydidean historiography, rhetorical theory and medical treatises.[3] Within their different contexts, these writings indicate a clear recognition that new understandings of words, and new ways of manipulating them, offer a perhaps uniquely productive means for generating innovation.

Greek literature exhibits varying degrees of self-consciousness about doing something new in word and thought. The Greeks not only innovated by creating a literature of extraordinary range and depth, but the development of their literary forms constantly gave them new forms and models for innovation. Within these new forms, the creation of new literary texts, whether in prose or verse, invariably exploits more or less deliberate

---

[1] Burr (1995) 33–45.
[2] 'There is nothing either good or bad, but thinking makes it so': Shakespeare, *Hamlet* Act 2 Scene 2. The classic ancient statement of cognitive relativism is Protagoras fr. 1, as expounded by Plato (*Tht.* 151e–152a). Euripides' moral relativism was parodied by Aristophanes: 'What's shameful if it doesn't seem so to those who do it?' asks the incestuous Makareus in *Aeolus* (Eur. fr. 19, cf. Ar. *Ran.* 1475).
[3] The relationship of historiography, particularly Herodotean, to contemporary intellectual currents is expounded by Thomas (2000).

mechanisms of innovation – improvisation, imitation, criticism, variation, reversal and so on. Words themselves illustrate a regular principle of innovation, in the way they recombine sounds and symbols that are part of a finite series to form wholly different phonemic and lexical units.[4] Poetry and prose demonstrate multiple ways in which existing elements of this kind – formulae, themes and images, as well as words – may be combined to produce something new. Out of such elements are created scenes, narratives and histories. Each verse or sentence of an epic poem, lyric song or prose history opens up new scenarios and new possibilities for readers or hearers to perceive, imagine and ponder. Written texts are supremely versatile and effective vehicles for exhibiting and provoking varieties of novelty.

Greek writings not only describe but sometimes self-consciously reflect styles of innovation that may be observed in other spheres of activity. Aristophanes' image of Agathon setting to work on constructing a new tragic drama uses a sustained metaphor of artisanal creation:

> Agathon the word-artist is just about . . .
> to lay the scaffolds for building a play.
> He's twisting the new (*neās*) beams of words,
> planing down here, gluing a song there,
> moulding a thought and shaping a metaphor,
> waxing it over and rounding it off
> and chasing flutings in it.[5]

Aristophanes' exuberant metaphor heralds the beginnings of the discipline of literary criticism, on whose terminology he wielded a significant influence.[6] The notion that one might appropriate terms and techniques pertinent to one activity in order to innovate in another is evident in other spheres. In Xenophon's *Cyropaedia*, when the young Cyrus is being instructed by his father in military stratagems, the importance of novelty in music (an echo of the famous Homeric dictum, p. 185 above) is transferred to the practical ends of military strategy:

---

[4] Lucretius follows in the footsteps of his Greek predecessors in expounding the notion (*D.R.N.* 2.688–99). *Elementa* is the Latin equivalent of Greek *stoikheia*, literally 'things proceeding in line' that combine in different permutations to form new structures of meaning and sound; cf. Pfeiffer (1968) 60–1. *Elementum* itself may derive from the letters L M N, the first three letters (so akin to 'ABC') of the 'second half' of the alphabet (Coogan 1974).
[5] Ar. *Thes.* 49, 52–7. Aristophanes regularly depicts the New Musicians and their circle in banausic terms: cf. Csapo (2010: 121) on the metaphors connected to Euripides in *Frogs*.
[6] Willi (2003) 87–94; O'Sullivan (1992); Hunter (2010) 3–8.

Constructions of novelty 209

You must not only make use of whatever you learn from others, but must yourself be an inventor of stratagems against the enemy, just as musicians play not only the music they have learned but seek to compose new pieces (*alla nea*). Now if even in music what is new and fresh (*nea kai anthēra*) is particularly sought after, new (*kaina*) stratagems in warfare are much more likely to be approved; for they can deceive the enemy even more successfully.[7]

Literary novelty involves a myriad of authorial techniques for adapting form, content, expression and effect. Epic composition varies epithets and manipulates formulae. Lyric poetry demonstrates productive adaptations of existing metrical forms for new kinds of expression – invective, political commentary, love poetry. Attic tragedy exploits the elision and redefinition of generic boundaries. Individual elements of style, character, narrative form, metre and emotion may all serve to produce an impression of novelty in a written work which in other respects is wholly conventional; to be recognisable as novel, a particular work need only be found to be original within the scope of its genre. 'New' texts may arise when different versions of a story or myth are presented, as when Euripides and Sophokles in their respective tragedies on Elektra present self-consciously variant interpretations of the story of Orestes' return (told earlier by Aeschylus in *Choephori*).[8] An author may revise a previous work to create something new: Euripides recast a second *Hippolytus* after the failure of his first, Aristophanes revised his *Clouds* and wrote two plays entitled *Wealth*. In these cases, the new emerges by means of conscious variations on or revisions to the earlier work.[9]

As a composition unfolds sentence by sentence or verse by verse, it imitates the unfolding of the new in lived experience. At the same time it presents an artfully constructed design, imposing a fresh pattern on and giving unique or idiosyncratic definition to thoughts, images or stories. In being repetitive and recurrent, verse recapitulates the cyclicality of periodic time; in being continuous and cumulative, prose reproduces the structure of linear time. By presenting at suitable junctures the prospect of its continuation or final resolution, a narrative tale projects intimations of the future; through techniques of foreshadowing, it anticipates new prospects

---

[7] Xen. *Cyr.* 1.6.38; the passage demonstrates the easy interchange between *nea* (reflecting the Homeric *neotatē*) and the more modern term *kaina*.
[8] Burian (1997); Baldock (1997) 96–110. Cf. Euripides'*Antigone*, written after Sophokles' play, which contrives a happy ending for Antigone and Haimon.
[9] I.e. these are innovations of the 'token' rather than the 'type'. In his discussion of innovation in a (post-)modern context, Eco (1985) raises this distinction, noting that classical aesthetics 'frequently appreciated as "beautiful" the good tokens of an everlasting type' (162).

and eventualities before they arrive. The beginning and end of a composition afford it a discrete identity, an autonomous existence that allows it to be identified, scrutinised and submitted to repetition, revision or reframing. The techniques of innovation and adaptation, widely acknowledged in the analysis of literary creations, can also be applied to the way in which innovators in the wider context of Greek cultural activities set out to 'make it new'.[10]

In his *Critique of Judgment* (1790), Kant articulates a distinction between mere 'novelty' and 'exemplary originality'. A composition that is simply different from what has come before may be considered new; but a great idea or work of art possesses a different order of newness, something that makes it both unique and a model for subsequent authors.[11] The extraordinary phenomenon of Greek tragedy presents a cultural innovation in its own right, with numerous instantiations of literary exemplarity. Yet until Nietzsche's *Birth of Tragedy* (1872) there was little attempt to account for the Greeks' creation of a new genre so brimming with innovative qualities – its fusion of genres, tropes and metres, its creative revisions of myth and history, its challenging reconceptualisations of ethics and philosophy.[12] Nietzsche lamented that the intellectualising approach of Euripides signalled the end of tragedy's greatness, drawing attention to the curious irony that innovation at its most self-conscious and perceptible can be felt to detract from rather than enhance true originality.

One can innovate by telling a new tale in an old way, or an old tale in a new one. Something new may even be said by simply repeating something that has already been said. The act of repetition brings a new perspective on what is repeated; repetition makes the listener re-evaluate a statement or theme in the light of their restatement.[13] Creativity via repetition recalls the starting-point of Greek literature, the oral formulaic framework of epic song. Within a range of mythical and compositional

---

[10] Insofar as all innovation involves adapting existing material, Kirton (2003) favours use of the term 'innovation-adaptation'.
[11] Kant (1987) 175, 186–7.
[12] Michelini (2009: 170) observes that the characteristic pluriformity and variegation of Euripidean drama is an extension of tendencies intrinsic to tragedy as an art form. Euripides is a notable exemplar of wilful innovation, and appears to highlight his innovations of myth by the use of *kainos*: McDermott (1991); Wright (2010) 179–81. Cf. Segal (2001) 141–8 on Euripides' *Helen*, referred to by Aristophanes as *hē kainē Helenē* (*Thes.* 850) with multiple intent – 'young', 'recent' and 'innovative'.
[13] 'The earnest man is earnest precisely through the originality with which he returns in repetition', writes Kierkegaard (1980 [1844]: 149). The fourth-century comic poet Xenarkhos (fr. 7.1–2 ap. Athenaeus 6.225c) is more cynical: 'Poets are all mouth: they create nothing new at all, but transfer the same old things from here to there.'

bounds, bards create new narratives, characters, episodes and expressions: epic improvisation presents a paradigm of the creation of new material from a set of rules. Where does repetition end and creation begin? Because the classics of Greek literature were preserved in writing, poets and authors could be read, studied and re-fashioned by posterity. The newness of their words, which had in their time both augmented and displaced the efforts of earlier authors, presented an exemplary source of inspiration for future generations.

NOVELTY IN THE AIR

In the late fifth century, verbalisation seemed to bring about new circumstances, perspectives and social or moral 'facts'. Words might be combined to create new versions of myth and history in the composition of tragedy and historiography, new and arguably artificial *hupotheseis* about human beings' physical nature for the purpose of medical knowledge and investigation, and 'new ideas' with which to dazzle and entertain the spectators of comedy while drawing their attention to matters of social urgency. The creative, persuasive power of words was variously viewed as positive, exciting, dangerous or frightening. The subservience of words to human manipulation and choice could also seem liberating: it lessened the inherent power of discourse by empowering individuals to re-invent norms of speech, and by subjecting it through rhetorical technique to systematic control of a kind that could be mastered. But the fact that the thoughts expressed by words were shown to be variable and manipulable also made them dangerously open-ended, potentially an obstacle to the traditional pursuit of *aretē* and to the practical political aim of establishing stable grounds for moral and social interaction. Pursued as an end in itself, novelty in thought and word might be felt to triumph at the expense of truth, good sense and traditional ethical norms.

In Xenophon's *Memoirs of Sokrates*, the sophist and polymath Hippias of Elis hears Sokrates discoursing with characteristic earnestness and spars with him:

'Still the same old sentiments, Sokrates, that I heard from you so long ago?'

'Yes, Hippias,' he replied, 'always the same, and, what's more amazing, on the same topics! You are so learned that I expect you never say the same thing on the same subjects.'

'I certainly try to say something new (*kainon*) every time.'[14]

[14] Xen. *Mem.* 4.4.6–14.

Elsewhere the sophist, after boasting to Sokrates about how much he has earned from his lectures, reveals that his Spartan audiences most like to hear him expound 'heroic and human genealogies and about how cities were founded in ancient times, and basically about antiquity (*arkhaiologiā*) in general'.[15] In what appears to be the proem to one such presentation, Hippias acknowledges that the novelty and variety after which he strives arise from recombining others' thoughts and utterances:

> Some of these things may have been said by Orpheus and Musaios in a brief and unsystematic way, others by Hesiod, Homer, and other poets, and others in works written by both Greeks and foreigners. I have brought together the most important and consistent of these sources, I shall make my exposition novel and variegated (*kainon kai polueidē*).[16]

In his *Clouds*, staged originally in 423 BCE, Aristophanes lays claim to originality in more extreme terms, maintaining that he aims for wholesale differentiation from his or other poets' earlier work:

> I don't try to fool you by repeating the same material time and again,
> but I always act the sophist and introduce new ideas (*kainas ideas*),
> all totally different from each other, and all brilliant.[17]

The comedies of Aristophanes, written over the course of the Peloponnesian War and during two decades thereafter, reflect many aspects of change in Athens in the period. *Clouds* provides particular witness to the reception of numerous kinds of innovation in the late fifth century – political and intellectual, social and material – for which the manipulation of language appeared to be a common basis. The play, which survives only in its subsequent revised, unperformed, version, treats newness in various forms as something to be pursued, ridiculed, feared, admired or rejected. It revolves around the moral and educational role of the sophists as represented by the caricature of 'Sokrates'. These itinerant teachers were popularly viewed with suspicion, and *Clouds* reflects genuine concerns on the part of Aristophanes' audience. New directions taken by fifth-century thinkers seemed inseparable from the rhetorical and literary methods whereby innovation was sought and fostered. In the words of the play's anti-hero Strepsiades ('Twisty'),

> These people teach anyone who pays them to win any argument whether it's right or wrong.[18]

---

[15] [Pl.] *Hipp. ma.* 285de.   [16] Hipp. fr. B6.   [17] Ar. *Nub.* 546–8.   [18] Ibid. 98–9.

The opening monologue by Strepsiades signals the ever-present background of war and its effects on social intercourse within Athens. An immediate contrast is drawn between the past and the present:

> The slaves are snoring – not like in the old days (*ouk an pro tou*).
> Damn you, war, for many things – not least because
> I can't even punish my slaves.[19]

Strepsiades' inability to sleep arises from his worries about the debts incurred by his spendthrift son Pheidippides. His solution is to urge him to enrol as a student in the Thinkery (*phrontistērion*) run by 'Sokrates', so that he might learn to hoodwink his debtors. Pheidippides prefers to associate with upper-class knights, and initially refuses to associate with 'those pasty-faced barefoot charlatans, god-forsaken Sokrates and Khairephon' (102–4). Strepsiades applies to become a student himself, though he is conscious that he is an unsuitable candidate because of his age:

> How on earth can I be expected to learn all those
> hair-splitting arguments at my age? I'm far too old,
> and my mind's certainly not what it used to be.[20]

When he first knocks on the door of the Thinkery, a student berates him 'By Zeus, you fool, don't bang on the door so thoughtlessly – you've just made an idea miscarry on the verge of birth.'[21] The student proceeds to describe some of the ideas that Sokrates has recently 'brought to birth', including a 'most ingenious' method for measuring the length of a flea's jump – by forming wax slippers for its feet, then counting up the number of slippers needed to cover a given distance.[22] This indication of experimental method offers a rare glimpse of empirical directions that may have seemed genuinely novel at the time. In another equally inventive and clever parody of scientific analysis, 'Sokrates' explains how a gnat's hum arises from air being forced through its tube-like body and rectum.[23]

Once admitted to the Thinkery, Strepsiades encounters various kinds of activity being pursued. Disciplines including astronomy, geometry, geography, theology, meteorology, metre and grammar are represented in a comically knockabout fashion. Whatever genuine intellectual content they suggest is crudely misconstrued by Strepsiades, whose inquiries are directed at finding out how his studies might bring material advantage:

---

[19] Ibid. 5–7; cf. the ironically repeated *kai pro tou* in *Eccleziazousae* (p. 95 above).
[20] Ibid. 128–30; the young (*neoi*) are in principle associated with receptiveness to new methods and ideas (see above, p. 100).
[21] Ibid. 135–7.   [22] Ibid. 148–52.   [23] Ibid. 160–4.

SOKRATES: Let's at least see if you can learn something about rhythm.
STREPSIADES: Rhythm? How is learning about rhythm going to buy me barley?[24]

On being shown a map with the location of hostile Sparta, he exclaims with rustic naiveté 'How close it is! Find a way of moving it further away.'[25] With the war continuing on different fronts, cartography may even have been a popular preoccupation.[26] But a giant portable map on stage may have struck the audience as a new device, comparable in effect to other Aristophanic novel effects which are more explicitly indicated as such, such as the flying dung-beetle in *Peace*, the weighing of words in *Frogs* and the chorus' dancing exit in *Wasps*.[27]

Allowing for comic exaggeration, the emphasis on the novelty of *tekhnai* of rhythm, measurement, grammar, geography and so on reflects the suspicion with which new intellectual structures were viewed. Precision was a feature of these disciplines, but the terminological detail and style could seem absurd. Excessive wordiness, unnecessary precision, or 'hair-splitting' detail are used to characterise new intellectual endeavours, as is a sophisticated new vocabulary.[28] In *Knights*, Demos parodies the kind of thing 'adolescents in the perfume market' might say, using new-minted words ending in *-ikos*:

> 'Brilliant (*sophos*), that Phaiax, how ingeniously he escaped death.
> He's cohesive (*sunertikos*) and penetrative (*perantikos*),
> inventive of new phrases (*gnōmotupikos*), clear and incisive (*kroustikos*),
> excellently repressive (*kataleptikos*) of the vociferative (*thorubētikos*).'
> Sausage-seller: And I suppose you are give-the-fingerative (*katadaktulikos*)
>   to such bletherative (*lalētikou*) types.[29]

A new concern for accuracy, manifest in different ways in the work of historians, grammarians, sculptors and medical thinkers, could be misinterpreted as a desire to confuse the public for illicit ends: 'I'll defeat you... by thinking up new thoughts (*gnōmas kainās exheuriskōn*)', boasts

---

[24] Ibid. 657–8.
[25] Ibid. 215–16. Maps were nothing new: Anaximander of Miletos (sixth century BCE) had drawn a world map which provided the basis for that of Hekataios, his fellow-Milesian, half a century later (Kahn 1960). Mapmaking had developed further by the time of Herodotos, who found the inaccuracy of Hekataios' map to be 'laughable' (4.36).
[26] Plutarch twice (*Nic.* 12.1, *Alc.* 17.3) paints a striking picture of men young and old, in the run-up to the Athenian expedition to Sicily in 415, enthusiastically sketching maps of the island and its topography in the sand.
[27] Trygaios, who is acting 'mad in a whole new way' (*Pax* 54–5, *mainetai kainon tropon... heteron kainon panu*), flies to Olympos on the dung-beetle 'venturing a novel act of daring' (*tolmēma neon palamēsamenos*, 94); the chorus of *Frogs* greets the word-scales (*Ran.* 1371–2) with 'here is another marvel (*heteron teras*), new and full of strangeness (*neokhmon atopiās pleōn*)'; Ar. *Vesp.* 1536–7: 'for no one has ever done this before, take a chorus in a comedy off dancing'.
[28] Willi (2003) 118–56.   [29] Ar. *Eq.* 1375–81; Willi (2003) 139–40.

Wrong Argument in his debate with Right.[30] Financial greed was the obvious motive, and Wrong Argument claims the credentials of a 'first discoverer':

> I was the first to think up (*prōtistos epenoēsa*)
> the idea of contradicting the laws and subverting justice.
> And this is worth more than a small fortune in cash,
> to be able to argue the weaker case – and still win![31]

The new ideas and methods seemed to challenge traditional religious views of the gods and their relationship to the natural world; the Cloud-goddesses, who personify insubstantial verbiage, are also given the attributes of controlling rain, lightning and thunder, functions traditionally attributed to the Olympian deities.[32] The newly atheistic (that is, 'kainotheistic') Strepsiades scorns Pheidippides for being slow, despite his youth, to grasp the lessons he himself imagines he has learned:

STREP: What stupidity believing in Zeus at your age!
PHEID: Why do you find that so funny?
STREP: Just amazed that a youngster like you holds antiquated views (*arkhaika*).[33]

Following his re-education in the Thinkery, Pheidippides strikes his father in the course of an argument and confidently claims that he can justify his behaviour. The Chorus invite him to speak, addressing him as 'instigator and engineer of novel discourse' (*kainōn epeōn*, 1397). Pheidippides exclaims:

> What fun it is to consort with new (*kainois*) and clever (*dexiois*) things,
> And to be able to scorn established customs.[34]

First he argues that it is customary for children to be beaten for their own good, and that old men are in their 'second childhood' (1410–17). He continues:

> Was it not a man who originally (*to prōton*) made the law,
> A man like you and me, and got men of old (*tous palaious*) to adopt it?
> So why am I less able to make a new (*kainon*) law in turn
> for tomorrow's sons, that they can beat their fathers in return?[35]

---

[30] Ar. *Nub.* 893, 896.   [31] Ibid. 1039–42.
[32] Ibid. 365–411. A further invention of 'new gods' is represented by Strepsiades' replacement of Zeus by Dinos ('Whirl'): ibid. 381, 828.
[33] Ibid. 818–21.   [34] Ibid. 1399–1400.   [35] Ibid. 1421–4.

He proceeds to argue that such behaviour is found 'in nature' and may accordingly be the basis for human law, and justifies him beating his mother as well.[36]

At this point Strepsiades repents of his original plan, and suggests doing away with Sokrates and Khairephon (1464–6), invoking 'Zeus of the Fathers'. Pheidippides' response is to echo what Strepsiades had said earlier:

Listen to that, 'Zeus of the Fathers'. How old-fashioned (*arkhaios*) you are![37]

Strepsiades subsequently abandons words and resorts to violence, burning down the Thinkery with the help of his slave, and pelting its adherents (possibly including his son) with stones. The dark anti-intellectual undertones of the ending attach to the surviving, unperformed text of the play. In the original stage production, Strepsiades probably succeeded in escaping his debtors and exiting in triumph. But the play was felt to promote sophistic immorality, and the revised parabasis of the extant *Clouds* reveals the author's dismay at his audience's insusceptibility to appreciating the subtle irony of his comic invention.

THE INNOVATIONIST TURN

Late fifth-century Athens exhibits a confident innovationism, in some areas reaching a feverish intensity during the second Peloponnesian War (431–404 BCE). Athens' power had grown steadily since the end of the Persian Wars, so that by the 440s a river of people, goods, ideas and *tekhnai* flowed into Athens and out again, coming from the Athenian sphere of dominion (*arkhē*) and far beyond. New drama and music was constantly being created and performed in the theatre and Odeion, new and magnificent temples were rising on the Akropolis and in the agora, new books and treatises were being published and sold in the agora, and new colonies were being founded and expeditionary campaigns conducted under Athenian leadership. The sources paint a picture of competition in innovative venturesomeness between poets and artists, musicians and sophists, politicians and generals. Some innovations, such as the use of new artillery weapons in war and Timotheos' avant-garde style of music, were destined to last. Others, such as Pythagoras' tripod (see p. 182) or Agathon's composition of a fictional tragedy (his *Antheus*), were one-off experiments.[38] All contributed to the atmosphere of pluralism, excitement

---

[36] Ibid. 1427–46.   [37] Ibid. 1468.   [38] *Antheus*: Arist. *Poet.* 1451b23.

and irrepressible vigour to which the abundant references to *to kainon* in a variety of written works, historical, dramatic and technical, bear explicit witness.

While Athens clearly played an exceptional role in admitting and disseminating novelty in a range of domains, Athenians' daily lives – their festivals and entertainments, trade and farming activities, religious and cultic practices – differed little from those of other Greeks. It has seemed paradoxical that Athens' elite cultural ambitions and accomplishments coexisted with 'a society which remained (like its landscape and polity) small-scale, complex, intricate and embedded in agrarian rhythms'.[39] As in the modern world, the pace of life and innovationist orientation will have differed markedly between urban centres and the countryside; and the paradox appears less intractable if, for both town and country in ancient Greece, the incidences of chance (*tukhē*) are seen to present recurrent novelties no less than deliberate innovation (*tekhnē*).[40]

Both chance and skill were instrumental in creating the conditions for generating novelty. Both contributed to the unprecedented military and economic supremacy that underpinned Athens' cultural hegemony that could seem a matter of wonder (*thauma*): 'Our power most certainly does not lack for witness', declares Perikles in the Thucydidean funeral oration delivered at the end of the first year of war, 'the proof is far and wide, and will make us the wonder of present and future generations (*tois te nūn kai tois epeita thaumasthēsometha*).' Verse was the traditional medium of praise, but hard-headed realism and historical truth could be better served by the modern vehicle of rhetorical prose:

We have no need of a Homer to sing our praises, or of any encomiast whose poetic version may have immediate appeal but then fall foul of the actual truth. The fact is that we have forced every sea and every land to be open to our enterprise (*tolma*).[41]

Athens' sea-power was at the root of its success. The city's command of the sea, firmly entrenched after the Persian Wars, encouraged commercial adventurousness and introduced Athenians to a host of novelties, material and otherwise. 'The size of our city attracts every sort of import from all over the world', says Perikles, 'so our enjoyment of goods from abroad

---

[39] Davies (1992) 305.
[40] Cf. MacLeod (1983: 124) on Thucydides' characterisation of war as a 'harsh schoolmaster' (*biaios didaskalos*): 'war itself is an inventor, and its inventions are events'.
[41] Thuc. 2.41.4; all translations are from Hammond (2009). The contrast is tellingly similar to Thucydides' own claim (1.22.4) to have composed a 'permanent legacy' rather than a 'show-piece' (such as the work of the 'most Homeric' Herodotos might be described).

is as familiar as that of our own produce'.[42] The author of the political treatise known as the Old Oligarch draws the connection between maritime dominance and novelty of experience:

> If one must also mention minor matters, it is through their command of the sea that, first, the Athenians have mixed with other peoples in various lands and discovered varieties of luxury foods. The delicacies of Sicily, Italy, Cyprus, Egypt, Lydia, Pontos, the Peloponnese and elsewhere are concentrated in one place, simply because of their rule of the sea. Secondly, through hearing every language, they have acquired one word from one language, one from another. Where other Greeks prefer to stick to their own language and diet and dress, Athenians employ a mixture drawn from the whole range of Greeks and non-Greeks.[43]

The sound of exotic foreign words and accents mingling with Attic Greek was as symptomatic of Athens' openness as the enjoyment of a variety of imported commodities.[44] In a parody of the Homeric Catalogue of Ships, the comic poet Hermippos lists in epic hexameters a cascade of luxury items brought into Athens by the god Dionysos (in the guise of an Athenian merchant):[45]

> From Kyrene he has brought silphium stalks and oxhides,
> from the Hellespont mackerel and all kinds of salt-fish,
> from Thessaly barley meal and ribs of beef...
> ... from Egypt comes rigged sails, sailcloth and
> papyrus-ropes, from Syria frankincense.
> Fair Crete furnishes cypress-wood for the gods,
> Libya provides masses of ivory for sale,
> Rhodes offers raisins and dried figs, which give sweet dreams.
> From Euboia he has brought us pears and fine apples,
> servantmen from Phrygia, mercenaries from Arkadia.
> Pagasai gives us slaves and tattooed men;
> hazelnuts and glossy almonds, accessories for a feast,
> are provided by Paphlagonians.
> Phoenicia gives us dates and wheat,
> Carthage provides blankets and embroidered cushions.[46]

Along with new foods and luxury goods, interstate exchange brought new ideas and practices to Athenians' attention. New forms of religious

---

[42] Ibid. 2.38.2.
[43] [Xen.] *Ath.Pol.* 2.7–8. Marr and Rhodes (2008: 3–6) outline the arguments for dating the pseudo-Xenophontian treatise to the 420s.
[44] Aristophanes revels in 'foreigner talk': Willi (2003) 198–225.   [45] Davidson (1997) 14.
[46] Hermippos fr. 63.4–6, 12–23.

worship – notably the cults of Asklepios and Thracian Bendis – followed commercial routes, arriving first at Peiraieus, which had become the busiest *emporion* of the Greek world.[47] Sophists and thinkers converged on Athens: Protagoras came from Abdera in Thrace, as did Demokritos a generation later; Euthydemos and Dionysodoros sailed from the island of Chios, as earlier had the poet Ion; Gorgias came from Sicily, Prodikos from Keos, Hippias from Elis, Thrasymakhos from Khalkedon on the Bosporos. Some of these travelled far afield, disseminating the innovative culture of Athens. When in the 440s a new Panhellenic colony was settled at Thourioi in southern Italy, Protagoras accompanied the expedition, among other things to draw up a new law code for the city.[48] Residents of the new colony included Hippias and Herodotos and the Athenian sophists Euthydemos and Dionysodoros.

Individuals noted for their innovative flair – politicians such as Alkibiades, dramatists such as Euripides and Aristophanes, musicians such as Timotheos – boldly declared the positive benefits of new methods and approaches. Others appealed to tradition in promoting their novelties. Athens' readiness to innovate could be acceptable even to traditionalists when presented as variety of experience (*polupeiriā*) aiming at the development of individuals' excellence (*aretē*), rather than the pursuit of the new for its own sake. For Perikles, the versatility displayed by Athenian citizens ensured the cultural supremacy of their *polis*:

In summary I declare that our city as a whole is an education to Greece (*paideusis tēs Hellados*); and in each individual among us I see combined the personal self-sufficiency to enjoy the widest range (*pleista eidē*) of experience and the ability to adapt with consummate grace and ease (*eutrapelōs*).[49]

With less solemn intent, Aristophanic comedy revels in the *poikiliā* and *kainotēs* of its enterprising Athenian characters. The chorus of *Knights* approves the way the Sausage-Seller defeats Paphlagon in 'multifarious (*poikilois*) schemes and wheedling speeches', and hail him as 'a multifaceted (*poikilos*) fellow, good at working out (*eumēkhanos*) what works in sticky situations'.[50] In *Birds*, the Hoopoe summons the flocks to greet Peisetairos:

---

[47] Garland (2001) 115–17, 118–22.
[48] D.L. 9.50; Muir (1982) connects Protagoras' presence with an innovative proposal recorded by Diodorus (12.12.4) to provide free public education to the sons of citizens.
[49] Thuc. 2.41.1. The antonym *dustrapelos* is used by Sophokles, in its sole occurrence in tragedy, of the heroically 'unadaptable' Ajax (*Aj.* 914): Knox (1961) 24–5.
[50] Ar. *Eq.* 686–7, 758–9.

> Come here and learn the news (*ta neōtera*) ...
> a shrewd old man has arrived,
> novel (*kainos*) in his ideas,
> an entrepreneur of novel (*kainōn*) actions.[51]

The sole allusion to beauty (*kallos*) in the Periklean funeral speech is a reminder of the visual dimension to innovation in the city:

> We pursue beauty (*kallos*) without extravagance, and intellect without loss of vigour; wealth for us is the gateway to action, not the subject of boastful talk ... [52]

Athenians and their visitors were surrounded by visible evidence of artistic activity, worthy of more than modest pride: the city's physical appearance exceeded its true power.[53] Athens' pursuit of home-grown cultural excellence could be distanced from the extravagant self-glorification associated with tyranny or barbarian grandiosity; but in conception, grandeur and execution, Perikles' grand vision impinged on Athenians' consciousness as having no equal in previous ages. The building programme required a huge outlay of money and materials, and employed an army of artisans;[54] and Pheidias' colossal statue of Athena, commissioned for the Parthenon, was symbolic of the attempt to extend the bounds of art and craftsmanship.[55] Athenians of the 420s saw works of unprecedented magnificence rising at the heart of the city, including the graceful Ionic temple of Athena Nike (constructed around 420–410) and the Erekhtheion with its Karyatid porch (421–406).[56]

The innovative dynamism of Athens created apprehension among its rivals, who resented encroachment on their interests and suspected imperialist designs. The city's openness, even in conditions of war, was constructed by Perikles as diametrically opposed to Spartan paranoia:

> We differ too from our enemies in our approach to military matters. The difference is this. We maintain an open city and never expel foreigners or prevent anyone from finding out or observing what they will – we do not hide things when sight of them might benefit an enemy: our reliance is not so much on preparation and concealment as on our own innate spirit for courageous action.[57]

---

[51] Ar. *Av.* 252, 255–7.   [52] Thuc. 2.40.1.
[53] Ibid. 1.10.2; Athens was also filled with *objets d'art* of more modest scale, including the mass of statuary that inspired St. Paul's description of Athens in the first century CE as 'stuffed with idols' (*kateidōlos*, Acts 17.16).
[54] Plut. *Per.* 12. 6.
[55] Pliny writes (*N.H.* 34.54) 'Pheidias is rightly judged to have revealed the true possibilities of sculpture and to have demonstrated its methods', one of a series of judgements derived from the third-century author Xenokrates.
[56] Pedley (1992) 254–7.   [57] Thuc. 2.39.1.

The innovationist turn 221

The potential benefit of such an approach was not lost on some, at least, of Athens' adversaries. At the start of the Peloponnesian War, the Athenians were described by the Corinthian envoy to Sparta as untiringly innovative in politics and war:

> They are revolutionaries (*neōteropoioi*), quick with new ideas and quick to put their thoughts into action... they will dare beyond their means, take risks defying judgement, and stay confident in adversity... they are unhesitant, while you are dilatory... if they do happen to fail in some attempt, another hope is born to fill the gap... it is in their nature to have no quiet themselves and to deny quiet to others.[58]

The envoy goes on to contrast the Spartans' traditionalistic attitudes to the Athenians' inventiveness (*epitekhnēsis*) and embrace of diverse experience (*polupeiriā*):

> [I]n the present situation, as we have just pointed out, your ways are old-fashioned (*arkhaiotropa*) compared to the Athenians'. In politics as in technology (*tekhnē*) the new (*ta epigignomena*) must always prevail over the old. The established traditions may be best in a settled society, but when there is much change demanding a response there must be much innovative thinking (*epitekhnēsis*) also. This is where the Athenians have great experience, and why their systems have undergone more reform than yours.[59]

In 415 BCE, in the course of the debate on the dispatch of an expedition to conquer Sicily, Alkibiades appealed to similar considerations in extolling the benefits of experience:

> Remember too that if the city is at rest its mechanism will seize like anything else out of use, and everyone's skill will atrophy, whereas constant campaigning will add to our experience and train us to fight our cause with action rather than rhetoric.[60]

The contrast he draws between action and words had superseded the more traditional linkage of both skills. Whereas the Homeric warrior was encouraged to be both 'a speaker of words and a doer of deeds', speech appeared to have gained an unwelcome ascendancy in the 'city of words'.[61] 'Speech is the shadow of deeds', wrote Demokritos, 'False and fair-seeming

---

[58] Ibid. 1.70.2–8. The 'misspoken' words of George W. Bush (5 August 2004) create an unwitting echo: 'Our enemies are innovative and resourceful and so are we. They never stop thinking about new ways to harm our country and our people, and neither do we.'
[59] Ibid. 1.71.3.
[60] Ibid. 6.18.6. In the event, the Syracusans prove more successful at sea thanks to their *epitekhnēsis* (see p. 175); cf. MacLeod (1983) 85.
[61] Hom. *Il.* 9.443. 'City of words': chapter title, Goldhill (1986) 57. On the antithesis of *logos* and *ergon* in Thucydides, cf. Parry, A.M. (1981 [1957]).

are those who do everything in words and nothing in action.'[62] Novelty in action was to be applauded, novelty in words was a source of mistrust. In the summer of 427 BCE Kleon belaboured his audience with the contrast between their traditional model of value and their current enslavement to words at the expense of deeds:

You like to be spectators of speeches and an audience of actions. Good speakers advocating some future course of action are all the evidence you need to judge it possible, and your judgement of past actions relies less on the facts which you have seen with your own eyes than on what you have been told by plausible detractors. You certainly win the prize for gullibility to novel arguments (*kainotēs logou*) and rejection of the tried and tested. You are slaves to any passing paradox and sneer at anything familiar... You are in effect looking for a different (*allo*) world from that in which we live, and you cannot even think clearly about our present circumstances.[63]

Kleon's exasperation at the Assembly is ironic in view of his own success as a demagogue.[64] Using methods and expressions reminiscent of Perikles (including the trope of remaining consistent in his views), he himself was felt to instantiate a new style of politics.[65] The Old Oligarch expressed distaste at the situation:

Nowadays any scoundrel who wants to can stand up and devise a way of getting what is in his interest and that of those like him. You might ask 'How would such a person recognise his own interest and that of the people?' But they know that his ignorance, immorality and favour are more profitable than the good citizen's virtue, intelligence and contempt.[66]

The way that war created new understandings of words and human values emerges most strongly in Thucydides' preface to his account of the civil strife (*stasis*) in Corcyra in 427 BCE. Echoing earlier remarks about the consistent way human beings respond to circumstances, he describes the doublespeak that resulted from the civil war:

It happened then and will forever continue to happen, as long as human nature remains the same, with more or less severity and taking different forms as dictated by each new permutation (*metabolai*) of circumstances. In peace and prosperous times both states and individuals observe a higher morality, when there is no forced

---

[62] Demok. B145, B82. [63] Thuc. 3.38.4–5, 7.
[64] Thucydides here uses 'new man' Kleon's words to unmask him as a hypocritical demagogue, since the passage's modernistic antitheses 'pander to those very tastes of the audience which he repudiates': MacLeod (1983) 93–5.
[65] Connor (1971) 120–1, 132–4. 'I am the same': Perikles at Thuc. 2.61.2, Kleon at 3.38.1. Fulkerson (forthcoming) explores in depth the Greek attitudes to changing one's mind (*metameleia* etc.).
[66] [Xen.] *Ath. Pol.* 1.6–7.

descent into hardship: but war, which removes the comforts of daily life, runs a violent school and in most men brings out passions that reflect their condition. So then civil war spread among the cities, and those who came to it later took lessons, it seems, from the precedents and progressed to new and far greater extremes in the ingenuity (*kainousthai*) of their machinations and the atrocity of their reprisals. They reversed the usual evaluative force of words to suit their own assessment of actions. Thus reckless daring was considered bravery for the cause; far-sighted caution was simply a plausible face of cowardice; restraint was a cover for lack of courage.[67]

The defeat of Athens in the Peloponnesian War was bound to close down many avenues of innovative endeavour. Demosthenes' remarks about Philip's *blitzkrieg* tactics suggest that this was the kind of 'innovation to end innovation' (see p. 177).

Negative attitudes to the new are detectable in other fourth-century writings. Rhetorical instruction put an emphasis on the creation of novelty, but Gorgias' pupil Isokrates sought to combat the pejorative associations of rhetoric by insisting on its intrinsic moral dimension.[68] In his *Against the sophists* of around 390 BCE *to kainon* is no longer the means to create appealing and deceptive representations, but has been reduced to a tool of rhetorical technique:

Oratory is good only if it has the qualities of fitness for the occasion, propriety of style and innovative treatment (*kainōs ekhein*).[69]

In the developed *tekhnē* of rhetoric, 'invention' (*heuresis*) might be sought by its practitioners within a circumscribed area. Isokrates could thus commend his own innovations and look forward to the technical innovators of the future:

I believe that all the arts, rhetoric included, will make the greatest progress if one admires and extols not the people who initiated the different kinds of endeavour but those who seek to perfect every detail of them.[70]

By systematising rhetoric, the power of the spoken word was controlled. Meanwhile Plato, in the *Phaedrus*, argued that writing posed a greater danger than speech to truthful communication. This increasingly widespread technology of script allowed words to take on a life of their own, divorced from the intentions of their producers:

---

[67] Ibid. 3.82.2–4.
[68] Teisias and Gorgias supposedly instructed orators on 'making trifles important and important things trifling through the power of words, and the old new and the new old': Pl. *Phdr*. 267ab.
[69] Isok. *Soph*. 13.   [70] Isok. *Paneg*. 10.

You might think the words spoke as if they had a mind of their own, but if you question them and want to know what they are saying, they just keep on repeating the same thing. And when you write something down one way, it is bandied around equally among those who have insight and those for whom it has no relevance, and it cannot choose to whom it should speak and to whom not.[71]

The argument is reminiscent of the fourth-century sophist Alkidamas' *On the Use of Written Words* or *On the sophists*, an *epideixis* composed with a different concern in mind, the retention of oral skills in the teaching of rhetoric.[72] The work reads like a futile, last-gasp reaction to the use of writing. By the date of its composition in the 390s, writing was as much a feature of rhetorical as of other forms of education. Alkidamas laments the decline of old-fashioned skills of improvisation and recognising *kairos*, and the turn towards nit-picking precision (*akrībeia*) encouraged by the written word. While writing has its uses, it shuts down the prospect of creative novelty:

So if someone wants to become a good orator rather than a mediocre wordsmith, prefers to be able to take advantage of the *moment psychologique* than to create a precise text, is keen to evoke favour in his audience rather than resentment, desires to present his excellent powers of memory and conceal his forgetfulness, and is eager to possess an oratorical ability equal to life's vicissitudes, would it not be reasonable for him to dedicate himself actively, at all times and in all circumstances, to improvised speech? Would he not be judged by sensible men to be a man of sense for using writing only for fun and as a sideline?[73]

[71] Pl. *Phaedr.* 275de.   [72] Alcid. fr. 1 Avezzù.   [73] Ibid. 1.34.

CHAPTER 10

So what's new?

> In short, nothing is being said now that has not been said before.
> Terence, *Eunuchus* 23–4

Given the profuse and disparate manifestations of the Greeks' imaginative interactions with the new, there can be no simple historical narrative of their engagement with novelty. What is discernible, however, is that over the classical period the sensibility of change as a cyclical and repetitive process, an assumption no less evident in Greece than in other traditional societies, yielded intermittently to a more innovationist outlook. The rapid growth of knowledge and the development of new *tekhnai* were advanced by the use of writing and as a result of the intensified interchange of people, goods and ideas; and the diversification of knowledge created an ever broader acknowledgement of the role and possibilities of doing and experiencing new things. The consciousness of growing human capacity, posited by Meier (1990) as an ancient equivalent of progress, together with an increased recognition of the benefits of novelty and change, led to a more explicit embrace of the new. In the terms suggested by Csapo and Miller (1998), the kinds of novelty allowed by 'aristocratic' perspectives on temporality were augmented by (and in some areas overtaken by) new kinds of novelty afforded by 'democratic' understandings of temporality. Negative sentiments in the face of change, such as the expressions of helplessness (*amēkhaniā*) found in early lyric poetry, recede in fifth-century writings. In their place, a positive confidence in human beings' ability to control their environment is expressed by medical authors, sophists and historians, and given forceful poetic expression by the 'ode to man' in Sophokles' *Antigone*.

These writings reflect a recognition that the new need not be something that simply happens; it can be brought about through human intention, effort and ingenuity. While human beings cannot control the workings of fate, it could be felt (to paraphrase Agathon) that contingency and skill go hand in hand. Linguistic considerations reflect this shift of attitude to novelty. By the late sixth century, the semantic range of *neos* has been extended from the predominantly temporal towards the more qualitative connotations associated with *kainotēs* and the manufacture of novelty. *Neos* means not just 'young' or 'recent', but 'new', as found in the Pythagorean statement that 'nothing is wholly new (*neon*)'. In this period, the word *kainos* makes its appearance for the first time in Greek texts. The import and creation during the orientalising period (eighth to sixth centuries) of beautiful, bright and highly finished 'new' objects of manufacture from the Near East may have contributed to the sense that something can be 'brand-new'. The derivation I have proposed for *kainos* (Chapter 3) raises a nexus of associations to manufactured artificiality, externality, brightness and technological elaboration. These notions do not displace the common associations of *neos* to youth, recency and natural, organic change, but they augment and complement them.

Greek society was famously agonistic; but competition was directed towards excellence, and only in some areas (such as *mousikē*) was innovation thought to contribute to that goal. However, the impulse to create new ideas and products was underpinned by the culturally approved competitiveness found in many contexts of Greek life, and was variously rewarded and incentivised in different spheres of technical and artistic activity. In the case of musico-literary products, the notion of novelty is insistently raised over the centuries from Homer to Plato (and beyond). The earliest bards do not vaunt their *tekhnē*, their songs come from the Muse; while new things could be the product of human devising, a sense of due humility might more often attribute their novelty to external sources, whether human or superhuman. The notion of invention as deliberate personal creation accompanies the increased use of terms such as *tekhnē*, *akrībeia* and *poiēsis*, words which indicate a recognition of the role of human effort, care and capability.

These qualities come into sharper focus with the use of *kainos*. Its first secure attestation in Bakkhylides relates to *mousikē*, as does its occurrence in one of the most forthright claims to novelty by Timotheos. Considered a value in epic, novelty becomes a demand in lyric poetry, and a programmatic pursuit for New Musicians. By the fifth century, *to kainon* is considered a desideratum in areas as widely removed from one another as warfare, the visual arts and dramaturgy. Distanced from temporal significations, the attribute of *kainotēs* holds greater promise of unexpectedness, wonder and salience. It proposes the existence of an intrinsic quality of novelty whereby the new no longer appears to depend on the old, but to oppose it, is no longer bound to yield to age, but brings with it a persistent (and to some observers, alarming) freshness. This usage heralds the recognition that some products – first and foremost the songs of Homer – are old, but do not age; that is, the earliest intimations of the idea of the classical.[1] Plutarch writes of the Periklean buildings on the Akropolis:

> They are all the more wonderful because they were created in a short time for all time. Each in their beauty was at that time and at once antique (*arkhaion*), but in their vigour each is even today fresh (*prosphaton*) and newly made (*neourgon*). A bloom of perpetual newness (*kainotēs*) rests on them, making them seem untouched by time, as if an ever-flourishing, ageless spirit is mingled with them.[2]

In Greek art and sculpture, the shift in the course of the fifth century from fluent creativity to a more self-conscious innovativeness is manifested in a tendency to ornateness and intricacy, calculated archaising and the pursuit of bizarre subjects and effects. The profusion of visual experience with which Greeks were presented in their daily lives was not matched by a high level of critical sophistication. The predominant criterion for judging works of art seems to have remained a naive representationalism, and innovation in this respect was sought out by artists and prized by their viewers. The opportunity to theorise about artistic creation in written form, exemplified by Polykleitos' *Kanōn*, gave pictorial and sculptural disciplines a new impetus to innovate and a new degree of intellectual respectability.

When the experience of change is a regular part of life, people often acquire a taste and expectation for the new. But when novelty can bring grave discomfort, and even be a matter of life and death as in the case of political revolution and social turbulence, it is apt to be viewed with alarm and mistrust. In matters of less urgent consequence, such as the arts of leisure, entertainment and associated *tekhnai*, it is more likely to be welcomed and appreciated. A specialist *tekhnē* demands innovation; but at the same time, the fact that it is a specialism circumscribes the scope and effect of such novelty. Where innovation has a limited impact and is subject to the control of experts, novel technical advances may be sought out and celebrated. On the other hand, when novelty is restricted to a particular discipline, it may not be much appreciated outside its proper domain; and it may be the case, as in the area of ancient medicine, that the desire to innovate will lead to arbitrary hypotheses and unsound procedures.

In many areas of life, there is no wholesale separation of technical from more general spheres. With the New Music, for instance, technical

[1] D'Angour (2005).   [2] Plut. *Per.* 13.

changes seemed too closely bound up with revolutionary social changes for conservative critics to approve innovations, even if these were a natural development of the discipline; the concern expressed by Plato and others goes much further than purely aesthetic disapproval. In warfare, the context most directly concerned with life and death, the relative inertia of the earlier centuries of the period indicates a psychological aversion to finding innovative ways of killing (on the whole) fellow Greeks; but after the Persian invasions this distaste starts to be overcome by the competitive imperative to obtain victory by all means. The eventual success of Philip of Macedon in this regard is, in the view of his arch-opponent Demosthenes, the kind of innovation to end innovation. Although the impulse to find new outlets for creativity, even in the pursuit of destructiveness, cannot be suppressed, a devotion to conquest and domination puts a brake on the pursuit of more life-enhancing forms of novelty.

To say or do something *anew* may be one way of saying or doing something new. Novelty builds on the past, whether by repeating and adapting it or by criticising and rejecting it. In practice, innovation generally proceeds according to well-tried principles: proven methods are applied to new ends, novel techniques are devised to satisfy existing requirements, differentiating elements are added to pre-existing structures, familiar ingredients are recombined to create something new. Whether the impetus is competition, necessity or individual initiative, innovation demands the productive interaction of the old and the new. From the viewpoint of practitioners of an art and of self-conscious innovators, the new is likely to come about as a result of incremental advances within the frame of their *tekhnē*; in the field of medicine *to kainon* is explicitly dismissed. But from the observer's viewpoint, *kainotēs* can be a source of wonder and bedazzlement, an epiphanic process. The notion of progressive discovery unaided by supernatural revelation is intimated by Xenophanes in the sixth century, but the gradualism and painstaking empiricism of Hippocratic medicine (demonstrated in the *Epidemics*) signal a remarkable intellectual reorientation.

In a society exposed to an increasing profusion of experience, innovation is often found to involve the cross-fertilisation of disparate methods and ideas.[3] The Hippocratic *On Ancient Medicine* indicates one such process: the author reiterates a concern about the derivation of new medical theories from philosophical speculations. Lasos of Hermione, by combining

---

[3] Within any given period, innovators often appear to be seeking solutions to similar problems: Miller, A.I. (2002) shows how in the early twentieth century both Einstein and Picasso sought to address in their different ways the problems of space and time.

considerations of choral formation with concerns about verbal and acoustic precision, was able to bring about a lasting reform of dithyrambic dance. The writings of Polykleitos of Argos show how new sculptural techniques might be influenced by geometrical and anatomical thinking. Arkhinos' proposal for a new official script for Athens meshes with literary and political considerations, as well as being informed by the technical analysis of vocal production.[4] Temple sculpture provides an explicit parallel to the novel 'architecture' of Pindaric odes; techniques of carpentry provide Aristophanes with metaphors for poetic construction; and the verbal and rhetorical explorations associated with the sophists of the 'Greek enlightenment' influenced innovative directions in medicine, rhetoric and music, and in philosophical, ethnological, historical and religious thinking.

Experiencing something new involves a capacity for internal change: a change in one's psyche or perspective, an impulse to see things through fresh eyes. Innovators are often individuals who can cope well with the psychological or conceptual defamiliarisation that is required to see things in a new light. Their activities are apt to disturb the status quo in their own field or in wider society. They are often marginal figures, whether by choice or by necessity; outsiders by birth or temperament, through accident or compulsion. They may elect to stand aloof, or they may be forced to adopt an outsider's perspective through being exiled or distanced from their society. Many Hellenic innovators exemplify one or other of these positions – Homer the peripatetic minstrel from Ionia, Hesiod the son of an immigrant who sailed from Asiatic Kyme to far-flung Askra. Thales of Miletos was said to be of Phoenician birth, Alkman of Lydian; Pythagoras fled from Samos to create his following in southern Italy, Herodotos of Halikarnassos emigrated to Thourioi before returning to work on his *Histories* in Athens. Demokritos of Abdera made his way 'to Athens, where nobody knew me';[5] most of the great sophists, such as Protagoras and Prodikos, Gorgias and Hippias, were *xenoi* in the polis in which they made their mark. Hippodamos and Timotheos became celebrated figures beyond their native Miletos. Solon travelled far from his native Athens, Euripides left his city to live and die in Macedon – where he is likely to have encountered other visitors such as Agathon of Athens, Timotheos of Miletos, Zeuxis of Herakleia and Khoirilos of Samos. Original thinkers and artists, such as Thucydides, Pheidias, Kinesias, Sokrates and Diagoras of Melos, experienced rejection in different ways and to different degrees by the city in which they were born or pursued their vocations.

[4] D'Angour (1999a).   [5] D.L. 9.36.

The products of Greek culture and imagination reflect a deep engagement with the processes of internal change, as well as with external metamorphosis. Homer depicts how the characters of Akhilleus and Hektor, and Odysseus and Telemakhos, change in the course of their experiences. Characters in Old Comedy such as Dikaiopolis, Strepsiades and Trygaios are shown to undergo experiences of transformation and rejuvenation. Greek mystery cults promised to transform the lives of initiates and give access to eternal *olbiotēs*. Performances of epic and tragedy were designed to transport audiences, affecting listeners' perspectives and emotions and instructing them both through intellectual engagement and by means of the kind of experience identified by Aristotle as *katharsis*. The new forms of education devised – the establishment of schools, the pedagogy of children in letters, music and gymnastics, and in due course the 'higher' education provided by sophists and philosophers – could alter both the structure of individual minds and the direction of social evolution. While the individuals who engendered the kinds of innovation that have left their mark on the historical record were on the whole exceptional and inspired men, the effusion of new ideas and behaviours demanded wider popular engagement with new techniques and ideas. So long as fundamental norms and values were not fatally threatened, the Greeks appear to have been ready to adopt and embrace all manner of innovations.

New ideas can be felt either to be adopted from 'outside' or generated within the framework of a native culture or individual mind. For the Greek heroes of epic, what is new most often seems to come from outside themselves: divinities provide benefits and demand honour for them. Homer and Hesiod take their own source of inspiration to be the Muse (or Muses); and in general, gods are given the credit for bestowing benefits on mortals in spheres in which the new is variously encountered, from music and divination to cereal farming and success on the battlefield. Other novelties are acknowledged as being derived from different cultures: Phoenician letters, Egyptian medicine and statuary and Babylonian mathematics represent some of the numerous non-Greek areas of knowledge – which, however, present possibilities for transformation and improvement into a new and appropriately Hellenic form. Even demonstrably native developments such as Dionysiac cult and musical 'modes' may be imagined to be, in origin, foreign importations. Thinkers such as Xenophanes and Herakleitos ('I searched myself') signal a new sense of intellectual self-confidence, with their acknowledgement that ideas and knowledge are internally generated within individuals' minds.

Whatever the provenance of the new, the way it is presented and perceived was recognised as equally or more important than any supposedly objective considerations. The Greeks understood and enjoyed the vitality of salience, whether experienced as dazzling brightness, intellectual admiration, or a sense of sheer wonder; and they set out to enjoy and create such effects of novelty in every facet of life. Ideas that are perceived as novel, as well as information about new events ('news'), have in all times and periods tended to command interest; but a fascination with new ideas and with matters that seem worthy of note (*axiologa*) is particularly characteristic of classical Greeks. During the fifth century in particular, with its military and political upheavals and extensive cultural interchanges, the Greeks will have had reason to feel that they were living (in the words of the alleged ancient Chinese curse) in 'interesting times'. Athens' leadership of a rapidly developing empire forced its citizens to engage with a multiplicity of diverse material realities and political possibilities. A thriving centre of unprecedented vigour, the city acted as the hub of a centripetal movement of people and ideas, which were in turn dispersed centrifugally across the Greek world. While we know far less about social and intellectual activity in Sparta or Corinth, Thebes or Syracuse, interactions with peoples to whom these *poleis* were allied or affiliated are likely to have given rise to new forms of thinking and experience in those cities.[6] But both to admiring and critical observers, the Athenians seemed to have a particular and unusually positive orientation to innovation and the new.

In parallel with the increasingly explicit embrace of novelty, the Greeks were familiar with the supposition or subterfuge that the new might in fact be 'nothing new'. Assimilating novelty to tradition, and viewing innovation as no more than renovation, can often operate as conscious or unconscious mechanisms for allowing individuals and collectives to come to terms with novelty: such strategies do not reduce innovativeness, but can reframe it in a way that may be felt to make it more acceptable. The desire to avoid presenting novelty for what it is may indeed be thought a characteristic way for Greeks to allow themselves to be innovative; but no less characteristic of the Greeks is their desire to claim novelty for creative endeavours and achievements. Far from precluding novelty, an intensive engagement with the past is often a stimulus to the generation of the new. Secure in the traditions that they inherited and adapted, revered or criticised, the Greeks embraced the new no less than they feared it, and sought out novelty even while they denounced it. The multiple ways in which newness recurs in

[6] Cf. Brock and Hodkinson (2000).

the historical, literary and artistic expressions of Hellenic imagination give witness to a complex and deeply ingrained fascination with the notion; and the elements present in the ancient understanding of the new – youthfulness, artifice, competition, differentiation, futurity and so on – form much the same set, if in different configurations and with different emphases, as those recognisable to us as indicating newness. Some scholars continue to take it as a given that the Greeks were 'in the grip of the past'.[7] The variety, salience and vigour of the Greeks' imaginative orientations to old and new demonstrated in this book can no longer admit the unqualified reiteration of such a premise.

[7] E.g. Grethlein (2010: 2): 'As B.A. van Groningen noted, the Greeks were in the grip of the past.'

References

Abbreviations for journal titles conform to those used in *L'Année Philologique*

CAH 5²   D.M. Lewis *et al.* (1992) *The Cambridge Ancient History*, 2nd edn, Vol. 5: *The Fifth Century B.C.* Cambridge.
DK   H. Diels and W. Kranz, eds. (1952) *Die Fragmente der Vorsokratiker*. 6th edn. Berlin.
FGE   D.L. Page, ed. (1981) *Further Greek Epigrams*. Cambridge.
IG   *Inscriptiones Graecae* I³ (various editors). Berlin.
KRS   G.S. Kirk, J.E. Raven, and M. Schofield (1983) *The Presocratic Philosophers*. 2nd edn. (1st edn. 1957). Cambridge.
OED²   *Oxford English Dictionary* (1989). 2nd edn. Oxford.
PEG   Albertus Bernabé, *Poetae Epici Graeci. Testimonia et Fragmenta. Pars II: Orphicorum et Orphicis Similium Testimonia et Fragmenta. Fasciculus 1* (2004). Munich and Leipzig.
PMG   D.L. Page, ed. (1962) *Poetae Melici Graeci*. Oxford.
PMGF   M. Davie, ed. (1991) *Poetarum Melicorum Graecorum Fragmenta*, vol. 1. Oxford.
TGF   A. Nauck, ed. (1889) *Tragicorum Graecorum Fragmenta*. Leipzig.

Albright, W.F. (1972) 'Neglected Factors in the Greek Intellectual Revolution'. *PAPS* 116.3: 225–42.
Anderson, W. (1966) *Ethos and Education in Greek Music: The Evidence of Poetry and Philosophy*. Cambridge, Mass.
Apfel, L.J. (2011) *The Advent of Pluralism: Diversity and Conflict in the Age of Sophocles*. Oxford.
Arendt, H. (1990) *On Revolution*. London.
Attridge, D. (2004) *The Singularity of Literature*. London.
Austin, C. and Bastianini, G., eds. (2002) *Posidippi Pellaei quae supersunt omnia*. Milan.
Austin, M.M. and Vidal-Naquet, P. (1977) *Economic and Social History of Ancient Greece: An Introduction*. Berkeley.
Baldock, J. (1997) *Greek Tragedy: An Introduction*. London.
Barker, E. (1946) *The Politics of Aristotle*. Oxford.

Bartley, A., ed. (2009) *A Lucian for our Times*. Newcastle-upon-Tyne.
Berkun, S. (2007) *The Myths of Innovation*. Cambridge, Mass.
Bertens, H. (1995) *The Idea of the Postmodern: A History*. London and New York.
Bertman, S. (2000) *Cultural Amnesia: America's Future and the Crisis of Memory*. Westport, Conn.
Betegh, G. (2004) *The Derveni Papyrus: Cosmology, Theology and Interpretation*. Cambridge.
Bicknell, P.J. (1968) 'Did Anaxagoras Observe a Sunspot in 467 B.C.?' *Isis* 59.1: 87–90.
Biles, Z. (2007) 'Celebrating Poetic Victory: Representations of Epinikia in Classical Athens'. *JHS* 127: 19–37.
Blau, S.K. (2003) 'A Little Extra Weight Goes a Long Way'. *Phys. Today* 56: 15.
Blundell, M.W. (1989) *Helping Friends and Harming Enemies: A Study in Sophocles and Greek Ethics*. Cambridge.
Boardman, J. (1956) 'Some Attic Fragments: Pot, Plaque, and Dithyramb'. *JHS* 76: 18–20.
  (1999) *The Greeks Overseas: Their Early Colonies and Trade*. New York.
Boedeker, D. and Raaflaub, K., eds. (1998) *Democracy, Empire, and the Arts in Fifth-Century Athens*. Cambridge, Mass.
Bowie, A.M. (1993) *Aristophanes: Myth, Ritual and Comedy*. Cambridge.
Bowra, C.M. (1966) *Landmarks in Greek Literature*. Cleveland and New York.
Braund, S. and Most, G.W., eds. (2003) *Ancient Anger*. Cambridge.
Brock, R. and Hodkinson, S., eds. (2000) *Alternatives to Athens: Varieties of Political Organization and Community in Classical Greece*. Oxford.
Bronk, R. (2009) *The Romantic Economist*. Cambridge.
Budelmann, F., ed. (2009) *The Cambridge Companion to Greek Lyric*. Cambridge.
Burckhardt, J. (1998 [1872]) *The Greeks and Greek Civilisation*. Ed. O. Murray, tr. S. Stern. Oxford.
Burian, P. (1997) 'Myth into *Muthos*. The Shaping of Tragic Plot'. In P.E. Easterling, ed., *The Cambridge Companion to Greek Tragedy*, 178–208.
Burkert, W. (1972) *Lore and Science in Ancient Pythagoreanism*. Tr. E. L. Minar Jr. Cambridge, Mass.
  (1985) *Greek Religion: Archaic and Classical*. Tr. J. Raffan. Oxford.
  (1992) *The Orientalizing Revolution: Near Eastern Influence on Greek Culture in the Early Archaic Age*. Cambridge, Mass.
  (1997) 'Impact and Limits of the Idea of Progress in Antiquity'. In Mittelstrass *et al.*, eds., 19–46.
Burr, V. (1995) *An Introduction to Social Constructionism*. London.
Bury, J.B. (1932) *The Idea of Progress*. London.
Buxton, R. (1994) *Imaginary Greece*. Cambridge.
  ed. (1999) *From Myth to Reason? Studies in the Development of Greek Thought*. Oxford.
Cairns, D., ed. (2001) *Oxford Readings in Homer's Iliad*. Oxford.
Caldwell, R. (1993) *The Origin of the Gods: A Psychoanalytic Study of Greek Theogonic Myth*. Oxford.
Cameron, A. (2004) *Greek Mythography in the Roman World*. Oxford.

Carter, J.B. and Morris, S.P. eds. (1995) *The Ages of Homer*. Austin, Tex.
Cartledge, P. (1990) *Aristophanes and his Theatre of the Absurd*. Bristol.
  (1998a) *Democritus*. London.
  (1998b) 'Writing the History of Archaic Greek Political Thought'. In Fisher and van Wees, eds., 379–99.
  (2002) *The Greeks: A Portrait of Self and Others*. 2nd edn. Oxford.
  (2009) *Ancient Greek Political Thought in Practice*. Cambridge.
Caskey, M.E. and Caskey, J.L. (1986) *The Temple at Ayia Irini* (*Keos*, vol. 2). Princeton, N.J.
Chadwick, J. (1985) 'What do we know about Mycenaean religion?'. In Davies and Duhoux, eds., 191–202.
Chadwick, J. and Baumbach, L. (1963) 'The Mycenaean Greek Vocabulary'. *Glotta* 41: 157–271.
Chantraine, P. (1968) *Dictionnaire étymologique de la langue grecque*. Paris.
Christensen, P. (2007) *Olympic Victor Lists and Ancient Greek History*. Cambridge.
Christie, J. and Johnsen, E. (1983) 'The Role of Play in Social-Intellectual Development'. *Review of Educational Research* 53.1: 93–115.
Clay, D. (1994) 'The Origins of the Socratic Dialogue'. In Vander Waerdt, ed., 23–47.
Cole, A.T. (1991) *The Origins of Rhetoric in Ancient Greece*. Baltimore.
Collins, D. (2004) *Master of the Game: Competition and Performance in Greek Poetry*. Cambridge, Mass.
Connor, W.R. (1971) *The New Politicians of Fifth-Century Athens*. Princeton.
  (1977) 'A post-modernist Thucydides'. *CJ* 72: 289–98.
Conte, G.B. (1986) *The Rhetoric of Imitation*. Ithaca.
Coogan, M. (1974) 'Alphabets and Elements'. *BASOR* 216: 61–3.
Cooper, F.A. (1968) 'The Temple of Apollo at Bassae: new observations on its plan and orientation'. *AJA* 72: 103–11.
Cousland, J. and Hume, J., eds. (2009) *The Play of Texts and Fragments: Essays in Honour of Martin Cropp*. Mnemosyne Supplement 314. Leiden and Boston.
Cowley, M. and Lawler, J.R., eds. (1972) *Leonardo, Poe, Mallarmé*. Princeton.
Crowther, N.B. (1992) 'Second-place finishes and lower in Greek athletics (including the Pentathlon)'. *ZPS* 90: 97–102.
Csapo, E. (2004) 'The Politics of the New Music'. In Murray and Wilson, eds., 207–48.
  (2010) *Actors and Icons of the Ancient Theatre*. Chichester.
Csapo, E. and Miller, M. (1998) 'Towards a Politics of Time and Narrative'. In Boedeker and Raaflaub, eds., 87–126.
  eds. (2007) *The Origins of Theater in Ancient Greece and Beyond: From Ritual to Drama*. Cambridge.
Csapo, E. and Slater, W. (1994) *The Context of Ancient Drama*. Michigan.
Csapo, E. and Wilson, P. (2009) 'Timotheus the New Musician'. In Budelmann, ed., 277–93.
Cuomo, S. (2007) *Technology and Culture in Greek and Roman Antiquity*. Cambridge.

Currie, B. (2004) 'Reperformance Scenarios for Pindar's Odes'. In Mackie, ed., 49–70.
  (2005) *Pindar and the Cult of Heroes*. Oxford.
D'Angour, A. (1996) 'How the Dithyramb Got its Shape'. *CQ* 47: 331–51.
  (1998) 'Dynamics of Innovation: Newness and Novelty in the Athens of Aristophanes'. Diss. London.
  (1999a) 'Archinus, Eucleides and the reform of the Athenian alphabet'. *BICS* 43: 109–30.
  (1999b) 'Ad Unguem'. *AJP* 120.3: 411–27.
  (2003) 'Drowning by Numbers: Pythagoreanism and Poetry in Horace Odes 1.28'. *GR* 50: 206–19.
  (2005) 'Intimations of the Classical in Early Greek *mousike*'. In Porter, ed., 89–104.
  (2006) 'The 'New Music': So What's New?'. In Goldhill and Osborne, eds., 264–83.
  (2007) 'The Sound of *mousike*: Reflections on Aural Change in Ancient Greece'. In Osborne, ed., 288–300.
  (forthcoming) 'Music and Movement in the Dithyramb'. In Kowalzig and Wilson, eds.
Davidson, J. (2006) 'Revolutions in Human Time: Age-Class in Athens and the Greekness of Greek Revolutions.' In Goldhill and Osborne, eds., 29–67.
  (1997) *Courtesans and Fischcakes*. London.
Davies, A.M. and Duhoux, Y., eds. (1985) *Linear B, a 1984 Survey*. Louvain-la-Neuve.
Davies, J.K. (1992) 'Society and Economy'. In *CAH* 2: 287–305.
Davison, J.A. (1958) 'Notes on the Panathenaea'. *JHS* 78: 23–42.
Dawe, R.D. (1978) *Studies on the Text of Sophocles*, vol. 1. Leiden.
Denyer, N. (2001) *Plato: Alcibiades*. Cambridge.
Detienne, M. and Vernant, J.-P. (1978) *Cunning Intelligence in Greek Culture and Society*. Tr. J. Lloyd. Sussex and New Jersey.
Devine, A. and Stephens, L. (1994) *The Prosody of Greek Speech*. Oxford.
Dillon, M. (2002) *Girls and Women in Classical Greek Religion*. London.
Dobrov, G.W. (1995) 'The Poet's Voice in the Evolution of Dramatic Dialogism'. In Dobrov, ed., 47–98.
  ed. (1995) *Beyond Aristophanes*. Atlanta.
Dodds, E.R. (1951) *The Greeks and the Irrational*. Berkeley.
  (1973) *The Ancient Concept of Progress and other Essays*. Oxford.
Donlan, W. and Thompson, J. (1976) 'The Charge at Marathon: Herodotus 6.112'. *CJ* 71.4: 339–43.
Dossin, G. (1953) 'Les Cabires'. *Nouvelle Clio* 5: 199–202.
Dougherty, C. and Kurke, L., eds. (2003). *The Cultures within Greek Culture: Contact, Conflict, Collaboration*. Cambridge.
Douglas, M. (2007) 'Conclusion: The Prestige of the Games'. In Hornblower and Morgan, eds., 391–408.

Dover, K.J. (1974) *Greek Popular Morality in the Time of Plato and Aristotle.* Oxford.
  (1987) Review of Ehrenberg (1951) in *Greek and the Greeks: Collected papers,* vol. 1 (Oxford), 279–82.
Dow, S. (1939) 'Aristotle, the Kleroteria, and the Courts'. *HSCP* 50: 1–34.
Drews, R. (1970) 'Herodotus' other "logoi"'. *AJP* 91: 181–91.
  (1976) 'The Earliest Greek Settlements on the Black Sea'. *JHS* 96: 18–31.
Dru, A., ed. (1938). *The Journals of Søren Kierkegaard: A Selection.* Oxford.
Dunbar, N. (1995) *Aristophanes' 'Birds'.* Oxford.
Dunn, F. M. (2007) *Present Shock in Fifth-Century Greece.* Ann Arbor.
Durkheim, E. (2006 [1897]) *On Suicide,* trans. R. Buss. London: Penguin Classics.
Eco, U. (1985) 'Innovation and Repetition: Between Modern and Post-Modern Aesthetics'. *Daedalus* 114.4: 161–84.
Edelstein, L. (1967) *The Idea of Progress in Classical Antiquity.* Baltimore.
Ehrenberg, V. (1951) *The People of Aristophanes.* Oxford.
Eisenstein, E.L. (1980) *The Printing Press as an Agent of Change.* Cambridge.
Eliade, M. (1971) *The Myth of the Eternal Return: Cosmos and History.* Princeton.
Falkner, T.M. (1995) 'Ἐπὶ γήραος οὐδῷ: Homeric Heroism, Old Age, and the End of the Odyssey'. In Falkner and de Luce, eds., 3–51.
Falkner, T. M. and de Luce, J., eds. (1995) *The Poetics of Old Age in Greek, Epic, Lyric and Tragedy.* Norman, Okla.
Fantuzzi, M. and Hunter, R. (2004) *Tradition and Innovation in Hellenistic Poetry.* Cambridge.
Feinberg, H. and Solodow, J. (2002) 'Out of Africa'. *Journal of African History* 43: 255–61.
Ferrill, A. (1985) *The Origins of War from the Stone Age to Alexander the Great.* London.
Finkelberg, A. (1998) 'On Cosmogony and Ecpyrosis in Heraclitus'. *AJP* 119.2: 195–222.
Finkelberg, M. (1998) *The Birth of Literary Fiction in Ancient Greece.* Oxford.
Finley, M. (1981) *Economy and Society in Ancient Greece.* Ed. B. Shaw and R. Saller. London.
Fisher, N. and van Wees, H., eds. (1998) *Archaic Greece: New Approaches and New Evidence.* London.
Forbes, C. (1952) 'Crime and Punishment in Greek Athletics'. *CJ* 47: 169–74.
Forbes Irving, P.M.C. (1990) *Metamorphosis in Greek Myths.* Oxford.
Ford, A. (2002) *The Origins of Criticism: Literary Culture and Poetic Theory in Classical Greece.* New Jersey.
  (2003) 'From Letters to Literature: Reading the "Song Culture"'. In Yunis, ed., 15–37.
Forrest, W.G. (1975) 'An Athenian Generation Gap'. *YClS* 24: 37–52.
Foucault, M. (1989) *The Archaeology of Knowledge.* Tr. A. Sheridan. London.
Fowler, B.H. (1989) *The Hellenistic Aesthetic.* Bristol.
Fraenkel, E. (1950) *Aeschylus: Agamemnon.* Oxford.
Frame, D.M., ed. and tr. (1958) *The Complete Essays of Montaigne.* Stanford.

Freeth, T., Jones, A., Steele, J.M. and Bitsakis, Y. (2008) 'Calendars with Olympiad Display and Eclipse Prediction on the Antikythera Mechanism'. *Nature* 454: 614–17.
Freud, S. (1914) 'Remembering, repeating and working-through'. *Standard Edition* 12: 147–56.
  (1926) 'Inhibitions, Symptoms and Anxiety'. *Standard Edition* 20: 87–156.
Fulkerson, L. (forthcoming) *No Regrets: Portrayals of Remorse and Consistency in Classical Antiquity*. Oxford.
Garland, R. (1992) *Introducing New Gods: The Politics of Athenian Religion*. Ithaca.
  (2001) *The Piraeus: From the Fifth to the First Century BC*. 2nd edn. London.
  (2004) *Surviving Greek Tragedy*. London.
Garnsey, P., Hopkins, K. and Whittaker, C., eds. (1983) *Trade in the Ancient Economy*. Berkeley and Los Angeles.
Geertz, C. (1983) *Local Knowledge: Further Essays in Interpretive Anthropology*. New York.
Gill, C. (1985) 'Ancient Psychotherapy'. *Journal of the History of Ideas* 46.3: 307–25.
Gingerich, O., ed. (1975) *The Nature of Scientific Discovery*. Washington, DC.
Goldhill, S. (1986) *Reading Greek Tragedy*. Cambridge.
  (1990) *The Poet's Voice*. Cambridge.
Goldhill, S. and Osborne, R. eds. (1999) *Performance Culture and Athenian Democracy*. Cambridge.
  (2006) *Rethinking Revolutions through Ancient Greece*. Cambridge.
Gombrich, E. (1960) *Art and Illusion*. London.
Goody, J. and Watt, I. (1963) 'The consequences of literacy'. *Comp. Stud. Soc. Hist.* 5: 304–45.
Gordon, R.L., ed. (1981) *Myth, Religion and Society: Structuralist essays by M. Detienne, L. Gernet, J-P. Vernant and P. Vidal-Naquet*. Cambridge.
Gould, J. (1980) 'Law, custom and myth: aspects of the social position of women in classical Athens'. *JHS* 100: 38–59.
  (2001) *Myth, Ritual, Memory and Exchange*. Oxford.
Gouldner, A.W. (1965) *Enter Plato: Classical Greece and the Origins of Social Theory*. New York.
Graham, D.W. (2006) *Explaining the Cosmos: The Ionian Tradition of Scientific Philosophy*. Princeton.
  ed. (2010) *The Texts of Early Greek Philosophy*. Cambridge.
Grant, M. (2000) *Galen on Food and Diet*. London.
Graziosi, B. (2002) *Inventing Homer: The Early Reception of Epic*. Cambridge.
Grethlein, J. (2010) *The Greeks and their Past: Poetry, Oratory and History in the Fifth Century BC*. Cambridge.
Gribble, D. (1999) *Alcibiades and Athens: A Study in Literary Presentation*. Oxford.
Guthrie, W.K.C. (1962) *A History of Greek Philosophy*, vol. 1: *The Presocratic Tradition from Parmenides to Democritus*. Cambridge.
Hahn, R. (2001) *Anaximander and the Architects: The Contribution of Egyptian and Greek Architectural Technologies to the Origins of Greek Philosophy*. Albany.

Hall, M.B. *et al.* (1975) 'The Spirit of Innovation in the Sixteenth Century'. In Gingerich, ed., 309–34.
Hallett, C.H. (1986) 'The Origins of the Classical Style in Sculpture'. *JHS* 106: 71–84.
Halliwell, S. (1989) 'Authorial Collaboration in the Athenian Comic Theatre'. *GRBS* 30: 515–28.
Hamel, G. (2000) *Leading the Revolution*. Cambridge, Mass.
Hammond, M. (1987) *Homer: The Iliad*. London.
 (2009) *Thucydides: The Peloponnesian War*. Oxford.
Hannah, R. (2009) *Time in Antiquity*. Oxford.
Hanson, V.D. (1995) *The Other Greeks*. New York.
Hardie, A. (2000) 'The ancient etymology of ἀοιδός'. *Philologus* 144: 163–75.
Harrington, S. (1996) 'Sanctuary of the Gods'. *Archaeology* 49.2: 28.
Hartog, F. (2001) *Memories of Odysseus: Frontier Tales from Ancient Greece*. Tr. Janet Lloyd. Chicago.
Harvey, D. and Wilkins, J., eds. (2000) *The Rivals of Aristophanes*. London.
Havelock, C.M. (1995) *The Aphrodite of Knidos and her Successors*. Ann Arbor.
Havelock, E. (1963) *Preface to Plato*. Cambridge, Mass.
Heath, M. (1990) 'Aristophanes and his Rivals'. *Greece and Rome* 37.2: 143–58.
Heath, T. (1981 [1921]) *A History of Greek Mathematics*. New York.
Hedreen, G. (2007) 'Myths of Ritual in Athenian Vase-Paintings of Silens'. In Csapo and Miller, eds., 150–95.
Heinimann, F. (1987 [1945]) *Nomos und physis*. Darmstadt.
Hemberg, B. (1950) *Die Kabiren*. Uppsala.
Hendry, M. (1997) 'A Coarse Pun in Homer? (*Il.*15.467, 16.120)'. *Mnemosyne* 50: 477–9.
Henrichs, A. (1975) 'Two Doxographical Notes: Democritus and Prodicus on Religion'. *HSCP* 79: 93–123.
Henry, W.B. (2001) 'Aeschylus, "*Isthmiastae*" 77–89 Snell'. *ZPE* 134: 12.
Herington, J. (1985) *Poetry into Drama: Early Tragedy and the Greek Poetic Tradition*. Berkeley.
Hess, R.S. (1993) *Studies in the Personal Names of Genesis 1–11*. Neukirchen-Vluyn.
Heubeck, A., West, S., and Hainsworth, J.B. (1988) *A Commentary on Homer's Odyssey*, vol. 1. Oxford.
Hexter, R. and Selden, D., eds. (1992) *Innovations of Antiquity*. London and New York.
Hignett, C. (1963) *Xerxes' Invasion of Greece*. Oxford.
Hirschmann, A.O. (1991) *The Rhetoric of Reaction: Futility, Perversity, Jeopardy*. Cambridge, Mass.
Hobsbawm, E., and Ranger, T., eds. (1983) *The Invention of Tradition*. Cambridge.
Hodgkin, L. (2005) *A history of Mathematics: From Mesopotamia to Modernity*. Oxford.
Hopkins, K. (1983) 'Introduction'. In Garnsey *et al.*, eds., ix–xxv.
Hopkinson, N. (1988) *A Hellenistic Anthology*. Cambridge.

Hornblower, S. (2002) *The Greek World*. 3rd edn. London.
Hornblower, S., and Morgan, C., eds. (2007) *Pindar's Poetry, Patrons and Festivals: From Archaic Greece to the Roman Empire*. Oxford.
Horstmanshoff, H., ed. (2002) *Kukeon: Studies in honour of H.S. Versnel*. Leiden.
Hose, M. (2000) 'Der alte Streit zwischen Innovation und Tradition: Über das Problem der Originalität in der griechischen Literatur'. In Schwind, ed., 1–24.
Hoyos, D. (2010) *The Carthaginians*. Oxford.
Huizinga, J. (1971 [1938]) *Homo ludens: A Study of the Play-Element in Culture*. Boston.
Humphreys, G. (1982) *Consciousness Regained*. Oxford.
Hunter, R. (2010) *Critical Moments in Classical Literature*. Cambridge.
Hyde, W.W. (1938) 'The Pentathlum Jump'. *AJP* 59.4: 405–17.
Ingalls, W. (1982) 'Linguistic and Formular Innovation in the Mythological Digressions in the Iliad'. *Phoenix* 36.3: 201–8.
Janko, R. (1982) *Homer, Hesiod and the Hymns: Diachronic Development in Epic Diction*. Cambridge.
Jeanmaire, H. (1939) *Couroi et Courètes*. Lille.
Jex-Blake, K. and Sellers, E. (1896) *The Elder Pliny's Chapters on the History of Art*. London.
Jouanna, J. (1999) *Hippocrates*. Tr. M. DeBevoise. Baltimore.
Kahn, C. (1960) *Anaximander and the Origins of Greek Cosmology*. Indianapolis.
  (1979) *The Art and Thought of Heraclitus*. Cambridge.
Kant, I. (1987) *Critique of Judgement*. Tr. W. Pluhar. Indianapolis.
Kennedy, G., ed. (1989) *The Cambridge History of Classical Literary Criticism*. Cambridge.
Kerferd, G.B. (1981) *The Sophistic Movement*. Cambridge.
Kierkegaard, S. (1980 [1844]) *The Concept of Anxiety: Kierkegaard's Writings* Vol. 8. New Jersey.
King, M. (2003) *The Penguin History of New Zealand*. London.
Kirk, G.S. (1970) *Myth: Its Meaning and Functions in Ancient and Other Cultures*. Cambridge.
Kirton, M.J. (2003) *Adaption-Innovation: In the Context of Change and Diversity*. London.
Klein, M. (1928) 'Early Stages of the Oedipus Conflict'. *International Journal of Psycho-Analysis* 10: 167–80.
Kleingünther, A. (1933) ΠΡΩΤΟΣ ΕΥΡΕΤΗΣ. *Philologus*, Suppl. 26, 1. Leipzig.
Knight, V. (1995) *The Renewal of Epic: Responses to Homer in the 'Argonautica' of Apollonius*. Leiden.
Knox, B.M.W. (1961) 'The *Ajax* of Sophocles'. *HSCP* 65: 1–37.
Kowalzig, B. and Wilson, P., eds. (forthcoming) *The Contexts of Dithyramb*. Oxford.
Kuhn, T. (1970) *The Structure of Scientific Revolutions*. 2nd edn. Chicago.
Kullmann, W. (2001 [1968]) 'Past and Future in the *Iliad*'. In Cairns, ed., 385–408.

Kurke, L. (1991) *The Traffic in Praise: Pindar and the Poetics of Social Economy.* Ithaca.
Lang, M. (1976) *Graffiti and Dipinti: The Athenian Agora*, vol. 21. New Jersey.
Lapatin, K.D.S. (2001) *Chryselephantine Statuary in the Ancient Mediterranean World.* Oxford.
Latacz, J. (2004) *Troy and Homer.* Oxford.
Lavecchia, S. (2000) *Pindari Dithyramborum Fragmenta.* Rome and Pisa.
Lesky, A. (1966) *A History of Greek Literature.* New York.
Lévêque, P. and Vidal-Naquet, P. (1996) *Cleisthenes the Athenian: An Essay on the Representation of Space and Time in Greek Political Thought from the End of the Sixth Century to the Death of Plato.* Tr. D. Curtis. New Jersey.
Lewis, S. (1996) *News and Society in the Greek Polis.* Chapel Hill.
Lichtheim, M. (1975) *Ancient Egyptian Literature*, vol. 1. Berkeley.
Lindberg, D. (2007) *The Beginnings of Western Science.* 2nd edn. Chicago.
Littlewood, A.R., ed. (1995) *Originality in Byzantine Literature, Art and Music.* Oxford.
Lloyd, G.E.R. (1966) *Polarity & Analogy.* Cambridge.
  (1968) *Aristotle: the Growth and Structure of his Thought.* Cambridge.
  (1979) *Magic, Reason and Experience.* Cambridge.
  (1987) *The Revolutions of Wisdom.* Berkeley.
  (1990) *Demystifying Mentalities.* Cambridge.
Lloyd-Jones, H. (1971) *The Justice of Zeus.* Berkeley.
  (1990) *Greek Epic, Lyric and Tragedy: The Academic Papers of Sir Hugh Lloyd-Jones.* Oxford.
Locke, J. (1972 [1689]) *An Essay Concerning Human Understanding.* Ed. P. Nidditch. Oxford.
Loraux, N. (1992) 'What is a Goddess?'. In Schmitt Pantel, P., ed., 11–45.
  (1993) *The Children of Athena: Athenian Ideas about Citizenship and the Division between the Sexes.* Tr. Caroline Levine. Princeton.
Lord, A.B. (2000) *The Singer of Tales.* 2nd edn. Ed. S. Mitchell and G. Nagy. Cambridge, Mass.
MacFarlane, K.A. (2006) 'Choerilus of Samos and Darius' Bridge: the Scope and Content of the *Persica*'. *Mouseion* 6: 15–26.
Mackie, C.J., ed. (2004) *Oral Performance and its Context.* Leiden.
MacLeod, C. (1983) *Collected Essays.* Oxford.
Maehler, H. (1997) *Die Lieder des Bakchylides.* Leiden.
Marr, J.L. and Rhodes, P.J. (2008) *The 'Old Oligarch': The Constitution of the Athenians attributed to Xenophon.* Oxford.
Mazur, P.S. (2004) 'Paronomasia in Hesiod *Works and Days* 80–85'. *CP* 99.3: 243–6.
McDermott, E.A. (1991) 'Double Meaning and Mythic Novelty in Euripides' plays'. *TAPA* 121: 123–32.
McGlade, J. and McGlade, J.M. (1989) 'Modelling the Innovative Component of Social Change'. In van de Leeuw and Torrence, eds., 281–97.
Meier, C. (1990) *The Greek Discovery of Politics.* Cambridge, Mass.

Métraux, G.P. (1995) *Sculptors and Physicians in Fifth-Century Greece: A Preliminary Study*. Montreal.
Michelini, A. (2009) 'The "Packed-full" Drama in Late Euripides: *Phoenissai*'. In Cousland and Hume, eds., 169–82.
Miller, A.I. (2002) *Einstein, Picasso: Space, Time and the Beauty that Causes Havoc*. New York.
Miller, M. (1997) *Athens and Persia in the Fifth Century BC: A Study in Cultural Receptivity*. Cambridge.
Miller, S.G. (2004) *Ancient Greek Athletics*. New Haven.
Mittelstrass, J., McLaughlin, P. and Burgen, A., eds. (1997) *The Idea of Progress*. Berlin and New York.
Morris, S. (1991) *Daidalos and the Origins of Greek Art*. Princeton.
Most, G.W. (1993) 'A Cock for Asclepius'. *CQ* 43: 96–111.
  (2003) 'Anger and Pity in Homer's *Iliad*'. In Braund and Most, eds., 50–75.
Muhly, J. *et al.* (1985) 'Iron in Anatolia and the Nature of the Hittite Iron Industry'. *Anatolian Studies* 35: 67–84.
Muir, J.V. (1982) 'Protagoras and Education at Thourioi'. *G&R* 29.1: 17–24.
Munn, M.H. (2006) *The Mother of the Gods, Athens, and the Tyranny of Asia*. Berkeley.
Munro, H.H. (1993 [1904]) *Collected Short Stories of Saki*. Ware.
Murray, O., ed. (1990) *Sympotica: A Symposium on the Symposion*. Oxford.
Murray, P. and Wilson, P., eds. (2004) *Music and the Muses: The Culture of Mousike in the Classical Athenian City*. Oxford.
Nagy, G. (1990) *Pindar's Homer: The Lyric Possession of an Epic Past*. Baltimore.
Nesselrath, H.-G. (1995) 'Myth, Parody, and Comic Plots: The Birth of Gods and Middle Comedy'. In Dobrov, ed., 1–28.
North, R. (1964) 'The Cain Music'. *Journal of Biblical Literature* 83: 373–89.
Ober, J. (1989) *Mass and Elite in Democratic Athens*. Princeton.
  (1996) *The Athenian Revolution*. New Jersey.
  (2008) *Democracy and Knowledge: Innovation and Learning in Classical Athens*. New Jersey.
Oliensis, E. (2009) *Freud's Rome*. Cambridge.
Ong, W.J. (1982) *Orality and Literacy: The Technologizing of the Word*. New York.
Osborne, R. (2006) 'Introduction'. In Goldhill and Osborne, eds., 1–9.
  ed. (2007) *Debating the Athenian Cultural Revolution*. Cambridge.
O'Sullivan, N. (1992) *Alcidamas, Aristophanes, and the Beginnings of Greek Stylistic Theory*. Stuttgart.
Otto, W. (1933) *Dionysos: Mythus und Kultus*. Tübingen.
Padel, R. (1990) 'Making Space Speak'. In Winkler and Zeitlin, eds., 336–65.
Papenfuss, D. and Strocka, V.M., eds. (2001) *Gab es das griechische Wunder? Griechenland zwischen dem Ende des 6. und der Mitte des 5. Jahrhunderts v. Chr.* Mainz.
Parisinou, E. (2000) *The Light of the Gods: The Role of Light in Archaic and Classical Greek Cult*. London.
Parker, R. (1996) *Athenian Religion: A History*. Oxford.

(2007) *Polytheism and Society at Athens*. Oxford.
Parry, A.M. (1981 [1957]) 'Logos and Ergon in Thucydides'. Diss. Harvard. New York.
Parry, M. (1971) *The Making of Homeric Verse: the collected papers of Milman Parry*. Ed. A. Parry. Oxford.
Pedley, J.G. (1992) *Greek Art and Archaeology*. London.
Pfeiffer, R. (1968) *History of Classical Scholarship*, vol. 1. Oxford.
Piaget, J. (1999 [1951]). *Play, Dreams, and Imitation in Childhood*. Tr. C. Gattegno and F.M. Hodgson. London.
Pöhlmann, E. and West, M.L. (2001). *Documents of Ancient Greek Music*. Oxford.
Pollitt, J.J. (1972) *Art and Experience in Classical Greece*. Cambridge.
  (1974) *The Ancient View of Greek Art*. New Haven and London.
  (1986) *Art in the Hellenistic Age*. Cambridge.
Porter, J., ed. (2005) *Classical Pasts: The Classical Traditions of Greece and Rome*. Princeton.
  (2007) 'Lasus of Hermione, Pindar and the Riddle of S'. *CQ* 57: 1–21.
Porter, M. (1985) *Competitive Advantage: Creating and Sustaining Superior Performance*. New York.
Powell, A., ed. (1995) *The Greek World*. London.
Powell, B. (1991) *Homer and the Origin of the Greek Alphabet*. Cambridge.
  (2002) *Writing and the Origins of Greek Literature*. Cambridge.
Prauscello, L. (forthcoming). '"Epinician Sounds" and their Reception: Pindar and Musical Innovation'. In P. Agocs, C. Carey, and R. Rawles, eds., *Proceedings of the Epinicians Conference* (London, July 2006).
Pretzler, M. (2009) 'Form over Substance? Deconstructing Ecphrasis in Lucian's *Zeuxis* and *Eikones*'. In Bartley, ed., 157–72.
Privitera, G.A. (1965) *Laso di Ermione nella cultura ateniese e nella tradizione storiografica*. Rome.
Probert, P. (2003) *A New Short Guide to the Accentuation of Ancient Greek*. Bristol.
Pucci, P. (1987) *Odysseus Polutropos: Intertextual Readings in the Odyssey and the Iliad*. Ithaca.
Renan, E. (1948) *Oeuvres complètes*. Paris.
Richardson, N. (1981) 'The Contest of Homer and Hesiod and Alcidamas' *Mouseion*'. *CQ* 31: 1–10.
Riginos, A.S. (1976) *Platonica: The Anecdotes Concerning the Life and Writings of Plato*. New York.
Rihll, T. and Tucker, J. (1995) 'Greek Engineering: The Case of Eupalinus' Tunnel'. In Powell, A., ed., 403–31.
Robertson, C.M. (1981) *A Shorter History of Greek Art*. Cambridge.
Rogers, E.M. and Shoemaker, F.F. (1971) *Communication and Innovations: A Cross-Cultural Approach*. New York.
Romm, J. (1992) *The Edges of the Earth in Ancient Thought*. Princeton.
Rorty, A. (1992) 'The Psychology of Aristotelian Tragedy'. In A. Rorty, ed., *Essays on Aristotle's Poetics*. New Jersey, 1–22.

Ruffell, I. (2000) 'The World Turned Upside Down: Utopia and Utopianism in the Fragments of Old Comedy'. In Harvey and Wilkins, eds., 473–506.
Rutherford, I. (1994–5) 'Apollo in Ivy: The Tragic Paean'. *Arion* 3: 112–35.
　(2001) *Pindar's Paeans: A Reading of the Fragments with a Survey of the Genre.* Oxford.
Rykwert, T. (1996) *The Dancing Column: On Order in Architecture.* Cambridge, Mass.
Sansone, D. (2009) 'Euripides' New Song: The First Stasimon of *Trojan Women*'. In Cousland and Hume, eds., 193–203.
Saxonhouse, A. (1992) *Fear of Diversity: The Birth of Political Science in Ancient Greek Thought.* Chicago.
Schefold, K. (1992) *Gods and Heroes in Late Archaic Greek Art.* Tr. Alan Griffiths. Cambridge.
Schein, S.L. (1970) 'Odysseus and Polyphemus in the Odyssey'. *GRBS* 11: 73–83.
Schmidt, J. (1967 [1876]) *Synonymik der griechischen Sprache.* Amsterdam.
Schmitt Pantel, P., ed. (1992) *A History of Women: From Ancient Goddesses to Christian Saints.* Cambridge, Mass.
Schumpeter, J. (1975 [1942]) *Capitalism, Socialism, and Democracy.* New York.
Schwind, J. P., ed. (2000) *Zwischen Tradition und Innovation: Poetische Verfahren im Spannungsfeld Klassischer und Neuerer Literatur und Literaturwissenschaft.* Munich and Leipzig.
Scodel, R. (2002) *Listening to Homer: Tradition, Narrative, and Audience.* Ann Arbor.
Seaford, R. A. (1994) *Reciprocity and Ritual: Homer and Tragedy in the Developing City-State.* Oxford.
　(2003) 'Aeschylus and the Unity of Opposites'. *JHS* 123: 141–63.
　(2004) *Money and the Early Greek Mind: Homer, Philosophy, Tragedy.* Cambridge.
Segal, E. (2001) *The Death of Comedy.* Cambridge, Mass.
Shear, J. (2003) 'Prizes from Athens: The List of Panathenaic Prizes and the Sacred Oil'. *ZPE* 142: 87–108.
Shelmerdine, C.W. (1995) 'Shining and Fragrant Cloth in Homer'. In Carter and Morris, eds., 99–108.
Sherratt, S. and Sherratt, A. (1993) 'The Growth of the Mediterranean Economy in the Early First Millennium BC'. *World Archaeology* 24.3: 361–78.
Smyth, H.W. (1906) 'Aspects of Greek Conservatism'. *HSCP* 17: 49–73.
Sommerstein, A.H. (1989) *Aeschylus: Eumenides.* Cambridge.
　(1996) *Aristophanes: Frogs.* Warminster.
Spivey, N. (1996) *Understanding Greek Sculpture.* London.
Spratt, D.A. (1989) 'Innovation Theory Made Plain'. In van de Leeuw and Torrence, eds., 245–57.
Stevenson, R.L. (2006 [1881]) *Virginibus Puerisque.* London.
Stewart, A. (2008) *Classical Greece and the Birth of Western Art.* Cambridge.
Storr, A. (1972) *The Dynamics of Creation.* Harmondsworth.

Strauss, B.S. (1993) *Fathers and Sons in Athens: Ideology and Society in the Era of the Peloponnesian War*. Oxford.
Struck, P.T. (2004) *Birth of the Symbol: Ancient Readers at the Limits of Their Texts*. Princeton.
Swift, L. (2010) *The Hidden Chorus*. Oxford.
Tanner, J. (2006) *The Invention of Art History in Ancient Greece*. Cambridge.
Thomas, R. (1992) *Literacy and Orality in Ancient Greece*. Cambridge.
  (2000) *Herodotus in Context: Ethnography, Science, and the Art of Persuasion*. Cambridge.
Thomson, G. (2004) *Aeschylus: The Oresteia*. New York.
Tilg, S. (2010) *Chariton of Aphrodisias and the Invention of the Greek Love Novel*. Oxford.
Valéry, P. (1938) *Variété IV*. Paris.
van de Leeuw, S.E. and Torrence, R., eds. (1989) *What's New? A Closer Look at the Process of Innovation*. London.
van Groningen, B.A. (1953) *In the Grip of the Past*. Leiden.
van Wees, H. (2004) *Greek War: Myths and Realities*. London.
Vander Waerdt, P.A., ed. (1994) *The Socratic Movement*. Ithaca.
Vernant, J.-P. (2006) *Myth and Thought among the Greeks*. New York.
Vernant, J.-P. and Vidal-Naquet, P. (1988) *Myth and Tragedy in Ancient Greece*. New York.
Vidal-Naquet, P. (1981) 'Recipes for Greek Adolescence'. In Gordon, ed., 163–85.
  (1986) *The Black Hunter: Forms of Thought and Forms of Society in the Greek World*. Baltimore.
von Reden, S. (1995) *Exchange in Ancient Greece*. London.
Wackernagel, J. (1953) *Kleine Schriften*. Göttingen.
Wallace, R. (2004) 'Damon of Oa: a Music Theorist Ostracized?'. In Murray and Wilson, eds., 249–68.
Waterfield, R. (1997) *Xenophon: Hiero the Tyrant and Other Treatises*. Harmondsworth.
West, M.L. (1966) *Hesiod: Theogony*. Oxford.
  (1967) 'The Contest of Homer and Hesiod'. *CQ* 17: 433–50.
  (1971) *Early Greek Philosophy and the Orient*. Oxford.
  (1978) *Hesiod: Works and Days*. Oxford.
  (1981) 'The Singing of Homer and the Modes of Early Greek Music'. *JHS* 101: 113–29.
  (1983) *The Orphic Poems*. Oxford.
  (1985) *The Hesiodic Catalogue of Women: Its Nature, Structure, and Origins*. Oxford.
  (1992) *Ancient Greek Music*. Oxford.
  (1993) *Greek Lyric Poetry*. Oxford.
  (1997) *The East Face of Helicon*. Oxford.
  (2001) *Studies in the Text and Transmission of the Iliad*. Berlin and New York.
  (2007) *Indo-European Poetry and Myth*. Oxford.

Wheeler, S. (1999) *A Discourse of Wonders: Audience and Performance in Ovid's Metamorphoses*. Philadelphia.
Whitmarsh, T. (2005) *The Second Sophistic* (*Greece and Rome* New Surveys in the Classics 35). Oxford.
Willcock, M.M. (1964) 'Mythological Paradeigmata in the *Iliad*'. *CQ* 14: 141–54.
Willi, A. (2003) *The Languages of Aristophanes*. Oxford.
Wilson, P. (1999) 'The *aulos* in Athens'. In Goldhill and Osborne, eds., 58–95.
  (2004) 'Athenian Strings'. In Murray and Wilson, eds., 269–306.
Winkler, J.J. and Zeitlin, F.I., eds. (1990) *Nothing to Do with Dionysos?* Princeton.
Winnicott, D. (1982 [1971]) *Playing and Reality*. London.
Winter, I.J. (1995) 'Homer's Phoenicians: History, Ethnography, or Literary Trope?'. In Carter and Morris, eds., 247–72.
Wolfram, S. (2002) *A New Kind of Science*. Chicago.
Woodhouse, W.J. (1898) 'The Greeks at Plataiai'. *JHS* 18: 33–59.
Wright, M. (2010) 'The Tragedian as Critic: Euripides and Early Greek Poetics'. *JHS* 130: 165–84.
Wyatt, N. (1986) 'Cain's Wife'. *Folklore* 97.1: 88–95.
Yener, K.A. (1995) 'Swords, Armor, and Figurines: A Metalliferous View from the Central Taurus'. *Biblical Archaeologist* 58: 41–7.
Yunis, H. ed. (2003) *Written Texts and the Rise of Literate Culture in Ancient Greece*. Cambridge.
Zeitlin, F. I. (2002) 'Apollo and Dionysos: Starting from Birth'. In Horstmanshoff, ed., 193–218.
Zhmud, L. (2001) 'ΠΡΩΤΟΙ ΕΥΡΕΤΑΙ – Götter oder Menschen?' *Antike Naturwissenschaft und ihre Rezeption* 11: 9–21.
  (2006) *The Origins of the History of Science in Antiquity*. New York.

General index

Aeneas the Tactician, 176
Aeschylus, 96, 102, 150
Agatharkhos of Samos, 155
Agathon, 19, 42, 106, 208
   Antheus, 216
ageing, 87, 137
agōnes. See competition; contests
Akhilleus, armour of, 69, 143, 149
Alexamenos of Teos, 36
Alkaios, 143
Alkamenes, 89
Alkibiades, 53, 100, 221
Alkidamas of Elea, 49, 166, 224
Alkmaion of Kroton, 56, 128
Alkman, 192, 229
alphabet, 109, 130
   Ionic, adoption of at Athens, 131
   letters LMN, 208
ambivalence, 1, 18, 28, 80, 136, 205
Anaxagoras, 56, 122, 125
Anaximander, 120, 182
Ankhu, 59
anomie, 31
Antikythera mechanism, 183
Antiphon, 160
Apelles of Kos, 156
Aphrodite of Knidos, 141, 151
Apollodoros (painter), 151
archaism, 89
Arion of Methymna, 182
Aristophanes, 20, 32, 52
   Clouds, 39
Aristotle, 37, 119
   law of non-contradiction, 86
   on music, 199
   on *thauma*, 28
Arkhilokhos, 26, 45
   loss of shield, 20
Arkhimedes, 183
Arkhytas of Taras, 108, 127, 128, 180, 182

art, illusionism in, 150
artificiality, 142
artillery, 175, 216
asigmatic song, 197
Asklepios, cult of, 97, 219
astonishment, 148, 149
Astydamas, 60
Athena, 32, 84, 134–41
   peplos of, 73, 148
Athens, 18, 38, 41, 73, 84
   innovation in. *See in particular* Ch. 9
Attic script, reform of, 31
Augustine, St, 33

Bakkhylides, use of *kainos* by, 72, 106, 226
banausic pursuits, 39, 84, 164, 165, 208
Bassai temple, 154
battle. *See* innovation in battle
beauty, 143, 144, 220
Bendis, cult of, 97, 219
birth, 32, 119, 136
brand-new, 23, 67, 81, 139, 226
brightness, 32, 81, 100, 107, 141, 142, *cf.* radiance
Burckhardt, Jakob, 162
Bury, J.B., 16
Byron, Lord, 129

Cain. *See qayin*
Carthage, 23, 177
Cartledge, Paul, 14
catapult. *See* weapons, new
catharsis. *See katharsis*
chance, 56, 217
change, 11, 21, 29, 31, 33, 39, 44, 121, 131
   antipathy to, 27
   from without, 129
classical, idea of the, 26, 141, 204, 227
cleverness, 94, 159, 215
coinage, 83, 98, 119
colonisation, 50, 131, 219

247

General index

competition, 35, 128, 174, 226, 228
  diachronic, 61
  poetic, 102
competitive advantage, 162, 171
competitiveness, 153, 179
complexity theory, 21
conservatism, 14, 42
contests, 102, 152, 153, 166, 195
contrarian tactics, 176, 177
Copernicus, 30
creativity, 29, 35, 166, 168, 169, 210
criticism, 34, 122, 154
Csapo, Eric, 17, 225
cultural amnesia, 29, 129
Cup of Nestor, 168
cyclicality, 33, 114, 137, 209
  cosmic, 47, 113, 114, 115
  in *Iliad*, 117

Daidalos, 150
Daktuloi, 81, 193
danger. *See* risk
death, as change of state, 119, 125, 135, 160
Demetrios of Phaleron, 164
democracy, 17
Demokritos, 50, 108, 126, 229
Demosthenes (general), use of light-armed troops, 175
Demosthenes (orator), 34, 53, 228
  on innovation in war, 177
  on Philip, 223
Diagoras of Melos, 229
differentiation, 21, 62
Dionysios I of Syracuse, 178
Dionysodoros, 176, 219
Dionysos, 48, 50, 54, 65, 130, 158
  birth of, 139
Dipylon *oinokhoē*, 168
discovery, 123, 194
dithyramb, 54, 158, 182, 195, 196, 201, 204
diversity, 21
Dodds, E.R., 2, 16
Drakon, 31
Dunn, Francis, 18
Durkheim, E., 31

eccentricity, 50, 52
eclipse, 45, 46, 47
Eco, U., 209
Edelstein, Ludwig, 16
education, 65, 165, 219
Egypt
  antiquity of, 101
  borrowings from, 16, 126, 130

Einstein, Albert, 228
Empedokles, 56, 121
empiricism, medical, 42, 56, 57
emulation, 60
envy, 61, 193
Epameinondas, 164, 176, 177
epic, 64, 65
'epistemophilic' instinct, 28
Erekhtheion, 165, 220
eternal recurrence, 112
etymological connections, 19, 66, 72, 80, 81, 117, 144, 226
Euphranor, 152
Euphronios, 153
Euripides, 45, 94, 202, 203, 210, 229
  Nietzsche on, 210
Euthydemos, 176, 219
excellence, 162, 170, 186, 211, 219, 226
experimentation, 128

face-to-face society, 39
fashion, 30
fiction, 60, 189, 216
first discoverers/inventors, 30, 82, 109, 132, 182, 199, 215
flying, 173, 195
foresight, 33, 44
freshness, 141, 187, 227
Freud, Sigmund, 136
futurity, 20, 43, 44

Glaukos of Chios, 180
glory, 162
glōttai, 65, 90
Gorgianic tropes, 154
Gorgias, 27, 65, 88
  on poetry, 202
Greek language, 90, 202
  tonal properties, 203
Greek miracle, 13, 62

Hahn, Robert, 15
handicraft, 139
Hephaistos, 69, 70, 138
Herakleitos, 50, 121, 123, 124, 125, 126
Herodotos, 41, 116, 130, 229
  account of Plataiai, 105
  on inventors, 180
  on tactics at Marathon, 174
  on wonders, 148
Heron of Alexandria, 183
Hesiod, narrative of regress in, 96
heurematographic treatises, 109, 132, 199
Hippias of Elis, 51, 108, 211, 212
  dating system, 12

General index

Hippocratic writings, 32, 43, 54, 55, 56, 57, 107, 155, 228
Hippodamos of Miletos, 37, 51, 165, 229
historiography, 44, 116
hoplites, 174
horsemanship, 79
Huizinga, J., 167
humoral theory, 57
humour, comic, 137

ideas
   cross-fertilisation of, 57, 155, 208
   generation of, 126, 135, 213
imagination, 42, 44, 155
improvisation, 167, 169, 204, 205, 208, 211, 224
incentives, 37, 162
individualism, 31
individuation, 136
initiation, Dionysiac, 158, 159, 160
innovation
   definition of, 25
   in battle, 177
   in music. *See* Ch. 8
   in poetry. *See* Ch. 8
   in war. *See* warfare
   lexicon of, 4–6
   mechanisms of, 34
   social, 5
innovationism, 2, 4, 14, 15, 16, 40, 184, 216
inspiration, 33, 35, 70, 169, 186, 230
invention, 114, 133, 139, 155, 165, 180, 182, 183, 217, 226
Iphikrates, use of peltasts by, 176
irony
   Demosthenic, 53
   Euripidean, 158
   Platonic, 97
   Sokratic, 148
   Virgilian, 23
Isokrates, 65

Julian the Apostate, 26

Kadmos, 80, 130
Kaineus, 64–84
   burial of, 78
   identified with spear, 78
   supposedly 'new man', 80
Kainon, to (Athenian lawcourt), 23
kainotheism, 147
Kallimakhos (sculptor), 154, 156
Kant, I., 210
katharsis, 30, 160, 189, 230
Kenites, 81
Khoirilos of Samos, 26, 57–8, 60, 62, 229

Kierkegaard, S., 42, 210
Klein, Melanie, 28
Kleisthenes, 15, 31
Kleon, 53, 222
Kratylos, 34
Kroisos, 44, 131
Kronos, age of, 86

Lasos of Hermione, 182, 197, 228
laws, new, 37
lexicon. *See* innovation – lexicon of
light, 32, 173, *cf*. radiance
Lloyd, Geoffrey, 15
Locke, John, on pineapple, 24
loss, 136, 137

madness, 65, 158, 214
maps, 214
Marsyas, 53, 54
medical ideas, 56, 57
Meier, Christian, 17, 225
memory, 113, 129
mentality, 15, 27
metalworking, 81–4
metamorphosis, 33, 64, 130
metaphor, 49, 98, 136, 141, 208, 229
Meton, 51
   Metonic cycle, 51
Miller, Margaret, 17, 225
Mimnermos, 124
mining, 73
mirror, 49
modernity, 31
money, 5, 15, 16, 85, 164, 199, 220
Montaigne, M. de, 29, 30
mourning, 29
multiplicity, 120, 132, 152, 179. *See* pluralism
music, Greek. *See* Ch. 8
Mycenaean Greek, 66
Mysteries, Dionysiac, 64, 128, 134, 159
myths, new, 62, 101

naval warfare, 174
Neapolis ('new city'), 23
Near East
   borrowings from, 25, 79, 81, 126, 129, 158
   influence of, 80, 108, 120, 226
neologisms, 65
new, shock of the, 141
new laws, 30, 37, 101, 131, 215
newfangled, 25, 55, 90, 147
newness
   concept of, 3, 5, 19, 21, 22, 28, 32, 43, 67, 73, 83, 105, 231
   perceived, 20, 23, 34, 87, 88
   stylistic, 156

news, 31, 34, 107, 136, 142, 145, 146, 147, 149, 189, 220, 231
Newton, Isaac, 21, 124
Nietzsche, F., 29, 210
Nikomakhos, 96
Nikostratos, 88
nostalgia, 30, 206
nothing new, 28, 32, 52, 53, 231
novelty
  and loss, 29
  constructions of. *See* Ch. 9
  in fifth-century Athens. *See in particular* Ch. 9
  literary, 59, 104, 129, 209
  negative associations to, 95
  organic, 137
  perceived, 61
  radical, 24
  temporal, 67
  unwelcome, 59

ode to man, Sophoklean, 44, 127, 225
Odyssey, 43, 68, 69, 126, 131, 144
Oedipus, 107
old age. *See* old and young
old and new, 30, 45, 85–107, 228
Old and New day, 89
old and young, 28, 95, 98–102
Old Comedy, 88
Old Oligarch, 218, 222
Olympic Games, 12, 145, 171
originality, 182, 191
  in poetry, 166, 205
origins, 32
Orphic doctrine, 142
Orsippos of Megara, 171
otherness, sense of, 14, 17, 20, 33, 49, 130, 131
Otto, Walter, 158
Ovid, 64

painting, 166
Palamedes, 131, 132
Panathenaic festival, 89
paradigm shift, 21
paradox of innovation, 62
parasol, 130
Parmenides, 33, 50, 108, 121
Parrhasios, 52, 152
past, grip of the, 62, 232
Paul, apostle, 34
Peloponnesian War, 30, 175, 212, 216
Periklean funeral speech, 34

Perikles, 30, 219, 222
personality, innovative, 50, 153
perspective, 155
Phaleas of Khalkedon, 37
Pheidias, 25, 27, 220
Pheidon of Argos, 132
Phemios, 184
Philip of Macedon, 228
Philolaos of Kroton, 92
Philoxenos of Kythera, 54, 199, 205, 206
Phoenician
  alphabet, 109, 130
  qart-hadasht, 'new city', 23
  traders, 82, 130
Piaget, J., 167
Picasso, Pablo, 228
Pistias, 180
pitch accent, 203
Plataiai, battle of, 104, 105
Plato, 65
  invention of alarm clock, 180
  Laws, 36
  on music, 53, 190, 205
  on *thauma*, 28
  Republic, 36
play, 162–70
playthings, 38, 102, 139
pluralism, 17, 49, 50
Plutarch, on Akropolis, 227
poetry, 26, 44. *See also* innovation in poetry
politics, 14, 15, 32, 221, 222
Polykleitos of Argos, *Kanōn*, 154, 165, 166, 227, 229
postmodernity, 31
Praxiteles, 151
precision, 57, 106, 154, 156, 224
prediction, 33
present, the, 31
Presocratic thinkers, 16, 41, 108, 112
Prodikos of Keos, 118, 229
professionalism
  in music, 204
  military, 175
progress, idea of, 16, 17
progressivism, 55
Prometheus, 12, 132
Pronomos of Thebes, 200
Protagoras of Abdera, 180, 207, 229
psychoanalysis, 7, 28, 29
psychology, 7, 29, 42, 167
psychotherapy, 160
Ptahhotep, 58, 59
Pythagoras of Samos, 112, 131, 229
  alleged bilocation of, 114
  alleged reincarnation, 114

General index

Pythagoras of Zakynthos, invention of tripod by, 182, 200
Pythagorean table, 90–8
Pythagoreanism, 47
Pythagoreans, 115

qayin, 64–84

radiance, 148
Ranke, Leopold von, 6
rationalism, 56, 140
recency, 67, 73, 88, 98, 188
reciprocity, 16
religion, Greek, 49, 97, 117
renovation, 30
reperformance, 167, 168
repetition, 52, 117, 167, 210
research, 55, 127, 128
resourcefulness, 139
Revelation, vision of the new in, 159
revolution, 30, 32, 39, 96, 202
reward. *See* incentives
rhetoric, 29, 55, 65, 203, 224
　contrasted with action, 221
　of novelty, 89
　of reaction, 41
riddles, 170, 197
risk, 5, 35, 100, 221
rites of passage, 29, 117
ritual, 117, 135

Saki (H.H. Munro), 100
salience, 7, 11, 24, 28, 29, 62, 121, 226, 231
Saxonhouse, Arlene, 17
Schumpeter, Joseph, 29
sculpture, 27, 150, 154, 227, 229
Seaford, Richard, 16
seasonality, 117
Second Sophistic, 10
self-consciousness, 153, 201, 207, 209, 210, 227
self-promotion, 55, 60, 61
Shakespeare, 25, 37
Sicilian campaign, 30
Simonides, 102, 131
skill, 19
slavery, 181
Smyth, H.W., 14
social innovation. *See* innovation – social
Sokrates, 52, 53, 54, 65, 96
Solon, 15, 31, 44, 104, 118, 131, 229
sophists, 42, 107, 132, 207, 212, 216, 219, 229

Spartan conservatism, 202, 221
Stevenson, Robert Louis, 99
Storr, Anthony, 3
strangeness, 90, 153, 214
Strepsiades, 18, 86, 175, 212
sun
　estimated size of, 125
　new every day, 123
　under the, 111, 126

technical skill (*tekhnē*), 26, 32, 37, 39
Teisias, 88
Telemakhos, 68, 185
temple construction, 30
temporality
　aristocratic vs democratic, 16–17
　and futurity, 67
　and *neos*, 80, 225
　on spectrum of 'new', 22–3
Thales, 50
Themistokles, 44
Theodoros of Samos, 180
Thourioi, 51, 219, 229
Thrasymakhos of Khalkedon, 97
Thucydides, 116
　Corinthian envoy's speech, 43
　historical aims, 107
　on Olympic Games, 171
Timanthes of Kythnos, 155
time, 33, 116
　brings the new, 12, 142
　historical, 17, 18
　natural, 32, 118
Timotheos of Miletos, 43, 54, 194, 201, 205, 226, 229
Tithonos, 160
trade, 82, 164
tradition, 14, 18, 40, 42, 194
　invention of, 40
tragedy, Greek, 17, 28, 29, 30, 106, 136, 158, 195, 202, 209, 210
transformation, 65, 136, 160, 229, 230
travel, 50, 131
Tubal-Cain, 81

unexpectedness, 33, 45, 46, 123, 226
utopia, 32

Valéry, Paul, 27, 115
van Groningen, B.A., 17, 41–3, 45
versatility, 219

warfare, 131, 162–79, 228
weapons. *See also* artillery
　new, 39, 67, 79, 81, 164, 177, 178, 179

Weber–Fechner law, 42
wine, old and new, 102, 103
Winnicott, D., 167
Wittgensteinian 'family resemblance', 6
women, 33, 93, 95
wonder, 50, 105, 134–50, 217
wordplay, 65
writing, 15, 167, 170, 208, 223

Xenophanes, 55, 122, 123, 126, 228

young and old. *See* old and young
youth, 87, 99, 101, 117, 137, 144, 158

Zeus Olympios, sculpture of, 27
Zeuxis of Herakleia, 52, 152, 153, 229

Index of Greek terms

admēs, 144
agalma, 150
agathos, 42
aglaos, 30
agōn, 166, 175
aiglā, 145
aitiai, 135
akrībeia, 106, 153, 156, 224, 226
allos, 20, 60, 209, 222
allotrios, 33
angeliā, 34, 145, 146
aretē, 32, 70, 170, 172, 186, 219
arkhaios, 30, 84, 87, 90, 95, 98, 216
  arkhaiologiā, 212
  arkhaiotropos, 221
arkhē/-ai, 32, 33, 41, 43, 54, 56, 108, 120, 135, 216
  ex arkhēs, 46
atalos, atalophrōn, 168
athurma, 33, 101, 139
atopiā, 52
atrekeia, 57, 107
auxēsis, 17
axiologos, 231

deinos, 148
dēmokratiā, 12
dunamis, 38

eiōthos, 52, 86
ekplēxis, 27, 148
elpis, 33, 123
  aelptos, 33, 44, 45
energeia, 38
epigignomena, ta, 37, 221
epitekhnēsis, 26, 221

genesis, 5, 32, 33, 134
gēraion, 125
gerōn, 87, 101, 103
graus, 87

grīphos, 197

heteros, 20, 124
heuresis, 33, 36, 56, 94, 132, 180, 223
  heurēmata, 33, 132
  heurēsiepēs, 194
hupothesis, 54

isonomiā, 12

kainos, 5, 21, 22, 71, 90, 95, 98, 105, 106, 130, 212, 223
  kainē hupothesis, 55
  kainizō, 72, 90, 147
  kainon, to, 226
  Kainon, to, 23, 96
  kainoō, 105
  kainopathēs, 106, 136
  kainopēgēs, 106
  kainopoiein, 153
  kainopoiiā, 6
  kainoteros, 66, 90
  kainotēs, 6, 21, 53, 141, 205
  kainotomeō, 26
  kainotomiā, 6, 13, 26, 36, 73, 153, 192
  ouden kainon, 32, 53
  ti kainon, 12, 28, 72, 106, 137, 195
  ti kainoteron, 34
kairos, 172, 224
kalos, 67, 143, 144
kathestōs, 86
khrēsimos, 180
kindūnos, 33
kīnein, 6, 37
  kīnēsis, 32
kleos, 70, 162
kompsos, 36, 55

lampros, 134, 145, 195
  lamprotēs, 32
liparos, 144

maniã, 33, 158
mellon, to, 16
metabolē, 6, 14, 32, 200, 222
mētis, 139

neios, 69
  neiatos, 69
neomai, 117
neos, 5, 22, 90, 95, 101, 103, 107, 112, 117, 185
  nea, 34
  nearos, 48, 191
  neognos, 137
  neokēdēs, 136
  neokhmos, 48, 101, 147, 157, 192
  neoktitos, 102
  neon (adverb), 23, 67
  neon, to, 137
  neopenthēs, 136
  neosīgalos, 193
  neosmēktos, 67
  neōsti, 20, 157
  neōtatos, 30, 68, 185
  neōtera, ta, 220
  neōtera prāgmata, 28
  neōterismos, 6, 30, 39
  neōterizein, 39
  neōteropoios, 221
  neōteros, 30, 39, 46, 90, 96, 103, 157
  neotēs, 16, 33, 144
  neoteukhēs, 67, 187
  neozuges, 58
ne-wo, 88
nomos, 37, 155, 205
nostos, 117
nūn, 19, 31, 48, 97, 103, 159, 194, 196

paideia, 65, 165
paidiã, 33
paignia, 33, 102
paizein, 170
palaios, 66, 84, 87, 96, 98, 105, 106, 107
  palai, 23, 90, 194

paronta, ta, 31
patrios, 31, 40, 42
phaos/phōs, 32, 134, 146
  phaos, es, 134, 137
pheggos, 134, 145
phthonos, 61, 193
phusis, 38, 155
poikiliã, 21, 33, 50, 94, 158, 191, 201, 219
  poikilogārus, 193
polu
  polu, to, 33
  polueidēs, 212
  polumētis, 139
  polupeiriã, 21, 219, 221
  polupragmosunē, 34
  polutlās, 49
  polutropos, 49, 132, 139
presbus, 87
pronoia, 33
prophēteia, 33
prosphatos, 141, 227
prōtos, 67, 215
  prōtistos, 215
  prōtopagēs, 67, 187

saphēneia, 107
sebas, 33, 138, 149
selas, 147
sophiã, 32, 94, 131, 146, 198
stoikheia, 56

tekhnē, 39, 102, 138, 151, 153, 169, 195, 205, 217, 221, 227, 228
thambos, 33, 149
thauma, 28, 33, 67, 105, 143, 144, 148, 149, 150, 168, 217
tolma, 33, 214, 217
tukhē, 19, 56, 217

xenos, 33, 153, 178, 179, 229

zētēsis, 36, 127

Index locorum

Acts
  17.16: 220
  17.21: 34
Aeschylus (Aesch.)
  Agamemnon (Ag.)
    1–7: 146
    20–22: 147
    960: 72, 90
    1071: 72, 90
  Eumenides (Eum.)
    80: 150
    394, 838, 871: etc.: 96
    396, 926: 96
    658–66: 140
  Fragments (fr.)
    78c, 85–8, 92: 102
    390: 180
  Libation Bearers (Cho.)
    492: 72, 90
  Persians (Pers.)
    394, 405, 838, 871, etc.: 175
  Seven against Thebes (Sept.)
    394, 838, 871, etc.: 106
Aeschylus, pseudo- ([Aesch.])
  Prometheus Bound (PV)
    96: 48
    149: 48
    391: 48
    982: 12
Akousilaos of Argos
  fr. 22: 78
Alexis
  Fragments (fr.)
    122: 103
    145: 138
Alkaios
  Fragments (fr.)
    140: 144
Alkidamas (Alcid.)
  Fragments (fr.)
    1 Avezzù: 224
    1.34 Avezzù: 224
Alkman
  Fragments (fr.)
    3: 192
    14c: 192
    30: 192
Anaxilas
  (ap. Ath. 14.18.10–12): 109
ANET
  365f: 142
Anth. Gr.
  9.713–42: 152
Antiphanes (Antiph.)
  Fragments (fr.)
    207: 206
Antiphon (DK 87)
  A6: 161
  B49: 44
  B64: 97
Apollodoros (Apollod.)
  Epitome (Epit.)
    1.22: 21
Apollonios of Rhodes (A.R.)
  Argonautica (Arg.)
    1.59–64: 77
    4.1310: 138
Aristophanes (Ar.)
  Assemblywomen (Eccl.)
    209–11, 214–28: 95
    338: 90
    876: 26
  Banqueters frr. 205, 233: 90
  Birds (Av.)
    252: 90
    252, 255–7: 220
    1373–6, 1382–90: 195
  Clouds (Nub.)
    5–7: 213
    98–9: 212
    128–30: 213

Aristophanes (Ar.) (cont.)
    135–7: 213
    139: 135
    148–52: 213
    160–4: 213
    215–16: 214
    365–41: 215
    381: 215
    398: 86
    476–80: 175
    546–8: 212
    547: 20, 73
    657–8: 214
    818–21: 215
    828: 215
    893, 896: 215
    969–72: 201
    984–5: 86
    1004–8: 51
    1008: 51
    1039–42: 215
    1178–84: 89
    1353–76: 186
    1399–1400: 215
    1421–4: 215
    1427–46: 216
    1468: 216
  Frogs (Ran.)
    1–5, 12–15: 52
    177: 137
    718–33: 98
    1150: 103
    1301–3: 202
    1314, 1348: 202
    1371–2: 214
    1475: 207
    1477–8: 86
  Knights (Eq.)
    686–7, 758–9: 219
    1331: 86
    1375–81: 214
  Peace (Pax)
    54–5: 214
  Wasps (Vesp.)
    120: 23
    876: 26
    1222–49, 1299–1325: 170
    1410: 102
    1480: 86
    1536–7: 214
  Women Celebrating the Thesmophoria (Thes.)
    49, 52–7: 208
    850: 210
Aristotle (Arist.)
  Fragments (fr.): 36

Metaphysics (Meta.)
    982b12–13: 28
    986a22–6: 91
    993b15: 201
    1011b13–14: 86
    1032a12–13: 38
Meteorology (Mete.)
    355a13–15: 124
Nicomachean Ethics (EN)
    1094b23–5: 6
    1096b6: 91
    1140a–17: 19
On the Generation of Animals (GA)
    746b7–8: 109
Physics (Ph.)
    198a9–10: 38
Poetics (Poet.)
    1449a10–15: 38
    1449a18: 155
    1451a36–b11: 26
    1451b23: 216
    1460b13–15: 38
Politics (Pol.)
    1252b33–36: 38
    1259a9–18: 51
    1264a1–5: 36
    1265a: 36, 38
    1266a34–40: 37
    1266a39–1267b21: 37
    1267b29: 37
    1268a6–8: 165
    1268a6–11: 37
    1268b33–8: 37
    1269a3–4: 42
    1269a19–28: 38
    1338b24–9: 175
    1341a24–32: 199
    2617b22–8: 51
    1342b: 199
Rhetoric (Rhet.)
    1406b12–13: 49
    1409b26: 201
Sophistici Elenchi (Soph. El.)
    183b29–33: 97
Aristotle, pseudo- ([Arist.])
  Problemata (Pr.)
    19.918b: 204
Aristoxenos (Aristox.)
  Fragments
    87: 197
  Harmonica (Harm.)
    1.123: 204
    1.18: 202

Index locorum

Arkhilokhos (Arkhil.)
  Fragments (fr.)
    5.4: 20
    120: 196
    122: 26, 45
Arkhytas (DK47)
  A10: 181
  B1: 128
  B3: 127
Artemon
  (ap. Athenaeus 14.637cf):
    183
Athenaeus
  1.25f–26a: 103
  4.174c: 180
  4.637cf: 183
  4.75: 181
  6.225c: 210
  631e: 200
  637b: 200
  8. 337f, 352a:
    201
  10.455bc: 197
  11.467: 197
  11.505a: 36
  12.543: 153
  12.543e: 152
  14.643d: 206
Augustine, St. (Aug.)
  Confessions (Conf.)
    11.15: 33

Bakkhylides (Bakkhyl.)
  5.160–2: 137
  5.169: 144
  5.48–9: 145
  19.1–10: 72
  Fragments (fr.)
    5: 194
Bible. See names of individual books

Callimachus (Call.)
  Epigrams (Ep.)
    28.4: 153
CEG
  454: 168
Cicero (Cic.)
  Tusculan Disputations (Tusc.)
    2.62: 176
Clement of Alexandria
  Stromateis (Strom.)
    1.18: 198

Deinarkhos
  5.2.1: 53

Demetrius (Demetr.)
  On Style (Eloc.)
    14: 156
Demokritos (Demok., DK68)
  A5h, A11p, A28a: 155
  A75: 118
  B9, B10b, B11: 155
  B25: 118
  B82: 222
  B145: 222
  B158: 109, 126
  B294: 99
  B295: 100
  B296: 99
Demosthenes (Dem.)
  4.10: 34
  9.48–51: 177
  15.9.1: 53
  25.20.1: 53
  35.1.1: 53
  Against Meidias
    112: 141
Dikaiarkhos
  A8: 112
  B8a: 71
  F33: 93
Diodorus of Sicily (D.S.)
  12.12.4: 219
  12.53.2–3: 27
  14.41–2: 178
  14.43: 179
Diogenes Laertius (D.L.)
  1–2: 182
  2.43: 61
  2.8: 125
  2.40.7: 73
  2.103: 180
  8.41–2: 93
  8.73: 52
  9.36: 229
  9.50: 219
  9.53, 4.2: 180
Dionysius of Halicarnassus (D.H.)
  7.72.2–3: 171
  de Compositione Verborum (Comp.)
    14.87–91: 197
    11.29–32: 202
Diss. Log.
  3.10 (2.410.30–411.1 DK): 152

Ecclesiastes
  1.3–11: 110
  1.9: 34
  1.13, 2.3, 3.10: 110
  3.1–8: 112

Eleg. adesp.
  27 West 1–8: 32, 170
Empedokles (Emped.)
  B17.10–13, 31–5: 121
  B23: 152
  B26: 121
Epicurus
  Letter to Menoikeus: 99
Epikharmos
  23B1 (275KA): 119
Euboulos
  Fragments (fr.)
    122: 103
Euripides (Eur.)
  Bacchae (Ba.)
    70–1: 158
    188–90: 157
    214: 157
    215–20: 157
    353–4: 65
    650: 158
    924: 159
  Cyclops (Cycl.)
    250–2: 20
  Danae fr.
    316: 134
  Fragments (fr.)
    19: 207
    285.1–2: 137
    291: 99
    494: 94, 95
    508, 509: 99
    638: 86
    833: 86
    862: 113
    945: 12
  Hercules (Herc. Fur.)
    38, 541, 779: 48
  Hippolytos (Hipp.)
    368: 137
  Ion
    475–7: 145
  Iphigeneia among the Taurians (IT)
    239–40, 340: 148
    1028–32: 94
  Medea (Med.)
    298–301: 94
  Orestes (Or.)
    239–40: 106
  Phoenician Women (Phoen.)
    528–30: 99
  Suppliants (Supp.)
    990–4: 145
  Trojan Women (Tro.)
    511–15: 194

    884–6: 147
    1256–9: 148
    1277: 106
Eustathius
  on *Il.* 1.264: 74
Ezekiel
  27.13: 82

FGE
  27.792–5: 102

Galen
  Glosses on Hippokrates 19 p.65 K, 1–2: 90
Genesis
  1.3: 142
  4.20–1, 4.22, 10.2: 81
  10.2: 82
Gorgias (Gorg.)
  Helen
    18: 152
    9: 203
Greek Anthology (Anth. Gr.)
  9.713–42: 152

Herakleitos (DK22)
  A13: 113
  B3: 125
  B6: 71, 123
  B7: 125
  B10: 121
  B18: 123
  B36: 124
  B40: 123
  B40, B47, B101, B55, B113: 123
  B51: 121
  B62: 125
  B64, B30, B76, B90: 124
  B84a: 126
  B88: 125
Hermippos
  Fragments (fr.)
    4: 113
    63.4–6, 12–23: 218
Herodotos (Hdt.)
  1.1: 83
  1.1.1: 149
  1.25: 180
  1.30.1: 131
  1.31.1: 104
  1.32: 44, 118
  1.51.3: 180
  1.74: 50
  2.100.3: 105
  2.53.2: 50
  3.41.1: 180

3.60: 149
3.80–3: 105
3.94: 82
4.36: 214
5.58: 131
6.112: 174
6.228: 174
6.229: 174
9.26: 105
9.28.6: 105
Hesiod (Hes.)
  Fragments (fr.)
    87: 75
  Theogony (*Thg.*)
    3–4, 31–2: 58
  Works and Days (*Op.*)
    11–26: 163
    42: 122
    109–201: 47
    423–36: 71
    643: 102
    650–62: 166
    778: 65
Hesiod, pseudo- ([Hes.])
  Fragments (fr.)
    357: 166, 191
  On the Idaian Daktyloi
    fr. 282: 82
  Shield of Herakles (*Sc.*)
    165: 150
    178–90: 76
Hippias (Hipp., DK86)
  Fragments (fr.)
    B6: 212
Hippocrates, pseudo- ([Hp.])
  On Ancient Medicine (*VM*)
    1.1–6: 54
    1.16–17: 56
    1.20–1: 55
    2.1–5: 55
    4.5–6: 56
    4.6–10: 56
    8.19–20: 56
    9.21–2: 57, 107
    12.12–13: 57, 107
    13.1–2: 55
    14.14–20: 56
    20.8–11: 155
  On Disease (*Morb.*)
    1.5: 57
    1.9: 57
  On Joints (*Art.*)
    4.182.15–20: 153
  On the Art (*Loc. Hom.*)
    46.342.4–9 Littré: 57

Homer. See *Iliad*, *Odyssey*
Homer, pseudo- ([Hom.])
  Battle of the Frogs (*Batr.*)
    116: 67
  Homeric Hymn to Aphrodite (*H. Hom. Aph.*)
    218–38: 160
    5.11, 12–15: 139
  Homeric Hymn to Athene (*H. Hom. Ath.*)
    28.4–7: 138
  Homeric Hymn to Demeter (*H. Hom. Dem.*)
    10: 149
    187–90, 275–83: 149
  Homeric Hymn to Hermes (*H. Hom. Herm.*)
    54–6: 169
    20–78, 80, 111: 139
Horace (Hor.)
  Art of Poetry (*AP*)
    93: 199
    205–301: 50
  Carmen Saeculare
    9–11: 125
  Epistles (*Epist.*)
    2.1.90–1: 2
  Odes
    3.1.1: 153
    3.1.2–4: 192

Iamblichus (Iambl.)
  Life of Pythagoras (*VP*)
    267: 93
    31: 114
Ibykos
  286: 160
Iliad (*Il.*)
  1.199: 149
  1.262–272: 75
  1.477: 117
  2.229–33: 68
  3.397–8: 149
  4.164–5: 44
  5.63: 44
  5.194: 67
  5.722–31: 143
  6.146–9: 116
  6.208: 170
  6.288–95: 69
  6.448–9: 44
  8.103: 99
  9.258: 69
  9.36: 69
  9.443: 221
  9.527: 91
  10.79: 99
  11.384–90: 70
  11.604: 44

Iliad (Il.) (cont.)
 11.632–7: 168
 11.656–803: 70
 11.784: 170
 13.342: 67
 14.108: 69
 15.469: 67
 17.36: 68
 18.434: 99
 18.462–617: 143
 18.467: 149
 18.468–608: 69
 18.610, 617: 69
 19.336: 99
 24.267: 67
 24.629: 149
 24.788: 117
Ion of Khios
 Fragments (fr.)
  3: 19
Isaiah
 42.10: 191
Isokrates (Isok.)
 Against the Sophists (Soph.)
  13: 223
 Antidosis (Antid.)
  2: 165
  13: 165
 Panegyricus (Paneg.)
  10: 223

Julian
 Epistles (Ep.)
  20.453b: 26

Khoirilos
 Fragments (fr.)
  1 *PEG*: 60
  2: 58

Lucian
 Zeuxis
  3, 7: 153
 Dream, or Life of Lucian (Somn.)
  9: 165
Lucretius
 D.R.N.
  2.688–99: 208
Luke
 5.37–8: 24

Mark
 2.22: 24
Matthew
 5.18: 28
 9.17: 24

Menander (Men.)
 Fragments (fr.)
  125: 104
Mimnermos (Mimn.)
 2.7–10: 99
 Fragments (fr.)
  12: 124

Nikostratos
 Fragments (fr.)
  30: 88

Odyssey (Od.)
 1.1–4: 49
 1.32–4: 126
 1.62: 65
 1.323: 149
 1.337–44: 184
 1.350–2: 185
 1.351–2: 68
 1.368–98: 185
 2.1: 117
 2.223: 20
 2.293: 68
 3.123: 149
 3.404: 117
 5.339–40: 65
 5.423: 65
 6.161: 149
 6.232–7: 144
 6.233–4: 138
 6.64: 67
 6.74: 143
 8.265: 168
 8.271: 111
 8.370–80: 168
 8.404: 67
 8.477–83: 186
 8.483: 58
 8.536–43: 185
 8.74: 58
 9.364–7, 399–412: 65
 10.63: 149
 13.298–9: 139
 17.381–5: 187
 19.275–6, 407–9: 65
 21.406–7: 69
 22.347: 58, 70
 22.347–57: 186
 23.160–1: 138
 23.184–204: 68
Orphic fragments
 72, 86: 142

Index locorum

Ovid (Ov.)
  Metamorphoses (*Met.*)
    1.1: 64
    12.189–207: 74
    12.524–6: 75

P.Derv.
  col. 4.7: 29
P. Köln
  21351: 160
P.Oxy. 1399: 60
Parmenides (Parm.)
  B1.5: 58
  B8.1–7: 120
Pausanias (Paus.)
  1.3.3: 152
  1.24.3: 139
  1.26.7: 156
  1.27.1: 150
  1.44: 171
  2.4.5: 150
  3.11.3: 165
  5.14.5: 139
  6.9.6: 109
  8.36.5: 139
  8.40.1: 156
  9.12.5–6: 200
  9.37.4: 103
  10.38.7: 156
  10.5.13: 104
PEG
  856F: 139
Philo Mechanicus (Philo Mech.)
  4.1 p. 49, 20: 154
Pindar (Pi.)
  Fragments (fr.)
    3: 104
    70b.1–8: 196
    70b.23: 159
    70b.9–18: 198
    128f: 77
    166: 76
    212: 102
  Nemean Odes (*Nem.*)
    8.20–21: 193
    8.21: 61
    9.8: 193
  Olympian Odes (*O.*)
    1.4: 59
    1.5: 59
    2.86–8: 194
    3: 172
    3.4: 71
    3.4–6: 193
    3.9–11: 193
    4.1–2, 4–10: 145
    4.5: 145
    7.11–12: 193
    8.69: 173
    9.48–9: 102
    9.49: 71
    9.80: 194
    10.93–4: 193
    13.18–19: 196, 198
  Paian (*Pa.*)
    9.1–6: 46
    9.19–20: 46
  Pythian Odes (*P.*)
    8.81–7: 173
    8.88–94: 173
    8.95–7: 145
Plato (Pl.)
  Cratylus (*Crat.*)
    402a: 121
    410cd: 113
    424de: 155
  Crito (*Crit.*)
    107d: 150, 152
  Euthydemus (*Euthyd.*)
    273d3: 176
  Euthyphre
    6bc: 48
  Ion
    530d6: 169
    531e1–3: 169
    535b–e: 189
  Laws
    665c: 205
    669e–670a: 205
    677cd: 114
    7.797bc: 101
    700a–701a: 204
    807e–808c: 180
    889d1–6: 38
  Meno (*Men.*)
    91d: 165
  Phaedo (*Phd.*)
    118a6: 97
    60e–61b: 65
  Phaedrus (*Phdr.*)
    246a–254e: 58
    267ab: 223
    267b1: 88
    275e: 224
    277b–278a: 170
    405c8–d6: 58
  Protagoras (*Prot.*)
    337d: 18

Plato (Pl.) (cont.)
  Republic (Rep.)
    602cd: 155
    328a, 328de: 97
    399de: 53, 205
    405c8–d6: 55
    424bc: 190
    424c: 205
    436b6–437a: 86
    596e–597e: 152
  Sophista (Soph.)
    236a: 31, 152
  Symposium (Symp.)
    178a5–c2: 141
    197e: 170
    206b, 206e: 135
  Theaetetus (Tht.)
    149a–d: 135
    151e–152a: 207
    155d: 28
    156e–157a: 23
    174a: 51
  Timaeus (Tim.)
    22b4–8: 101
    37c6–38b5: 121
Plato, pseudo- ([Pl.])
  Epinomis (Epin.)
    987d: 128
  Hippias Major (Hipp. ma.)
    282a: 150
    285de: 150, 212
  Hippias Minor (Hipp. mi.)
    366c–368a: 51
Pliny
  Natural History (N.H.)
    5.112: 120
    7.198: 180
    34.54: 220
    34.92: 156
    35.56.9: 154
    35.58: 154
    35.60: 151
    35.62: 151, 153
    35.64–5: 152
    35.69: 152
    35.72: 152
    35.74: 155
    35.129: 152
    36.20–1: 151, 154
Plutarch (Plut.)
  Alkibiades (Alc.)
    17.3: 214
  Aristides: 105
  Lysander: 125

Moralia (Mor.)
  45c: 154
  346a: 152
  539c: 201
Nikias (Nic.)
  12.1: 214
On the Fame of the Athenians (Glor. Ath.)
  2 (Mor. 346a): 151
On the Opinions of the Stoics (De absurd. Stoic. opin.)
  1057D: 77
Pelopidas (Pel.): 176
Perikles (Per.)
  2.1: 165
  12.6: 220
  13: 227
Solon: 89
Plutarch, pseudo- ([Plut.])
  On Music (Mus.): 192, 199, 200, 201
PMG
  378: 195
  788–91: 204
  791.211–12: 202
  795.2: 73
  796: 201
  851b: 191
PMGF
  222 i.9: 78
Polybius
  12.13.11: 164
Porphyrios of Tyre (Porph.)
  Life of Pythagoras (VP)
    19: 112
  On Abstinence (Abst.)
    2.18: 150
Poseidippos
  Lithika
    1.24–9, 2.28: 142
Prodikos
  B5: 132
Psalms
  96.1, 98.1, 149.1: 191

Quintilian (Quint.)
  Institutes of Oratory (Inst.)
    12.10.5–6: 153

Revelation
  21.1–5: 159

Samuel
  2 Samuel 21.16: 79
Satyrus (Sat.)
  Life of Euripides (Vita)
    22: 194

Semonides (Sem.)
   1.11–12: 99
Simonides (Sim.)
   Fragments (fr.)
      581 *PMG*: 102
      602 *PMG*: 102
Solon
   Fragments (fr.)
      18: 131
Sophokles (Soph.)
   Ajax (*Aj.*)
      914: 219
      646–9, 669–77: 118
   Antigone (*Ant.*)
      100–3: 47
      104–5: 47
      148–57: 48
      332: 148
      332–68: 127
   Electra (*El.*)
      685: 149
   Oedipus at Colonus (*OC*)
      1224–38: 137
   Oedipus Tyrannus (*OT*)
      155–7: 107
      290: 107
      1182–5: 107
   Trachiniae (*Tr.*)
      1277: 106
Stesikhoros (Stes.)
   Fragments (fr.)
      233: 138
      S17: 124
Stobaios (Stob.)
   4.52.22: 137
Strabo
   8.3.30: 27
   11.14.5: 82
   14.2.9: 51
Straton
   1.1–7, 48–50: 90
Suda
   s.n. Khoirilos: 60

TFG 1, no.60
   T2a: 61
   Tb: 61
Thales
   A22: 126
Theognis (Thgn.)
   425–8: 137
   527–8: 99
   789: 20
Thrasymakhos
   B1: 97

Thucydides (Thuc.)
   1.6.5–6: 171
   1.10–12: 220
   1.22: 113
   1.22.4: 107, 217
   1.70.2–8: 221
   1.71.3: 26, 37, 221
   1.138: 44
   2.12.3: 44
   2.38.2: 218
   2.38–9: 175
   2.39.1: 220
   2.40.1: 220
   2.41.1: 18, 219
   2.41.4: 217
   2.61.2: 222
   2.77: 175
   2.84–5: 175
   3.38.1: 222
   3.38.4–5: 53
   3.38.4–5, 7: 222
   3.94–8: 175
   4.33–6: 175
   4.90–6: 175
   4.100.2–4: 175
   5.71: 174, 175
   6.18.6: 26, 221
   6.89.6: 53
   7.29–30: 109
   7.36: 175
   7.50.4: 26
Timotheos
   PMG
      791.202–3: 202
      791.230: 201
      796.2: 73
      802: 201

Virgil
   Aeneid (*Aen.*)
      1.12: 23
      4.260: 23
Vitruvius (Vitr.)
   4.1.6: 165
   4.1.9–10: 154
   4.1.10: 156
   7 *praef.* 11: 155
   7 *praef.* 12: 166
   10.8: 183

Xenarkhos
   Fragments (fr.)
      7.1–2: 210
Xenophanes (Xenoph.)
   B18: 123

Xenophon (Xen.)
  Agesilaus (*Ages*)
    1.25–8: 178
  Education of Cyrus (*Cyr.*)
    1.6.38: 209
  Hellenica (*Hell.*)
    3.4.16–19: 178
    4.5.10–16, 6.4.12: 176
  Hiero
    9.10: 165
  Memorabilia (*Mem.*)
    1.1.1: 73
    3.10.9–10: 180
    4.4.6–14: 211
    4.4.14: 73
  On Revenues (*Vect.*)
    4.27–9: 73
    6.1: 40
Xenophon, pseudo- ([Xen.])
  Constitution of Athens (*Ath.Pol.*)
    1.6–7: 222
    2.7–8: 218
    3.82.2–4: 223

Zenobius (Zenob.)
  1.14: 150
  2.51: 109